THE ACHIEVEMENT OF BRIAN FRIEL

ULSTER EDITIONS AND MONOGRAPHS

General Editors
Elizabeth McIntyre
John McVeagh
Robert Welch

ULSTER EDITIONS & MONOGRAPHS
ISSN 0954-3392

THE
ACHIEVEMENT OF
BRIAN FRIEL

Edited by

Alan J. Peacock

Ulster Editions and Monographs: 4

COLIN SMYTHE
Gerrards Cross, 1993

First published in 1993 in Great Britain by
Colin Smythe Limited, Gerrards Cross, Buckinghamshire SL9 8XA

British Library Cataloguing in Publication Data

A catalogue record for this book is available from
the British Library

ISBN 0-861340-349-5

Produced in Great Britain
Printed and Bound by T.J. Press, Padstow

CONTENTS

ACKNOWLEDGEMENTS

Thanks are expressed to the Publications Committee of the University of Ulster for financial assistance, and to the Faculty of Humanities for practical and financial support; also, to the Librarian and Staff of the University Library. I am also indebted to The National Library of Ireland and the Libraries of Trinity College and University College, Dublin for use of their facilities. In particular, I would like to thank the General Editor of the Series, Professor Robert Welch, for his generous support and advice during the preparation of this volume.

Acknowledgements are made to Faber & Faber Ltd. for permission to publish extracts from the following of Brian Friel's works:

Aristocrats
Dancing at Lughnasa
Faith Healer
The Freedom of the City
Living Quarters
Lovers
Making History
Philadelphia, Here I Come
Translations.

ABBREVIATION

SP   *Selected Plays of Brian Friel*, edited with an Introduction by Seamus Deane (London, Faber and Faber, 1984).

CHRONOLOGICAL CHECK-LIST OF PUBLISHED PLAYS

The Enemy Within — First performed by the Abbey Theatre, Dublin, at the Queen's Theatre on 6 August 1962.

Philadelphia, Here I Come! — First performed at the Gaiety Theatre, Dublin on 28 September 1964.

The Loves of Cass McGuire — First performed at the Helen Hayes Theatre, New York on 6 October 1966.

Lovers — First performed at the Gate Theatre, Dublin on 18 July 1967.

Crystal and Fox — First performed at the Gaiety Theatre, Dublin on 12 November 1968.

The Mundy Scheme — First performed at the Olympia Theatre, Dublin on 10 June 1969.

The Gentle Island — First performed at the Olympia Theatre, Dublin on 30 November 1971.

The Freedom of the City — First performed at the Abbey Theatre, Dublin on 20 February 1973.

Volunteers — First performed at the Abbey Theatre, Dublin on 5 March 1975.

Living Quarters — First performed at the Abbey Theatre, Dublin on 24 March 1977.

Aristocrats — First performed at the Abbey Theatre, Dublin on 8 March 1979.

Faith Healer — First performed at the Longacre Theatre, New York on 5 April 1979.

Translations — First performed by Field Day Theatre Company in the Guildhall, Derry on 23 September 1980.

Three Sisters — First performed by Field Day Theatre Company in the Guildhall, Derry on 8 September 1981.

The Communication Cord — First performed by Field Day Theatre Company in the Guildhall, Derry on 21 September 1982.

Fathers and Sons — First performed at the Lyttleton Theatre, South Bank, London on 8 July 1987.

Making History — First performed by Field Day Theatre Company in the Guildhall, Derry on 20 September 1988.

Dancing at Lughnasa — First performed at the Abbey Theatre, Dublin on 24 April 1990.

The London Vertigo — First performed at Andrews Lane Theatre, Dublin on 23 January 1992.

INTRODUCTION

ALAN PEACOCK

Writing in the *Irish Times* on November 4th, 1989, Fintan O'Toole made the following observation:

The decade now drawing to a close has been one in which the Irish Theatre has produced more masterpieces than at any time since the Revival upped and died 60 years ago. Pre-eminently, this has been due to the extraordinary flowering in mid-career of Brian Friel and Tom Murphy. Friel, quite suddenly, produced 'Faith Healer', 'Aristocrats' and 'Translations'. Murphy . . . gave us 'The Gigli Concert' and 'Bailegangaire'.

This can be set against Friel's own view, voiced in the March 17th, 1972 issue of the *Times Literary Supplement*, of the then state of Irish theatre:

. . . in Ireland, as I write this, in the capital's three largest theatres, Boucicault capers on the Abbey stage, Cinderella on the Olympia, Robin Hood on the Gaiety. Some enterprising impresario should book Nero and his fiddle for a long Irish season.

Friel had been recalling the 'high seriousness' which the audience 'in the first quarter of the century' brought to the theatre: 'we recognised then that the theatre was an important social element that not only reflected but shaped the society it served; that the dramatists were revolutionary in the broadest sense of the word; and that subjective truth — the artist's truth — was dangerously independent of church and state.'
   At this point he was on the brink of the transformation in his dramatic outlook which was to lead to the triumphant series of plays to which Fintan O'Toole refers. *The Freedom of the City* in the following year was to initiate the attuning of Friel's dramatic concerns and practice to the pressure of political events, particularly the Northern 'Troubles', in a way that, in the article cited, he had prescribed for Irish drama generally. *The Freedom of the City* and, in 1975, *Volunteers* are not by any means unqualified successes, but they represent, as is now clear, a necessary coming to terms with

contemporary history if the author, identified at the end of the
TLS article as 'novelist' (*sic*) and 'author of *Philadelphia, Here I
Come*', was to outgrow the possibility of such tagging: for still, in
1975, the 1964 *Philadelphia . . .* remained his most achieved play.
The remarkable output between, say, *Living Quarters* (1977) and
Translations (1980) consolidated his status as a major dramatist,
coinciding with, and indeed centrally generative of, the decade of
'masterpieces' in Irish theatre which Fintan O'Toole identifies.

The aim of the present volume is to throw light upon the particular achievement of Friel himself. The crucial, central period is
one obvious focus. In his *A Critical History of Modern Irish
Drama, 1891–1980*, D. E. S. Maxwell notes how 'Over the eighteen
years from 1964, Friel has written the most substantial and impressive body of work in contemporary Irish drama. Its variety,
from the late seventies taking on new strengths, is to be seen in
Philadelphia, Lovers (1967), *Crystal and Fox* (1968), *The Freedom
of the City* (1973), *Aristocrats* (1979), *Faith Healer* (1979), *Translations* (1980) and *The Communication Cord* (1982)'.[1] Taking stock
however in 1973, with only the work up to *The Freedom of the City*
for consideration, the same writer was already able to conclude
that among contemporary Irish dramatists 'Friel has unques-
tionably the body of work most distinguished by its substance, integrity and development . . .'[2] In addition to *Translations* and its
'antidote' (*SP* 21) in *The Communication Cord*, the eighties have
seen further developments: witness his *hommage* to Chekhov in an
'Irishised' version of *Three Sisters* (1981) and a related exercise in
historical and cultural analogy in *Fathers and Sons* (1987); and his
linguistic and historical preoccupations, which so notably inform
Translations, are significantly exercised once again in *Making
History* (1988).

The essays which appear in this volume were largely commis-
sioned in 1989 — an appropriate year for taking stock of Friel's
career. It was the year of his sixtieth birthday, and a year in which
he had been able to close the decade with the touring success and
London production of *Making History* in a way which echoed the
reception of *Translations* at the beginning. The reception of these
two plays in particular, within and beyond Ireland, sealed his
reputation as an Irish dramatist of international stature. In 1989
also, the BBC, uniquely for a modern dramatist, put on a radio
season of his work; while, in his rôle as a public figure in Ireland,
he was completing his term as Senator and had seen Field Day
Theatre Company, of which he was a founding director, establish
itself as a notable cultural force in the North West. Since then, in

1990, with characteristic unpredictability he has produced *Dancing at Lughnasa*, a haunting, ambivalent and strangely inspiriting examination of parallel Christian and pagan traditions co-existing in the Ireland of the 1930s. Its popular and critical success in Dublin, London and New York had notably re-asserted Friel's standing as a dramatist within and beyond Ireland.

The focus in what follows is on Friel as writer and dramatist, though the conjunction, in the above details, of regional, national and international career-markers exemplifies a consistent pattern in his writing and thinking, where questions of general or universal relevance are characteristically predicated on bed-rock notions of allegiance to a given locale and community. Friel's success, in terms of national and international acclaim, has grown centrifugally out of a principled adherence to a commitment to the local, the 'parochial', the regional. This perspective is unshakable in Friel, and if his career has developed or 'moved on', it has done so not in the sense of leaving early influences, roots and allegiances behind, but in terms of a steady expansion of intellectual purview which never loses sight of primary calls upon an individual's loyalty. In this, he is at one with Seamus Heaney, similarly an intellectual and artist of national and international significance, but with tap-roots in specific rural locales of County Derry. As Friel himself has put it: '. . . the world has become much smaller and we should now view ourselves not in an insular but in a world context. . . The canvas can be as small as you wish, but the more accurately you write and the more truthful you are the more validity your play will have for the world.'³

The local affiliation is perhaps the most visible aspect of Friel's programme. Tyrone (of his earliest years), Derry (to which his family moved in 1939 when he was ten) and Donegal (where he visited and holidayed as a child and now chooses to live) provide the characteristic territory of his dramas, as of his early short stories; Donegal assumes an increasing prominence in the later drama, echoing the domiciliary pattern of his life. By contrast, his intellectual horizons are broad, learned and eclectically defined. In historical terms, his drama ranges through sixth century Iona, sixteenth-seventeenth and nineteenth century Ireland and, by translation and analogy, nineteenth century Russia, fifth century Athens and ancient Rome; linguistically, four languages are directly used, English, Irish, Greek and Latin — plus, obliquely, Russian. Conceptually, he utilizes, e.g., linguistic and translation-theory (in *Translations*) and, in *Making History*, provides a dramatic meditation on the integrity of historical narrative. Simultaneously, the whole of his drama may be seen as a continuous examination of Irish culture and politics in the broad sense: analytical, analogical, but not hortatory, doctrinaire or propagandist. He is not a 'political' dramatist in this latter sense, and it is a simplification of a complex, sceptical and humane artistic outlook so to view his practice. He is in fact a man of definite political views. He maintains a broadly nationalist outlook on recent historical events in Northern Ireland; and he is simultaneously concerned about other aspects of Irish life, North and South — the power of the clergy, for instance, and the prospect of Ireland 'becoming a shabby imitation of a third-rate American state.'[4] Like Heaney, however, like Longley, like the late Stewart Parker (the only other contemporary Northern dramatist who might begin to be compared with him in intellectual élan, and formal invention and virtuosity as a dramatic *writer*) and like other contemporary Irish writers he is scrupulously aware of the pitfalls and consequences of a writer's partisan involvement in contemporary politics *in the work*; he is however, in the drama, profoundly interested in the total human situation in which politics have meaning — hence his proclivity to transcultural analogy and historical perspective.

Friel's outlook generally in his drama is not susceptible to monolithic redaction or simplistic pigeon-holing. He is at his best when at furthest stretch in terms of the referential complexity of the drama — as in *Translations*: an Irish nineteenth century hedge school is the setting, cultural erosion under colonial pressure is the theme, the demise of a language is the focus, while Greece, Rome, Carthage and the decline of humanism are a central part of the play of ideas. Yet, and here is the particular achievement of the play, this is popular drama, premièred in 'provincial' Derry, but uncompromising in its intellectual seriousness and in the dramatic conventions which it requires the audience to accept. Friel has emerged progressively as a dramatist of ideas. The achievement of the last decade, from *Translations* to *Making History*, has explicitly reinforced the fact that Friel is an intellectual, a deft handler, like Stoppard, of technical vocabularies relating to particular disciplines, who is able to mobilise them for his own, often ironic, purposes. The equivocal use of 'expert' testimony in *The Freedom of the City* was an early instance of this technique; and Friel can deploy a technical jargon with complex, tragic irony in the mouth of Dodds, the sociologist in *Freedom . . .* , or in the spirit of intellectual farce, as in the case of Tim Gallagher's doctoral work on 'Discourse Analysis with Particular Reference to Response Cries' in *The Communication Cord* (1982).

These plays make exhilaratingly explicit a preoccupation with the dubieties, the duplicities, limitations and simultaneous analytical, expressive and transcendent qualities of language which is ubiquitous in Friel's drama. It is an aspect of his work which is treated, from different perspectives, by a number of the essays in the present work. The power of naming and its political or metaphysical consequences; the problematics of self-definition through language and the tyranny of imposed definitions at a personal, social or national level; emotional inarticulacy at the individual level and cultural aphasia at the national; authentic and inauthentic narrative — these are the kind of themes which insistently feature in Friel's drama.

Crucially, though, these issues are not pursued as abstractions. Within the humane scope of this drama, the idea-content is always predicated on recognizable, intimate human experience within a given familial or social circle. Society is always *there*, a robust 'given'. It may, in its manifold groupings and manifestations, be variously probed, criticised, idealised, ridiculed; it is however never dismissed. Friel, throughout his career, resists the absurdist, the nihilistic — in short, the Beckettian option. In a lecture published in 1968, he showed himself sharply aware of the perspectives afforded by contemporary dramatic practice:

What modern dramatists are saying is this. They say, with Nietzsche, that God is dead and that all traditional values died with Him. They say that man can create new values only by becoming God — that the only alternative to nihilism lies in revolt. They say, with Camus, that this revolt is born of the spectacle of irrationality, confronted with an unjust and incomprehensible condition. They say that the Church as a divine institution is an absurdity. . . They say that the conventions, morals and values of social organism that we know are suspect.[5]

Waiting for Godot is quoted as the exemplar of this syndrome. Friel's reaction is telling. He is fully willing to assimilate the dramaturgical lesson: 'the days of the solid, well-made play are gone' — that is, the plays which work with structural neatness to the cosy resolution of a given problem: 'these plays are finished because we know that life is about as remote from a presentation-problem-resolution cycle as it can be.' Having been asked, however, to talk about 'the Theatre of Hope and Despair', he embraces the former option. Dramatists, amid all the dubieties 'have this function: they are vitally, persistently, and determinedly concerned with one man's insignificant place in the here-and-now world. They have the function to portray that one man's frustrations and hopes and anguishes and joys and miseries and pleasures with all the accuracy and truth that they know; and by so doing help to make a community of individuals.' This conviction, against the grain of contemporary European drama as he sees it, that the individual, the community can be the dramatic location of non-reductive examinations of the human conditions is the measure of his stature. He is thinking beyond the parochialisms of modernism.

The position is broadly humanistic, though 'accuracy and truth' and a commitment to the 'here-and-now world' imply a certain specificity — and hence his composite, fictional locale of Ballybeg, the representative Donegal town within which his drama, since *Philadelphia, Here I Come!*, is characteristically set: it has a con-vincing social and regional character, but without any limiting or distracting reference to any particular place. By the same token, Friel's plays are set within recognisable social, historical and cultural circumstances: often in fact within the unitary Catholic society represented by Ballybeg. This might be misinterpreted as a failure of imagination on his part, a reluctance to write beyond his own community. In fact, the opposite is the case. A given, stable set of social relations allows, paradoxically, for universalisation. The fact that the religious ethos is, arbitrarily, Catholic means that religion is not an issue: the plays may then work at an essentially secular level. Familial myth, authority and social identity are, for instance, examined and subtly exploded in *Aristocrats* within an upper-middle-class milieu; it is however not the great-house culture of the Protestant Ascendancy, familiar from so much Anglo-Irish literature in various genres. It is in fact a Catholic family which is depicted, entailing less accumulated socio-literary complication, and hence transposable in its implications to other families in other places.

Friel does not seek one-for-one topicality or correspondence with documentary or historical fact in his drama. His plays are acts of imagination. Their preoccupations are characteristically ethical, philosophical or metaphysical as much as political, social or historical. In fact, as Friel's career develops and diversifies, it becomes increasingly difficult to discover broad, stable, categor-ised lines of development. A number of possible models present themselves: the shift, seen in the earliest radio pieces and plays, from the natural world which is often the setting of the short stories to the social world as a predominant background for human self-realisation; the development, from *The Enemy Within* (1962) to *Crystal and Fox* (1968), of a drama concerned with various kinds of 'love' (Friel's own categorisation or with individual 'character'

(George O'Brien's heading)[6] — giving way, from *The Freedom of the City* (1973) onwards, to a drama more directly involved with the socio-political world, where a social organism or group such as the family takes the place of the complex individual psyche as the human focus. This development, broadened into an historical perspective, may be seen as reaching its culmination in 1980 with *Translations*. *Translations* in turn is a nodal text for Friel's pre-occupations with language in its complex cultural significances, its manifold realisations, its glories and duplicities. The theme had already been prominently introduced in *The Freedom of the City*, and the interrelationship examined in *Translations* between language and national history and destiny was to be taken up as a central issue in *Making History* (1988). Meanwhile, through the eighties, Friel had explored the possibilities of 'translation' in the broadest sense with the comic contemporary reprise of the pre-occupations of *Translations* in *The Communication Cord* (1982), the trans-cultural analogising of his version of Chekhov's *Three Sisters* (1981), and the extension of this vein in *Fathers and Sons* (1987). Again, these developments of the eighties had been prefigured in the seventies with *Living Quarters* (1977), Friel's adaptation of Euripides' *Hippolytus*.

Each new work tends to set us riffling through the corpus and discovering newly apparent patterns of development and possible referential grids. *Crystal and Fox* (1968) to take a further example, with its portrayal of Fox Melarkey's obscure, grim compulsion to reduce his world and that of his companions to stark, ruinous bedrock, may have seemed, on first appearance, a cryptic study in obsessive behaviour and apparently gratuitous cruelty, radically diverging from the vein of *Philadelphia, Here I Come!* and *Lovers*. Looked at backwards however from, say, *Faith Healer* (1979), and its study of Frank Hardy's self-destructive questing after a not easily definable goal, its metaphysic seems clearer. Similarly, the recent *Dancing at Lughnasa*, with its mixing of pagan and Christian elements, its probing of primal needs and ritualised extremes of behaviour within the prim world of thirties Ireland, may refer us back to the violent, primitivistic myth-puncturing vision of West of Ireland life (mutilation, sexual repression, cruelty to animals) in *The Gentle Island* (1971) or, again, to *Faith Healer* and its final scene of communal, ritualised slaughter of a human 'victim'.

To make such connections, however, is to make only limited comment on plays whose central preoccupations require complex exegesis. The above comments on some of the thematic consti-tuents of *Dancing at Lughnasa*, for instance, would not bring out the primary impact of the play as a notably entertaining, amusing and, at one key moment, electrifying theatrical experience. The scene where the four sisters launch themselves progressively into a spontaneous, wild, Dionysiac dance, as carefully choreographed in Friel's stage instructions and faithfully interpreted in Patrick Mason's Abbey Theatre production, was a piece of pure theatre: Ireland's finest theatrical *writer* had brought off the core scene in his drama entirely in non-verbal terms. Friel's dramatic imagination and technical invention continue to out-flank expectations. It is a dramaturgy at once profoundly adventurous and simultaneously keyed to the thematic content of the individual play. The use of dance within the anthropological view of Irish society in *Dancing at Lughnasa* is as bold and integral as the dramatic separation of Public and Private Gar in Friel's first major success in *Philadelphia, Here I Come!*

The pattern and scope of Friel's development is not, therefore, amenable to easy encapsulation. His career is a complex pattern of subtle continuities and new departures; and the *oeuvre* is now an extensive one. In its attempt to survey and assess this achievement, the present volume follows a particular strategy. The idea is to bring to bear a variety of academic and professional approaches calculated to respond to particular aspects of his work and thought. Thus, the contributors range from playwright, poet, theatre critic and theatre director, with their particular practical and professional insights, to academics from various disciplines with relevant specialisms to offer. These include literary theory, Irish history, fiction, drama and social history; and there are also contributions from writers with particular interests in the various languages and literatures which constitute the extended literary and cultural context of Friel's work. Within these different professional and disciplinary approaches, various critical views and methodologies are apparent.

Thus, although the book provides a wide-ranging survey of the development of Friel's career, it is not constituted on a strict play-by-play linear chronology. The focus is essentially on the drama, and in particular the body of dramatic work in the public domain in the form of published volumes (i.e., excluding for the most part early plays and radio and TV scripts which are available only in typescript). One contribution deals with the short stories in relation to the dramatic work. The organisation, within a broad chronological frame-work, is essentially thematic; and it is a feature of the book that key works find treatment in more than one essay, and hence are illuminated by comment and interpretation from different critics, approaching the work from distinct disciplinary and professional standpoints. The titles of the individual essays indicate the particular tangents at which their authors come to Friel's work. By these means, it is hoped to give some sense of the breadth, quality, and dramaturgical and intellectual richness of the work of Ireland's leading dramatist in a survey which ranges from *The Enemy Within* (1962) to the latest published play, *The London Vertigo*. It is a remarkable achievement and, as the success of *Dancing at Lughnasa* powerfully suggests, it is only the achievement *so far*.

' "DONGING THE TOWER" – THE PAST DID HAVE MEANING': THE SHORT STORIES OF BRIAN FRIEL

JOHN CRONIN

The great short story writers tend, naturally enough, to be associated with their most masterly tales: Joyce and 'The Dead'; Lawrence and 'Odour of Chrysanthemums'; Sean O'Faolain and 'A Broken World'; Frank O'Connor and 'Guests of the Nation'. It may not be entirely without significance that one does not tend to think of Friel and his stories in this way. Admirably skilful as many of them are, no great classic of the form leaps to mind at mention of his name. An early reviewer of his second collection, *The Gold in the Sea*, while he commended the general competence of the performance, also noted that 'we do not, finally, have much sense of a searching or transforming view of life behind these tales', and concluded the review with what, in view of Friel's subsequent career, can be seen as a canny perception that it would not be in this genre that Friel would most effectively express his genius:

Although they often impress, they remain disparate and self-contained, and thus their effect, when collected, is a muted one. The talent is there, but it is not yet in full possession of its characteristic and identifying mode.[1]

The 'characteristic and identifying mode' was, as we now know, to be found subsequently in the drama, and the result is that commenting on the short stories a quarter of a century later, from beyond the major achievement of the plays, is a rather daunting task. It is inevitable that, viewed from the impressive heights Friel has scaled in the theatre, the early work in the stories will seem, however unfairly, somewhat diminished and shrunken by comparison. Pointless, ultimately, to view the stories in complete isolation from the plays and yet, enshrined as they are in two neat volumes, *The Saucer of Larks* (1962) and *The Gold in the Sea* (1966), they seem somehow to demand separate consideration in their own right.

In the main, the stories precede the plays, if we exclude such early efforts as the two radio plays, *A Sort of Freedom* and *To This Hard House*,

1

and two early stage plays which Friel seems keen to disown, *A Doubtful Paradise* and *The Blind Mice*. The two radio plays were broadcast by the Northern Ireland Home Service of the BBC in 1958 and both were, as D.E.S. Maxwell indicates, somewhat similar to the short stories:

Friel wrote these plays while he was still primarily occupied with the short story. They recall 'The Illusionists,' 'The Flower of Kiltymore,' 'The Gold in the Sea,' whose characters are similarly engaged in their various degrees of compromise with disappointment and the hard life. The plays, however, do not achieve their design with the authority of the stories. In both of them there is perhaps some uncertainty about their intention . . . With the disappearance, too, of the stories' narrative and description, the dialogue has to assume new obligations that it is not yet able to fulfil. There is no equivalent to the mediating voice that in the stories suggests directions of understanding and sympathy.[2]

As this suggests, Friel had yet to achieve an effective transition from the private art of the short story to the public art of the theatre. He himself remarked the distinction between the two kinds of literary endeavour in the course of a public lecture in 1967:

The dramatist does not write for one man; he writes for an audience, a collection of people. His technique is the very opposite of the short story writer's or the novelist's. They function privately, man to man, a *personal* conversation. Everything they write has the implicit preface, 'Come here till I whisper in your ear'.[3]

This echoes both Flann O'Brien's tongue-in-cheek account (in *At Swim-Two-Birds*) of the play as something 'consumed in wholesome fashion by large masses in places of public resort' and Frank O'Connor's description (in *The Lonely Voice*) of the short story as 'a private art to satisfy the standards of the individual, solitary, critical reader', an art which rings 'with the tone of a man's voice speaking'. Whereas Friel the dramatist was to prove a daring and exciting innovator, as a short story writer he is strictly in the traditional line of development from such as O'Faolain, O'Connor and fellow Northerner, Michael McLaverty. His Field Day associate, Seamus Deane, has noted this:

Brian Friel is, technically speaking, a traditional writer. The dislocations and the nuanced egoism of many modern texts are sternly avoided, even rejected here.[4]

The reader of the stories, then, experiences first of all a sense of familiarity. Neither matter nor manner is strange in the best modern way. Predecessors in the form come frequently to mind as we read.

Friel's first published story, 'The Child', scarcely more than a vignette, had appeared in *The Bell* in July, 1952, and his literary debt to that most famous Bell-man, Sean O'Faolain, is evident in a number of the stories. It emerges clearly, for example, in the calculatedly genial tone of the mild, anti-clerical mockery indulged in by Thomas, narrator of 'The Highwayman and the Saint', a story which vividly recalls O'Faolain's 'Childybawn'. 'The Death of a Scientific Humanist' is yet another successful venture by Friel into O'Faolain's favourite territory of urbane satire against the inhumane rigidities of Catholic Church dogma. Least satisfying among Friel's stories are the quasi-autobiographical, first-person tales which incline to neatly formulaic closures, often reminiscent of correspondingly contrived climaxes in the stories of Frank O'Connor. O'Connor's favoured comic ploy, the innocent child's viewpoint on the strange world of the adults, is often in evidence, with correspondingly cloying effects. 'The First of My Sins' seems to owe much to O'Connor's well-known 'First Confession'. Stories like 'The Fawn Pup', revolving around the remembered teacher-father figure, smack of the incidental hilarities of the 'R.M.' stories of Somerville and Ross, while 'Segova, the Savage Turk' produces an even flimsier comedy, scarcely lifting the central episode of the boy narrator's disastrous shaving of his body hair much beyond the level of comic triviality. 'Ginger Hero', the final story in *The Gold in the Sea*, inevitably challenges comparison with Michael McLaverty's classic tale, 'The Game Cock', though the reticent McLaverty would hardly have found the rather contrived sexual climax of Friel's story much to his taste. A contemporary reviewer of *The Saucer of Larks* suggested that these early stories suffered from the dictates of a particular house-style:

If the reader is left faintly dissatisfied it is perhaps because too many of the stories fall so neatly into the formula of slightly dotty recollection now so popular with the *New Yorker*.[5]

It would, clearly, serve little real purpose to dwell unduly on the weaker, more derivative aspects of prentice work by a writer who had yet to discover his true medium. More to the point to note the emergence in this early work of themes and preoccupations which were to come to full artistic fruition later, in the plays. The best of the stories at once identify Friel's chosen territory of Tyrone and Donegal and also effectively explore his deeply-felt involvement with the shaping themes of love, language and a torturing nostalgia for an irretrievable past. All of these concerns cohere powerfully in 'Among the Ruins', a story in which a family sets out together, at the wife's suggestion, to revisit the father's birthplace in Donegal. The serious issues probed here are lightly carried on an eminently credible thread of narrative, with the two children squabbling in the car, the wife efficiently organising the picnic food, and the father, Joe, at first reluctant to risk this trip into his past but gradually becoming more and more excited by the prospect of revisiting once familiar and much-loved surroundings:

'I don't see the point,' he had said. 'I don't see the point at all.'

But she had persisted, and that night and the next day his stubbornness gave way to a stirring of memory and then to a surprising excitement that revealed itself in his silence and his foolish grin. And now that they were about to set off, there was added a great surge of gratitude to her for tapping this forgotten source of joy in him. She knew and understood him so well.[6]

The place names, always of central importance in Friel's writing, come back to Joe as they drive westwards: Corradinna, Meenalaragan, Glenmakennif, Altanure. They recall boyhood vigour and youthful joy in the natural scene. The reality, when they eventually arrive at Joe's humble birthplace in Corradinna, is a dreadful anti-climax – a ruined house, a trickle of water instead of the remembered river, and the 'bower' where the child Joe hid with his sister gone forever. The past, full of intensely experienced and vividly remembered joy, is desecrated by the drab, ruined realities of the present. The journey has, clearly, been a frightful mistake:

Was that his childhood? Why, Joe wondered, had he been so excited about the trip that morning? What had he expected to find at Corradinna – a restoration of innocence? A dream confirmed? He could not remember. All he knew now was that the visit had been a mistake. It had robbed him of a precious thing, his illusions of his past, and in their place now there was nothing – nothing at all but the truth.[7]

Forced by his wife's insistence that he explain to her the youthful fun he so clearly recalls, Joe can only lamely recount what now seem ludicrously silly word games played with his sister in the long ago:

'What did we laugh at?' An explanation was necessary. We must have laughed at something. There must have been something that triggered it off.

'Are you not going to tell me?' Margo's face had sharpened. She stood before him, insisting on a revelation.

'Susan and I –' he mumbled.

'I know,' she said quickly. 'Susan and you in the bower. Once you got there together, you laughed your heads off. And I want to know what you laughed *at*.'

'She would make up a word – any word, any silly-sounding word – and that would set us off,' he said, clutching at the first faint memory that occurred to him. 'Some silly word like – like "sligalog," or "skookalook". That sort of thing.'

' "Skookalook." What's funny about that?'

'I don't know if that was one of them. I meant just any made-up word at all. In there, in the bower, somehow it seemed to sound – so funny.'

'And that's all?'

'That was all,' he said limply.[8]

The story briefly veers towards possible tragedy, with the sudden disappearance of the little boy, Peter, who wanders away to play on his own. The panic-stricken Joe eventually finds the child:

Peter was so engrossed in his play that he was not aware of his father until Joe caught him by the shoulder and shook him. He was on his knees at the mouth of a rabbit-hole, sticking small twigs into the soft earth.

'Peter! What the hell!'

'Look, Daddy. Look! I'm donging the tower!'

'Did you not hear me shouting? Are you deaf?'

'Let me stay, Daddy. I'll have the tower donged in another five minutes.'[9]

Impatiently, Joe drags the child away from his game of 'donging the tower' and, as they drive homewards, Joe ponders on what the day has brought in the way of disenchantment. He realises that he should not have gone back to Corradinna 'because the past is a mirage – a soft illusion into which we step to escape the present'. He is saved from despair by the sudden recollection of the odd phrase used by his little son to describe his solitary game at the rabbit burrow, 'donging the tower'. A seemingly meaningless word embraces a moment of private joy and Joe is granted a consoling sense of a continuity transmitted to him through the child's baby-talk:

Through the mesmerism of motor, fleeing hedges, shadows flying from the headlights, three words swam into Joe's head. 'Donging the tower.' What did Peter mean, he wondered dreamily; what game was he playing, donging the tower? He recalled the child's face, engrossed, earnest with happiness, as he squatted on the ground by the rabbit hole. A made-up game, Joe supposed, already forgotten. He would ask him in the morning, but Peter would not know. Just out of curiosity, he would ask him, not that it mattered. . . And then a flutter of excitement stirred in him. Yes, yes, it did matter. Not the words, not the game, but the fact that he had seen his son, on the first good day of summer, busily, intently happy in solitude, donging the tower. The fact that Peter would never remember it was of no importance; it was his own possession now, his own happiness, this knowledge of a child's private joy.[10]

The story ends with a brave assertion, and with a neatly generalised simplicity which, later, the plays will constantly call in question:

The past did have meaning. It was neither reality nor dreams, neither today's patchy oaks nor the great woods of his boyhood. It was simply continuance, life repeating itself and surviving.[11]

This comforting nostrum will be rejected in play after play. In *Philadelphia, Here I Come!*, Gar struggles in vain to persuade his father that the boat they fished from sixteen years earlier was a blue boat and that his father had suddenly sung 'All Round My Hat I'll Wear a Green Coloured Ribbono'. His father insists that he never knew that song and that the boat may have been brown in colour, not blue at all. In the play, Friel has found, in the brilliant device of the two Gars, Public and Private, a vehicle for the expression through savage comedy of many painfully conflicting views of the past and, at the end, old Madge, pragmatic voice of present reality, is not permitted any placebo about the comforting continuity of the generations:

When the boss was his (Gar's) age, he was the very same as him: leppin, and eejitin' about and actin' the clown; as like as two peas. And when he's (Gar) the age the boss is now, he'll turn out just the same. And although I won't be here to see it, you'll find that he's learned nothin' in-between times. That's people for you – they'd put you astray in the head if you thought long enough about them.   (*SP* 98)

Cass McGuire is another stalwart who does battle against the dangerous lure of the past, determined not to be trapped by its delusive seductions. She holds out as long as she can against the pressure from Trilbe and Ingram before she yields to them by sitting in the winged chair and retreating with them from grim reality into a world of fantasy. In Act 2, she had railed against 'this gawddam going back into the past!' and asked 'who the hell knows what happened in the past!' and had fought against the temptation to flee the unbearable pain of the present:

CASS: (*to Trilbe*) Leave me alone, will you? (*To audience*) They think they're going to run me back into the past but by Gawd they're not . . . I live in the present, Harry boy, right here and now. Where are you? Stick with me.
TRILBE: Catherine!
CASS: Go away! Gooks . . . real gooks living in the past, but not Cass McGuire.[12]

In the end, she can accommodate herself to the hideous reality of her existence in Eden House only by joining Trilbe and Ingram in their escapist, illusory world of dream and story-telling.

Crystal and Fox offers perhaps the most ferocious comment of all on the human tendency to retrospection, with Fox setting about the appalling business of refashioning his early idyll with Crystal by killing Pedro's beloved dog and even betraying his own son to the police. 'Among the Ruins' is, indeed, uncharacteristically reassuring about the onslaughts of time, and a later story, 'The Wee Lake Beyond', provides an altogether bleaker view of the relationships between the generations, a view much closer to that of the plays. Unrepresentative though 'Among the Ruins' may be, however, in the optimism of its conclusion, it is entirely typical of Friel's stories in its deeply felt involvement with a beloved locality. As Joe drives back to his birthplace in Donegal, the petty irritations of squabbling children and his wife's nagging objections to his fast driving all fall away, as he sees once again the hills and valleys he roamed as a boy:

At this moment, I don't give a damn, he thought without callousness; at this moment, with Meenalaragan and Pigeon Top on my left and Glenmakennif and Altanure on my right. Because these are my hills, and I knew them before I knew wife and children.[13]

This note of strong personal involvement with beloved places, this habit of uttering their names in a kind of litany of passionate reminiscence, is everywhere in the stories, as it is also, later, in the plays. As D.E.S. Maxwell notes:

The 'real' world of Brian Friel's short stories reaches from Kincasslagh in the west of Donegal through Strabane, Derry City, and Coleraine to Omagh and County Tyrone. Alongside, at times superimposed on, these actual places are the imagined towns, villages and country districts – Beannafreaghan, Glennafuiseog, Corradinna, Mullaghduff. These are composites and extensions of reality, given substance by an intense receptiveness to the atmosphere of a day or season, to the run of landscape, the play of light and shade, all the tangibles that localize a time and place. The vibrant solidity of the settings is perhaps the strongest single impression left by the world of these stories, memorable because never merely a background décor.[14]

The Sergeant in the title story of *The Saucer of Larks* 'had been twenty years in Donegal but there were times when its beauty still shocked him', and it is, indeed, the startling beauty of Glenn-na-fuiseog, the 'valley of the larks', which moves him to try to persuade the visiting German police officers to disobey their superiors by leaving untouched the grave of the German airman whose body they plan to disinter. The recitation of the names of much-loved places in the stories prepares us for the potent naming and cataloguing of places in plays such as *Faith Healer* and *Translations*.

Not surprisingly, when Friel turned to plays in place of short stories, characters, themes and preoccupations made familiar in the stories tended to surface in the new medium as well. Indeed, one can clearly sense the impulse to the dramatic form already manifesting itself in the liveliness of the dialogue assigned to some of the characters in the stories. In 'Straight from His Colonial Success', for example, the conversation between stay-at-home Joe and the friend, Bryson, who has returned from abroad bringing with him a tantalising flavour of exotic places and a cosmopolitan sophistication, powerfully presages many of the exchanges between the two Gars in *Philadelphia*. The vigorous alternation of mood and attitude in the short story is ener-getically handled and Joe's pathetic efforts to recapture the elusive image of a younger, brasher Bryson bring the occasion much closer to the generally pessimistic mood of the plays than to the rather facile optimism of 'Among the Ruins'. Some of the memorably dominant characters in the plays have already been given, as it were, a kind of trial run in the stories. Thus, the gallantly despairing Cass McGuire is clearly prefigured by the title character of 'Aunt Maggie, the Strong One'. Aunt Maggie, like Cass, is consigned to an old people's home at the end of her days. Like Cass, she smokes too much. Like Cass, she professes an unconvincing independence of her relatives. Here again, as in *Philadelphia*, the past is evoked by mention of a song which the narrator's father used to sing. When story and play are considered together, one can readily sense how the gallant, loud-mouthed, doomed Maggie has broken out of the smaller confines of the story form and mutated into the figure of Cass McGuire, who voices a similarly resolute outlook on life but does so through dramatic encounters with a wider range of characters. The story had allowed Maggie to respond only to her nephew, Bernard, and the smaller form's insistence on concentration and sharpness of focus had required that Maggie be encountered by the reader only at the moment of her death, when all her battles have finally been lost. In the play, in the form of Cass McGuire, she will be given longer to rage against the dying of the light.

Sometimes, an entire story, and not merely a single character, will develop towards dramatic form. 'The Highwayman and the Saint' becomes the play, *Losers*, with remarkably little in the way of addi-tional business or detail. Just one new character, the sickeningly pious Cissy Cassidy, is added, to become Mrs Wilson's companion in cant, and the poem hilariously recited by the unfortunate Andy during his constantly frustrated attempts at love-making becomes Gray's 'Elegy Written in a Country Churchyard' in place of 'The Highwayman' by Alfred Noyes. The short story, which is very much a satire in the O'Faolain manner on sexual repression and craw-thumping religiosity, is very close indeed to the play it becomes. The move here between the two forms has been accomplished with striking ease, almost as though the near-farce of the story had already achieved as much in the way of dramatic form as was necessary to its somewhat limited targets. On the other hand, the process by which a very different type of story, 'Foundry House', was eventually transformed into the play, *Aristocrats*, seems altogether more complex. Friel is engaging here not with the stock Aunt Sallies already much targeted by such predecessors as O'Faolain and O'Connor, but with concerns closer to his own searching imagination, so that, this time, the move to dramatic form opens up much greater possibilities. While some of the story's most effective details, such as the eerily recorded and tinny voice of the missionary nun in Africa, are retained and developed in the play, *Aristocrats* casts its net much more widely, to explore at greater length issues which can only be hinted at in the more constricted form of the short story. Here again, the essential distinction is between the short story's necessarily sharp focus on a single character, the subservient Joe Brennan, and the greater freedom granted by dramatic form for the searching exploration of numerous figures and many issues. In 'Foundry House', the Hogans are described as 'one of the best Catholic families in the North of Ireland' and their decline appears to derive from the decision of their son and daughter to enter the celibate world of the religious, with the daughter finally exiled to distant Africa and the son a priest in another part of Ireland. The ruinous sterility of the offspring of the Big House is clear. We are told about 'fat, blue-eyed Claire, who had blushed every time she passed the gate-lodge' and the epicene quality of the son, Fr Declan, is hinted at throughout. Joe Brennan and Fr Declan are the same age, thirty-three, but already Joe is the father of no fewer than nine children. When the priest opens the front door of the Foundry House to admit the stolidly matter-of-fact Joe, the contrast between the two men is pointed up sharply:

Father Declan was fair and slight, and his gestures fluttering and birdlike. The black suit accentuated the whiteness of his hair and skin and hands.[15]

Fr Declan's fingers are depicted 'playing arpeggios' over the recording machine which Joe has brought at Mrs Hogan's request, and he stands 'poised as a ballet dancer before the fire'. When the recording sent by Sr Claire from Africa is being played to the assembled company, the first person addressed is the priest, whose languid pose is noted even by the uncritical Joe:

She addressed the priest first, and Joe looked at him – eyes closed, hands joined at the left shoulder, head to the side, feet crossed, his whole body limp and graceful as if in repose.[16]

The robust health of Joe's nine offspring is constantly emphasised, being noted in particular by Mrs Hogan, and contrasts forcefully with the general sterility and decline of the Hogans. The old father, terror of Joe's youth, is by now an almost paralysed hulk. The shocking climax of the story is reached when he utters his one strangled cry on hearing his daughter's voice on the tape-recorder:

The dead purple of his cheeks was now a living scarlet, and the mouth was open. Then, even as Joe watched, he suddenly levered himself upright in the chair, his face pulsating with uncontrollable emotion, the veins in his neck dilating, the mouth shaping in preparation for speech. He leaned forward, half pointing toward the recorder with one huge hand.
    'Claire!'[17]

For all its powerful contrasts, however, the story suggests no explanation for the Hogans' decline, other than the celibate state of their two unimpressive offspring. When Friel casts this material into play form, he effects radical alterations. To begin with, he shifts the location significantly. Foundry House in 'the North of Ireland' becomes instead 'Ballybeg Hall, County Donegal, Ireland' and the O'Donnell family, who replace the Hogans here, are professional people, long involved in the legal system of the country at senior level. Traces of the effeminate Fr Declan survive, perhaps, in the son, Casimir, whose hectic, overstated behaviour creates a kind of feverish excitement throughout. As he tries to explain to Eamon in Act 3, he has long been aware of his own oddity:

I discovered a great truth when I was nine. No, not a great truth; but I made a great discovery when I was nine – not even a great discovery but an important, a very important discovery for me. I suddenly realized I was different from other boys. When I say I was different I don't mean – you know – good Lord, I don't for a second mean I was – you know – as they say nowadays 'homo-sexual' – good heavens I must admit, if anything, Eamon, if anything I'm – (*Looks around.*) – I'm vigorously hetero-sexual ha-ha.   (*SP* 310)

The embittered Eamon, now married to the alcoholic daughter, Alice, though he once loved her older sister, Judith, outlines the family's professional decline to the American researcher, Tom Hoffnung, in caustically comic manner:

And of course you'll have chapters on each of the O'Donnell forebears: Great Grandfather – Lord Chief Justice; Grandfather – Circuit Court Judge; Father – simple District Justice; Casimir – failed solicitor. A fairly rapid descent; but no matter, no matter; good for the book; failure's more lovable than success. D'you know, Professor, I've often wondered: if we had had children and they wanted to be part of the family legal tradition, the only option open to them would have been as criminals, wouldn't it? (*SP* 295)

Most significantly, perhaps, Friel suggests in the play that the decline of the O'Donnells is somehow related to their culpable detachment from the violent affairs of nearby Northern Ireland, thereby giving to the issue a political colouring totally lacking in the short story. When Tom Hoffnung quizzes Alice about Eamon and Judith, it emerges that Eamon has lost his Dublin diplomatic post through his involvement with the Civil Rights movement in the North, and that Judith brought about her father's first stroke by taking part in the Battle of the Bogside and fighting with the police. In reply to Tom's question concerning her father's attitude to the Civil Rights campaign, Alice replies:

ALICE: He opposed it. No, that's not accurate. He was indifferent: that was across the Border – away in the North.
TOM: Only twenty miles away.
ALICE: Politics never interested him. Politics are vulgar. (*SP* 272)

Direct involvement in the vulgarity of politics runs counter to the family's careful avoidance of commitment in the past, as Eamon's savagely comic account makes clear, when he advises the American that his proposed book about Catholic Big House influence should be turned into fiction rather than fact:

A great big block-buster of a gothic novel called *Ballybeg Hall – From Supreme Court to Sausage Factory*; four generations of a great Irish Catholic legal dynasty; the gripping saga of a family that lived its life in total isolation in a gaunt Georgian house on top of a hill above the remote Donegal village of Ballybeg; a family without passion, without loyalty, without commitments; administering the law for anyone who happened to be in power; above all wars and famines and civil strife and political upheaval; ignored by its Protestant counterparts, isolated from the mere Irish, existing only in its own concept of itself, brushing against reality occasionally by its cultivation of artists; but tough – oh, yes, tough, resilient, tenacious; and with one enormous talent for – no, a *greed* for survival – that's the family motto, isn't it? *Semper permanemus*. (*SP* 294)

This comprehensive indictment of the O'Donnells as 'Castle Catholics' carefully indifferent to the political struggle of their co-religionists in the North is a far cry from the vignette of the Hogans supplied by the more exiguous short story form. Furthermore, *Aristocrats* provides Friel with yet another opportunity for airing his favourite view of history as a creation of the fertile imagination rather than a record of identifiable fact. The amiable but literal-minded Tom Hoffnung is peddled a litany of historical improbabilities by all and sundry but particularly by

Casimir. His brain reels in the presence of the string of notables who, according to Casimir, visited Ballybeg Hall in its great days. Chesterton, John McCormack, Gerard Manley Hopkins, Cardinal Newman, Yeats . . . will the line stretch out to the crack of doom? Hoffnung establishes to his own satisfaction that mere chronology makes all this impossible but, when Casimir appeals to Eamon for support for his fantasies, Eamon comfortingly replies that 'there are certain things, certain truths, Casimir, that are beyond Tom's kind of scrutiny'. That there is a truth greater and more complex than mere historical fact is Friel's most constant assertion, repeated in play after play, from *The Freedom of the City* to *Making History*. He had spelt out the notion quite explicitly in the course of an account of his own boyhood, where he recalled a fishing trip on which his father had taken him at the age of nine. This vivid personal reminiscence lies behind many such moments in the plays and powerfully echoes such short stories as 'The Wee Lake Beyond':

And there we were, the two of us, soaking wet, splashing along a muddy road that comes in at right-angles to Glenties main street, singing about how my boat can safely float through the teeth of wind and weather. That's the memory. That's what happened. A trivial episode without importance to anyone but me, just a moment of happiness caught in an album. But wait. There's something wrong here. I'm conscious of a dissonance, an unease. What is it? Yes, I know what it is: there is no lake along that muddy road. And since there is no lake my father and I never walked back from it in the rain with our rods across our shoulders. The fact is a fiction. Have I imagined the scene then? Or is it a composite of two or three different episodes? The point is – I don't think it matters. What matters is that for some reason. . . this vivid memory is there in the storehouse of the mind. For some reason the mind has shuffled the pieces of verifiable truth and composed a truth of its own. For to me it is a truth. And because I acknowledge its peculiar veracity, it becomes a layer in my subsoil; it becomes part of me; ultimately it becomes me.[18]

The stories occasionally hint at the past's complexities but it is the plays which most memorably provide space for the multiple perspectives required to shuffle the pieces of verifiable truth and extract from them their peculiar veracity. Where the protagonists of the stories assert, sometimes a little desperately, that 'the past did have meaning' and seek to recapture that meaning in a phrase such as 'donging the tower' or in the chance survival of a name, as in the closing lines of 'Kelly's Hall', it was to be in the public art of the theatre that Friel would set in exciting opposition to one another the many voices which would, between them, embrace the complexity of his particular vision of truth.

In a typically self-deprecatory piece of jocosely imagined interview, Friel has posed for himself a set of stock questions and answered them with characteristic modesty:

When did you know you were going to be a writer? The answer is, I've no idea. What other writers influenced you most strongly? I've no idea. Which of your plays is your favourite? None of them. Which of your stories? Most of them embarrass me.[19]

Embarrassment is needless. The stories, early as they are and, often, clearly derivative in tone and theme, nevertheless contain frequent hints of necessary explorations to come. Reading them, we are, as it were, watching the dancer exercising at the barre before he moves into the spatial freedom of his essential art.

THE PENALTIES OF RETROSPECT: CONTINUITIES IN BRIAN FRIEL

NEIL CORCORAN

In the introduction to his edition of Brian Friel's selected plays in 1984 Seamus Deane outlines an account of the career which is, it seems, the more or less generally accepted one. The pattern proposes a radical break at the time of *The Gentle Island* (first performed in 1971); that play constitutes the rejection of the earlier work and the beginning of a new theatrical phase 'in which the emotions of utter repudiation would replace the half-lights of exiled longing'.[1] The earlier work, that is to say, for all its local satisfactions, is enmeshed in moods and pre-occupations which can be too easily and availably recuperated by an almost unexamined Irish and Irish-American emotionalism and commercialism; the later work (registering the shock of the Northern crisis after 1968) turns away from the glamour and seductiveness of those well-worked Irish theatrical themes and sails out dangerously into the uncharted waters of a more deeply perturbing and perturbed consciousness of self and society. These perturbations eventually register most acutely in an explicitation of language itself as theme, and they issue in the indubitable masterpiece of *Translations* (1980), with its practical and symbolic significance in the founding of Field Day, part of whose cultural-political programme it may be thought to articulate and incarnate.

In what follows here I have no great wish to revise this contour: it seems to me the proper one, the proper way of reading Friel and the proper way of understanding the way the dramatist has responded to the urgencies and responsibilities of his own historical and political moment. But in thinking again about Friel's beginnings as a playwright, I want to think too about those elements in his work which have retained a continuity from origin to protean present. Deane adumbrates an account of how the later Friel is a re-writing of the earlier; in this essay I want to retain a consciousness of that perception, but also to inquire more closely into the possibilities for interpretation of what Edward Said, the pre-eminent theorist of textual origins, puts at its pithiest in his book *Beginnings*: 'The beginning as primordial asceticism has an obsessive persistence in the mind, which seems very often engaged in a retrospective examination of itself'.[2] The mind in Friel's plays, from *The Enemy Within* to *Making History*, from his St

14

Columba to his Hugh O'Neill, is in an almost constant process of such retrospective examination: individuals and communities are caught up into an entanglement in their pasts, which is an entanglement in re-imagined, or invented, origins and sources. In the earliest work this entanglement takes the form of another contribution to the large Irish literature of exile; in the later it is carefully plotted into the Field Day programme of cultural re-examination and the desire to create that famous 'fifth province' of the imagination. From Columba's 'I remember everything', when he remembers Ireland from Iona for the benefit of his newest novice, Oswald, to Hugh's 'To remember everything is a form of madness' towards the end of *Translations*, Friel's plays inscribe a kind of arc in which, despite the intensification after *The Gentle Island*, the features of remembrance itself, of personal and cultural retrospect, form the staple focus of attention.

Friel's much-debated structural experimentation may also be read as a formal enactment of the theme of retrospection. In *Philadelphia, Here I Come!* the two Gars, Public and Private, are certainly a way of dramatising Gar's alienation, the virtual schizophrenia of character and reaction into which he is forced by his cultural and domestic circumstances; but they also allow the spilling over onto the stage of the fantasising by Private Gar of what might have been said, what could have been said, a kind of immediate reconstruction of the past as one would wish it to have been had one been capable of directing it (in this, *Philadelphia* has something in common with that popular myth of the 1960s, Keith Waterhouse's *Billy Liar*). In *The Loves of Cass McGuire* Cass does, in a sense, direct the play's action, since she addresses the audience and insists on giving her version of events: what we see is, partly, Cass's reconstruction. In 'Winners', the first of the one-acters in *Lovers*, and in *The Freedom of the City*, the action we witness is inevitably a retrospective action, mediated through commentary (the Commentators in *Lovers*; the judicial tribunal, the academic and the balladeer in *Freedom*), since the central characters in the drama are dead before the action begins. In *Living Quarters* 'Sir' is the directorial or dramaturgic mediator of the characters' own volitional reconstruction of the past: what we witness is not 'what happens' but what happens in the characters' retrospective recollection. And in *Aristocrats* the discarnate voice of the past is audible on stage as the bedridden father groans through his loudspeaker (terrifying his son) and as the sister, long disappeared to Africa, speaks through her tape in the voice of a child. These are all dramatic structures in which the past is brought into immediate contact with the present: to exert its hold over it, or to return as the fantasy of repression.

I want to think about the origin of these patterns of retrospect in

Friel's plays from *The Enemy Within* to *The Gentle Island* with a view to both identifying a central significance in the first phase of his *oeuvre* and also suggesting some of the ways in which the asceticism of this origin (in Said's terms), this austere first prompting to the act of writing, remains persistent and vibrant, as a besetting and enduring preoccupation.

In *The Enemy Within* St Columba on Iona is read as battling with homesickness and constantly tempted by the first community of his family to return to the faction-torn Ireland of his high-born origin. A man enmeshed in attachments he longs to revoke, he is the type of the Irish exile: displaced, uneasy, failing to belong, nostalgic for an original place which may be only an imagined or invented place, a place become the solace for the depredations of age and failure. To this extent, Friel's Columba is at one with Seamus Heaney's in his early poem 'Gravities':

> Blinding in Paris, for his party-piece
> Joyce named the shops along O'Connell Street
> And on Iona Colmcille found ease
> By wearing Irish mould next to his feet.[3]

Heaney's poem here perhaps does not realise how locked into its own affectionate tropes it is. The signals of attachment are also rituals of entrapment: an almost heroic poignancy becomes transparent onto absurdity and affectation; the private dream of loss and origin crystallises out into the public gesture of self-display; pain becomes 'party-piece'. These are surely the other ambivalences also sounded when Friel's Columba begins to sob an ambivalent response to his tempters at the end of the play (his brother and nephew have come to Iona to urge him to lead them into battle against their enemies in yet another Irish skirmish):

Get out of my monastery! Get out of my island! Get out of my life! Go back to those damned mountains and seductive hills that have robbed me of my Christ! You soaked my sweat! You sucked my blood! You stole my manhood, my best years! What more do you demand of me, damned Ireland? My soul? My immortal soul? Damned, damned, damned Ireland! – (*His voice breaks.*) Soft, green Ireland – beautiful, green Ireland – my lovely green Ireland. O my Ireland –[4]

Is it possible for an actor to speak such lines without histrionics, without registering some falsity in the emotion? This is a rhetoric of hyperbole (the personification, the repetitions, the exclamations, the neat antithesis of 'damned' and 'lovely') which signals the worked-up, the over-indulged, the party-piece for one's own benefit. Manifestly in the play, it is not the Ireland of present faction-fighting that Columba is attracted to (that is merely the Ireland he feels responsible to, the succubus of familial and social *pietas*), but the Arcadian lushness of his first world, an Ireland of his childhood, a *vrai paradis*.

In *Philadelphia, Here I Come!* and *The Loves of Cass McGuire* – plays which, as many commentators have noted, are companion pieces (in the way that *Translations* and *The Communication Cord* are later) – this element of the histrionic is given its explicit threatrical representation in the pseudo-Brechtian alienation or pseudo-Beckettian 'experimental' effects of those plays. Gar O'Donnell's twinned self in *Philadelphia*, and Cass's direct communication with the audience, are insistences that all selves are performed selves, that even in relation to the most profoundly perturbing emotions of separation, loss and displacement, we struggle with the ambivalences of private grief and public show, with the necessity to speak a language which disguises rather than articulates pain, and with the solving temptation to cliché, fantasy and delusion. In a vivid dramatisation of almost stylised retrospect, Gar invents himself remembering before he actually leaves; he remembers on behalf of the self he is yet to bring into being in America; his retrospect is initiated in prospect; he provides himself with an interior flashback in a play whose partly naturalistic conventions are breached not only by the audacity of the splitting of Gar into two but also by the O'Neill-like pathos of the enacted flashback. When his 'friends' leave, and in the terror of isolation and the anxiety about the different future he is giving himself, Gar knows the truth of his own most characteristic mental manoeuvres:

No one will ever know or understand the fun there was; for there *was* fun and there *was* laughing – foolish, silly fun and foolish, silly laughing; but what it was all about you can't remember, can you? Just the memory of it – that's all you have now – just the memory; and even now, even so soon, it is being distilled of all its coarseness; and what's left is going to be precious, precious gold . . . (*SP* 77)

Even in the act of recognising his glamourising of a past which is not yet actually past, Gar is programming himself into retrospective nostalgias; in the alchemy of transformative memory even the dross of Ballybeg, with its non-communicating father and son and its squalidly fantasising and unfulfilled young men, will become the gold of reminiscence. These lines therefore lend a further depth of irony to the potentially accurate analysis of Gar's new world (and New World) offered by the hopelessly self-deluded and alcoholic schoolmaster Boyle. America he says, is 'a vast, restless place that doesn't give a curse about the past; and that's the way things should be. Impermanence and anonymity – it offers great attractions'. But not if, like Gar, you prepare to carry your past out with you before you go, and in full, intelligently articulate consciousness of the trap you are laying for yourself. As Gar's song has it, 'Philadelphia, here I come, / Right back where I started from'.

Gar is preoccupied, however, not only with remembrance of his present circumstances but also with a kind of vanishing point of all remembrance: he wants to remember an undiscoverable origin, his own origin in the mother he has never known, the mother who died shortly after his birth. When he goes to pack his suitcase, he finds in it the newspaper of the day on which his parents married; and, the stage direction carefully tells us, he 'puts the newspaper carefully inside the folds of a shirt'. He folds his past into his future and takes it with him. It is worth thinking a little more about Gar's thinking about his mother, not only because so much commentary on the play concerns itself (for perfectly obvious reasons) with the father / son relationship, but also because the absent mother is a notable feature of Brian Friel's work (though one not, so far as I know, much remarked on). In plays which repeatedly present nuclear families, and the strains and tensions of familial life, families are repeatedly lacking a mother: she is often either dead or insane or both. In 'Winners', the first of the two *Lovers* plays, the girl's mother has suffered permanent nervous collapse as the result of the death of one of her twins. In *The Gentle Island* the remembered mother is a young suicide. In *Living Quarters* the dead mother has been a frequently absent invalid. In *Aristocrats* the remembered mother is another suicide. In *Faith Healer* Grace's mother is 'a strange woman who went in and out of the mental hospital'. And in *Translations* the opening scene-setting for the hedge-school emphasises that 'there is no trace of a woman's hand', since the hedge-school master's family also lacks a mother. This is, indeed, a pattern, and a striking one.

In *Philadelphia* Gar fictionalises a mother, with the aid of the recollections of Madge the maid (who has acted as a kind of surrogate mother for Gar, but rather confusedly, it would appear, since Gar's relationship with her is a markedly flirtatious one). The fiction makes the lost mother a radical antithesis to his father. Where the father was forty when they married, the mother was nineteen; where the father comes from tame, petit-bourgeois Ballybeg, the mother comes from the wilderness of Bailtefree, 'beyond the mountains'; where the father sits in Gar's imagination as the helpless burden of incommunication, the mother seems intimately connected with Gar's frequent quotation of the opening of Burke's *Reflections on the Revolution in France*: 'It is now sixteen or seventeen years since I saw the Queen of France, then the

Dauphiness, at Versailles; and surely never lighted on this orb, which she hardly seemed to touch, a more delightful vision . . .'. Spoken as a kind of consolatory mantra, the Burkean idealisation of Marie-Antoinette, doomed queen, has its bitter appropriateness to Gar's alienation. For Burke, the 'delightful', regal feminine represents the glory that has gone from the world, and the origin of his counter-revolutionary text. For Gar (the drop-out student of history at UCD), the Burkean text writes itself into his fantasy of maternity, supplying for a vanished source, inscribing his life into a pattern of what we might (thinking of Burke) be allowed to call a kind of psychologically reactionary retrospection: the fetishised past dominates the present and blocks all hope of development. The pattern is dramatised with great tact, economy and ironic pathos when Private Gar's imagining of his mother is interwoven with Public Gar's recitation of the prayers for the dead. This kind of lyrical invention or re-creation of an alternative moment and mood is a frequent occurrence in Friel, but rarely managed any better than here:

PUBLIC: O God, the Creator and Redeemer of all the faithful, give to the soul of Maire, my mother, the remission of all her sins, that she may obtain . . .

PRIVATE: She was small, Madge says, and wild, and young, Madge says, from a place called Bailtefree beyond the mountains; and her eyes were bright, and her hair was loose, and she carried her shoes under her arm until she came to the edge of the village, Madge says, and then she put them on . . .

PUBLIC: Eternal rest grant unto her, O Lord, and let perpetual light shine . . .   (*SP* 37)

The invention here is rapt, entranced and devotional; the repetition of the conjunction, with its quasi-biblical associations, creates a dignified rhythm of pathos, while also suggesting that the invention could go on, ecstatically, for ever, that there could be more and more for Gar not genuinely to remember. But the public liturgy into which this private rhetoric of loss intrudes is absolute in its insistence on that loss: 'she' is merely what Gar turns her into.

The accumulation of detail in Gar's speech glosses the lost mother with an almost legendary status; and the detail that obtrudes most poignantly and individuatingly is the mother's peasant carrying of her shoes until she reaches the civility of the village. Her deeply attractive wildness of undress contrasts radically with Gar's father's overdressing: he memorably wears his hat at the table. This is 'peasant' too, of course, but insultingly unattractive to Gar; and this contrast of social decorums may act as the register of how Gar understands his mother. She represents the lost value of a fundamental alternative to the repressive (and repressively weak) patriarchy he endures. I would hesitate to claim, without examining this pattern more closely in the later work, that the absent mother always has this kind of significance in Friel; but where she is remembered by a son, as she is notably by Casimir in *Aristocrats*, the degree of attachment to what is read as the alternative to a repressively authoritarian paternity is certainly similar. Friel's characters are paradigmatically lacking such alternatives, except in their fantasy lives. And how significant it is that when the missing mother in *Faith Healer* is recalled by Frank, her son-in-law, it is as a sage or holy fool. In his recollection she rises briefly out of the depths of her dementia to discuss obsession. Her husband's obsession, she says, is 'order' (that fascistic word); her daughter Grace's is 'devotion'; and she asks Frank what his is. He does not reply; but at the end of the play I think we are intended to read his final word as what that reply would have been had he articulated it: 'At long last I was renouncing chance'. The essence of his life as healer (and metonymic artist / creator), his 'obsession', has been the risk-taking of chance, pitting himself against uncertainty and self-doubt: and Grace's mother, I believe we are to assume, *knows this* before she relapses into 'demented' silence. It is the moment in Friel when the absent or silenced mother as the source of an alternative authority, the authority of comprehending (and potentially forgiving) wisdom, becomes explicit; and it emphasises the extent to which Friel's characters inherit and must contend with this primal loss.

Gar's entrapment in the rôle of son – the rôle, after all, which we see played out in its sad duplicate by both Private and Public Gar – is given its finally ironic rendering when we realise that what Gar is actually going off to in America is a second sonhood, a further filiality, in the home of his childless maternal aunt and her husband. The flashback in which we witness Gar's 'impetuous' decision to return with them to the States is heavy with this corrosive irony, since it is the day on which Gar's former girl-friend, Katie, is marrying another man. The day which forecloses Gar's immediate potential for an alternative future in a *chosen* family is the day on which he commits himself to the probable renewal elsewhere of the constrictions of his *given* family. Needless to say, the vulgarian maternal aunt bears no resemblance whatever to Gar's fantasies of the lost mother. *Philadelphia, Here I Come!* is a play in which ordinary late adolescent prospects are devoured by retrospect.

In its companion piece, *The Loves of Cass McGuire*, prospects have all long since been devoured: the Irish-American exile returned is the exile radically disabused of her fantasies of the Ireland she left behind,

but impelled by that into the creation of a further fantasy of retrospection, the fantasy now of the life she has had in America. This fantasy,
indeed, like those of the other inhabitants of Eden House (the anything
but Arcadian old people's home in which her family puts her) is
performed with not only a theatrical but an operatic flourish: Friel's
stage directions allow Cass's ruminative monologue to be set to the
strains of Wagner's *Liebestod*, that last word in the poignant refinement, the alchemy, of loss and longing into artistic triumph. Cass's
performance of herself is a kind of triumph of the creative act, the
transformation of her reality into a fictive artifice which may uniquely
offer solace in a life bereft of all alternatives (except the bottle). There
is perhaps an impulse towards the sentimental in *The Loves of Cass
McGuire*, with an uncertainty about exactly how we are to judge Cass's
self-performance, about whether the retreat into fantasy is actually
being celebrated by the play as the only recourse in a life of such
depredation and desperation; and, if it is being so celebrated, about
whether this is in some way figurative of the fantasy and compensatory element in even the greatest art (Wagner, for instance). If something of this does figure in the ground of the play, then, unlike *Faith
Healer*, it is liable to seem altogether too frail a structure to bear such a
weight of significance.

Cass's performance of her quasi-operatic rhapsody, however, is at
one with her directorial inveigling of the play's audience: she insists on
telling this story that appears from its title, after all, to be hers: 'they'll
see what happens in the order *I* want them to see it; and there will be
no going back into the past'.[5] For Cass, however, much as she tries to
prevent it with talk to the audience, the constant slippage into the past
is unavoidable; and the only way the past can be endured is by
transforming it into a fantasy or dream of retrospection. The Yeats
line which accompanies the retrospect, however – 'Tread softly because you tread on my dreams' – is ominously admonishing: the
fantasy knows the precariousness of its own construction. The 'loves'
of Cass McGuire are all fantasy loves, the gloss of possibility written
over the world as it was and is for her: 'Connie and father and Harry
and Jeff and the four kids and Joe and Slinger . . . and I love them all so
much, and they love me so much; we're so lucky, so lucky in our love'.
When Cass has successfully translated herself into this fantasy world,
a world in which she is the success story where her brother Harry, the
true bourgeois Irishman, is the failure to be pitied and accommodated,
then she has returned herself to an impossible origin. Early in the play,
when she has been temporarily accepted by a Harry innocent of her
nature and proclivities, she sentimentally insists that 'This is what it
was all for – to come home again'. At the end of the play, expelled

from Harry's home to Eden Home, she has made herself a home out of delusion; and the play's last line has its ringingly poignant irony: 'Home at last. Gee, but it's a good thing to be home'. If the true paradises are the paradises we have lost, then the attempt to rediscover them in the world outside our constructions of them is doomed to Cass's kind of retrospective inversion. Her last home, the fiction she creates inside her own skull, is therefore a mirror of the first home she remembers, crouched inside her railwayman father's signalbox, hiding from the world outside.

The three plays which followed *Cass* – *Lovers*, *Crystal and Fox* and *The Mundy Scheme* – seem to me markedly less interesting and successful than the rest of Friel's work, although they too make their contribution to the pattern I am describing here. In *Winners*, the first of the two *Lovers* plays, the retrospective structure compels its audience to listen to the doomed young lovers' talk of their future through the knowledge that no such future will happen for them; and when, in the second play, *Losers*, the aging 'lovers' are played by the actor and actress who have been the commentators in *Winners*, we are invited to read their fate as, at least potentially, that of the young lovers too. The play thereby folds in on itself in a kind of self-retrospection whose ironies are embodied in the chillingly (in)appropriate titles: the 'winners' are the dead, who can suffer no depredation; the 'losers' are those condemned to repeat familial and genetic patterns, the woman Hanna becoming, in the appalled and hardened Andy's view, 'a younger image of her mother'. *Crystal and Fox* is, I think, a baffling play whose apparent generic shifts make for an ultimate uninterpretability, even unintelligibility. Although the play seems to me over-plotted and under-characterised, Fox himself, perhaps in some ways an early sketch for Frank Hardy in *Faith Healer*, clearly corresponds to the typology of retrospection I have been defining here: clearly and not merely deludedly, like Cass, but almost insanely, since his fixation on how things once were with Crystal is the dominating *punctum* of his life, a life which (along with the lives of those he comes in contact with) he is willing, indeed eager, to wreck in order to recover the first place of primordial happiness, that first place which is, of course, almost certainly an imagined or invented place. The attempt to return himself to paradisal bliss ('heaven's just around the corner') results in acts of extreme cruelty to others and also, inevitably, in the loss of the one thing necessary to his paradise, Crystal herself. Retrospect for Fox Melarkey is unambivalent loss; and the tone of his recall is not so much poignant as merely absurd, a self-delusion he invites someone else, fatally to its own success, to share. But the play's inability to realise Frank with any coherence, to account for a psychology or motivation, leaves the theme uneasily stranded in a limbo of lost connections, blurring its focus in an undecided confusion of naturalism and expressionism.

The political satire of *The Mundy Scheme* is something of an exception in Friel's work to date (although it perhaps looks less exceptional now that we have the brilliant, brittle farce of *The Communication Cord* to compare it to), and its patterns and figures are distinct from those I have been describing here. Nevertheless, there is undoubtedly some correspondence between them and the nature of the Mundy scheme itself, a scheme to transform the west of Ireland economically by converting it into a vast cemetery for the Western world – bringing life by importing death, as it were. This is primarily a blackly hilarious exemplum of cynical political mercenariness and venality; but we are presumably at liberty to read it too as a trope for an ultimate cultural retrospection. The Irish West, mythologised in Synge, Yeats and the Revival, demythologised in its depopulation and touristic despoliation, the focus of so many desires, failed dreams and aspirations, becomes here not only a metaphoric but a literal graveyard: not inappropriate, perhaps, to what one of the play's ministerial characters calls 'a nation of chronic necrophiliacs'.

During the course of these relatively unsuccessful plays, Friel has nevertheless been resolutely working outwards from a psychological to a more inclusively social anatomisation. His work has moved from Gar's divided consciousness to whatever symbolic resonance we are to attach to the fact that Fox's final reckoning with Crystal takes place at a crossroads 'at the hub of the country' (underneath a signpost naming Dublin, Galway, Cork and Derry), and to his first treatment, in *The Mundy Scheme*, of the political theme proper (however embarrassed that play is by Friel's lack of the true satirical invective necessary to sustain his caricatures in a more than merely cartoon-like, *Spitting Image* kind of dramatic life). In *The Gentle Island* the psychological and the social are more radically meshed when the idea of 'home' examined in *The Loves of Cass McGuire* is brought into relation with another well-tested Irish theme, the relation between the urban and the rural, between Dublin and the West. The fusion of these themes at this stage in Friel's career is (literally) explosive: the play climaxes in the violence of a gunshot. It is, we might say, a sound which echoes through all of his subsequent work, in which physical violence rather than fantasising delusion now becomes the outcome of various kinds of retrospection.

The gentle island of the play's title is the imaginary Inishkeen, off the coast of Donegal. The play begins as all the islanders except the Sweeney family are leaving for voluntary exile in Glasgow, Kilburn

and Manchester: the old island ways are being brought to their conclusion by economic necessity. Manus, the paterfamilias, refuses to
believe in such a conclusion. His household consists of his sons Joe and
Philly and Philly's wife Sarah: the couples are childless, in what proves
to be the nodal point of the play's tensions. The island on the day of its
depopulation is being visited by two Dublin teachers, Peter Quinn
and Shane Harrison, whose apparent (though understated) homosexuality is the reagent for the catastrophe. If the Sweeneys are the last of
what Inishkeen, the 'gentle' western island, has been, then Peter and
Shane, the urban tourists, are presumably what it is to become, if it is
to become anything other than a desert. The island is caught, therefore,
at its moment of transition: from an agricultural and piscine economy
worked by an indigenous peasantry (on the verge of becoming the
unskilled labour force of the industrial Britain of the early 1970s) to the
tourist economy of the urban middle classes. Retrospect and prospect
are therefore brought into confrontation. Manus's backward look, his
desire to keep things as they were, confronts Shane's certainty that this
way of life has had its day: Shane the engineer, who can mend the
Sweeneys' broken appurtenances of modern living (the record player,
the radio), is the representative of the coming world. Sarah's child-
lessness acts as the focus of conflict since Manus, in order to sustain
any credibility in his conception of a potential future for an inhabited
Inishkeen, must have grandchildren; in Sarah's version of her marriage
it is Philly who is incapable of providing her with a child (the heavy
but submerged implication is of course that he too is homosexual).
Manus's intellectual and emotional conception of the island's future is
dependent on Sarah's literal conception of a child, a conception which
Philly, Manus's son, is incapable of provoking.

This is not merely a fanciful way of putting it, since *The Gentle Island*
is a play whose psychological and social themes are ultimately located
in sexuality. Sarah, from the depths of an extreme loneliness, makes a
pass at Shane and is rejected. She subsequently sees, or believes she
sees (the audience is unsure how much of this is reality and how much
jealous, over-determined fantasy), Shane and Philly making love in the
boathouse after their return from a fishing expedition. She urges
Manus to exact revenge and, when he proves incapable, she herself
shoots Shane, paralysing him: robbing him, presumably, of his
sexuality. The motifs of thwarted sexuality implicit in *Philadelphia* and
Cass here break through the surface into theatrical, perhaps even
slightly melodramatic, explicitation: the violence stirring at the root of
retrospection in the earlier works now has its direct consequence in
physical and sexual maiming. This gentle island harbours anything
but gentle passions: Friel, once again, proves himself expert in the

finely judged ironic title; it is Sarah who tells Peter, the musician infatuated with his fiction of the island's old ways, that the name 'Inishkeen' translates as 'the gentle island'. The otherness of homosexuality is the spur which provokes the islanders into a revelation of their true sexual and moral natures.

Whether Sarah is telling the truth about what she has seen or merely inventing it is a question thrown into some relief by our gradually learning the story of Manus's lost arm. He has earlier claimed that it was lost in an accident in a mine in Butte, Montana; but we learn eventually that it was hacked off by the brothers of his wife-to-be in a vengeful skirmish years before on this 'gentle island'. The woman was pregnant with Philly and after the birth of her second son, Joe, she committed suicide, throwing herself off an island cliff. Manus's retrospective fiction is a self-promoting fiction of his own heroism, but it is also a way of keeping his myth of the island free from the violence which actually comes to appear endemic to it: Sarah, in shooting Shane, is merely following one of its age-old traditions. The Sweeney cottage is furnished with the flotsam and jetsam deposited on the island by shipwrecks along its coast: we may read this as a trope for the duplicitous detritus which Manus carries around in his emotional life, for those desperate fictions which help him endure. Shane instinctively recognises his plight:

We give support to his illusion that the place isn't a cemetery. But it is. And he knows it. The place and his way of life and everything he believes in and all he touches – dead, finished, spent. And when he finally faces that, he's liable to become dangerous.[6]

The irony of Shane's insight, however, is that when it comes to it Manus is even more spent than he realises, too spent to be truly dangerous: the danger to Shane comes from a source he has not imagined. Shane's insight, however, may derive not only from the outsider status given him by his sexuality but also from his own lack of any origin to be retrospective about: an orphan brought up in a children's home, he is cut off from that nexus of familial intrication that debilitates so many characters in Brian Friel's theatre. When Peter wants to insult him during a kind of lovers' spat, he is registering Shane's saving grace as well as his disablement: 'Your affections have always been as uncertain as your origins!' Such uncertainty of affection and attachment allows Shane to stand clear of the retrospection of others: of Manus's fictions, of Peter's acculturated sentimentalities. But it does not, of course, save him from Sarah's bullet: privileged insight into causation has never been any prophylactic against physical violence, either in family life or in political history.

It seems to me that this lesser-known and in many ways melodramatic and incompletely realised play brings to fulfilment the earliest themes of retrospection and its penalties in Brian Friel, and that in doing so it also seeds some of the later work. Undoubtedly there is a new energy of repudiation after this, as Seamus Deane proposes, but there is also a continuity of preoccupation. If *The Freedom of the City* and *Volunteers* turn to explicitly political themes in the wake of post-1968 Northern Ireland, *Living Quarters*, *Aristocrats* and *Faith Healer* return to the entanglements of family and sexuality, and to the way a past presses its claims upon a present. In *Living Quarters* the paterfamilias commits suicide on learning that the son has been his own new wife's lover; in *Aristocrats* the family is in permanent struggle to grow free of its origin in a family and a house; in *Faith Healer* Frank is drawn back to his first Irish place, which he has initially repudiated, in an ambivalent act of piety to origin which is near-suicidal and does in fact culminate in his murder. The representative or exemplary status of the central characters of these plays (Frank Butler in *Living Quarters* is a commandant in the Irish army, newly and heroically returned from an engagement with the U.N.; in *Aristocrats* the family is the diminished survival of a Catholic Big House; in *Faith Healer* Frank is a figure for the Irish artist-in-exile-and-return) does indeed move Friel's work up to a new pitch of address and scrutiny and political resonance, but originary shapes and structures maintain their priority. Brian Friel, two of whose primary loyalties are to Chekhov and to ancient Greek theatre (*Living Quarters* is explicitly 'after *Hippolytus*'), seems to me a dramatist of centripetal development; in the way some of his plays fold in on themselves, his *oeuvre* too, for all its prolific exuberance of imagining and invention, turns inwards and downwards in the reworking of a tight nexus of preoccupying interests.

I want to end this essay by proposing that the pattern of *The Gentle Island* also persists, but with a new shock of historical and linguistic insight and without the taint of melodrama, in Friel's finest play, *Translations*. In *The Gentle Island* Manus's first language is Irish, and the fact of the Irish language makes other occasional appearances in Friel's earlier work. When Cass McGuire, Irish-American, proposes a toast in Irish in Harry's house, his wife Alice thinks she is speaking German; and Fox makes insulting jokes against Irish speakers in his opening 'on-stage' remarks in *Crystal and Fox*. Before *Translations* the Irish language was little more than this attenuated interruption in Friel, but perhaps just enough of an interruption to make it clear that the other culture represented by Inishkeen does have a linguistic contour and origin too. In *Translations* Friel re-presents that origin at its point of near-terminal collapse, by making contemporary Irish English transparent to, or retrospective on its Gaelic past. The relationship between past and present in *Translations* has often been read as an allegorical one: for Deane, approvingly, it is 'a play about the tragedy of English imperialism as well as of Irish nationalism';[7] for Edna Longley (disapprovingly) it is a barely disguised play about the British army in Northern Ireland;[8] for Declan Kiberd it is 'a covert exploration of the attempt by post-Whitaker Ireland to convert tradition into modernity without betrayal'.[9]

The play's use of the making of the 1833 survey is open enough to allow such variant readings; but its providing of Friel with the opportunity for historical and linguistic retrospection makes *Translations* a kind of fulfilling retrospect on his own career too. I am not sure that it has ever been noticed how even certain characters' names in *Translations* correspond to those of *The Gentle Island*, both plays having a Sarah and a Manus. Manus with his two in some ways antithetically opposed sons, Philly and Joe, may be thought to recur in the Hugh of *Translations* with his sons, Manus and Owen. And the tragedy of *Translations* is precipitated, as is the crisis of *The Gentle Island*, by sexuality: Sarah's frustration, and Philly's possible act of sex with Shane, may be thought to correspond with Maire's frustration with Manus and her liaison with Yolland in *Translations*. The disturbing interruption from outside the contained community, the interruption which results in acts of love and acts of violence, and precipitates catastrophe, is represented by the intransigently other in both cases: homosexuality in *The Gentle Island*, the English army in *Translations*.

At the end of *Translations*, then, Hugh is not only articulating an attitude to the situation of that play but expressing the ideal of an alternative to patterns of retrospection and repression, types of enslavement to the past, which have formed a template for Brian Friel's work from the beginning, from the asceticism of his origins to the superb theatrical ramification of *Translations*. 'To remember everything is a form of madness': yes, many (most?) of Friel's characters have their forms of madness. But memory can be redemptive too, if I read Hugh's closing speeches correctly. In them he recommends the persistence of the past under forms necessary to the present: specifically, the labour to make ancestral and affiliative feeling survive into conditions which may seem entirely hostile, but are unavoidable except by further acts of physical violence condemned to repeat the patterns of a fossilised past. The cultural survival Hugh recommends is an act of subtlety, stealth and subversion, an act of reclamation in which retrospect may create the conditions of a fulfilling future. A lesson in both reasoned necessity and necessary survival, it cuts radically across the heroic modes towards which others of the play's characters (Owen, Doalty) are being, however understandably, impelled at its close. And Hugh's comprehension of this dual necessity is sanctioned by his mock-heroic story of his own behaviour in 1798, when he turned tail before any fighting, despite his fine and pious feeling. The capacity to recollect one's own past in the mock-heroic mode is the pre-condition of Hugh's wisdom. It is a capacity given to no earlier characters in Brian Friel's plays (its antithesis is Manus and his arm); but it is the condition beyond the terrible frustrating, inhibiting and disconsolate patterns of their existences, which alone could offer them renewal.

THE FIFTH PROVINCE

ELMER ANDREWS

Everything is fiction. There is no such thing as reality, only versions of reality. Science is fiction, politics is fiction, history is fiction. So runs a line of postmodernist thinking that underlies much of Brian Friel's dramatic writing. It's a line of thinking that might well be expected to have a demoralising effect on the creative writer, since it calls into question traditional notions of art's unique capacity for conveying timeless truths. The modernist saw the world as chaotic yet believed the artist still retained power to convert disorder into the perfect order of art. But where does postmodernism leave art? What is art supposed to do now? If there is nothing to reveal but fiction, how can fiction tell us about anything other than itself? Thus, postmodernist 'metafiction': self-conscious fiction which draws attention to the fact that it is fiction. The conjuror, it would seem, can no longer perform the trick without declaring that it is a trick.

The trick is narrative, and the problematics of narrative have always intrigued Friel. His plays are full of writers, chroniclers, history-men, stage directors, translators, story-tellers and 'artists', whom we watch in the very process of constructing their narratives. Yet, however problematic reality may be for Friel, plot and character are not entirely done for in his plays. He warns of all the impostures of narrative, but insists we are still watching a group of human beings or a window on time. The mendacity and unreliability of fiction do not stop it having a social function. The abolition of the signified does not mean the abolition of power. Meanings produce practices and generate behaviour. The control of meaning *is* power. Art does not match life, but that doesn't have to be the only subject matter. Indeed, it is in that mismatch that the artist may aspire to a spontaneously revolutionary vocation: in re-writing the accepted version of reality he may open up new horizons of possibility.

The conviction that everything is fiction, that truth is forever elusive, can lead to pessimistic resignation, a sterile conservatism. But for Friel it is when we think of reality as fixed and final, when we forget that meanings are produced and that they serve the interests of particular social groups, that we begin to 'fossilise'. The virtue of fiction lies in what its detractors so often accuse it of doing: it tells us entertaining

29

lies; it stimulates us with things that are not, then and there, literally true; it exercises our imaginations. Play and story are the best ways we have of doing that. If play and story did not convey meaning there would be no urgent need, a need as old as Plato, to expose their insanity. But nobody need suppose they were ever fact.

A writer who understands the artificial nature of reality is more or less obliged to enter the process of making it. Friel's increasing preoccupation with the social and political nature of this project has promoted the search for a public rôle. Field Day, which he helped to found, was set up with no less an ambition than that of reconstructing reality. Field Day writers 'seek – consciously and with conviction – to exploit the traditional connection between Irish literature and politics, for the sake of the idea of a new Ireland'.[1] Field Day asks us to unlearn the Ireland that we know, the received ways of thinking about it, and to learn new ones. One of the central Field Day concepts is that of the 'Fifth Province' – 'a place for dissenters, traitors to the prevailing ideologies in the other four provinces'.[2] This is the neutral realm of the imagination, where the symbol may mediate between subject and object, where actualities need not be so terribly insisted upon as they normally are in Ireland.

Restricting myself to the six plays that were first performed in the 1970s, I would like to consider what, for Friel, constitutes an authentic fiction. How far do these plays represent a challenge to conventional modes of perception and habits of mind? With what degree of stringency is Friel's ethical and political stance taken or maintained in the presence of uncertainty?

In *The Gentle Island* (1971), as in many other of his plays, Friel focusses on a small group of individuals surrounded by a disintegrating world. He homes in on the point of crisis, the point at which an old order is on the verge of collapse, and choices have to be made. The central problem which Friel, along with a good many other Irish writers, faces is how to negotiate between the past and the future, how to reconcile traditional value and the search for individual freedom and authenticity, how to avoid the danger of fossilisation on one hand, and the danger of postmodern dehumanisation on the other. What transpires on the ironically named 'gentle island' epitomises the crisis of culture in the larger island of Ireland: the unresolved conflict between Tradition and Modernity. It's an old theme of Friel's. Gar O'Donnell in *Philadelphia* (1964) must make up his mind between staying at home in the repressed, small-town backwater of Ballybeg and jetting out to the excitements of the New World. In that play, the modern world has tragically failed to satisfy Aunt Lizzie's emotional needs; and Ballybeg, for all its limitations, still exerts a powerful hold on the restless Gar. (Ben Burton represents a third alternative by challenging the very terms of the debate and hinting at a universal malaise: 'Ireland–America–what's the difference?' [*SP* 64] he asks.) In *The Gentle Island* the choices are as finely balanced, but grimmer than ever. The departing islanders face an uncertain future in the urban gehenna where work will be hard, families will be split up and the old stabilising certainties will no longer hold. Those who remain will not only continue to face the hard life of the island, but it is made clear to us that there is not likely to be anything in the public world of urban exile to match the shocking violence and treachery of the claustrophobic island world.

The play is, in fact, a bitterly ironical re-working of certain romantic fictions of the past. This island is home to no rural idyll. Though its 'gentleness' is what first impresses Peter's urban sensibility, it turns out to be a place seething with frustration and violence, and blighted by an ancient 'curse'. Its inhabitants, devious, desperate and vicious, are lurid contradictions of the popular fiction of the Noble Peasant. Ironically, the only positive human values come from the city: it is Peter who brings sympathy and understanding into the violent amorality of Friel's anti-pastoral; and it is Peter's friend, Shane, who turns the cold douche of common sense on Manus's fervid pieties and Peter's touristic enthusiasms alike. Most ironic of all is Friel's treatment of the family, that traditional bastion of moral value. Family life in *The Gentle Island* is a hotbed of ugly passions, unspoken rivalries, guilty secrets, and unresolved mystery. We never know exactly what happens on the island. There is a range of competing versions of events, but Friel declines to exercise his authorial privilege to fix and finalise. Rather, he exploits uncertainty and ambiguity. As Manus says: 'There's ways and ways of telling every story. Every story has seven faces' (*GI*, p. 56).[3] The episode where Manus and his daughter-in-law Sarah exchange accounts of how Manus lost his arm is one of Friel's early Pinteresque experiments in the use of contrapuntal narratives as a means of strict psychological notation. Manus, seeking a strong self-image, boasts he lost his arm in a mining accident in Butte, Montana. Sarah tells us he lost it in a sordid fight on the island when he was attacked by two men whose niece he had got pregnant. According to Sarah, Manus is a reactionary old dinosaur whose brutishness has made it impossible for his son, Philly, to relate naturally to a woman. Manus, however, presents himself as a devoted husband. Sarah says the only reason he has remained on the island is that there were no jobs for one-armed labourers in America or England: Manus, on his own account, repeatedly champions an atavistic law of 'belonging' and the sanctity of roots:

They belong here and they'll never belong anywhere else! Never! D'you know where they're going to? I do. I know. To back rooms in the back streets of London and Manchester and Glasgow. I've lived in them. I know (*GI*, p. 10).

Manus's island images tend to float free of reality altogether and assume an independent, talismanic force. He well knows the power of story. Story-telling is a kind of magical ceremony and requires certain objective conditions for its magic to work. Thus, Manus refuses to tell Peter the story of the Monks: 'Some night I'll tell you. No man can tell a story right in the middle of the day' (*GI*, p. 26). To Shane, Manus's version of the island is both false and dangerous. Shane knows that he and Peter 'give support to his (Manus's) illusion that the place isn't a cemetery. But it is. And he knows it. The place and his way of life and everything he believes in and all he touches – dead, finished, spent. And when he finally faces that, he's liable to become dangerous' (*GI*, p. 37). The romance of primitivism is another joke ('Look at the act I have – the simple, upright, hardworking island peasant holding on manfully to the *real* values in life, sustained by a thousand-year-old culture, preserving for my people a really worthwhile inheritance' [*GI*, p. 37]), as is the mystique of eloquence which keeps the old values alive ('And now, as di-varsion, I'll tell youse the old tale of the white-headed harper from the townland of Ballymaglin in the barony of Kildare' [*GI*, p. 37]).

Shane is the only one who acknowledges the fictional nature of reality. He speaks of life as a story, a game or a play, and expresses himself in a highly self-conscious manner, deliberately mixing idioms, breaking the rules, refusing the magical function of story which Manus so passionately affirms. Shane is a chameleon-like, truly ambiguous character, the ambiguity extending even to his sexuality. He is the antithesis of Peter who wants 'the calm, the stability, the self-possession . . . no panics, no feverish gropings. A dependable routine' (*GI*, p. 52). In the end, the playboy Shane's antics are as intolerable to the natives of the 'Gentle Island' as Christy Mahon's are to the Mayo peasants. Shane's behaviour is an affront to ancient piety, and deep springs of violence are activated by his transgressive, Dionysiac behaviour. When the others come upon him singing and dancing frenziedly to a gramophone record of 'Oh! Susanna' in mock celebration of 'a memorable holiday I once had on a heavenly island one divine summer' (*GI*, p. 40), Sarah slaps his face 'viciously' (*GI*, p. 42) and Joe and Philly punch him to the ground. In the end, he has to be executed. The attempted murder is justified by hearsay only. Manus is apparently prepared to commit murder with no more evidence than the testimony of a woman who has consistently been his chief adversary up to this point. Sarah's version of what happened in the boathouse sets in motion a jealous woman's deadly plan of revenge against the man who had rejected her earlier advances and stolen her husband. Deeply resenting Manus's patriarchal law, under which she has been made to feel a failure because she has not borne a child, Sarah cunningly manipulates the old man, leading him to make a scapegoat out of Shane: Shane has to be punished for seducing Philly from his sacred duty of siring Manus's grandchildren and bringing back life to the island graveyard. Stories, we see, are constructed to satisfy particular needs, not some standard of objective truth. Stories give shape and utterance to our deep wishes and fears: they stir us to our most feverish gestures, sacrifices and betrayals.

The world of the play is a demoralised version of the absurdist vision. Friel puts greater emphasis on the absurdists' concern with the irrationality of life than their affirmation of human resourcefulness and resilience. Something of the playfulness of Vladimir and Estragon is present in Shane, but generally Friel's is a dark and nihilistic view of human relations, showing more interest in the demons within than in the potentially liberating human qualities. He offers no hope for the future, no possibility of fundamental change. This is what comes, Friel shows, of assuming an unchanging, essential human nature. No history: no politics. Instead, a notion of eternal recurrence: Manus is a Sweeney, a version of the ancient Sweeney who was caught between two worlds, the ancient and the modern. The island exodus strikes one of the emigrés as another 'Flight of the Earls' (*GI*, p. 4). Yet another paradigm is suggested by the story of 'the Monks' which tells of two young monks who were turned to stone because they fell in love with the old monk's niece and tried to escape with her from the island. The story establishes the ritual pattern, the key elements of which – youth's disruptive sexuality, conflict between old and young, the need to escape, the evil curse which negates the effort to escape – have their obvious contemporary parallels. The stories of the niggerman's torture, of the war dead who fell burning from the skies or were washed in by the tide, of Manus's horrific mutilation, of the sickening end of Mary's little dog, of the many storms and wrecks along the coast – these are all further instances of an endless, dark necessity.

In this play we see Friel struggling to find a form which would allow him to dramatise this supernatural world view and at the same time incorporate a judgement of it. The play, in fact, epitomises the problem which we find Friel struggling with throughout the 70s: how to satisfy the demands of both realistic enactment and rational critique. In *The Gentle Island* we constantly feel the pressure of the schematic parable behind the ostensibly realistic speech and situations. It is, in the end, a rather schematic play working to overturn the schema of conventional expectation and traditional value.

Most of Friel's plays are history plays or memory plays, fixing either on public events (Columba on Iona, Bloody Sunday, the Ordnance Survey of 1833) or private traumas, but always on the moment of crisis, the Fall, the moment which is taken to be the origin of and key to all subsequent moments. In *The Freedom of the City* (1973) he turned to Bloody Sunday, an episode which quickly and deeply embedded itself in the ideology of republicanism, assuming the status of a mythic reiteration of earlier sacred foundational acts (in, say, 1798 and 1916), the recollection of which serves the purpose of integrating and justifying republican consciousness. Thus, one option for the artist was to use his art to contribute to the common fund of hallowed traditions, orthodox pieties and idealised self-images whereby one particular social group maintains its sense of identity. At the other extreme, however, he could resist the process of stereotyping social formation and social action; instead of repeating the regressive movement which always fixates on the past, he could open up a progressive movement toward new meaning. Let us see where on this axis *Freedom* might be located.

Certainly, Friel's play, as Heaney has said of his own poetry, bears the 'watermarks and colourings' of a Northern, Catholic, Nationalist sensibility. But without denying the implications of his own background and experience, Friel aims for depth and completeness in his depiction of the rebellious oppressed, so that between author and audience common recognition will emerge, a supervening bond above and beyond ideas. Thus, Friel's civil rights marchers are not republican mouthpieces nor committed revolutionaries, but very ordinary people whose ambitions are remarkable for their innocence – that is, for being so stringently de-politicised and non-sectarian. Michael, one of the three marchers who end up taking refuge from the tear-gas in Derry's Guildhall, doesn't want to change the system at all, only his place within it. He has all the respectable middle-class susceptibilities, including an exaggerated respect for authority; and he is tragically naive. Skinner, the aimless ne'er-do-well has more insight, but none of the discipline nor commitment of a true revolutionary. He died, as he lived, he reflects, 'in defensive flippancy' (*SP* 150). Skinner is the anarchic, Dionysiac spirit who leads Lily beyond social constraint. For a moment Lily is unburdened of her manifold responsibilities and freed into a dimension of pure play. The endless, human capacity for play, we see, is one means whereby the determinism of the universe may be held at bay. In emphasising this kind of broadly human rather than a strictly political potential, Friel suggests a project of universal freedom from which no creed or class need feel excluded. (He could hardly have

chosen a more 'Orange' name for one of his characters than Lily!)
Friel's agitators are redeemed of all doctrinal prejudice, racist nationalism, class oppression and totalitarian ambition. They represent a
morality that does not lie in formulated code nor explicit programme,
but respect for the rich variousness of life. The play ends in death, but
the possibility of fluidity and experiment has also been affirmed.

Friel's problem is that while using such partial or limited characters
as Michael, Skinner and Lily, he must find a dramatic structure which
will allow him to bring out the implications of particularised experience. The relationship between meaning and experience, as the play's
sharp juxtapositions of conflicting versions of the same event are
designed to show, is intensely problematic. It is a problematic from
which Friel seeks to claim immunity by exploiting the naturalistic
illusion in his presentation of the private reality of Michael, Skinner
and Lily. The play is on the side of the concrete and specific: abstraction is the real enemy. This opposition is enforced by the two quite
different modes of characterisation employed for the personal and
public lives. The Judges, Press Officers, Policemen, Professors, Priests
and Balladeers are remote and dehumanised, bereft of any of the compelling human characteristics so sensitively and lovingly delineated in
the central trio. The public world, though it quite literally calls the
shots, is emphatically less real. In *Philadelphia*, Public and Private
interact closely with each other; they are recognizably two sides of the
same personality. But in *Freedom* the dialectic between private and
public has broken down completely. The meanings produced in the
public domain proliferate in violent disregard of the private reality
which alone can justify them, and on the side of which we are aligned
from the start.

But Friel in the end seems to lose faith in what he is doing, and
gives up on realistic speech. Determined that the story of Michael,
Skinner and Lily should disclose abstractable meanings after all, he has
the three characters, before they die, slip out of the flexible, idiomatic,
private language he has so brilliantly devised for them, into the
abstract and impersonal language of the public world:

MICHAEL: I knew they weren't going to shoot. Shooting belonged to a
totally different order of things. And then the Guildhall Square
exploded and I knew a terrible mistake had been made. And I
became very agitated, not because I was dying, but that this
terrible mistake be recognized and acknowledged . . .

LILY: And in the silence before my body disintegrated in a purple
convulsion, I thought I glimpsed a tiny truth: that life had
eluded me because never once in my forty-three years had an
experience, an event, even a small unimportant happening

been isolated, and assessed, and articulated . . .

SKINNER: And as we stood on the Guildhall steps, two thoughts raced
through my mind: how seriously they took us and how
unpardonably casual we were about them; and that to match
their seriousness would demand a total dedication . . .

                                                          (*SP* 149–50).

The fate of the three characters is directly related to social forces, but
social forces construed as the instruments of an inexorable fate. The
social formation in *Freedom* has precisely the same determining function as the 'curse' in *The Gentle Island*. *Freedom* ends as it began with the
deaths of the central trio. Is Friel colluding with a magical view of
reality? Surely not. The play, I would wish to argue, demonstrates
empathy with the mentality of powerlessness, but also represents what
Heaney calls 'a coming to consciousness',[4] an objectification of a certain, negative, alienating habit of mind. Friel's framing technique (a
more skilfully deployed break with the conventions of naturalism than
the sudden polemicisation of Michael's, Skinner's and Lily's speech)
serves the purpose of foregrounding a particular way of viewing
history – one which, in fact, brings history to a standstill and promotes
the recognizably Gaelic, Catholic, Nationalist idioms of myth,
tradition, piety and martyrdom. Such a way of viewing history may
have the purpose of both integrating and justifying a social group,
but it may also condemn that group to a demoralising cycle of
recurrence and eternal defeat. History is no longer an open-ended
process of transformation: action must always ultimately conform to
the terms established by the foundational act or 'curse'. What Friel
proposes is a relation between the object of perception and the mode of
perception. In choosing to foreground a particular form of imaginative
projection in a context of tragic waste, he is warning against, not
reinforcing, a group's predisposition to recollect itself in terms of such
gambits of despair.

In *Living Quarters* (1977) the principle of determinism is psychological, but as hopelessly imprisoning as the social determinism which
governs *Freedom* or the evil magic which controls the pattern of events
in *The Gentle Island*. Friel's characters, like those in classical Greek
tragedy, act in fulfilment of an ancient curse. Indeed, *Living Quarters* is
written 'after Hippolytus'. In Derek Mahon's poem, 'The Last of the
Fire Kings', the 'fire-loving people' require their fire king 'Not to
release them / From the sacred curse / But to die their creature and be
thankful'.[5] Friel's characters, likewise, see themselves as tied to a wheel
of fire, irrevocably bound to immolation.

All the characters in *Living Quarters* (with the exception, of course, of
Commander Frank Butler, who is dead in the fictional present) are

entranced by the moment of failure, betrayal or defeat in the past. The past absorbs them more completely than the need to confront the present. At a time when it behoves them to find some new principle of order, when some new creative charge is needed to rescue them from total disintegration, they have all retreated from the challenge of reality into a lost time before the Fall, a time when they could still enjoy a sense of 'belonging', a shared system of value. With the bankruptcy of the old structures they have refused the responsibility of choice. 'Opportunities' existed only in the past, but they have been 'squandered' (*SP* 242). Since their present is regarded as devoid of possibility, the characters have all fallen into a state of Joycean paralysis. To confirm their hopelessness they have invented Sir. Sir is no impresario of alternatives but a meticulous enforcer of the literal facts. He allows only one version of the past, that which faithfully reflects the chronological order of events. Elements of a situation such as mood and atmosphere, the submerged wishes, hopes and fears which do not find expression in the dominant discourse but which are none the less real, do not count with him. He is the champion of rational empiricism and common sense. For him the outcome of events is more important than the precise nature of the events: the end determines the means; process is subordinated to the need for closure. The characters re-live the past 'as if its existence must afford them their justification, as if in some tiny, forgotten detail buried there – a smile, a hesitation, a tentative gesture – if only it could be found and recalled – in it must lie the key to an understanding of *all* that happened' (*SP* 177). However, Sir's primary function is to ensure that no new meaning *does* emerge. He acknowledges that his version *is* a version ('What I would like to do is organise those recollections for you, impose a structure on them, just to give them a form of sorts' (*SP* 178)), but the other characters show no more than a token resistance to Sir's version in which they are inscribed. At the beginning of Act II Sir is not on stage and they have their chance to seize their momentary freedom and re-direct the course of events. They could, perhaps, displace the central importance of Frank's death altogether, evoke more pleasurable and vitalising memories, shift the focus of interest from a past event to present or future possibility. This is their chance to let other incidents come to consciousness and exert a complicating pressure. But the opportunity is missed. As Sir, in his usual patronising tone, confides to Charlie later, 'they're always being true to themselves. And even if they've juggled the time a bit, they're doing no harm' (*SP* 225). Sir fulfils the dual role of both creature and master of the other characters: 'And yet no sooner do they conceive me with my authority and my knowledge than they begin flirting with the idea of circumventing me' (*SP* 178). Ironically, the play itself emphasises not the invention and change of which Sir complains, but impotence and passivity – the schoolboyish deference to authority suggested by Sir's name. Sir is there as the sign of man's powers of invention, but paradoxically those very powers of resourcefulness and ingenuity are placed in the service of myths which incarcerate rather than liberate.

Friel acknowledges that man and society are alterable, and emphasises the disastrous consequences of always living in the past. But, absorbed by the psychology of defeat and the point of view of the victim, with its opportunities for both nostalgia and melodrama, he fails to evolve a dramatic form capable of including and expressing the anticipation of new freedoms. The focus is consistently on the past: there is no strong sense of the present, nor of the futural dimension of experience. Motivation begins to sound very like mystification: the characters keep returning to the past 'out of some deep psychic necessity' (*SP* 177). Not only are all the characters subject to exactly the same compulsion to live in the past, but the past is seen in essentially the same way by each of them. This homogenisation of memory may be seen as yet another distorting strategy of reactionary domination, another instance of Friel's (unconscious) connivance in his characters' denial of change and possibility.

Volunteers (1975) concerns a group of political internees who for the last five months have been on a daily parole to assist the excavation of a Viking site that is soon to be buried under a multi-storey hotel. They have volunteered for the job, have been ostracised by their fellow internees and eventually learn that they are to be killed by their comrades back in the cells. Nothing can avert this inexorable fate, as nothing could avert the tragic climax in *Freedom* or *Living Quarters*, or placate the evil spirit which presided over *The Gentle Island*.

The Viking parallel heightens the suggestion of determinism. One way of viewing the diggers' plight and, beyond that, the whole contemporary Troubles, is to see them as part of a timeless continuum of sacrifice and martyrdom rather than the product of a specific network of social relations. One of the diggers, Keeney, spells out the terms of the parallel when he ponders the circumstances of the ancient Leif's death:

Maybe this poor hoor considered it an honour to die – maybe he volunteered? Take this neck, this life, for the god or the cause or whatever . . . he was – to coin a phrase – a victim of his society . . . Maybe he was a casualty of language. Damnit, George, which of us here isn't? (*V.* p. 26)[6]

Whatever Keeney's own motives may have been for joining the 'movement', he speaks now with scant respect for the willing victim. He also takes us to the heart of Friel's theme by seeing the individual's relation to his society as fundamentally a matter of language, of which 'story' he happens to believe. Keeney, like Hugh in *Translations*, knows that the individual can become imprisoned in 'a linguistic contour which no longer matches the landscape of fact' (*SP* 419).

We recognise Keeney as the latest in a line of fiction-specialists, impresarios, symbol-conscious commentators, obsessive rôle-players, protean spirits, anguished doubters, dreamers with an almost compulsive resourcefulness. Keeney, along with his vaudevillian feedman Pyne, tells Leif's story in a variety of ways (the limitations of scientific knowledge and archaeological discovery leaving free space for the story-teller's invention). Keeney probes the significance and value of the mind's inventive power while apparently remaining outside any particular version or story himself. The tendency of the stories toward parable and allegory, and the way Keeney is used to spell out their secret meanings ('So that what you have around you is encapsulated history, a tangible précis of the story of Irish man' (*V*. p. 31)), reveal the strain between inner and outer, enactment and assessment, the particular and the general. Friel's talent for rendering individual speech realistically is compromised by the literary quality of the dialogue. Once again Friel's difficulty has been to find a form which would embody the private reality and at the same time accommodate larger insights than those which any of his limited and partial characters are capable of.

Pyne's story of Leif's death is of a punishment killing for Leif's exogamous relationship with an American Indian woman. The story is a version of what Heaney calls the tribe's 'exact and intimate revenge'[7] against the man who dares to transgress traditional pieties. Keeney, like Manus in *The Gentle Island*, is concerned that Pyne tells his story to best effect (' "Once upon a time" – keep up the protection of the myth' (*V*. p. 51)) and congratulates him on his performance at the end ('Not bad, Pyne. Fairly trite melody but an interesting sub-theme' (*V*. p. 52)) Compulsive story-teller that he is, Keeney takes it upon himself to speak for the recalcitrant Knox. In this version, Leif was a man who for money and companionship carried messages between two groups of 'subversives' (*V*. p. 57). Keeney apparently tells the story against Knox for it prompts the latter to an angry outburst against Keeney. Butt also has a version – or rather, several versions – of Leif's death, all of which Keeney can predict. To each of the stories of dispossession and deprivation recited by Keeney Butt assents with a resounding 'Yes' (*V*. p. 58). Keeney, however, though he can reel off the stories without even having to think, cannot subscribe to any of them. 'I'm sure of nothing now' (*V*. p. 58), he says. He finds the greatest difficulty in sustaining faith, or even interest, in any particular fiction. He no longer has 'a confident intellect': 'my paltry flirtations are just . . . fireworks, fireworks that are sparked occasionally by an antic disposition' (*V.* p. 57). Keeney is the disillusioned volunteer, demoralised by the elusiveness of certainty, yet, in the vitality and playfulness of his language, continuing to embody unquenchable, if unruly, human spirit. Paralysed by his intuitions of life's meaninglessness, and no doubt acknowledging his obsession with coded language, he caricatures himself as Hamlet: 'Was Hamlet really mad?' (*V.* p. 66) he keeps asking, the query echoing through the play like the quotation from Burke in *Philadelphia*. Keeney would understand Heaney's self-criticism in *North*: 'skull-handler, parablist / smeller of rot / in the state, infused / with its poisons, / pinioned by ghosts / and affections, / murders and pieties'.[8] Keeney's dilemma is that he wants to break out of passivity and acceptance, but he is inhibited from doing so by an overwhelming sense of futility and despair. As a result, he represents a diffuse, anarchic energy that has no positive or constructive ambition. George the foreman recognises in Keeney the most 'dangerous' kind of subversion of all: 'But Keeney – a danger-man, Butt, a real danger-man. No loyalty to anyone or anything' (*V.* p. 63).

What prompts Keeney's most ferocious outburst is the reception the pathetic Smiler receives when he returns after his attempted escape. He is fussed over, given tea and one of Knox's best cigarettes, while Butt 'drapes a very large sack round Smiler's shoulders. It is so long that it hangs down his sides and looks like a ritualistic robe, an ecclesiastical cape' (*V.* p. 59). Keeney comments on this idolisation of the victim:

He's an imbecile! He's a stupid, pig-headed imbecile! He was an imbecile the moment he walked out of this quarry! And that's why he came back here – because he's an imbecile like the rest of us! Go ahead – flutter about him – fatten him up – imbecile acolytes fluttering about a pig-headed victim. For Christ's sake is there no end to it? (*V.* p. 60).

The real object of Keeney's disgust is the incorrigible Irish respect for sacrificial immolation, the notorious martyr-complex which inhibits realistic, forward-looking action.

Leif is installed in the same idolising discourse:

PYNE: Never harmed man nor beast.
KEENEY: And generous – give you the shirt off his back.
PYNE: The bite out of his mouth.
KEENEY: One of nature's gentlemen.
PYNE: A great husband – a great father.
KEENEY: May the hard-core rest light on him.
PYNE: We'll never see the likes again (V. pp. 66–7).

But, again, Keeney insists on generating another, less innocent, less reassuring, version of Leif:

KEENEY: All the same boys –
PYNE: What?
KEENEY: Is there a look of the mother's side of the house about the set in
        the jaw?
PYNE: The Boyces of Ballybeg? . . .
PYNE: He favoured the mother's side all right.
KEENEY: Right and bitter.
PYNE: And notionate, too.
KEENEY: Man, they held grudges for generations. And in drink –!
PYNE: Balubas!
KEENEY: Be Jaysus they'd fight with their shadow (*V*, p. 67).

Through Keeney, Friel draws attention to the masks of illusion, and questions the idols of false consciousness. Keeney stops short of initiating any progressive movement towards the emergence of new meaning, but his *skepsis* may be the prerequisite to the opening onto other possible worlds which transcend the narrow limits of the play's fictional world.

It is the experience of difference and division which, above all, characterises the world of Friel's play. The internees are separated from the rest of society; the diggers are ostracised by their comrades back in prison, and divided amongst themselves. The dominant order is no monolithic unity either, but riven by class division. Friel's main interest is in the way meanings maintain themselves or are fought for in a world bereft of consensus. Artistic truth, he insists, has no valid claim on absolute value. The aesthetic mode, we are shown, is historical and materialist, not universal and eternal. He symbolically deconstructs the notion of art having no relation beyond itself in the story of the priceless jug which George has pieced and glued together from fragments unearthed by Smiler: 'A little patience – a little art – and there he is in all his pristine dignity' (*V*. p. 15), says George proudly. It is not long, however, till the ostensibly self-sufficient art-object is at the centre of a fierce dispute: Where does it belong? Whose is it? What does it signify? To the diggers it is a symbol of Smiler: 'This is Smiler, George; Smiler restored; Smiler full, free and integrated' (*V*. p. 46). At the end, however, Butt realises that when he and his fellow internees leave the site, the jug will be left in the hands of George and Professor King, and that it is they who will become the designators and custodians of its meaning. Rather than let this happen, Butt drops and smashes the jug. Refusal of any meaning (symbolised by the broken jug) is preferable to the false image of perfection represented by George's 'well-wrought urn'.

In *Aristocrats* (1979), as in *Living Quarters* or *The Gentle Island*, an old order is disintegrating. At this critical juncture questions are precipitated about the real value of this hitherto privileged centre of meaning and identity, and a younger generation is faced with the challenge of finding the means to make shift in a less congenial world. With a stroke of savage humour, Friel reduces traditional authority to a disembodied voice through a baby-alarm. Father's voice is crotchety and hopelessly confused, but still able to elicit reflex fear. With the head of the house fallen into decrepitude, and Ballybeg Hall in a state of terminal decay, how is this 'aristocracy' (actually a family of upper middle-class Irish Catholics) to be remembered, and what of the future? Tom Hoffnung, the American academic over to write the official history of the Irish aristocracy is, like Sir, the proponent of an empirical kind of truth. Eamon knows what the conventional assessment would be:

What political clout did they wield? (*Considers. Then sadly shakes his head.*) What economic help were they to their co-religionists? (*Considers. Then sadly shakes his head.*) What cultural effect did they have on the local peasantry? Alice? (*Considers. Then sadly shakes his head.*) We agree, I'm afraid. Sorry, Professor. Bogus thesis. No book   (*SP* 281–2).

But Eamon also believes that the true meaning of the aristocracy cannot be assessed in these terms. He objects to Tom's project because he assumes that the outsider could not possibly appreciate Ballybeg Hall's symbolic worth. It is Eamon, the boy from the village who married into 'aristocracy', who has the most to lose if the family home is sold, or if the chronicler does not represent it fairly. With disarming candour, Eamon acknowledges the appeal of 'aristocracy' to 'all that is fawning and forelock-touching and Paddy and shabby and greasy peasant in the Irish character' (*SP* 318). To such, the Big House is 'irresistible' because it represents 'aspiration' (*SP* 319). This, Eamon believes, Tom could never understand: 'There are certain things, certain truths . . . that are beyond Tom's kind of scrutiny' (*SP* 309–10).

Eamon pursues an aristocratic dream of toughness, tenacity and endurance, from which Tom maintains a sceptical distance throughout: 'It's your fiction' (*SP* 294), Tom says. Later, when Eamon adds 'discipline' to his list of aristocratic virtues, Alice, his wife, offers the further qualification: 'I'm the alcoholic, remember' (*SP* 324). Sometimes Eamon himself has trouble sustaining the dream, as when he asserts the central position in his 'fiction' occupied by Mother (whose memory has been suppressed in the collective family consciousness because of her dubious origins as an actress) by virtue of her great beauty:

And a racing beauty by all accounts. No sooner did Yeats clap eyes on her than a sonnet burst from him – 'That I may know the beauty of that form' – Alice'll rattle it off for you there. Oh, terrific stuff   (*SP* 295).

Eamon's language here repays some attention. It displays a kind of pleasurable excess over precise meaning, a libidinal gratification within his mythologising structures, a wayward energy which disrupts and opposes the original intention. Eamon cannot speak of the dream without giving way to playful irony. His speech serves to demonstrate that there is no meaning which is not always somehow dispersed, divided and never quite at one with itself.

Yet another kind of 'truth' is represented by Casimir who confounds both the factual chronicler (Tom) and the romantic idealist (Eamon). Casimir's 'truth' blurs the line between fact and fantasy. With him, nothing is fixed or final. He is kin to other Protean, playful spirits of Friel's, such as Shane and Skinner. He is the wise fool. There is some doubt as to whether Helga and the children whom he is always telephoning actually exist at all:

EAMON: Casimir pretending he's calling Helga the Hun. All a game. All a fiction.
ALICE: Oh shut up!
EAMON: No one has ever seen her. We're convinced he's invented her. (TOM *laughs uncertainly*.)
TOM: Is he serious, Claire?
EAMON: And the three boys – Herbert, Hans and Heinrich. And the dachshund called Dietrich. And his job in the sausage factory. It has the authentic ring of phoney fiction, hasn't it?
CLAIRE: Don't listen to him, Tom   (*SP* 278).

The deliquescence of Casimir's world, we come to see, is the condition of his survival in diminished circumstances. His game of imaginary croquet offers a salutary reminder of the limits of fact as well as fantasy. Down-to-earth Willy is drawn into the game initiated by Casimir, and imagines himself to be winning: 'His elation is genuine – not part of the make-believe. And his triumph has given him a confidence' (*SP* 300). These stage directions emphasise the positive effects of play. By breaking with the normal rules and routines, by our willingness to experiment, we can open up lost or buried channels of feeling. Through play we can experience a freeing of self and glimpse the means of a future transformation of our condition. But the croquet-playing episode concludes by emphasising the limits of play. When Willie, flushed with his success, goes to have a drink of wine, only to find the bottle empty, Eamon comments: 'Imagine it's full. Use your peasant talent for fantasy, man' (*SP* 301) – another of Eamon's ironic slightings of the ubiquitous peasant propensity to dream as a compensation for deprivation and failure.

Casimir survives because of his playfulness and his constant readiness to adjust to change. But he is no mere illusionist. His negotiations with the world are based on recognition of his own limitations:

> I made a great discovery when I was nine . . . I suddenly realised I was different from other boys . . . That was a very important and a very difficult discovery for me . . . But it brought certain recognitions, certain compensatory recognitions. Because once I recognized – once I acknowledged that the larger areas were not accessible to me, I discovered – I had to discover smaller, much smaller areas that were   (*SP* 310).

Casimir's play is not sterile escapism but the means of self-discovery.

Another kind of 'truth', another version of 'aristocracy', is represented by eldest sister Judith's hard-headed realism. Countering Eamon's idealisms, Judith speaks for the reality of decline, poverty and sickness. She is the one who has taken responsibility for Father and for looking after Ballybeg Hall. To Judith, the old order is simply not worth preserving. She, it appears, has for long been in revolt against her class. In remaining 'indifferent' to the violence in the North, and in regarding politics as 'vulgar', the Catholic 'aristocracy' has, in her view, rendered itself socially irrelevant. For the first time Friel includes a serious counter-movement which opposes itself to defeat and inevitability. The possibility of renewal and continuance – even heroism – is affirmed. The future, we see, depends on Judith's determination that she and her family confront reality and come to terms with their diminished circumstances; on Casimir's recognition of both possibility and limitation; on the family's instinct for life which Eamon is so impressed by; on the younger generation's awareness that any adequate version of reality cannot consist entirely of either Tom's mechanical facts or Eamon's romantic vapours; on the adaptability which Claire, the youngest sister, shows in marrying the local greengrocer. Dumb Uncle George, like dumb Sarah in *Translations*, is one of Friel's odd, waiflike creatures who, because they are without language, are continually in danger of being written out of the social reckoning altogether. Both Sarah and Uncle George respond to the 'warmth' and 'concern' of others. Sarah learns to speak with Manus's help and encouragement, and is frightened into dumbness again by Lancey's rough interrogation. Uncle George, seeing the heroic effort going on around him to resist 'fossilisation', is finally touched into life and language by the gesture of magnanimity when Alice assures him of a place in the new order by inviting him to come and live with her and Eamon in London.

The play as a whole may be seen as a giving voice to the suppressed forces for change in society and the individual. It is a play about survival, and survival, we are shown, depends on the ability to subsume respect for the past within a dynamic sense of the future. The play ends on the very moment of transition (which, in Friel's great play of 1980, is also the moment of 'translation'). That moment is elevated to become life's eternal moment. Knowledge of life as perpetual process is the prerequisite of authentic existence. Uncle George enters:

He puts his small case on the ground and his coat across a chair and sits with his hands on his lap. He has all the patience in the world. As he sings Casimir glances over the house. Claire begins to hum. One has the impression that this afternoon – easy, relaxed, relaxing – may go on indefinitely (*SP* 326).

The play not only affirms Becoming over Being, but emphasises irrepressible human spirit in the face of the brute facts of death and defeat. That energy is given expression throughout in the non-discursive form of Chopin's music which drifts in and out of the action, and in the song which concludes the play. For even when the provisional version offered by an artist seems pessimistic and despairing we can still be invigorated and extended by the energy of perception and invention which went into the making of the version, and without which there would be no plays, no games and no songs. The play is, finally, a celebration of the human impulse to turn the negative aspects of everyday life into positive form.

Faith Healer (1979) is another memory play, a set of recreations of the past from three different points of view. But where the memory of all the characters in *Living Quarters* was contained within the same dramatic structure, *Faith Healer* is divided into four distinct parts. There is no Sir and and no ledger to ensure that the representation follows a preordained plan: each character is freer to construct his or her own version of the past. Thus, there is no single event which forms the undisputed common point of reference for all other events in the lives of the three characters. Each character, that is, has a different centre of meaning, and so produces a different version of the past.

The play consists of four monologues spoken by Frank the faith-healer, Grace his wife (or is she his mistress?) and Teddy, Frank's business manager. Each character gives his or her version of what is essentially the same story. But there are stories and there are stories. The past lives on in three different versions of it, in each of which certain details are repressed or displaced, others highlighted or exaggerated, according to personal need and emotion. The characters never interact directly with one another: being is a fundamentally private affair. Our concentration is fixed entirely on the three voices, on the very process whereby they encode a consoling or justifying fiction, on the deep rhythms of personality to which they give utterance. Frank's speeches concentrate on his troublesome gift, as he debates its nature, recollects his successes and failures. Grace's monologue emphasises the personal life, and betrays her deep and manifold resentments of Frank, of his gift which removes him from the world of ordinary feeling and relation, and makes him seem inhuman at times. The dominant note of Teddy's speech is one of confusion and exasperation: first, as a result of his inability to maintain the pretence that there was only a 'professional relationship' between himself and Frank and Grace (there is the suspicion, for example, that Teddy and not Frank may be the father of Grace's baby); second, because Frank's artistic temperament continually eludes and defies Teddy's efforts at rational control: 'God! Bloody artists!' (*SP* 357, 361) is Teddy's refrain. All three characters confront what is enigmatic, and in dramatising what is a constant source of worry or resentment or exasperation for them, Friel produces a play of compelling and mysterious power, defying ultimate interpretation.

Reality is both stubborn and malleable. Conscious fantasy and illusion are both ways of transforming what is intractable in life. On a more esoteric level, so is faith-healing. And so is art. The faith-healer is Friel's image of the artist. Friel ponders the nature of Frank's gift – a gift which lies outside conscious control and is notoriously unreliable. If Frank cured a man, we are told, that man became for him a 'successful fiction' (*SP* 345). Grace recognises that she, too, is one of Frank's 'fictions': 'O my God I'm one of his fictions too, but I need him to sustain me in that existence – O my God I don't know if I can go on without his sustenance' (*SP* 353). At the end, exhausted and impotent, Frank plots his supreme fiction – his own death at the hands of his own people. Sham or shaman: not even Frank himself can be sure which he is. He may not always be successful, but the faith-healer's work preempts determinism for sometimes he is successful. The faith-healer / artist occupies a borderland between hope and despair. He makes it impossible for his people to settle for either – or for any fixed meaning or attitude. As Frank says, he denies the people who come to him 'the content of a finality' (*SP* 337).

The strikingly unusual form which Friel has devised for his play may be seen as an attempt to enact and enforce this denial of the satisfactions of completion and closure. The play proclaims its own impotence by continually contradicting and deconstructing itself. Friel's fragmentary form is an open-ended one that is amenable to the disarrangings and re-arrangings of subjective fantasy and, as such, offers the playwright a way of countering the notion of finality and fixity. We find outselves not a little bewildered amongst a variety of versions of what happened because Friel makes no effort to provide a hierarchical index to the conflicting discourses. The play dramatises the abolition of a centre, of a given and accepted authority. We, the audience, become the producers of the play's meaning. For this is, in Roland Barthes' terms, a 'writerly' as opposed to a 'readerly' text, one which forces each member of the audience into an active, productive role rather than that of a mere passive consumer. We are involved in the process which Hugh in *Translations* calls 'interpreting between privacies' (*SP* 446). As we construct our own meanings we may, if we remain alert to what we are doing, learn something about our own principles of structuration, our own allegiances and suppressions, which normally we may only be half aware of. For the play declares the paradox of Friel's wanting to be an artist without making his readers or spectators feel they are being trapped into one particular version of things. The play, while constantly pursuing its own kind of sense, disrupts the forms of conventional drama so that Friel can demonstrate his own freedom from control, his 'disinterestedness'. Thus, he creates an artistic space wherein he can live with ambiguity and uncertainty. The danger of this tactic is that the play amounts to nothing more than whimsy; in refusing authoritarianism the playwright can all too easily fall into coyness, false naiveté and sentimentality. These are certainly to be found in Friel, but hardly at all in this play. The form is basically static, but it serves Friel's purposes brilliantly. Modulating expertly between the lyrical, the comic and the tragic, he has given us a drama of remarkable vibrancy and variety.

In the neutral territory, the 'Fifth Province' of art, Friel seeks to reestablish the imaginative relation of observation to belief, and so sustain the complexity of human possibility against dangerous and deadening abstraction. His plays do not propagate any particular 'truth' so much as explore the conditions of 'truth'. He seeks to create an aesthetic out of the tentative. *Faith Healer*, his culminating play of the 1970s, epitomises his reluctance to allow any particular statement absolute authority. He is suspicious of completion and a singularity of experience which would prove definitional. The restless, neurotic self (Casimir, Keeney, Shane, Skinner) becomes a central strategy for survival and resistance to determinism. The plays of the 1970s are an assertion and a celebration of the resistant spirit whose acts of transformation, like the playwright's art, are a means of survival, of resistance to the ignominies of the world's injustice and violence. Storytelling and play-acting are positive acts. The very fact that a story is told suggests that something has been overcome; it is a sign of hope.

Of the Irish language, Hugh in *Translations* says: 'Yes, it is a rich language . . . full of the mythologies of fantasy and hope and self-deception. . . It is our response to mud cabins and a diet of potatoes; our only method of replying to . . . inevitabilities' (*SP* 418–9). Fiction inhabits the gap between the real and the ideal, mediating between what is and what might be. Friel's plays of the 1970s explore what constitutes an authentic response to 'inevitabilities': fiction, we are shown, must keep the ideal and the real in close and creative relationship; and it must know itself to be fiction, a provisional ordering. Only by so doing can fiction avoid 'fossilisation' and remain constantly open to change.

'FIGURES IN A PEEPSHOW': FRIEL AND THE IRISH DRAMATIC TRADITION

DESMOND MAXWELL

(i)

Yeats's phrase about the peepshow[1] may sound derogatory or dismissive. It is not so intended. The figures he has in mind are Don Quixote, Hamlet, Lear, and Faust. They occupy our minds not because of any thought or discourse they express. They are memorable because of what Yeats calls their 'action', their 'visibility'. He means this quite literally: we see them doing things, Hamlet is 'a mediaeval man of action'.

Beyond that, however, Yeats is placing them within his notion of the hero and of drama, especially tragic drama. He distinguishes, not with entire consistency, between 'personality' and 'character', the latter consisting in superficial individualising. Personality is to be found in dramatic characters who are not defined by idiosyncrasies. Their nature is legendary, mythic, evoking an essential spirituality in human experience. That is the property of the tragic hero whose destiny is to resolve by action conflicts on which thought will merely speculate, defiant of any but his own law, moved by passion that 'asks no pity, not even of God'.[2] The outcome is 'tragic joy', a celebration of the spirit confronting terror and loss.

The passage in *On the Boiler* alludes also to Yeats's theories about the rôle of speech in drama. Yeats inveighs against the kind of dialogue he considered Shavian, carrying no more than opinions debated around some 'issue', though he recognised that 'in certain plays' Shaw raised it from banality to philosophy. Synge's 'highly coloured musical' prose was more to his taste, but only verse could command the full amplitude of the poetic speech he advocated for the stage.

'The theatre began in ritual', he wrote in 1899, 'and cannot come to its greatness again without recalling words to their ancient sovereignty'.[3] Language extends beyond the informative, the expository, the contentious. Yeats takes it as the agent to re-instate ritual, leading drama 'to inhabit as it were the deeps of the mind'.[4] Other possibilities beckoned. Yeats knew and experimented with the power of masks, gesture, dance, music, even at one point disparaging the 'difficult irrelevant words' of *Fighting the Waves*. But language remained paramount.

49

Yeats's somewhat rarefied prescriptions for an Irish drama did embody an Irish content, drawing on history, heroic legend, and folk life. In the end they were fully realised only in his own plays, the dramatic quality of which is still questionable. In 1919 he said that the drama which had displaced his own 'has been to me a discouragement and a defeat'.[5] The Abbey had become 'a people's theatre', its medium prose, its subjects rural and, increasingly, small-town life. Yeats's early enthusiasm had envisaged large audiences attracted to his own as much as to realist plays. He saw the times as propitious for expressing an 'impulse that was in the people themselves . . . at that precise stage in their history when imagination, shaped by many stirring events, desires dramatic expression'. The artistic flowering would be 'a part of that popular imagination'.[6]

Yeats was perfectly aware that the 'stirring events' – Parnell's disgrace and death, for instance – had their profoundly disheartening aspects: and that the Gaelic popular movement was liable to produce a good deal of dogma and fulsomely propagandist writing. He withstood the dogma, defending Synge against the charge that his unflattering portrayals of country people defamed Irish purity. Some of his early plays – *The Countess Cathleen*, *Cathleen ni Houlihan* – have a clearly political content. They were remedial works, attempts to subsume the simplicities of propaganda into the subtleties of art. None of this advanced the heroic verse drama to which he aspired. Yeats turned to the cultivation of 'an audience like a secret society where admission is by favour and never to many'.[7]

Yeats was by no means wholly blind to the virtues of the Abbey's achievement, but the prose style of, say, Padraig Colum, was too remote from his preconceptions for his ear to catch its muted poetry. Despite his growing distance from the Abbey, Yeats's ideas did influence its development. The kind of realist theatre which evolved – through Synge, Colum, O'Casey – has inflections which move it towards poetic transformations of its material, away from a straightforward traffic with, in Yeats's words, 'the sensation of external reality'. Irish drama acknowledges an ideal of poetic drama active in later imaginations in quite other ways than Yeats's. It is, indeed, around the work of Yeats and Synge that its definitions clarify.

The Abbey grew out of the Irish Literary Theatre and the Fay brothers' Irish National Dramatic Company, neither of which had a theatre of its own. The Field Day Theatre Company, founded by Brian Friel and Stephen Rea[8] in 1980, is similarly unaccommodated, though so far without its predecessors' desire for a house. It produces a new play annually[9], opening in Derry, then touring the country – one of Yeats's unfulfilled ambitions for the Abbey – North and South, in whatever theatres or halls it can find: a vagabonding that suits the Company's title. Apart from these trifles, there are more binding resemblances of intent and circumstance between the past and the present ventures.

Friel's work belongs to the artistic revival of the 1960s, strongly located in the North. That revival may have associations with the political upheaval which at last effectively challenged the authoritarian Northern state. These 'stirring events', like Yeats's, were both exhilarating and dispiriting, from the fall of the Stormont government to the political stalemate of paramilitary violence and the attempts to 'contain' it. Whatever connection there may be here between the artistic and the political, it was part of Field Day's motive to address the social and cultural assumptions underlying the turmoil. Since its inception, it has extended its operations to the publication of a series of pamphlets, analytical commentaries on political and cultural themes; and an anthology of Irish writing in both languages, from the earliest times to the present, is about to appear.

The essence of Field Day remains its drama, and in that mode the analytic defers to parable and metaphor, acts of imaginative paraphrase. It is a political drama, but one which looks to other implications than the simple nationalism – or loyalism – available at the start of the Irish dramatic movement. The genesis and the nourishment of Field Day are Northern; its vision is of 'the island's cultural integrity which would operate as a basis for an enduring and enriching political settlement'.[10] Field Day is also, like Yeats, expectant and trustful of an audience. It is not an audience to be wooed by the populist 'relevance' of community theatre, nor condescended to by 'culture' mongering. The relationship between theatre and audience is to be, ideally, a mode of discourse. The theatre 'goes to the people not for their sake but for its own – but in the conviction that it will eventually be for their benefit if they are sufficiently to its benefit'. If both parties get it right, the audience 'does not find *otherness* in the theatre. It only finds the self it knows'.[11]

Regarded as a composite, a single, continuing testimony, Brian Friel's plays occupy both the zone of Field Day's interest and a recognisable dramatic tradition.

(ii)

Friel's stage is diversely inhabited. A young man on the eve of emigrating to America revolves his home life, friendships, and alien future (*Philadelphia, Here I Come!*). An old woman returns from sixty years

American exile to a family now at odds with all her memories of it (*The Loves of Cass McGuire*). Attempting to repossess the past as he remembers it, a travelling showman sets about the destruction of the reality, his rundown show (*Crystal and Fox*). Around the enquiry into the killing of three locals by British soldiers after a Civil Rights march accumulate the myths and the actuality of the event (*The Freedom of the City*). A Catholic Big House in its decline is host to its heirs and their images of their house's presence in their lives (*Aristocrats*). A faith healer and his two associates give their riddling versions of episodes from his nomadic life, his return to Ireland and his violent death (*Faith Healer*). During the British Ordnance Survey of Ireland in the 1830s, a small rural community embodies the clash between a confident imperialism and a depleted Gaelic culture (*Translations*).

These summaries, necessarily partial, suggest that despite the variety of situations there are unifying perceptions of them. Recurring words identify a cluster of circumstances which monitor the characters' lives: past, memories, home, community, exile, image, versions, myths, actuality. A play now disowned by Friel, *A Doubtful Paradise* (1959), makes a rudimentary reconnaissance of these points of reference.

Willie Logue is acting overseer in the Derry Post Office. He has futile hopes of promotion, children on their individual paths to disaster, and vast but defective cultural pretensions. Years of bogus refinement and ill-considered ambitions for his family constitute the illusion which distances and solaces a drab reality. This, as his wife sees, is the cause of their misfortunes. Willie's own occasional glimmerings of sense come to nothing. All of his life falls into the focus of his self-deception.

Although *A Doubtful Paradise* does not make anything of the social realities to which Willie's fantasies are an alternative, one can conjecture latent connections between the two in the 1950s original of his Derry. Its Catholic majority suffered the heaviest of generally heavy unemployment, atrocious housing, virtual disenfranchisement locally, and a civic administration with a gerrymandered Protestant majority. Doíre had become, so to speak, Derry and, officially, Londonderry. Thus seen, Derry provides the unsightly images of an urban community economically and politically oppressed, pervasive in the only other play Friel has set in Derry, *The Freedom of the City*. The never-never land of Willie's illusions is left unrelated to that real life.

Willie nevertheless anticipates a number of Friel's protagonists. They too seek to impose upon their lives some reassuring vision of its state. The difference is that their circumstances are not only the cause of their disaffection. Those very circumstances, intractably present, reviewed, aligned with the more malleable past of fond memory, have to be reconstituted into a tolerable version of their plain fact. So, as Cass McGuire succumbs to the make-believe cultivated by the residents of Eden House, the American low life of her bawdy reminiscence is transmuted into a fairy tale of opulent marriage and happy homecoming. Characters and events, re-cast, are made over into a fiction: 'our truth', the might-have-been made valid by her telling of it. Though the solace is real for Cass, the play makes its unreality bleakly clear.

The subjective distortions by which people manipulate their condition into a semblance of love or personal dignity are a motif which Friel explores with increasing subtlety and depth. Some of the later plays – *The Freedom of the City, Volunteers, Translations, Making History* – place it in an overtly political context. Even in the early plays, which work essentially with the personal relationships of an enclosed group – family, parish – Friel's peepshow has a solidly depicted social background in which the shifts and chicaneries of Irish politics and politicians are part of the private alienation. Gar O'Donnell in *Philadelphia* cannot sustain the boisterous mood that would befit his departure, perfectly aware though he is of all that is mean-spirited in Ballybeg. Its voice is Senator Doogan, advocate of ambition and advantageous marriage: his daughter is not for the likes of Gar. Private, the *alter ego* of Gar's Public self, unseen and unheard by the other characters, mocks, extravagantly, the masquerades of the circumspect politician:

You know, of course, that he carries one of those wee black cards in the inside pocket of his jacket, privately printed for him: 'I am a Catholic. In case of accident send for a bishop'. And you know, too, that in his spare time he travels for maternity corsets; and that he is a double spy for the Knights and the Masons; and that he takes pornographic photographs of Mrs D. and sends them anonymously to reverend mothers. (*SP* 45)

This comic exhuberance, sparking many of the exchanges between the two Gars, betokens an anarchic spirit, or, more soberly, an urge to self-disclosure, self-realisation, inhibited by Ballybeg's Victorian mores of social decency. The same spirit is epitomised in Gar's mother, Maire, dead in giving birth to him, touchingly, but only by hearsay, recalled:

She was small, Madge says, and wild, and young, Madge says, from a place called Bailtefree beyond the mountains; and her eyes were bright, and her hair was loose, and she carried her shoes under her arm until she came to the edge of the village, Madge says, and then she put them on.

(*SP* 37)

Gar's memory of Madge's memory seeks to coalesce with memories directly his own. The local Canon and Gar's father, S.B., are at their weekly chess. 'I had you cornered', says the Canon, setting Private off into a popsong parody. Then, Mendelssohn's violin concerto on his gramophone, Private thrusts his face between the two players:

D'you know what the music says? It says that once upon a time a boy and his father sat in a blue boat on a lake on an afternoon in May, and on that afternoon a great beauty happened, a beauty that has haunted the boy ever since, because he wonders now did it really take place or did he imagine it? There are only the two of us, he says; each of us is all the other has; and why can we not even look at each other? (*SP* 89)

Brought into the open by Public, it elicits no memory from S.B.

If these memories could be verified, connected, they would make up a truth complementing the more manifest reality of Ballybeg: 'the boys' ' endless reminiscence of imaginary seductions, futile street wanderings, cold, locked doors, drawn blinds. Even within that present there are moments of healing union: Ned's gauche presentation of his belt as a farewell gift; the comic-tender declaration of Gar's love, treasured though frustrated, to Kathy Doogan. These are counterparts of the lost innocence and spontaneity remembered, a pastoral freshness 'beyond the mountains', 'in a blue boat on a lake'. They have the imaginative power absent from Willie Logue's arbitrary affectations. Gar's effort is to consolidate these idyllic emblems, present with past confirmed, into the community of a Ballybeg 'distilled of all its coarseness', more earthily, 'not such a bad aul' bugger of a place'. Inevitably the effort will fail.

The neo-Arcadianism is potentially sentimental, but balanced by the 'coarseness'. It succeeds, too, because the figments of the past are seen to be capricious; the elusiveness of their promise is not blinked. And because the feelings which insist upon the promise represent an admirable defiance, however unavailing, of the conventions inhibiting both the individual and the community that might be. Gar's central longing is to elicit a relationship from merely living with his father. They are bound by silences neither can break, relieved only from a stock of commonplaces. In the Public / Private exchanges Gar displays the eloquence stifled with S.B. It is this eloquence which confers upon his versions of the past the only reality they have.

Fox Melarkey in *Crystal and Fox* is eloquent too, superficially with a showman's patter. Deeper feeling re-lives a time when he and Crystal 'raced across the wet fields in our bare feet'. For Fox it is an enchanting ideal of life, a time of instinctive responsiveness to each other, unencumbered by their ramshackle show. Reaching for the irrecoverable – or some quality it represents – Fox ruthlessly dismantles his present, the rattletrap van and the stage turns. He wonders if Pedro's performing dog might not prefer 'to all the sugar cubes in the world just one little saucer of arsenic'; and administers the poison.

The final object of destruction is himself. Self-accused, wrongly, of informing on their son, he loses Crystal. Fox is a masker, testing the panacea for discontent of Swift's dictum that 'happiness is the perpetual possession of being well deceived'. His quest has a desperate hope in view – 'I want to live like a child', in some primal simplicity – which leads him to reject the human ruses for dissembling reality. Like the rickety wheel, he thinks at last, 'the whole thing's fixed, my love – fixed – fixed – fixed'.

Crystal and Fox is a more sombre and more violent play than its predecessors. *The Gentle Island* reinforces this darker tone. Cass, Gar, Fox are all in their way concerned with aspects and the nature of love – family, romantic – within mainly domestic boundaries. The Gentle Island is Inishkeen, off the Donegal coast, an entire community being abandoned by its inhabitants. Two Dublin holiday-makers arrive. Peter invests the island with his notions of bucolic tradition, hardy endurance, vernal purity. Shane sees its life as an anachronism, mockingly enacting a cowboy, a 'plantation darky'. The summer spent by Sarah, a local, on the Isle of Man, another false Hesperides, is a comment too. The play's narrative deconsecrates the myth of Irish pastoral innocence. Like its history, the island is a place of atavistic brutality, literally paralysing mutilation, thwarted sexuality.

These two plays totally subvert the verbal defences, and the sources their fictions draw on, which, fragile though they are shown to be, have for Gar and Cass a transitory magic, whistling in the dark. Peter and Shane are violently dispossessed of their assurances. The islanders too, for all the starkness of Inishkeen, are being dispossessed: of some sense of belonging, to farm, region, culture, leaving for Glasgow, London, Manchester to become 'Paddys slaving their guts out in a tunnel all day'. In *The Freedom of the City* the three victims, Michael, Lily, and Skinner, have led lives of dispossession in their home town, and are finally dispossessed of life itself.

The play surrounds them, dead on stage at the opening, with the heavy furniture of the Mayor's Parlour, battlemented walls above, where the Judge sits, with the apparatus and vocabulary of a judicial enquiry, sociological generalisations, the intrusive media. All that, and what we see in the Mayor's Parlour as Lily, Skinner and a reluctant Michael disport themselves, are worlds apart. As they talk, a tracery of experience emerges. Lily's artless accounts of ghetto life convey her world of the streets around her, their doings her conversation, indifferently of hardship and high spirits.

However miserable, it has reassuring familiarities, collapsing now into problematic shapes. Her easygoing stoicism falters once. Quizzed by Skinner on why she marches, Lily answers out of the actuality behind her ingenuous brave talk:

LILY: Did you ever hear tell of a mongol child, Skinner?
SKINNER: Where did you hide the brandy?
LILY: I told you a lie about our Declan. That's what Declan is. He's
           not just shy, our Declan. He's a mongol . . . And it's for him I
           go on the civil rights marches . . . Isn't that the stupidest thing
           you ever heard? Sure I could march and protest from here to
           Dublin and sure what good would it do Declan? But I still
           march – every Saturday. I still march. Isn't that the stupidest
           thing you ever heard?
SKINNER: No.   (*SP* 155)

Michael has his sights on middle-class security, full of Civil Rights rhetoric, missing the days of marches 'dignified' by 'doctors, teachers, accountants'. 'Shite', says Skinner.

Skinner is the ringmaster. He abuses the furnishings, plunders the civic drink, summarily dispatches a Council agenda, teasing Michael, inveigling Lily into his mischief. Led towards any statement of belief, he backs off: 'But we'll discuss it some other time. And as I say, if you're passing this way, don't let them entertain you in the outer office'. To Lily he makes the only declaration breaching this defensive flippancy. Lily marches, he says, because she's obscurely aware of outrage at the hardships so vividly apparent in her uncalculating tales; because, 'in a vague groping way', she has awakened to a sense of 'hundreds, thousands, millions of us all over the world . . . It's about us – the poor – the majority – stirring in our sleep. And if that's not what it's all about, then it has nothing to do with us'. For the rest, he is an iconoclastic drop-out, securing for himself an apartness from society and commitment, rebuffing or blandly assenting. Asked by Michael, 'Are you for civil rights at all?' he replies, 'Course I am. I'm crazy about them. A little drop?'

Lily, Michael and Skinner have one release, *in articulo mortis*, from their vernacular to a heightened avowal of self-realisation. The play's final posture recalls it. The trio, hands aloft as during their stylised, formal statements, are mute. The silence summons their 'last words', above 'a 15-second burst of automatic fire'. Their now unspoken words perhaps outspeak Auden's 'lie of Authority'. The play's images and its language are dealing with individuals dwarfed by great institutions. It records the defeat, even the futility, of three silenced voices. Their lives have kept going on illusions which transpose indignity to a chimerical autonomy of the spirit: Michael's enchantment by 'dignified' protest; Lily's fantasy of cosy domesticity; Skinner's camouflage of taking nothing seriously. It is a response to circumstance which wins sympathy, respect indeed. Among the victims, speech ranges from Declan's (off-stage) 'shyness' to Skinner's spiel. The duckspeak of affronted officialdom, brute facts and brute force, prevail. Language is paramount, crucially embodying the clash between the powerful and the dispossessed.

In *Aristocrats*, Eamon, married from poverty into the O'Donnell Big House, has ruined his career by involvement in the Civil Rights Campaign; Judith, eldest daughter of the house, now nurse to her father, paralysed by a stroke, had taken part in the Battle of the Bogside: 'great betrayal; enormous betrayal'. But politics, in a strict sense, is a background murmur in a family chronicle of decline. Over the baby-alarm in his bedroom, the father's incoherent voice and memory relay travesties of the figure – 'such power, such authority' – he had been. Anna, now a nun in Africa, sends a tape-recording of saccharine recollections of long-vanished family evenings. Listening to it precipitates the father's death and the postponement of the marriage between the youngest daughter, Claire, and an ageing merchant. The Letterkenny exchange is a barrier against Casimir's phone calls to his wife and family in Germany. All these are disembodied, erratic communications, to which Uncle George adds his abrupt, speechless entrances and exits.

Aristocrats is scanning the archaelogy of a house, its latest heirs looking back on lives demeaned by the autocratic father and the house itself, claustrophobically introverted. 'Carriages, balls, receptions, weddings, christenings, feasts, deaths, trips to Rome, musical evenings, tennis – that's the mythology' retailed by Eamon's grandmother, a Hall servant. It is supplemented by Casimir's impossible memories of Yeats and other notables (in Eamon's translation, 'Shakespeare, Lenin, Mickey Mouse, Marilyn Monroe') and the prodigious gathering in Vienna of grandfather O'Donnell, Liszt, George Sand, Turgenev, Mendelssohn, Balzac . . . The reality is further from Casimir's extravanganzas than the less princely eminence of Eamon's account: 'a family without passion, without loyalty, without commitments; administering the law for anyone who happened to be in power; above all wars and famines and civil strife and political upheaval; ignored by its Protestant counterparts, isolated from the mere Irish, existing only in its own concept of itself . . . but tough – oh, yes, tough, resilient, tenacious; and with one enormous talent for – no, a *greed* for survival'. (*SP* 294)

The Freedom of the City and *Aristocrats*, with *Volunteers* and *Living Quarters*, written between 1973 and 1979, constitute a group of related plays. They are echo-chambers for many registers and modes of speech, ordered by the plays into the antagonisms and the confounding search for interior and bonding harmonies of the kind we have seen. The events on which they discourse are often themselves equivocal, to the parties concerned, at times to the audience. As early as *The Gentle Island*, are we to believe Sarah about Manus's treatment of his wife, or Manus? In *The Freedom of the City* the court, the balladeer, the media deliver their separate distortions. Casimir's fabrications cast doubt even on the existence of his German family. His croquet game, played with imaginary implements, takes on a life of its own. Facts are facts: illusion, misrepresentation, beguiling fictions demur. The individual seeks to discover and affirm a self within a system – paternal, social, political (in *Volunteers* some such group as the IRA) – bent on exacting conformity.

Faith Healer enfolds these tensions into its tale of Frank Hardy's healing powers. His fickle endowment will sometimes cure, sometimes not, all beyond his will. In the boldly demanding form of four monologues, the play gives a riddling account of the lives of its three characters: at the beginning and end by Frank, who we gradually learn is dead; in between by Grace, his wife (or mistress), also now dead, and by Teddy, his manager. At the close he confronts savagery, the menace of an axe, a crowbar, a mallet, a hayfork. Approaching the cripple in the Irish pub yard, sure that he will fail – 'if you do nothing for him, Mister, they'll kill you' – he is submitting to his gift in a mortal test which becomes a kind of sacrificial victory:

And as I moved across that yard towards them and offered myself to them, then for the first time I had a simple and genuine sense of homecoming. Then for the first time there was no atrophying terror; and the maddening questions were silent. (*SP* 376)

The story teases us with matters of plain fact. What is the truth of the episode at Kinlochbervie? The characters convert it each into their own event – the cruel birth of Grace's stillborn child, or Frank's hearing there of his mother's death; the idyllic weather in Teddy's mind, 'all blue and white and golden', or Grace's 'heavy wet mist'. Each account has its private validity. As Frank seeks to mend the deformed, the narrators order the circumstances of an event into conformity with the 'truth' they decree for it. Frank's power can alter reality; theirs produces illusions which compose a reality their author has chosen, interior and secure.

Yeats called poets 'transformers of the world', and Frank Hardy is literally, in another of Yeats's terms 'a shape-changer': of 'the crippled and the blind and the disfigured and the barren'. His, he says, is 'a craft without an apprenticeship, a ministry without responsibility, a vocation without a ministry'; and he asks, 'Was it all chance? Or skill? Or illusion? Or delusion? Precisely what power did I possess? Could I summon it? When and how? Was I its servant?'

Skill, illusion, control: the properties, not always biddable, to which the artist addresses himself, and to analagous ends. Sartre has a remark to the effect that in order for an event to become real it must be told as a story. The process may involve a cavalier treatment of events, of the daily world of phenomenal experience. ('Observed facts', said Yeats, 'do not mean much until I can make them part of my experience'.) The words that tell the story offer themselves as the equal of reality, possibly its creator, when they affect the way we see things. The fictions of the artist are a superior form of the illusions of ordinary resort: superior because they alter the contours of the world of fact, not necessarily to our comfort, by dislodging our perception of it; and because, unlike the illusions of everyday, they are made objective, dispassionate, by the discipline of form.

Frank Hardy's story is a parable of the work and the mysterious powers of the artist, enhancing, deceptive, dangerous. The telling of his story makes no concessions to any expounding of a parable. *Faith Healer* is absorbed in its immediate occasion. It never relinquishes the three lives at issue, their backgrounds, their squalid surroundings, their flux of dependences and rejections. Both the comic and the sombre spirits are observers. Teddy's monologue modulates with total assurance from the grotesquely funny account of Rob Roy the Piping Dog as Dedicated Artist – 'Morning, noon and night he'd sit there blowing the bloody thing and working them bellows with his back leg' – to the grief and loss of Kinlochbervie, Grace's child, 'that little wet thing with the black face and the black body, a tiny little thing, no size at all – a boy it was'. After Frank's triumphant performance in Llanblethian an old farmer whom he has cured pays tribute, 'and whatever way he said Glamorgan it sounded like the whole world'. The remark applies to *Faith Healer*, which leaves the parable to disengage itself from the particular histories.

(iii)

'Bloody words', says the Older Man, 'you can't change the world by words.' 'What other way can you change it?' the Younger Man returns. 'I tell you we can make this country – this world – whatever we want it to be by saying so and saying so again'. The exchange occurs in Denis Johnston's *The Old Lady Says 'No!'*; and Johnston has a note to the play – "The Republic still lives" is not the expression of a pious hope, but is in itself a creative act, as England knows to her cost'.[12]

The play is a reductive look at the banalities of 'liberated Ireland' (c. 1929), which has defaulted on the ideals of its rebels and political prophets, Tone, Emmet, Grattan, *et al*. Its language is a witty pastiche of styles: the diction of nineteenth-century patriotic verse, a histrionic quality in Emmet's declamations, echoes of Synge and O'Casey, contemporary Dublin demotic. The mundane pursuits of the passers-by accosted by 'Emmet' are entirely at odds with Emmet's ardours; as are their manners of speech. Grattan's statue, commenting on the life around his pedestal on College Green, has available only a diction inappropriate to the scene. *The Old Lady* opens with a playlet, put together by Johnston, of romantic fragments from Mangan, Moore, Ferguson and others of that sort. It ends with other borrowed words, spoken by 'some of Dublin's greatest contributors to the World's knowledge of itself'. Though there is perhaps a note of lament for squandered innocence, self-deceptions exposed, *The Old Lady* is not asking us to compare Glorious Past with squalid present. The play is alive with a sense of language evolving, exhausting and renewing itself, both receptive to and exercising itself upon the social environment. The collage of tongues is so deployed that it constitutes a means of enquiry into the sentiments they are used to express.

In turning to political history Johnston entered a substantial body of Irish drama. Yeats, though outside it, is not altogether out of sight. *The Countess Cathleen* is attached to his myth of the benevolent custodianship of the Big House. In the revised ending of *The King's Threshold* Seanchan dies, probably because Terence MacSwiney had just died on hunger strike. *Purgatory* is venting Yeats's contempt for the Ireland of the Free State. Some public figures and events had the stature he thought necessary, and his poetry admits them. Maud Gonne/Helen, Parnell/Cuchulain are among its recurrent occupants. But recent history as dramatic material he considered on the whole 'a spume that plays/Upon a ghostly paradigm of things'. In his plays Yeats was after archetypes of human experience, a world of prodigious characters and deeds. He draws not on the passing show around him nor on documented history but on the pre-history of legend.

Deirdre of the Sorrows, Synge's only treatment of legend, imbues its tragic love story with the mordant ironies admired but less success-fully pursued by Yeats. Insofar as it deals with Conchubor's kingly ambitions, the treacheries which they permit him, and their readiness to nullify mere individuality, it is a political play. Conchubor's claim on Deirdre is that she should 'be my queen in Emain . . . I've sense left not to lose the thing I've bought with sorrow and the deaths of many'. Like Johnston, though in a different way, Synge is establishing a dual view of the action: the kind of triumph comprehensible to political force – Naisi's murder; and the thwarting of that triumph by an act whose motive is sacramental, imaginative, telling an entirely other story. When Deirdre submits to, indeed helps to engineer, the fate prophesied for her, she has the quite conscious design of transcending Conchubor's power. Defeat, murder and suicide will become the victory of 'a story will be told for ever'. Lily, Michael and Skinner, observed by a different dramatic eye, assert none of the epic grandeur which Deirdre so confidently declares. But their words, like the words Deirdre invokes – and to severe pragmatic judgement with equal futility – persist beyond death in testimony against the sentence of the governors.

Synge stated his problem with the 'saga people' in a letter to Maire O'Neill in December 1906, that 'they seem very remote; one does not know what they thought or what they ate or where they went to sleep'. *Deirdre* supplies the tangibles. Synge earths the play in a sensual love and a sensuous world of woods and rivers, mud, the tracks and pathways of the glens. Both Synge and Friel we may for the moment call, in their distinctive ways, quite simply 'realist', though the term will have to acquire qualification. It is the dominant style of Irish drama, and characterises its plays on political-historical subjects. Lennox Robinson, whose plays almost epitomise the common run of Abbey theatre, took up the genre in *The Lost Leader* (1918) and *The Dreamers* (1915).

The hypothesis of the former is that Parnell is alive and living in the west of Ireland as Lucius Lenihan. Whether he is really Parnell or speaking as a figment of his own imaginings, Lenihans's appeal for a uniting of factions puts to shame the squabbling politicians of 1928. The weakness of the play is that Lenihan's identity remains just a problem, not a mystery and a symbol; and his rhetoric falls a good deal short of its obligations. *The Dreamers* takes into serious regard Emmet's maladroit rebellion and his love affair with Sarah Curran. In Robinson's account, the dream has not prepared itself for the assault on reality, though it leaves a residue of faith which is more than illusion. Robinson's inspection of the events is in part deflationary too, showing Emmet's followers uselessly drinking and brawling among themselves. The vapouring Clitheroe and the carousing mobs of O'Casey's *The Plough and the Stars* come to mind. Well beyond the achievement of his few forerunners – with Robinson one might instance St John Ervine (*Mixed Marriage*, 1911) – O'Casey extended into urban, political life the kind of drama initiated by Synge, a surface realism whose solidity is evaded and questioned by a highly stylised poetic prose. We shall return to O' Casey's 'Dublin Trilogy'.

Brian Friel's most recent work[13] has included *Translations* and *Making History*. Both are set in a historical past, a crucial period of political and cultural change whose ubiquitous stresses are shown at work in a small, localised group.

Imperial Rome and Homer's Troy – Virgil's Tyrian towers in the play's last speech – are references in *Translations*. Though in that perspective all empire is transient, here it is ascendant. *Translations* takes place in a hedge-school in Baile Beag/Ballybeg, where the polyglot Hugh teaches Greek and Latin through Irish. A contingent of sappers is engaged in the first comprehensive mapping of Ireland, which entails the anglicising of the Gaelic place names. Owen, Hugh's younger son, is assisting the project, a job which he sees as an academic exercise, not the collusion with a dispossessing colonialism his brother considers it to be. Maire, a local girl, falls in love with Lieutenant Yolland, who is bewitched not only by her but by a place and a language he can no more understand than Maire, equally entranced by 'England', can his. Their love, thriving on shared incomprehensions, participates in the divisions which on their wider stage are a dispute about cultural and political sovereignty. With Yolland's disappearance, British army correctness gives way to a programme of escalating reprisals. Sarah, the mute girl who had been learning to speak, reverts to silence.

Baile Beag, becoming Ballybeg, is an imperfect Eden, the corrupt smell of potato blight portending its other disasters. Its inhabitants speak Irish (and are to be taken as doing so on stage). This, with their schooling in Latin and Greek and general ignorance of English, is fertile in metaphor. In the world of Jimmy Jack Cassie Homeric deities, Diarmuid and Grania, and his neighbours cohabit in an exuberantly comic union of fact and legend. It is a place not wholly certain of its civil being, 'imprisoned', as Hugh puts it, 'in a linguistic contour which no longer matches the landscape of . . . fact'. The fact that was is now being reduced by the deletion of its familiarising names. The anglicised names and their originals echo through the play in a litany of lament for the Gaelic topography – the *'desiderium nostrorum* – the need of our own. Our *pietas'*. The loss of the names pre-figures the loss of the language itself:

Yes, it is a rich language, Lieutenant, full of the mythologies of fantasy and hope and self-deception – a syntax opulent with tomorrows. It is our response to mud cabins and a diet of potatoes; our only method of replying to . . . inevitabilities. (*SP* 418–19)

That Ordnance Survey was part of nineteenth-century England's utilitarian, bureaucratic imposition of its rule over Ireland. It had none of the abrupt conclusiveness of the suppression of the 1798 rebellion; or of the Irish defeat at Kinsale in 1601, the locus of *Making History*. As in *Translations*, a love story reflects the broader historical entanglements. Here it is the marriage of Hugh O'Neill, Earl of Tyrone, into the New English, to Mabel Bagenal, daughter of the Queen's Marshal. Coming to Dungannon as O'Neill's bride she abandons her own community for a society of which she cannot be wholly a member. Hence the occasional burst of gibing edginess within the tenderly playful relationship.

Archbishop Lombard, O'Neill's self-appointed biographer, has no time for the cultural niceties compromising such a relationship, nor for the Duke of Lerma's verdict on the Irish: 'Constantly at war – occasionally with the English – but always, always among themselves . . . fragmented and warring tribes'. For Lombard, O'Neill is to be presented as the hero unblemished, leading a united nation and a combative faith against heretical foreign oppression. It is thus that O'Neill has traditionally appeared in Irish political hagiology. The O'Neill of *Making History* is a much more equivocal and more credible character. His nine youthful years among the English nobility – 'Days without blemish', he calls them – will have no place in Lombard's account. They are a mark of separateness, registered in his normal 'upper class English accent'. To English eyes O'Neill is a Judas, in Ireland a Janus, perhaps even a Proteus. Certainly he declares two aims, 'almost self-cancelling': to keep his compatriots 'in touch with the life they knew before they were overrun . . . honouring [its] rituals and ceremonials and beliefs'; and 'to open these people to the strange new ways of Europe'. He demands that Lombard tell 'the truth' – 'Kinsale was a disgrace'; and O'Neill, in his own avowal, is 'The schemer, the leader, the liar, the statesman, the lecher, the patriot, the drunk, the soured, bitter émigré'.

Lombard, however, is 'making' history into the story of a holy crusade, a Gaelic demi-god, an embodiment of nationhood: 'Now is the time for a heroic literature' to raise an abject people. Another time may allow another history, the 'narrative pattern' it imposes on facts equally determined by politically desirable ends. But O'Neill in Rome, burlesqueing the illusory conspiracies ('Operation Turf Mould') is burlesqueing the whole heroic concept. The final scene counterpoints the 'truth' of Lombard's panegyric with whatever the truth may be of O'Neill's fulsome submission to the Queen after Kinsale, now recalled in Rome:

([O'Neill's] *English accent gradually fades until at the end his accent is pure Tyrone*)

LOMBARD: Son of Feardorcha, son of Conn Bacagh, son of Conn Mor, noblest son of noble lineage, who was fostered and brought up by the high-born nobles of his tribe –

O'NEILL: I do with all true and humble penitency prostrate myself at your feet and absolutely submit myself to your mercy, most sorrowfully imploring your commiseration and appealing only to your clemency –[14]

Making History – in a way the story Lombard will not tell – is about the stratagems of transcribing – selecting? shaping? perverting? – historical facts in order to establish a version of reality whose 'truth' is verified by its acceptance. O'Neill is a case in point. Many of the shibboleths and prejudices of contemporary Irish politics look back to just such mythologised pasts. With *Translations*, *Making History* is about the power of language, whether to possess by naming, or to re-create the historical past as it can the personal.

(iv)

In 1904 Yeats was lamenting the decay of the English spoken in Ireland. He argued that the only greatness achievable by a realist play must 'arise out of the common life' and its language. He meant the kind of language which is the source of Synge's dramatic speech, and seems to be attributing Synge's success in large measure to the vivacity of his – fast disappearing – models in Wicklow and the west of Ireland. Yeats goes on to ask, 'Is it possible to make a work of art, which needs every subtlety of expression if it is to reveal what hides itself continually, out of a dying or at any rate a very ailing, language and all language but that of the poets and the poor is already bed-ridden'.[15]

Some forty years later T. S. Eliot concluded that Synge's language 'is not available except for plays set among that same people'[16] – nor even, it might plausibly be added, for them, since that people no longer exists. In the event Eliot designed his plays in the genre of drawing room comedy and on the speech of educated people. The resulting verse became more and more indistinguishable from prose.

Neither Yeats nor Eliot arrived at a form which would restore verse on the twentieth-century stage. But Eliot's reading of Synge permits a more encouraging lesson than does Yeats's. Yeats's question about bedridden language is enforcing the answer 'no'. An alternative answer is that common speech, however different from, even inferior to, the hibernicised English on which Synge worked, is amenable to the metamorphoses of art. Synge's example is the use he made of his linguistic source, cultivating from it a quite artificial dramatic rhetoric. Beckett's variations on a wholly different vernacular have achieved an equally powerful dramatic speech, formalised in a repetitive, circling diction and syntax. O'Casey had shown earlier that the vernacular of his time and place was 'available' to the transforming imagination.

Irish drama has been a long experiment with the boundaries of realist theatre. Accepting the Abbey's proscenium stage, its best work extends the 'painted stage' a dimension beyond the simple imitation of reality in setting and décor and naturalistic dialogue. The effects it creates are poetic, though not in the ways recommended by Yeats; and their primary agent, as he advocated it should be, is language. The reason for this elevation of the word may be political as well as aesthetic. In the early years Frank Fay argued that a commitment to Irish was essential to a national theatre, but recognised that in practice English has superseded it. The long commerce with Gaelic had given the invading tongue a distinctively hibernicised character. It was sanctioned, in Synge's words, as 'English that is perfectly Irish in essence'. The plays of Yeats's 'Abbey period' (1898 – 1912) belong to what Seamus Deane has called a programme for turning a history of political defeat into a history of artistic triumph. An imperative part of that is to secure English to the expression of Irish imagination and sensibility, to possess, as it were, the dispossessing language.

Whatever accounts for this 'sovereignty of words', it has not been unanimously approved. One of Michael MacLiammóir's motives in founding the Gate Theatre was to improve 'the lack of visual sensibility of a nation whose ears had always been its strongest point of aesthetic perception'. More recently, Emelie Fitzgibbon concedes that 'the great predominating fashion in Ireland for verbal theatre is still, unfortunately, the presiding design',[17] rather in the resigned tone of E. M. Forster conceding that, yes, a novel tells a story. The disapproval is on the grounds that language and its dramatists are disadvantaging themselves by relegating directors, designers and so forth. The record does not bear this out.

Synge himself sought a quite literal authenticity. Cottages and shebeens are precisely represented on the stage: 'nets, oil-skins, spinning wheel . . . pot-oven'; 'counter on the right with shelves . . . many bottles and jugs . . . a settle . . . a table . . . a large open fireplace with turf fire'.

They are the particular furnishings of particular places, but with exits 'through the Meadows of Ease, and up the floor of Heaven to the Footstool of the Virgin's Son'. Pegeen Mike, 'in the usual peasant's dress', commonplace to the Widow Quinn, has 'poetry talk' too, 'the light of seven heavens in your heart alone'. The 'real' time of *The Playboy of the Western World* is an evening and a day, its passage is through 'the elements and stars of night'. In *The Playboy* dualities immediately engage us: of the romantic, or the romanticising, and the mundane; and of a stage scene, familiar, recognisable, yet discomposed.

It is only in his story that Christy Mahon murders his father, but for his audience the fiction becomes the event. When he is exposed, it is the power of words which masters his Da – 'Go on, I'm saying . . . Not a word out of you' – and sends him, a hero again, to go 'romancing through a romping lifetime'. The play closes with Christy restored to his 'poet's talking, and such bravery of heart'. His enchantments, however, carry their deceits. He wins not the lady but the crazed, ugly father. Pegeen is returned to the 'lonesomeness' which is a constant motif in their courtship. She is again 'a girl you'd see itching and scratching, and she still with a stale stink of poteen on her', no longer Christy's 'the Lady Helen of Troy with a nosegay in her golden shawl'.

We are constantly aware of the gaps, opening and closing, between the statement of words and what we see: transparent lies, fictions that come true, are exposed, find a new truth. The drama relies upon this interplay of correspondences and incongruities between language and the facts it purports to describe. Christy's imaginative fiction is on the verge of enthralling the community (whose encouragement was part of its creation) and its – relatively – settled ways of church, family, local boundaries: 'That's a grand story', 'he tells it lovely'. For the villagers, eloquence, both exciting and unsettling, is in the end not enough. 'There's a great gap', Pegeen says bitterly, 'between a gallous story and a dirty deed'. The pragmatic community rejects poetry for its former ways – 'By the will of God, we'll have peace now for our drinks'. For the artist Christy, forger of other worlds, society has no room. Off he goes with his captivating, threatening fancies.

Synge's plays revolve around small communities and fugitives of one sort or another: in *The Tinker's Wedding* a district clustered round a church, a tinkers' camp; in *The Well of the Saints* a similar district and two blind beggars precariously on its fringes. All are a stage for the antagonisms between private freedom and agreed conventions, anarchic imagination and calculating prudence, dream, actuality, and their compromises. Their effect is to mythologise and fantasticate action and character. Though commonly regarded as straightforwardly realist, O'Casey's Dublin trilogy continues this line.

Farce and absurdity pervade O'Casey's plays. Knockabout routines and tumbledown rooms establish a metaphor of a collapsing society. In *The Shadow of a Gunman*, Seamus Shields's braces – 'they'd do Cuchullian, they're so strong' – snap as he counts the spoons in their erratically filled boxes.

The sparsely furnished tenement rooms in *Juno and the Paycock* are rapidly supplied through the Boyles' illusory inheritance, the stage reduced at the end to emptiness and 'chassis'. In *The Plough and the Stars* the pub scene has the ludicrous choreography of the fights that come to nothing, the baby abandoned on the floor. All these antics imbue with their clownishness the surround of great happenings – Easter 1916, the Anglo-Irish war, the civil war – and the language partners the antics.

The dialogue of Captain Boyle and Joxer is vernacular mock-heroic – 'I seen things, I seen things, Joxer, that no mortal man should speak about that knows his Catechism'. Through it are refracted events inviting heroic interpretation diminished by association with the language to absurdity. Farce is always poised to break in upon a world whose structures seem destined to fail their serious pretensions. The nihilism of which Joseph Wood Krutch accuses O'Casey, his failure to give a persuasive dramatic voice to the socialist beliefs he actually held, is at root a scepticism about the institutions which form themselves around ideals – family, church, political party, trade union. There is not one 'happy family' in the plays; Jerry Devine is as interested in becoming Union secretary at £350 a year as in his 'principles'; the Covey spouts from Jenersky ideas in which O'Casey believed, and which he gives to a windbag.

The only community in which O'Casey represents any collective endurance is the anarchic tenement life, communes vagabonding from room to room. The life which has vigour, however disorderly and feckless, is the life which has a language for itself. Abounding in verbal traps and malapropisms, expansive with alliteration and assonance, the language belongs to the tenement world of shifts and expedients – working, in Beckett's phrase, on 'the principle of disintegration . . . surrounded by the doomed furniture'.[18] The principle is at work not only in the bravura comic passages. It operates also in a prose capable of reaching into intensities of despair, grief, outrage, not necessarily when O'Casey is displaying his fineries. The 'hearts of stone' speech, of which he thought well enough to use it twice, has none of the reverberation of Bessie Burgess's 'I got this through you, you bitch, you'; or, in the British bombardment of Dublin, Fluther Good's 'The whole city can topple home to hell'. Toppling, city, home, and hell are reference points in the topography of O'Casey's world. They 'place' the tenement / commune, which in its fragmenting way stubbornly coheres, resisting the manifestoes of romantic love and of the grand abstractions of politics: an aspect, worked through, of Yeats's 'Easter 1916', 'where motley is worn'.

Synge and O'Casey are the major founders of a tradition whose features are apparent in the work of contemporary Irish dramatists. Synge's west of Ireland is the west of Ireland, O'Casey's Dublin is Dublin. It is by just this concreteness and particularity that the plays, at root, work, by the uniqueness of each set of characters and situation. We should not read the plays into an undifferentiated, homogenised mass because they reveal kinships of attitude and theme and a certain coherence in their authors' aesthetic. They identify their localities not by guidebook landmarks but by the individual tones of voice which argue the naming of places: Deirdre / Conbchubor, Fluther Good / Clitheroe, though it is never just a duality. The locations become a home for fables and metaphors of the shaky armistices, negotiated through illusions, dream, art, between the supposedly given, objective 'out there' and the mediating self.

The same is true of Tom Murphy's Galway, Frank McGuinness's Derry, and Friel's Ballybeg. His plays are excursions around ways of designating, in time and space, where one is. The intent of his characters is to make a place habitable, transmuting its possessiveness, which cannot be exorcised merely by leaving it, into a sense of belonging, an idea of 'home' at once communal and unconstricting. We might see his plays not so much as 'figures in a peepshow' – though that conveys the necessary artifice – as figures in a landscape both contemporary and reminiscent.

FRIEL'S 'EMBLEMS OF ADVERSITY' AND THE YEATSIAN EXAMPLE

CHRISTOPHER MURRAY

To associate Friel with W. B. Yeats may appear to some a luckless undertaking. It may be that Yeats now gives the wrong vibes in Ireland, for one hears him referred to by young readers as remote, aristocratic, élitist, and so on. Among some more sophisticated readers one hears of a Yeats who begins more and more to resemble the Milton castigated a generation ago by Eliot and Leavis, a damaging and dangerous influence. The trouble with this sophisticated criticism is that it can become the Philistine's *vade mecum*. It can serve to justify prejudice born of sheer laziness; it can preempt fair judgment based on literary criteria. In recent years the swing that has rehabilitated Milton (sustained by people such as Christopher Hill and David Norbrook) would appear simultaneously to have downgraded Yeats. We should learn from this, however, the vanity of critical wishes. Ideology, conscious or unconscious, cannot leave the dyer's hand unstained; the critic should not take sides. As I refuse assent to any régime which sends Yeats into disgrace so I must insist on the propriety of making certain associations between Brian Friel and W. B. Yeats positively and without embarrassment. I may be discussing the anxiety of influence but without anxiety on my own part. As I see it, and as I wish to argue, Friel's greatness as a dramatist may more fully be appreciated when the courage of his endeavours is seen and measured in relation to the ideas and dramatic achievements of Yeats.

Given the obvious discrepancies between Yeats's poetic drama and Friel's far more Chekhovian art, it would be fatuous to speak of direct influence. In the catalogue of possible influences, indeed, Yeats would be named long after Synge and O'Casey in the Irish tradition and after Eliot, Arthur Miller, Ibsen and (above all) Chekhov in the wider field of modern drama and dramaturgy. To place Friel in either of these traditions would yield useful results; to refer to Yeats is to refer to an example rather than an influence. Yeats is relevant because of his life-long struggle to keep faith with his deepest artistic convictions. I should like in the essay that follows to inspect this fidelity under three headings: politics, language and form. My method will be to use these three headings as bases for seeing Friel as establishing in his own drama a comparable struggle and a comparable integrity.

1

When Conor Cruise O'Brien wrote some years ago about the unhealthy intersection of literature and politics he advanced Yeats as one of his most cautionary offenders.[1] *Cathleen Ni Houlihan*, first staged in 1902, proved, demonstrably, an inspirational text for nationalists. Dr O'Brien cited admirers of the play who testified to its importance in creating the spirit of the 1916 rebellion and, indeed, in creating recruits. Given such testimony it was a simple matter for him to answer unequivocally and positively Yeats's anguished question, 'Did that play of mine send out / Certain men the English shot?'[2] There is a good deal in Dr O'Brien's article to suggest his indifference (it can hardly be ignorance) towards the nature of 'imitation' in drama; he fails to make any distinction between histrionic performance in a theatre and what he takes to be equally histrionic performance on the streets. It is a failure, of course, which may be related to Dr O'Brien's equation elsewhere in his writings of politics and performance: in *To Katanga and Back*, for example, and in his revealing play *Murderous Angels*. It means that Dr O'Brien is prisoner of his own metaphor. More accurately and more damningly, he shows an inability to understand the nature of metaphor and especially of dramatic metaphor. It is not an uncommon plight, especially among historians. For this reason Dr O'Brien's rather crude equation between art and reality offers a useful means of introducing and discussing the political argument surrounding Brian Friel's plays.

When asked in interview about *The Freedom of the City*, 'are you afraid that in certain circumstances an audience might take a very crude and a very blunt political message from it?' Friel immediately thought of Yeats: 'That wouldn't worry me anyway. "Have I sent out certain young men?" – that sort of thing wouldn't worry me at all.'[3] He conceded, however, that he wrote the play out of 'some kind of heat and some kind of passion that I would want to have quieted a bit before I did it.' The experience of Bloody Sunday 'wasn't adequately distilled in me.' This admission, nevertheless, cuts across the fact that *The Freedom of the City* began as a history play concerned with evictions. It was in that early stage entitled *John Butt's Bothy*. In 1973, when *The Freedom of the City* was about to have its première (at the Abbey Theatre), Friel told Eavan Boland in interview that he still regarded the new play, 'like its embryo, as being a study of poverty'.[4] Poverty, too, is a political question. Thematically, it fuels the play just as history fuels Yeats's play. At the same time, Friel's play is polemical where Yeats's is inspirational. The bond between them lies in the matter of audience: both demand an audience sufficiently informed about Irish affairs to respond to the images provided. It has to be borne in mind here that Friel was writing after the events of Bloody Sunday, whereas Yeats wrote *Cathleen Ni Houlihan* fourteen years in advance of 1916: the tone of the author is altogether different. Yeats, as visionary, deploys a dream figure to mobilize the hero into a political decision; Friel, as realist, sits in judgment on action already taken against his three heroes. Friel's task, as artist, was to control by technical means the volume of feeling released by actual events. His skilled attempts to do this went for next to nothing with the reviewers. Irish reviewers complained of frustration at being deprived of empathy with the three central characters whose deaths are revealed in advance. The Brechtian devices Friel employs to destroy conventional illusionism – the abandonment of plot for narration, the use of the sociologist as interrupter of the flow of sequential narrative, the use of songs, the constant use of irony, and so on – were lost on such reviewers.[5] The art of the play was thus missed while its political content was superficially digested. The major irony here is that *The Freedom of the City* is as much about perception, about discriminating the real and factual from the metaphysically pre-conceived and supposed, as was Brecht's *Galileo*. It was, perhaps, much less surprising that Clive Barnes should have attacked the play on Broadway as if it were a simple piece of propaganda, seeing as 'far-fetched, indeed impossible' the finding of the tribunal in the play. A better informed reviewer would have been aware that such a finding had indeed been officially published in the *Widgery Report*.[6] Barnes's reaction resembles Dr O'Brien's response to Yeats's *Cathleen Ni Houlihan*. Both are very quick to use the emotive category 'propaganda'. As will appear below, neither Yeats nor Friel was ignorant of the danger of writing propaganda (however defined); the art of each is seen in his superiority to that danger.

Just as *The Freedom of the City* did not find its proper audience (the play closed after nine performances on Broadway) neither did *Volunteers* two years later. It went down to all sorts of hostile reviews in Dublin, and did not transfer elsewhere. Nevertheless, while Friel was castigating the society of Southern Ireland by a complex association of a Viking site and republican prisoners volunteering against orders to do the dig, reviewers looked for a clear declaration or 'point',[7] not to say a propagandistic line. Seamus Heaney pointed out that such reviewers (and he had in mind Gus Smith in the *Sunday Independent*, who had urged Friel to 'dig deeper') were really deflecting the play's severities by demanding a 'great play' on the 'subject of internment'.[8] The rebuke was well directed, and Heaney went on to describe Friel's achievement in Yeatsian terms: 'Friel would assent to the Yeatsian proposition that "we traffic in mockery". . . . The play is not a quarrel with others but a vehicle for Friel's quarrel with himself, between his heart and his head. . . . It is more about values and attitudes within the Irish psyche than it is about the rights and wrongs of the political situation.'

It was over *Translations*, however, that the political argument over Friel's work was to come to a head. It is fair to say that the reviewers liked it, in Derry, in Dublin, in London and New York. Friel had found (or created) his audience. But as time passed a certain hostile criticism began to come forward to challenge and subvert the enthusiasm. Some of this antagonism came from historians, some from critics of a more literary persuasion but saying much the same thing, namely, that Friel had written a dangerous and disingenuous play. The most virulent of such attacks to date has come from Lynda Henderson who says of *Translations*: 'Its seductiveness adroitly disguises its dishonesty. It is dishonest to both the cultures it represents.'[9] Since Ms Henderson advances no analysis to support her contention, what she claims remains a shrill and ill-considered piece of rhetoric. It is not the case, of course, that *Translations* 'represents' any culture, much less 'both the cultures'. Edna Longley is perhaps more subtle in her dislike of the play, as one would expect from a literary critic of such Leavisite strenuousness. Ms. Longley sees the play as sectarian, however: 'Friel, then, translates contemporary Northern *Catholic* feeling into historical terms'[10] (my emphasis). This is an extraordinary claim, because no such terminology invades the play. Why, one wonders, does Ms. Longley have to say 'Catholic'? Is it that the play frightens her? Does she have to resort to name calling because Friel 'explores the ethos of a particular community exclusively in relation to British dominion over the native Irish'? Even there, in the latter quotation, Ms. Longley loads the critical dice. Exclusively? But is it not the central axis of the plot that it is the 'native Irish' who will not tolerate the proposed marriage of the English lieutenant to the Irish peasant girl? The 'dominion' comes, necessarily, which is to say tragically, when the British soldiery take reprisals. The play exemplifies a mechanism, not a thesis. The dismaying fact is, however, that criticism such as Ms Longley's exemplifies a lack of objectivity. Contextualizing Friel with polemicists such as Seamus Deane and Tom Paulin, she cannot see the play as other than a Field Day pamphlet.

Edna Longley relies to a considerable extent on Conor Cruise O'Brien and John Andrews. Andrews, author of *A Paper Landscape*, which Friel has gratefully acknowledged as a significant source for *Translations*,[11] was the first historian to offer reservations about the play. Ms. Longley quotes him uncritically. What Andrews actually says in the symposium reported in *The Crane Bag* gives little grist to her political mill. He does complain of certain anachronisms in the play, but he comes to the conclusion that this is not at all a simple matter implying the rigging of a case: 'Every anachronism is thrown into relief by a corresponding non-anachronism' (p. 121), so that one got 'an extremely subtle blend of historical truth and – some other kind of truth' (p. 122). Andrews recognises that as literary artefact the play is elaborating metaphor (the map making), and, although he sees the lover Yolland as 'improbably and anachronistically classless' in seeking Maire's blistered hand and thereby ignores a pastoral tradition in such matters which is best exemplified by Prince Florizel's courting of the supposed peasant girl Perdita in *The Winter's Tale*, Andrews concedes that every character in *Translations* is 'treated fairly' (p. 121). In short, as historian Andrews is aware that the mode of the history play is different in kind from history itself, and he accepts, without perhaps being much interested in the topic, its validity. What he has to say can and should fuel a debate on the nature and scope of the history play but cannot fairly be invoked in condemnation of *Translations*.

Another historian, Sean Connolly, considerably less aware than Andrews of the nature of literary modes, conventions and traditions into which he blithely wades, has taken issue with *Translations* as not just anachronistic but as 'a distortion of the real nature and causes of cultural change in nineteenth-century Ireland so extreme as to go beyond mere factual error.'[12] This 'distortion' is then advanced as evidence of Friel's failure as dramatist: 'it is not Friel's reading of history that limited his achievement, but the poverty of the artistic resources he brings to his task, substituting caricature and political cliché for the recreation of experience' (p. 44). There is, of course, no coherence in Connolly's argument, interesting though it is in other respects. It does not follow if a writer 'distorts' factual or cultural (are these the same?) data that he compensates, as it were, by supplying larger-than-life rôles and operatic language. Is Shaw's *Saint Joan* renowned for such compensations? On the contrary, that play is flippant in its refusal to provide audiences with the slightest sign of nineteenth-century theatre comforts. Shaw wanted his audiences to be disturbed and to think rather than to immerse themselves in romantic escapism. And this is the emphasis of the modern history play ever since Shaw, its founder. Connolly, however, does not specify what 'artistic resources' he bewails and the inference is that he fails to recognise those on view, particularly the central convention of a single language to represent both Irish and English.

The unsatisfactoriness of much of the preceding commentaries on

Translations is seen once more in Brian McAvera's critique in *Fortnight*. Essentially, what he has to say is that Friel did not write the play McAvera thinks he should have written. Thus 'the play cops out.'[13] McAvera does not say out of what, nor, indeed, does he establish whether Friel set out to present a political argument in the first place. McAvera, while sensitive to the play's complexities, ends up, like Lynda Henderson, accusing Friel of dishonesty.

To date, *Making History* has not attracted the same sort of hostility as *Translations*. It may well do so, as it is clearly a political allegory for the current situation in Northern Ireland. For some people, accordingly, *Making History* will be a 'dangerous' play. This is the root of the matter. To what extent is the artist free to express his vision of political conflict and destruction? Where does 'responsibility' enter to inhibit his vision of reconciliation? Yeats fought for the artistic freedom of the theatre on both a specific, personal level and a general, philosophical level. Somewhat ironically, he found that to steer a course true to his convictions brought him into conflict with the nationalists on the one hand and with the Lord Lieutenant on the other. His early defence of Synge against those who claimed *In the Shadow of the Glen* was anti-nationalist is revealing:

I am a Nationalist, and certain of my intimate friends have made Irish politics the business of their lives. . . . But if some external necessity had forced me to write nothing but drama with an obviously patriotic intention instead of letting my work shape itself under the casual impulse of dreams and daily thoughts I would have lost, in a short time, the power to write movingly upon any theme. I could have aroused opinion, but would not have touched the heart.[14]

When the Abbey opened in 1904 *In the Shadow of the Glen* was in the first bill alongside *Cathleen Ni Houlihan*. Juxtaposed, the two plays attempt a definition of what the national theatre was about. 'To me it seems that ideas, and beauty and knowledge are precisely those sacred things . . . that a nation must value even more than victory.'[15] But in order to establish such a theatre, 'We have to free our vision of reality from political prepossession.'[16] Synge became the acid test of Yeats's commitment to the independence of art in the theatre, especially when the nationalists rioted in outrage at *The Playboy of the Western World* in 1907. Prior to his similar defiance of the Abbey audience over O'Casey's demythologizing of 1916 in *The Plough and the Stars*, this was Yeats's finest hour. It was as author of *Cathleen Ni Houlihan*, moreover, that he claimed the right to be heard. The victory he won then, in 1907, costly though it was, assured the artistic freedom of the Abbey.

On the other hand, if one is to talk of unhealthy intersections it has to be stressed that drama has always been a dangerous business, which has called forth censorship wherever theatre has thrived. It is easy to muzzle a theatre by law but it is not like turning off a tap; it is not possible to supply art again at will. The history of theatre offers many examples of the debilitation of drama through censorship; it takes a long time for drama to recover its energies once these are officially curtailed, as happened in England with the introduction of the Licensing Act in 1737. The issue is a vital one for consideration here because censorship is what lies behind the sort of criticism which wags the head over *Cathleen Ni Houlihan* or *Translations* as 'dangerous' plays. A censored theatre is an affront to civilization. Once again, Yeats's example indicates how the fight was and must be carried on against censorship. Following the defiance of Cardinal Logue in staging *The Countess Cathleen* in 1899, and the defiance of the nationalists in keeping *The Playboy* on the boards in 1907, Yeats faced up to Dublin Castle with the production of *The Shewing up of Blanco Posnet* in 1909. Shaw's play had already been banned in England by the official Censor (still operating under the 1737 Licensing Act), but the latter had no jurisdiction in Ireland. Shaw offered the play to the Abbey; the Lord Lieutenant, in an unusual move, threatened the removal of the theatre's patent if the production was not cancelled. Lady Gregory describes Yeats's stand before the Lord Lieutenant's office: 'Yeats spoke very seriously then about the principle involved; pointing out that we were trying to create a model on which a great national theatre may be founded in the future.'[17] Although the objections to Shaw's play were mainly moral Yeats and Lady Gregory saw plainly that its suppression would be a political act since the Lord Chamberlain had no authority over Irish theatres and the Lord Lieutenant had historically no real rôle as censor. In their joint press statement, accordingly, they emphasized the implications of the attempted censorship of Shaw's play, adding: 'The Lord Lieutenant is definitely a political personage, holding office from the party in power, and what would sooner or later grow into a political Censorship cannot be lightly accepted.'[18] They won their point and the play went on, to international attention (Joyce was at the première for *Il Piccolo della Sera*), an important landmark in the establishment of freedom of expression in the modern Irish theatre.

Brian Friel is heir to this freedom. As artist he has the responsibility to use it in such a way as to explore national identity without giving way to incitement to hatred or the like. His priority has always been to serve art. In interview, when asked whether the Field Day project did not depend on nationalism and the achievement of a united Ireland he replied: 'I don't think it should be read in those terms. I think it should lead to a cultural state, not a political state. And I think out of that cultural state, a possibility of a political state follows. That is always the sequence.'[19] Being part of a cultural movement in which other members write pamphlets does not mean that Friel cannot tell the difference between art and propaganda. James Fenton, critic for *The Sunday Times,* may at first glance seem to give aid and comfort to the anti-Frielites when he said of the first night of *Translations*: 'I took the piece as a vigorous example of corrective propaganda.'[20] But then Fenton forced himself to ask, 'propaganda for what?' and had to admit that there was nothing narrow or bigoted in the appeal:

The audience at the Guildhall in Derry included most political viewpoints, and it was an official Unionist who initiated the standing ovation. Dubliners had turned out *en masse,* but the bulk of the response was local and without apparent sectarian bias. The excitement of the audience was palpable. Applause punctuated speeches in a way that London only witnesses in opera houses. As a former political correspondent, I am a connoisseur of fake standing ovations. The ovation this production received was genuine.

It may well be that Dr O'Brien would be little impressed by Fenton's testimony; more likely, he would find it as ominous as he finds the effect of the première of *Cathleen Ni Houlihan,* and there will be others who will quickly concur. The case needs no apology. Neither is it an excuse for timidity, however. The fact of the matter is that in theatre the 'intersection' of art and politics can be quite healthy.

This point can readily be shown from the history of drama and theatre. Aristotle's argument on *catharsis* in the *Poetics* was an attempt to answer Plato's condemnation of drama as incitement to public disorder. The metaphor Aristotle uses to justify tragedy is in itself medical: *catharsis* means purgation in a physical sense, with the effect of restoring wellbeing. Puritans who have advanced variations of Plato's objections to theatre have ever since been answered by variations of Aristotle's socio-aesthetic. That the theatre acts as a safety valve as well as an agent of consciousness raising has secured its otherwise doubtful position in modern society. Ernest Blythe hardly stands out as a literary critic, but his comments on the rôle of the Abbey Theatre in Irish society are quite significant, coming from a highly political figure who ended up managing a national theatre. For example, Blythe credits the early Abbey playwrights with creating the political consciousness of the people: 'Most of those who built Sinn Féin and the Irish Volunteers were directly or indirectly influenced by Abbey plays in which the ideal of patriotic endeavour and sacrifice shone out, such as "Kathleen Ni Houlihan" by W. B. Yeats.'[21] At a later time the plays of O'Casey and Denis Johnston 'did much to soften asperities, to provoke laughter without cynicism and to re-establish healthy and tolerant public opinion.' The matter of partition, Blythe said, which was too controversial to be discussed coolly in public, 'got its best publicity in popular plays produced in the Abbey.' He envisaged that 'in future still other matters which could be sources of misunderstanding and division may well be combed out on the stage and rendered innocuous by thorough ventilation there.' The hope of rendering weighty and contentious issues 'innocuous' is, of course, something no serious playwright would accept, and here Blythe's limitations as a commentator on the justification of theatre may be glimpsed. Nevertheless, Blythe makes plain the tradition which sustained the Abbey in a positive way; he answers Conor Cruise O'Brien with the long-standing example of the 'healthy' intersection at the national theatre of performance and politics. Out of that tradition Brian Friel emerged as dramatist in 1962, when *The Enemy Within* was staged at the Abbey.

It goes without saying that Yeats was the prime mover and policy maker behind the development of the Abbey Theatre. It may be neces-sary to stress here, however, that Yeats saw his work at and for the theatre as his main life's work. When he accepted the Nobel Prize for Literature his address was not on lyric poetry but on the Irish Dra-matic Movement. Further, Philip Edwards has drawn a parallel be-tween Yeats's work as dramatist and Shakespeare as forger of a national consciousness. Each of them wrote historico-mythic plays. 'For each of them, the past of the nation is of intense importance, but, while that recovery of the past is meant to strengthen the nation in its future development, the past becomes a myth of foreboding, not so much a path to the future as an indignant repudiator of the future.'[22] It can be said, in turn, that the enterprise of Field Day and its cultural ambitions follow on from Yeats's design. Understandably, since he is a modest man, Friel has found difficulty in even suggesting such a parallel. But in one interview, at least, he is reported as invoking Yeats: 'The purpose of Field Day, he says, after tiptoeing round it . . . is to provide a brave and vibrant theatre that in some way expresses his country. He thinks of Yeats and the Moscow Art Theatre.'[23] Yet Friel is also on record as declaring: 'I do not believe that art is a servant of any movement.'[24] In attempting to reconcile these two convictions, theatre as articulator and moulder of public consciousness through carefully chosen metaphors and images and drama as the most profound form of self-expression, Friel shows himself a worthy successor of Yeats. To invoke the 'unhealthy intersection' clause in relation to his serious political plays (for nobody, noticeably, has anything much to say about the political farces, *The Mundy Scheme* and *The Communication Cord*) is to pay Friel this compliment, however ill-considered.

2

In 'The Reform of the Theatre' Yeats said: 'if we are to restore words to their sovereignty we must make speech even more important than gesture upon the stage.'[25] 'Sovereignty' is, perhaps, not the happiest of substantives in the Northern Irish vocabulary at present and yet it may serve as accolade for Friel's dramaturgy. Friel's drama is a literary form just as surely as was Yeats's. The plays read well; the dialogue does not usually suggest gesture, movement, or action. Rather, it seeks to define feeling. There is a consonance with Yeats's dictum: 'Without fine words there is no literature.'[26]

Friel, however, has never written in verse. Therefore, insofar as he is in the Yeatsian tradition he follows those who, like Synge, wrote their plays in prose. Ulf Dantanus has traced in Friel's short stories a sensibility and a sense of place which he relates to Synge: 'A careful reading of Friel's stories strengthened by some occasional comments he has made elsewhere clearly shows that Friel . . . approaches his subject with the same sensitivity and caution as Synge did.'[27] Yeats, however, perceived Synge and Lady Gregory as working towards the same poetic aim as himself: 'You and I and Synge', runs the famous Open Letter to Lady Gregory, 'not understanding the clock, set out to bring again the theatre of Shakespeare or rather perhaps of Sophocles. . . . We thought we could bring the old folk-life to Dublin, patriotic feeling to aid us, and with the folk-life all the life of the heart.'[28] So long as we can reconcile Sophocles' Thebes with Synge's Aran Islands we may find Yeats's theatre of the heart sufficiently meaningful to include also Friel's Ballybeg. For Synge, as for Yeats, Irish drama should first and foremost be 'literature', as he told Frank Fay: 'The whole interest of our movement is that our little plays try to be literature first – i.e to be personal, sincere, and beautiful – and drama afterwards.'[29] As if to emphasize how closely they agreed, Yeats declared in that same year (1904): 'Our plays must be literature or written in the spirit of literature.'[30] Friel's pronouncements on dramatic language are few, but he has displayed a fondness for quoting Eliot's 'Tradition and the Individual Talent' in relation to the need for the artist to display a separation between the man who suffers and the mind which creates, and this certainly argues a primarily literary, third-voice view of drama. Moreover, Friel's practice suggests, *mutatis mutandis*, an interest in language and style comparable with Synge's.

What concerns Friel most, however, is to reconcile style with accent. Style by itself could lead to preciousness or artificiality: a risk run by any successor of Synge. The most evocative passages in *Philadelphia, Here I Come!*, for example, are rich in descriptive detail attuned to a prose rhythm delicately adjusted, as in Private Gar's evocation of the crucial moment in the past:

– do you remember – it was an afternoon in May – oh, fifteen years ago – I don't remember every detail but some things are as vivid as can be: the boat was blue and the paint was peeling and there was an empty cigarette packet floating in the water at the bottom between two trout and the left rowlock kept slipping and you had given me your hat and had put your jacket round my shoulders because there had been a shower of rain. And you had the rod in your left hand – I can see the cork nibbled away from the butt of the rod – and maybe we had been chatting – I don't remember – it doesn't matter – but between us at that moment there was this great happiness, this great joy – you must have felt it too – although nothing was being said – just the two of us fishing on a lake on a showery day – and young as I was I felt, I knew, that this was precious, and your hat was soft on the top of my ears – I can feel it – and I shrank down into your coat – and then, then for no reason at all except that you were happy too, you began to sing: (*Sings*) . . . (*SP* 82–3)

In such passages language certainly aspires, as Pater said of all art, to the condition of music. The rhetoric is skilful, the images precise, the rhythm accelerating and weighed with feeling (not 'a shower' but 'a shower of rain', not 'your hat felt warm' but 'your hat was soft on the top of my ears'). The language has the effect of good poetry: it is over-heard rather than simply heard. Of course, the context and setting give this speech maximum effect, since it is delivered while its addres-see is on his knees in meditative posture, at a point in the action where Gar is working himself up to the doomed effort to make contact with his father through this memory; his halting, embarrassed description will contrast powerfully with this earlier, lyric evocation. As style and accent accord, the gap widens between private feeling and public discourse. The play becomes the tragedy of an impossible language. Yet the audience is witness to its reality and poetic truth.

The whole of *Faith Healer* is an exercise in rhetoric in this way. It is all overheard. The audience is affected directly by the narrating voice mediating an experience emotively. The skill called for in such writing – where dialogue is not in question – is considerable, being the modern equivalent of the Elizabethan 'set speech'. The most seductive of Friel's plays in this regard is *The Loves of Cass McGuire*. Appropriately, much use is made in this play of Yeats's poem 'He Wishes for the Cloths of Heaven', which the old pair, Ingram and Trilbe, intone as their siren-song to fantasy. Cass, being hard-bitten and toughened in the restaurant trade in New York, is at first contemptuous of these sirens and their invitation to spread her dreams under their feet. But the action of the play moves towards the decisive moment when Cass sinks into the winged chair and succumbs to their 'truth'. Here, again, the language approximates to music – and there is, counterpointing Cass's re-creation of her past, the Tristran and Isolde story, intoned by Ingram and Trilbe – and Friel presents Cass's tragic plight transformed into a new mode. The language sings in a context of utter desolation. The Yeatsian refrain ('But I, being poor, have only my dreams' etc.) is entirely ironic in Friel's use since in Yeats there is some 'other', some lover even if estranged, whereas Cass, we realise, is alone and has only her vulnerable dreams to sustain her. What Friel does here, one might say, is to use *The Shadowy Waters* to portray the lower depths.

Although part of Friel's technique is, then, to elaborate two distinct and separate languages ironically opposed he does set a certain amount of store on accent itself. I mean by 'accent' here fidelity to local experience and its expression, a veritable hallmark of Irish drama. Yeats had turned to Lady Gregory for help with the 'accent' for *Cathleen Ni Houlihan* and Synge, too, expressed his indebtedness to Lady Gregory's language in *Cuchulain of Muirthemne* in developing the 'dialect' of his plays. Are there floorboards, then, through which Friel eavesdropped, as Synge, and presumably Lady Gregory (though not in unison), eavesdropped on the conversations of Irish people? That notion of authenticity, with its colonial and class implications, has long gone. Nevertheless, Friel has more than once commented on the need for the Irish writer to find a language true to Irish experience. For instance, he remarks on the tradition from Farquhar to Behan which shaped not a stage-Irish dialect so much as a pitching of the voice in an English way:

They had to do that if they were to practise their craft. . . . Ultimately they were maimed.

But there's a big change now. What many are doing is writing for ourselves. Not in any insular or parochial sense but they want to be heard by their own people. And if they're overheard by anyone else, that's a bonus.[31]

In another interview the shift in point of view from 'they' to 'we' indicates that Friel includes himself among those writers 'writing for ourselves':

What I am talking about however is the relationship of this island to the neighbouring island. We have all been educated in an English system, we are brought up in school reading Wordsworth, Shelly [*sic*] and Keats. These are formative influences on our lives . . . . We must accept this . . . that there is a foreignness in this literature; it is the literature of a different race. . . .

If I can quote from the play [*Translations*], 'we must make them our own'. We must make them (English language words) distinctive and unique to us. My first concern is with theatre and we certainly have not done this with theatre in Ireland. The only person who did so in this country was Synge. Nobody since him has pursued this course with any persistence or distinction and indeed this is one of the problems of the theatre in this country. It is a new and young discipline for us and apart from Synge, all our dramatists have pitched their voice for English acceptance and recognition. This applied particularly to someone like Behan. However I think that for the first time this is stopping, that there is some kind of confidence, some kind of coming together of Irish dramatists who are not concerned with this, who have no interest in the English stage. We are talking to ourselves as we must and if we are overheard in America, or England, so much the better.[32]

The aim, then, is a form of English which would avoid stage-Irish on the one hand, standard English on the other. It excludes Gaelic itself. Friel's position recalls that stated by Yeats in 'A General Introduction for My Work', where Yeats feels torn between his 'hatred' for the English tradition and his awareness that 'everything I love has come to me through English; my hatred tortures me with love, my love with hate. . . . Gaelic is my national language, but it is not my mother tongue.'[33]

Obviously, *Translations* is the key text here. Even in the early stages of composition Friel knew that this play 'has to do with language and only language'.[34] This preoccupation has been much examined since *Translations* was first staged in 1980. A text less noticed, however, and perhaps equally revealing on this point, is Friel's version of *Three Sisters* (1981). A major reason for the undertaking was the quality of existing translations in English. If Irish actors used a standard English version of *Three Sisters* they must 'assume English accents because it's English music', Friel decided. 'As English as Elgar. The officers say "Jolly good. Wasn't it splendid." '[35] The task was to provide a new text for the actors 'so that they can assume a language that can simply flow out of them. . . . It's all a question of music. The audience will hear a different music to anything they've heard in Chekhov before.' Not exactly music to a psaltery, of course, but for all that a music akin to Yeats's quest for the tune underlying Irish speech. So far as *Three Sisters* is concerned the task was a form of naturalization of cadence, as seen, for example, in the repetitions and diction of this speech by Irina in Act Three:

I'm so unhappy, Olga. My God I'm so unhappy. I'm sick working in the county council office. I can't go on working there. I won't go on working there. It's far, far worse than the post-office. I dread and detest every second I spend in it. I'm twenty-three, Olga. I'll soon be twenty-four. And it has all been work, work, work. I've become desiccated in mind and in body. Look at me – I've got thin and ugly and old. I'll soon be twenty-four and what have I to show for it? Nothing, nothing, nothing. And time is slipping away. And every day that races past I feel – I *know* I'm losing touch with everything that has even the smell of hope about it – no, no, even worse than losing touch – sinking, being sucked down into a kind of abyss. I am despairing, Olga. Do you understand what I'm saying? I am desperate. I see no reason to go on living. I see no reason why I shouldn't end it now.[36]

The touch is delicate here, from the characteristic 'My God' in the second sentence down to the emphatic rendering contained in 'even the smell of hope' towards the end. There is a scruple between 'despairing' and 'desperate' as between a slightly embarrassing confession of weakness and a frank admission of finality. There is psychological pressure behind the rhetorical manoeuvre in the last two sentences, culminating in the bare phrase 'end it now'. The deep notes sounded are not all that remote from the speeches of loneliness and mutability heard in *The Tinker's Wedding* or *Deirdre of the Sorrows*.

3

In his 'Extracts from a Sporadic Diary' Friel stated that the crux with the writing of *Aristocrats* was 'as usual with me – with its form.'[37] Years earlier he had declared: 'the days of the solid, well-made play are gone.'[38] Form for Friel, accordingly, is something to be elicited from the content as it discloses itself in composition; the search for form is a search for meaning. In this area comparison with Yeats is not to be forced: each is in pursuit of an individual articulation of persistent themes. In particular, one has to distinguish Yeats's concept of the hero, Aristotelian, aristocratic and sublime, from Friel's modern, realistic depiction of Prufrockian man, interiorized and anti-heroic. In spite of this formal difference, however, it is noteworthy that Friel's protagonists are all marked with a certain arrogance, a disdain of common standards which would earn them a fairly respectable place on Yeats's great wheel of the phases of being (in *A Vision*). From Columba of Iona through the likes of Fox Melarkey, Skinner, Keeney,

Frank Butler, Francis Hardy and all the way to Hugh O'Neill, the hero in Friel is in some measure aristocratic. Frank Hardy probably speaks for all when he says in *Faith Healer* that when he was most himself, 'I knew that for those few hours I had become whole in myself, and perfect in myself, and in a manner of speaking, an aristocrat, if the term doesn't offend you.' (*SP* 333). What else is this sense but the sense of 'unity of being'? That quest, undertaken on an individual, community, and national level, running through Friel's oeuvre, may be seen as a tragic compulsion as doomladen and moving as the attempts of Cuchulain or of the Old Man in *Purgatory*.

Formally also, there is the distinction between Yeats's favouring of the one-act play and Friel's far greater adherence to the full-length, realistic form. Nevertheless, Friel's aims have never been circumscribed by the conventions of social drama. The plays invariably strain towards a world elsewhere, whether in Edenic youth or in a re-invented, 'mythic' history; there is always a 'land of heart's desire' advancing its dubious claims.

The essential resemblance, however, lies in the dramatization of what Yeats called 'the deeps of the mind'.[39] This concentration of the dramatic action on spiritual interiors inevitably drew Yeats to the Japanese Noh form, an artistic dead end into which Friel sensibly did not follow him; Friel's form is illuminated, nevertheless, by reference to Yeats's enterprise. *Philadelphia, Here I Come!*, with its division of the central character, marks Friel's first venture into 'the deeps of the mind'. Private Gar, he says in the opening stage direction, 'is the unseen man, the man within, the conscience . . . the *secret thoughts*, the id' (*SP* 27, my emphasis). Private Gar, in interaction with his public self, provides the means of dramatizing the inside of a character's head. The split indicates a telling schism in the modern Irish psyche – the counterpart, in its humble way, of the polarity presented by Yeats in Cuchulain and Conchubar in *On Baile's Strand*, with the important difference that Friel's inner character is hidden, secret and (to others on stage) invisible. What Friel is saying parallels what Yeats was saying: that the self cannot be fully realised in any attempt to know fulness or integration. Comic though the presentation of Private Gar is he signifies a tragic failure in Irish life to bring to bear upon relationships a union of mind and body. Tragically, likewise, Cass McGuire recognises that her only option in Eden House, as a result of the futility exposed as her lot, is to retreat into the deeps of her imagination and thereby transcend the facts. It is an ironic and a cruel choice, implying Friel's rejection of the socio-economic forces that shape consciousness. He will not accept things as they are (except, perhaps, in *Aristocrats*, his most positive play). The dramatic form signifies this non-acceptance.

A romantic vision, therefore, sustains Friel's dramaturgy. At the core of every play is another secret story, as Seamus Deane has shown. 'The function of the hidden story, when it is uncovered, is to transform the stage as public exhibition area into the stage as private and sacral area.'[40] I see this secret play, however, as a dream play, a Yeatsian rearrangement. Yeats wrote interestingly in 'Certain Noble Plays of Japan' about the paradox of intimacy in the theatre. He had discovered, through watching the miming and dancing of Michio Ito, that whereas the performer was very close to his audience (in a drawing room) and dispensed with all but the simplest stage trappings, the effect was one of distance:

Because that separation was achieved by human means alone, he receded but to inhabit as it were the deeps of the mind. One realised anew, at every separating strangeness, that the measure of all arts' greatness can be but in their intimacy.[41]

In a nutshell, this describes the paradoxical effect of Friel's experimental form. Obviously, Yeats's use of mask, chorus and dance is not replicated and has to be laid on one side here; this is not to say they do not exist in tentative fashion in at least some of Friel's plays. In what follows the focus is solely on 'the deeps of the mind'.

In *The Loves of Cass McGuire* we are at first brought into close, intimate relation with the central character, who breaks down the theatre's fourth wall and addresses us directly; by the end of the play, as she registers the horror of her situation, the direct addresses stop and she recedes away from us, literally into a world of her own. The effect is to draw us with her and yet independent of her; we inhabit her world of memory transformed. In *The Freedom of the City*, where a complex use of time and space provides a startling series of shifts between objective accounts of experience and subjective but contrasting realization, the core lies in the area in between these two modes, an interlude set in another world when the three central characters speak, as it were, after death and describe in a new language the meaning of their deaths: their speeches are subjective, but out of character, and *'they speak calmly, without emotion, in neutral accents'*. (*SP* 149) Some commentators have difficulty with these speeches, finding them unbelievable or a breach of convention. But that is precisely the point. They do breach the convention heretofore observed by these speakers. These are three people speaking from the dead: we are no longer in the realm of realism. The same point can be made about *Living Quarters* and *Faith Healer*. In each of these there is a special use of time, as a dead person (in *Faith Healer* two dead persons) inhabits both the past and (theatrically) the present.

Living Quarters, while apparently written in a meticulously realistic style, is actually among the most experimental of Friel's plays. In narrative terms, it provides a version of the Phaedra story, with the focus on the Theseus figure, Commandant Frank Butler. But the innovation is that as the play itself opens Butler is dead and what follows is a reconstruction in which Butler is both there and not there. In one way, the play is about thresholds which are crossed from one area, one world of experience, into another: the audience is brought by the performance into this second, inner world. The terms Friel uses to describe this state, inhabited by the characters at certain times, are quite Yeatsian, 'reverie' and 'memory' being the significant ones. In his essay 'The Tragic Theatre' Yeats wrote of the hero's passionate moments when the audience entered a mood of contemplation, of reverie, in which universals were encountered:

Tragic art . . . the confounder of understanding, moves us by setting us to reverie, by alluring us almost to the intensity of trance. . . . We feel our minds expand convulsively or spread out slowly like some moon-brightened image-crowded sea. That which is before our eyes perpetually vanishes and returns again.[42]

As the directorial figure Sir tells us at the outset of *Living Quarters*, Friel's whole play is merely a contemplation. The characters are not actually present but have gathered in their minds to reconstruct this fatal day: 'although they're now scattered all over the world, every so often in sudden moments of privacy, of isolation, of panic, they remember that day, and in their imagination they reconvene here to reconstruct it.' Yet, Sir continues, 'reverie alone isn't adequate for them' (*SP* 177). They have compiled a ledger, a script of the drama, and have conceived also 'the ultimate arbiter' of that script, Sir himself, whose position as bookholder they nevertheless challenge in a concerted attempt to alter the events of that fatal day. The fundamental conflict in *Living Quarters*, then, lies between Sir and the characters, which means it lies between and within their own imaginations. This, in short, is a dream play.

A parallel can be found in Yeats's *The Only Jealousy of Emer*. Essentially, what is presented there is a play-within-the-play. In Yeats, Emer is audience to the drama of Cuchulain's afterlife. When she tries to reach him she is told: 'He cannot hear – being shut off, a phantom'.[43] He dwells in another world, where memory agonizes and remorse forbids release. Emer, on certain terms, can intervene and unlock the prison of Cuchulain's consciousness, but he remains unaware of her presence. The whole play is built on that irony. The drama remains private, its secret uncommunicated to the man who is saved. In *Living Quarters* there is no play *except* this ironic play-within-the-play. When Anna, the Phaedra figure, tries to intervene early on and disclose in time her awful secret she is told by Sir (here the counterpart of Yeats's supernatural Figure of Cuchulain): 'it is the memory of those lost possibilities that has exercised you endlessly since and has kept bringing you back here, isn't that so?' (*SP* 206). Thus when Sir insists on the scene he wants to reconstruct, Anna and the others who are not in that scene '*begin to drift away, each encased in his privacy*' (*SP*208). This emphasis recurs at the catastrophe when the confidant, the ineffectual Father Tom Carty, tries to rouse the others to intervene and save Frank from suicide. Frank's son Ben (the Hippolytus figure) '*remains encased and intact in his privacy*', while his sister Helen looks at the priest '*as if he were a stranger*' (*SP*241). In short they are '*all isolated, all cocooned in their private thoughts*'. And '*No one responds*' until the suicide takes place off stage, after which they '*relax and emerge from their cocoons*' (*SP*242). But it is a '*slow awakening*' and they are '*still not quite out of their reveries*'. In contrast to *The Only Jealousy of Emer* the mythic hero is not saved. The drama hinges instead upon the enduring aftermath of his death, paradoxically permanent in the minds of those around him, his 'audience'. The real audience, distanced from all this, must find their way to the core.

The paradox just mentioned might be summed up on its thematic level in Yeats's line about the risen Christ in *The Resurrection*: 'The heart of a phantom is beating!'[44] On the theatrical level, the bringing together of past and present, invisible and visible, in such a way as to implicate the audience in the dissolution of realism, can be found in many of Yeats's other plays, eg. *The Dreaming of the Bones, The Words Upon the Window-Pane* and, most powerfully, in *Purgatory*. In the latter two, Noh elements are slight and unnoticeable but the drawing of an audience into the deeps of the (suffering) mind is still the effect.

Faith Healer provides another illuminating example of Friel's use of Yeatsian form. When this play opened in London at the Royal Court the critic Robert Cushman offered the asinine comment: 'I suspect that if rolled out into an ordinary play, with action and dialogue and suchlike adornments, Mr Friel's story would not seem wonderfully interesting.'[45] Where, one wonders, does this leave not only the whole of Yeats's dramatic corpus but *Waiting for Godot, Six Characters in Search of an Author* and *The Birthday Party*, to confine the argument to but three experimental plays. It is not the story but the conditions of its creation that *Faith Healer* presents to its audience. Cushman's critique, based on the criteria of the well-made play, entirely misses, as such criticism must, the theatrical power of Friel's play.

As in *Living Quarters*, the central character in *Faith Healer* is actually dead when the play opens. This is just the first and most daring risk the playwright takes here. Dead men proverbially tell no tales, and yet Frank Hardy's rôle is to tell his tale in such a way as to make the audience share in his sense of fate. Compounding the problem, Grace, whose version of events usefully adjusts what we learn from Frank, is herself also dead, as we discover only at the end of Teddy's narrative. Using monologue alone, Friel confronts the technical difficulty of re-creating the lives of these three characters in narrative; it is all a telling of tales, with the breach of secrecy which that phrase implies. The tales conflict, contradict, repeat, confuse, and refuse to be entirely reconciled.

What *Faith Healer* enacts, with audience participation, is the reality of Frank Hardy and his history. We first see and hear Frank, then we hear about him from two independent narrators. The technique here is to have a speaker refer to Frank as if we had not seen him already, e.g. Grace says: 'I wish you could have seen him . . . he had a special . . . magnificence' (*SP* 350–51). Then she will use the demonstrative in such a way as to demand intimacy with his character: 'And when you speak to him he turns his head and looks beyond you with *those* damn benign eyes of his, looking past you out of his completion, out of *that* private power, out of *that* certainty that was accessible only to him' (*SP* 343, italics added). We begin to form a relationship towards Frank which is analogous to Emer's relation to the dead Cuchulain: his 'privacy' defines that relationship.

Faith Healer progresses inwards, towards a re-creation of Frank Hardy's consciousness. This is done, formally, by an incremental accumulation of perspective, until his reappearance to speak the final monologue renders him powerfully on the verge of some discovery which is the audience's discovery also. Thus Grace ends her account of the fatal evening in the Ballybeg lounge bar with an image of Frank's being swept into a play-within-a-play from which she was excluded. Having cured the deformed finger Frank said to her: ' "That's the curtain-raiser". . . and I wasn't there for him' (*SP* 352–53). Teddy's description of the same scene broadens the picture to include both Grace and Frank: 'And it was like as if I was seeing them for the first time in years and years – no! not seeing them but *remembering them*' (*SP* 367). Here Teddy, in the present, is recounting a moment in the past which in turn he sees as a recollection of an earlier, happy time for Grace and Frank. When we recall that they are now dead their happiness is perceived as occupying a remote place, distanced from the audience. Teddy seems to suggest this when he goes on to describe Grace and Frank as occupying the centre of 'that big circle round that big lounge', while he himself was 'sitting there just outside the circle, sitting there very quiet, very still' (*SP*367, 368), like the actual audience. When Frank reappears for the final monologue he is described as not so 'aloof' or 'detached' (*SP*370) as in Part One, and, indeed, he addresses the audience with more intimacy than before. Paradoxically, he moves closer *to* the audience while drawing the audience back into that circle of attention created for him by the narratives of Grace and Teddy. As Frank's own narrative reaches its climax, '*he moves very slowly down stage*' (*SP*376), closer to the audience, in imitation of the movement within the narrative: 'And as I moved across that yard towards them and offered myself to them . . .'. The demonstrative *that* conveys the reality already established: the stage is now the yard; *them* evokes the four men about to kill him, but *them* is also the audience, made witnesses individually and collectively (in that strange way in which theatre communicates) to his extinction as a blackout follows his final line, 'At long last I was renouncing chance' (*SP*376). It is an extraordinary moment in the theatre, '*Pause for about four seconds. Then quick black*', which enforces a sense of sharing. At the Irish première at the Abbey Theatre (28 August 1980) a palpable silence registered this moment with an intensity to be associated with the greatest tragic art. 'We feel our minds expand convulsively or spread out slowly like some moon-brightened image-crowded sea.' Before our eyes Frank Hardy recedes from us into the deeps of the mind. The moment of his self-realization is also and simultaneously the moment of his death. But being dead already he is like Yeats's Swift in *The Words upon the Window-Pane* re-enacting an abiding crisis, or like Yeats's Christ re-enacting Calvary in a dream.[46] Of all the reviewers of *Faith Healer* I have seen Robert Hewison alone seems to have understood this Yeatsian correspondence, when in his perceptive critique for the *TLS* he remarked:

Brian Friel uses his three forms of rhetoric to convince us of one case, that the imagination, willed or unwilled, can be so strong that it is possible to create the conditions under which people can recreate themselves. . . . The irony is that the faith healer, the artist, finds the mystery of his talent a cross too hard to bear. Beneath the modernism of Friel's exploration of the nature of fiction lies a Catholic symbolism which resolves itself in the faith healer's sense of a necessary sacrifice.[47]

That sense of 'necessary sacrifice' takes us right back to the roots of Yeats's tragic drama, to *The Countess Cathleen* and, indeed, to *Cathleen Ni Houlihan*. Essentially, however, Frank Hardy exists in a kind of Yeatsian purgatory which the actor must re-enter nightly and which the audience cannot remedy. Instead, the audience shares the process, the ritual, the experience emotionally and intellectually, knowing as they assist at that they cannot actually assist, 'Mankind can do no more.'[48]

Finally, in Friel's most recent play *Dancing at Lughnasa* the form for the first time aspires to and includes what for Yeats was the essence of lyrical expression in drama: the dance. Starting with *Four Plays for Dancers* (1921) Yeats attempted to find a new language for the bridging of two worlds, one actual and the other supernatural, and to make their interaction palpable. Inspired by the Japanese Noh drama, as translated by Ernest Fenollosa and edited by Ezra Pound in 1916, and shown the possibilities of dance by Michio Ito, Yeats created what he termed a new, eclectic form, 'distinguished, indirect and symbolic',[49] for the purpose of dramatizing 'the deeps of the mind'. Although his experiment could not be called entirely successful, and although Yeats soon modified his ambitions and compromised with realism (for example, in *The Resurrection* and *The Words Upon the Window-Pane*), to the last he persisted in the belief that dance was integral to his design. In the prologue to his last play, *The Death of Cuchulain*, he has his alter ego say: 'I wanted a dance because where there are no words there is less to spoil' (*CP* 694). At the end of *Dancing at Lughnasa*, likewise, Friel's commentator says: 'When I remember it, I think of it as dancing. . . . Dancing as if language no longer existed because words were no longer necessary.'[50] The whole play enacts the interaction of the actuality of village life with the spiritual and emotional longings of the Mundy family, on the brink of dissolution. Dance is the core of the play: in the background are the two pagan forms, the Celtic dance in honour of Lugh, god of arts and crafts, and the African dance in honour of Obi, 'our Great Goddess of the Earth' (p. 47); in the play itself there are the wild, Dionysiac dance of the five sisters with '*a sense of order being consciously subverted*' (p. 22) and the quieter (Apollonian?) ballroom dancing to a Marconi radio with the visiting godhead of Gerry Evans (ironically considered). The two kinds of dancing express the souls of the women and measure their constrictions against the amplitude offered by the so-called 'savage' ritual beyond the realistic horizon. The poverty and hostility of the orthodox Catholic culture, its inability to sustain the spiritual lives of these five women, are highlighted by the imagery of the dance and its broad anthropological implications. Friel has succeeded in finding a dramatic form which beautifully integrates body and soul while it laments the transience of that integrity.

Yeats is Ireland's greatest man of the theatre. James W. Flannery's study, *W. B. Yeats and the Idea of a Theatre* (1976), is an acknowledgement and a reinforcement of that conviction. Yet to a lot of people, theatregoers among them, Yeats is still an esoteric figure whose plays are too remote from ordinary concerns to make them interesting. That view is being seriously challenged now, not only in the steady stream of books exploring and applauding the range and liveliness of Yeats's theatrical ideas but in the recent revival of interest in the plays in production at the Lyric Theatre, Belfast, and the Peacock Theatre in Dublin. In particular, the production of the Cuchulain cycle at the Peacock in September 1989 showed the variety and richness of style to be found in that five-part story of life, death and the afterlife, heroically considered. Over the next few years, plans and finances are drawn up to carry on this reinstatement of Yeats as national dramatist, so that in time it is likely that his work will generally be seen for what it is, in ambition and in achievement.

It is in that expectation that this essay seeks to pay tribute to Brian Friel as a worthy inheritor of Yeats's legacy to the Irish theatre. Friel's greatness as a playwright is established, but the nature of his art, it seems to me, is not always or not clearly understood. If those who have a problem with Friel's work also have a problem with Yeats there isn't much more to be said. Those who have a problem with Yeats alone can increase their appreciation of Friel's achievement if they take the trouble to take note of Yeats's persistent experimentalism. Those who have a problem with Friel on political grounds must look a little further abroad than Northern Ireland and learn to consider the wider circumference of world theatre, as Yeats himself encouraged through his interests in Gordon Craig, Adolphe Appia, Maeterlinck and the symbolists, not to mention the Noh tradition of Japan. Katharine Worth has indicated, in *The Irish Drama of Europe from Yeats to Beckett* (1978), how necessary it is to see Yeats and other Irish dramatists in this wider perspective. Without that perspective we are doomed to a provincialism which denies freedom by insisting on labels and credentials. Thus to associate Friel with the Yeats who is equally at home among the modern symbolists as in the nationalist tradition is to liberate him and his work for the consideration which is his due. Only then will it be fully seen how he enriches while he draws upon the Yeatsian tradition.

THEATRICAL TEXT AND LITERARY TEXT

THOMAS KILROY

We write plays, I feel, in order to populate a stage. It is this curious desire to move about actual living bodies, to give them voice and the mantle of character in a conspiracy of play, which distinguishes playwriting from all other kinds of writing. It is also the element which makes the place of Drama in Literature so problematical. This is a form of writing which employs a physical medium, that of the human body and its physical environment, to communicate with others. The very surrender of creativity to a third party runs counter to the whole principle of literary method which is based upon the strict control of a single authority.

Yet there have always been playwrights who have insisted by their practice that their plays be accepted as literary as well as theatrical texts. Brian Friel is one such. His plays arrive in the theatre scrupulously finished. He would have little patience, I think, with the notion that improvisation, workshops or extended rehearsal discussion could contribute very much to the actual business of writing a play. Certainly any treatment of his extraordinary technical skills should be framed by this acknowledgement: his is a sophisticated literary intelligence. Many of his effects are close to those of the novelist and short story writer. His plays consistently test the histrionic adaptability of these techniques, whether or not they can be made to work on stage. I want to look at two of the more 'literary' of Friel's plays, *Living Quarters* and *Aristocrats* and end with the play *Faith Healer* in which Friel challenges the very nature of conventional dramatic action itself.

There is nothing as desolate as an empty stage. It is an intense model of all desert places unwarmed by human presence. But the intensity derives from artifice, not nature, from the eye of the voyeur, the ear of the eavesdropper, the expectant imagination of the bystander. Somewhere within this nexus is the dynamic of playwriting and it is removed from the territory in which most literary works are plotted and executed. Dramatic technique is simply anything which serves to excite the expectancy of a theatre audience and then proceeds to satisfy it.

All dramatic technique begins with the first image that is imposed upon the empty stage. As playwrights we are defined by that first image. We are what we are by where we choose to make things happen.

In particular, this helps to place us in relation to our tradition. The more audiences are consoled by the familiar on the rise of the curtain, the more traditional the playwright. In the Western European tradition the most familiar of these first images foisted upon the stage is that of the *domus*, the house, home, room, palace or cabin, at any rate some version of the human domestic. This is merely a concession (again given the nature of our European tradition) to the fact that the human drama has been seen to exist in its most vital form within the cell of the family. Those playwrights, particularly in this century, who have radically departed from this in a bewildering display of different settings have been attesting to the displacement of the family from its traditional place of eminence in the human story.

Brian Friel is not radical in this way. Most of his plays are firmly set within the family and in the community which radiates out from it, his Ballybeg, an imaginative portion of Ireland which has attained a ripe identity so extensively has he employed and developed it over the years. Kitchen in the home of County Councillor S. B. O'Donnell. Commandant Frank Butler's living-quarters. Ballybeg Hall, the home of District Justice O'Donnell. The hedge-school, old byre, habitation of Hugh Mor O'Donnell. These are solid properties precisely because they come to the stage already carrying the weight and ramification of fully imagined families.

Actors love playing Friel for the same reason that they love playing Chekhov. They can feel the immersion into a world which is fully in place and fully knowable. Actors crave security and here they can sink into the embrace of kinship and neighbourliness. Stephen Rea, in conversation with me, has talked of this 'sense of people who are well used to living together' in the work of his friend.

But there is something else. Although an intensely private writer whose plays are a gentle lifting of the veil on inviolable privacies, Friel nevertheless presses these images into images of Ireland itself. Obviously there are variations in the degree of political urgency between one play and another. But the general tone of the plays is referential in this way; it has a kind of loving attentiveness to the broader fate of the people of Ireland and their culture. Pre-eminently in the theatre of our time, Friel is a custodian of certain public values, those of tradition and place, of kinship and tribe, of all those necessary pieties which allow people to live with some decency in close proximity to one another. I can recognize this the more clearly because I have none of it myself in my own work.

Part of the excitement in September 1964 for someone of my generation watching the first production of *Philadelphia, Here I Come!* was in the recognition that a staple Irish formula was being reinvented before our eyes. There had been meticulously observed plays set in Irish country kitchens before this. There had been Irish plays of non-comprehending fathers and dreamy sons, of comic house-keepers, lonely school-masters, big-shot neighbours and prudent, arid priests. There was even a characteristic Irish style of naturalism (which so infuriated Yeats) matched by, perhaps engendering a whole school of naturalistic Irish acting. All of this was based upon a close attention to surface character and a usable stage speech which accurately mimicked the vernacular. It was a style badly in need of infusion.

Friel was heir to all this in the sixties. What marked him apart from the best of his predecessors, T. C. Murray, say, or Paul Vincent Carroll was not so much his material (since it arose in the first instance out of a similar background) but what distinguishes all first-rate writers: the range of his sensibility. Yet, with some exceptions, he was to remain loyal to this inherited tradition: that branch of naturalistic Irish drama which originated in and took its inspiration from rural Catholic Ireland and which had dominated Irish theatre, not always happily, throughout the late twenties, the thirties, forties and fifties. It is a measure of Friel's integrity that one is always assured of the value of tradition even when he is pressing it into change or registering its obsolescence. Historically (as opposed to the individual reputation) I believe that Friel's importance will be seen in the way he received this youthful tradition (scarcely four decades old when he began writing for the stage) and opened it up to the enquiry of a mind schooled in modern theatre and literature. In this way he exhausted some received forms or, perhaps more accurately, his writing coincided with their demise and he has given them a fitting departure. Certainly it would be difficult to conceive of anyone writing another peasant play, without irony or distancing, after *Translations*.

It is now commonplace to talk about *Living Quarters* (1977) as a not entirely successful trial-run for the later, more popular *Aristocrats* (1979). To do so is to distract attention from Friel's remarkable application of literary narrative technique to the stage. One play, it is true, leads into the other. Both plays are built upon family reunions. Each reunion is the occasion of the death of a father; in each the mother is already dead before the rise of the curtain. Each father is authoritarian in a family of three sisters and a brow-beaten, errant son. Each play ends with the dispersal of the family. Even the attendant figures duplicate one another. There is the comic male neighbour husband-suitor. And, finally, there is the narrating or choric outsider whose viewpoint of events is Friel's principal distancing device, perhaps his most contentious use of a fictional device in his plays.

Sir, in *Living Quarters*, the stern ring-master of events with his ledger of completed but endlessly repetitive actions, is the more obtrusive of these choric figures and the one who has met with most resistance from audiences. Tom, the American researcher in *Aristocrats*, because he is integrated into the action rather than left as a cold observer of it, is generally understood to be an improvement. I cannot see it like that.

The first (and only) production of *Living Quarters* failed to find a place, a style for the figure of Sir in what was offered as a surround of naturalism. The chilling mechanics of the play failed to lock and whirr and run out to full, terrifying effect. But what appears to be cosy naturalism in the family scenes is, in fact, high stylization in need of a studied, highly theatricalised presentation. Among his other roles Sir is a projection of the imagination of that group of people assembled on a May day in a remote corner of Donegal to act out, again and again, that brief, dire collision of the Butler family. It is one of the points of the play that once the imagination has called up a record, a register, a ledger of events past the results take on an implacable momentum. It is as if the imagination were a way of freezing time or of generating that force which the ancients called Fate. For imagination here read theatrical imagination. Nowhere in Friel is the potential impersonality of theatre, its bending of human will to serve action, to serve effect, so beautifully imbricated, so clinically impaled.

> SIR: And in their imagination, out of some deep psychic necessity, they have conceived this (*ledger*) – a complete and detailed record of every-thing that was said and done that day, as if its very existence must afford them their justification, as if in some tiny, forgotten detail buried here – a smile, a hesitation, a tentative gesture – if only it could be found and recalled – in it must lie the key to an understanding of *all* that happened. And in their imagination, out of some deep psychic necessity, they have conceived me – the ultimate arbiter, the powerful and impartial referee, the final adjudicator, a kind of human Hansard who knows these tiny little details and interprets them accurately. And yet no sooner do they conceive me with my authority and my knowledge than they begin flirting with the idea of circumventing me, of foxing me, of outwitting me. Curious, isn't it? (*SP* 177–78)

There are two passages at the beginning of *Living Quarters* which illustrate Friel's handling of fictional narrative on the stage. The text is a cool modernist one in which the narrative, over such a short span, has the density and pith of complex prose fiction. There is information here, terse, complete but there are also multiple shifts in perspective as well as a testing of character. There is also that element, so rare in drama, so essential to first-rate novels, the presence of a formidable auctorial mind which is a constituent of the writing itself. This is the element that James understood, in *The Art of Fiction*, to be the ultimate criterion of literary art, 'the quality of the mind of the producer'.

These two passages are rather like prologues to the play proper since they involve minor characters, a kind of sharp sketching of the strict geometry of what is to happen, a precise notation of tone. The first has to do with Father Tom, the pathetic alcoholic priest, friend and honorary uncle of the Butler family. In the early part of *his* plays, Synge removed the priest as a figure of irrelevance, the irrelevance of established Christianity, in order to clear space for the bare moral action which was to follow. Friel does something similar here. The space in which the Butler family re-enact their tragedy, for all its Donegal sign-posting, is elemental, secular, devoid of conventional consolations. In short, it is the pure space of the stage. Indeed the text might be further sharpened by the excision of some of its realistic labels and references.

Father Tom belongs to the world of weak Irish half-truths, evasiveness, easy feeling, the inability to face the truth. It is a world that Friel understands as few other writers and one for which he has compassion. Here, however, he is pitiless. Father Tom stalks Sir and tries to see into his ledger. Like any weak man the priest believes or hopes or blusters that moral transformation can be simple. Sir strips him to the core.

TOM: Sir
SIR: (*Busy*) What is it, father?
TOM: I don't suppose it would be a breach of secrecy or etiquette if I – if
         you were to let me know how I'm described there, would it? You
         know – something to hang the cap on – 'good guy', 'funny guy', 'bit
         of a gossip'. Which of my many fascinating personas should I
         portray?
SIR: (*Still busy*) You'll be yourself, father.   (*SP* 179)

The persistence of the priest is that of the man who itches at his own petty foibles until they swell into profound failure. In a very true, Faustian sense he is the creator of his own tormentor. To this scene Friel adds the mute presence of Anna, the young wife whose adultery is the instrument of the play's action, a strangely immune presence in the play who alone, with Sir, is allowed to be an observer. Sir is reading from his ledger.

SIR: 'The children used to call him Uncle – Uncle Tom'
TOM: (*Delighted*) Tina still does – occasionally.
SIR: '"Is Uncle Tom coming with us?" they'd say. And he did. Always.
         Everywhere. Himself and the batman – in attendance.'
TOM: That's one way of –

SIR: '– and that pathetic dependence on the Butler family, together with his excessive drinking make him a cliché, a stereotype. He knows this himself –'

TOM: Cliché? For God's sake –!

SIR: '– but he is not a fool. He recognizes that this definition allows him to be witness to their pain but absolves him from experiencing it; appoints him confidant but acquits him of the responsibility of conscience –'

TOM: That's not how –! O my God . . .

SIR: 'As the tale unfolds they may go to him for advice, not because they respect him, consider him wise –'

TOM: (*Sudden revolt*) Because they love me, that's why! They love me!

SIR: '– but because he is an outsider who represents the society they'll begin to feel alienated from, slipping away from them.'

TOM: (*Beaten*) Outsider?
(*Anna goes to Tom and puts her arm around him.*)

SIR: 'And what he says won't make the slightest difference because at that point – the point of no return – they'll be past listening to anybody. At that point all they'll hear is their own persistent inner voices –' And so on and so forth.

TOM: (*On the point of tears*) O my God – O my God –

SIR: It's your role.

TOM: No, it's not. No, no, no, it's not.

SIR: And to have any role is always something.
(*Anna begins to lead Tom away.*) (*SP* 180)

The second passage replicates this one but in the different mode of comedy. Sir's antagonist this time is Charlie, one of those Friel clowns, bumbling and honest and attractive, who light up the edges of even the bleakest scene. Ever-reliable, handyman, bit of a gaum, simple, loyal lover, Charlie is the eternal spear-carrier and scene-shifter in the everyday drama. As befitting a play in which theatre itself is a controlling metaphor, his scene with Sir is based upon the old acting game of shifting about for the high ground, the brightest spot, manoeuvring for centre-stage. Charlie desperately wants to be a player in the action but, like Tom, he is insulated from some layer of knowledge, some fundamental implication of what is happening, that protects him, in turn, from the suffering:

CHARLIE: Tell you what: suppose I just sat about, you know, and looked on, I'd –

SIR: There are no spectators, Charlie. Only participants.

CHARLIE: Promise you – wouldn't open my mouth –

SIR: If your turn comes, I'll call you.

CHARLIE: Could keep an eye on the ledger for you.

SIR: Charlie.

CHARLIE: Oh, well – see you later – good luck. (*SP* 181)

To speak, then, of this play as some kind of exercise in preparation for *Aristocrats* is to confuse, so to speak, chalk and cheese. Passing from one to the other is like moving from hard-edge to impressionism, from a cold metallic surface to a rush of warmth and colour. It is relatively easy to account for the greater popularity of *Aristocrats* in this way. For all its charting of disintegration, *Aristocrats* is written with all the considerable charm of Brian Friel. *Living Quarters*, in contrast, is one of the harshest plays that he has written. It looks forward, not so much to *Aristocrats*, as to the masterpiece *Faith Healer*. It is arguable that Friel discovered the extraordinary narrative tone of the later work – grievous and elegiac but also lyrical and marmoreal – in the narratives of *Living Quarters*. The narratives of *Living Quarters* are multiplex; in *Faith Healer* the narratives have been soldered into monologue.

There is a further point about *Living Quarters*. Friel effects something quite unsettling with the old formulaic material of the Irish family (if this is a version of *Hippolytus* it is also a version of *Autumn Fire*). He puts it under scrutiny which painfully exposes its inefficiency when faced with the utter isolation of the tragic individual. By fixing it within a narrative that is as discriminating as anything in prose fiction Friel creates a distance between us and the family. This forces us to look upon the happenings through the impersonal, comfortless eye of Sir, a viewpoint which the modern theatre does not often tolerate but which would have been entirely acceptable in the theatre of the Greek fifth century. The disintegration of this family is beyond condolence; it can only be attended on like a clean ritual. By contrast, the *dénouement* of *Aristocrats*, with its running-down of plot into the natural dispersal of people, is consolatory.

The question is: why should novelistic narrative with its information, its reliability or unreliability, its pressing of opinion, its lapel-tugging insistence, be such a problem in the contemporary theatre? In the past theatre has always found ways of admitting editorializing or commentary whether by way of soliloquy, aside, chorus or choric character. Is it that modern audiences feel manipulated? Is it a matter of entertainment? Or laziness? Assuredly a theatre which seeks to make its audience think has a better chance with people who read than with people who don't. The pleasures of such drama, in other words, are literary as well as theatrical. I am not suggesting that Brian Friel has suffered through a resistance to his more literary writing but aspects of his work have been neglected for this reason. *Living Quarters* is a case in point. It is a seriously neglected work. On the other hand, there has been far less difficulty with that other literary feature of his plays: the use of stories or story-telling as a form of dramatic action.

I have tried to write elsewhere (*TLS* March, 1972) of the way in which the anecdote resides at the centre of Irish fiction giving a vocal rhythm to the Irish novel which has at least partially displaced the deep social preoccupation in classical fiction elsewhere. The fiction of Joyce, Flann O'Brien and Beckett is like a vast anthology of anecdotes, of voices constantly talking and telling, even to the point of dementia. And while our culture may have had no indigenous, native theatre prior to the eighteen-nineties it did have the *seanchai*, a distinctively histrionic artist with his repertoire, his own audience. It was inevitable with such an oral tradition that the told-tale should be subsumed not only into the literary short story (see Walter Benjamin on Leskov) but into the novel and emerging drama as well. Our classic play, *The Playboy of the Western World*, is not just a comedy about a story-teller and his story. It is also about the awesome effects upon his listeners when his story fails to pass the test of authenticity. It is a parable of the limitation of theatrical illusion. It is about that strange curtain which separates performance from actuality.

Brian Friel is a superb creator of story-tellers. They are not only expert in delivery, in all the skills of an actor in full-flight, mimicry, timing, playing upon the audience as upon an instrument – even their body language is enlisted in the way Friel has written the parts. Story-telling in Friel's plays may offer succour, consolation, relief, renewal but it can just as easily offer deception of the self, of others. Like every substantial writer of fiction, Friel has a healthy scepticism about the nature of fiction itself or at least the uses to which it can be put. Frequently the virtuoso story-teller in a Friel play is an outsider, his or her gift a kind of scar or wound, a misfortunate or fatal gift. More subtly than any other Irish playwright Friel has transcribed this national skill into the theatrical medium. That is why we often have to enlist a literary or quasi-literary vocabulary in talking about some of the plays.

Friel's complex attitude to his own culture, his celebration of it as well as his critique, may be seen to good effect here in his use of the patterns and cross-patterns of story-telling. Ours is a culture of gossip. It may partly account for our exceptional population of fiction readers and our splendid theatre audiences, particularly in rural Ireland. But such an appetite for the imaginative representation of life brings with it its own recoil. There is, for instance, the escape from the ugly factuality of life. The widening of this gap between the hyperbolic, the fanciful and the prosaic or earthbound may be comic or tragic. It is one of Brian Friel's main themes and the authority of the story-teller one of his main devices in the pursuit of it. Whole sections of dialogue in the plays appear to be composed of compacted story-telling, speaker vying with speaker, the dramatic conflict in the competitiveness between the different tellings. It is as if what is, is partial, incomplete, dissatisfying until refracted or filtered through this verbal athleticism.

Because both plays are plays of reunion, *Living Quarters* and *Aristo-crats* are both made up of this story-telling grist. Each stage of present action has to be bolstered up or tempered by versions of what has happened in the past. When people come home they have stories to tell and stories to listen to. It is the process by which a family re-establishes its codes, a way of recovering intimacy. But this linkage provided by stories is extremely tenuous and can never get around the testing of feeling in the here and now. This is the hard bone running through both plays, the way in which Friel subjects stories and story-tellers to the strict demands of immediate plot.

Some items so recalled have a spectral, numinous or epiphanic qual-ity like the picnic at Portnoo in *Living Quarters* or the mother's song in *Aristocrats*. Other recountings are more robust in the sense that they generate direct, even brutal conflict. There are, for example, the competing versions of the house's history in *Aristocrats*: the official history of patient Tom's research, the funny, hysterical ramblings of Casimir, the hurt, angry, street subversiveness of Eamon. The much-admired dying-fall at the end of this play is based upon the exhaustion of story-telling. There are no more stories to be told. Or the capacity to listen to them has gone. Willie, the comic outsider, attempts one and it stands like an interrogation mark in the air. The others drift into song, the song of a dead mother who cannot be recalled with sufficient clarity to make up an anecdote. Singing is like an aftertaste of feeling. But the song is a ballad; it, too, tells a story. Like Willie's anecdote it is a story which floats away on the air in diminuendo, a matter of incon-sequence in the light of everything that has happened except that it catches perfectly the unwinding of the bonds between those people on the stage.

Faith Healer, in my view, is the one theatrical text of our time which unmistakably takes its place with the best of Beckett or Synge or the Yeats of *The Herne's Egg* and *Purgatory*. That is to say, it is a sublime work of the imagination in which the distinction between theatrical text and literary artefact ceases to be of account. It is profoundly affecting and intellectually satisfying both in the theatre and within the individual mind of the reader. This is but another way of remarking upon the play's formal perfection, the perfect congruence of passionate feeling and the controlling mind of a first-rate artist. Very few plays are written with this high degree of literary skill. Even the very best of them too often show their stage effects, marvellously effective, indeed, within the sounding chamber of the theatre but contrived and rhetor-ical on the cold page. In part, the consummate writing in *Faith Healer* is the more evident because Friel has consciously eschewed the usual notion of what dramatic action should be, the direct inter-play between characters. Instead he offers four monologues that are allowed to stand in austere, frontal engagement with the audience.

There has been a persistent tendency in modernist literature towards the monologue, the elimination, the erasure of others, of the Other. Speech pruned of answers. A retreat into privacy, that most valued, most sought after and most threatened condition in our century. *A Portrait of the Artist As a Young Man* ends in the privacy of Stephen's journal. *Dubliners* ends within the dwindling and yet rapidly expanding consciousness of Gabriel Conroy. *Ulysses* ends with the monologue of Molly Bloom. *Finnegans Wake* is the total monologue which has subsumed all other voices into itself, a great mastication and regurgitation of words. This retreating in Joyce is a paradigm of one important strand of twentieth century fiction and an equally important one of its drama.

Finnegans Wake, in its histrionics, exemplifies two recurrent features of the theatrical monologue: its self-containment and its obsessiveness. Both present severe technical problems to the playwright. The hermetic, excluding nature of monologue is inherently nondramatic. Friel deals with this by making his three witnesses give conflicting evidence on the same events. It is like a serial Chinese puzzle. If you believe one witness of the three you cannot believe the other two. All are given to omission, partial truths or downright lying. The important thing is not whether the statements are true or false but the degree of falsehood and its motivation, whether the deceits are self-serving or other-serving, black, white or grey. The creation of this nest of evasion and concealment is critical to Friel's purpose in the play.

A monologue is a worrying of hidden or half-hidden obsessions into conscious life, that is to say, into speech. In Friel's play, not unexpectedly, these obsessions are those of the story-teller. In an earlier draft the play consisted of a single monologue, more or less that first monologue as it now exists in the finished, published play. That early monologue, however, did include a shortened version of the end of the present play, the dawn encounter in the yard with McGarvey and the wedding guests. In the further writing, Friel detached this from the opening monologue, postponing it for effect to the end of the play.

What are missing from that first draft, however, are the two nuggets, the two haunting stories of the completed play: the miracle, if such it was, in the old Methodist Hall at Llanbethian and the bloody miscarriage at Kinlochbervie. In discovering these through the process of writing, Friel broke through the fixity of the single monologue into a form of engagement between the three characters, even if that engagement or sharing is the source of contradiction. There are differing

versions of these incidents offered by Frank, Grace and Teddy. The
versions contradict or modify one another. Yet the play in its totality is
an assurance of an essential truth in each monologue: the transcendent
heights to which Hardy's art can aspire and the squalid shit to which
he can descend as a man.

To be theatrical a monologue has to possess its audience as a confidant. The literary analogy is the Browning dramatic monologue where
meaning, if it is to exist, is a product of shared consciousness between
the speaker and reader and the hidden, ventriloquial poet. In the theatre
persuasion must come not only through the voice but also through the
scene. What scene does a single speaking voice inhabit? Where can it
achieve greatest credibility but where the stage is a stage, no more, no
less? This autonomous space, reflecting nothing beyond itself, this
Nowhere Land dressed with a few props is where the monologue is
best situated as it is, with differing levels of artistry, in Beckett,
Shepard and Pinter. Here are the *Faith Healer* stage-directions:

The stage is in darkness. Brief Pause.

Then out of this darkness comes FRANK's incantation, 'Aberarder,
Aberayron . . .' At the end of the second line bring up lights very slowly . . .

Three rows of chairs . . . not more than fifteen seats in all . . .

Note: Stage directions have been kept to a minimum. (*SP* 331)

We discover GRACE HARDY on stage, the same set as Part One, with the
rows of seats removed. She is sitting on a wooden chair beside a small
table . . . (*SP* 341)

We discover TEDDY on stage – sitting beside the table – the same table as
in Part Two; but TEDDY's chair is more comfortable than GRACE's.
(*SP* 353)

The poster is gone. The set is empty except for the single chair across which
lies Frank's coat exactly as he left it in Part One.

We discover Frank standing down stage left, where we left him.
(*SP* 370)

Friel's scenes are set, respectively, in one of the Faith Healer's drab
halls, in Grace's digs on Limewood Grove, in Teddy's equally awful
digs on some other Grove or Crescent just around the corner in London. The Hardy poster presides over the first three scenes, Grace and
Teddy share the same table and there is a general melting of particu-
lars one into other the way reality bleeds into fiction, fiction bleeds into
reality. In the end one has to concede that all the scenes simply happen
upon a stage, that the naturalistic props are like remnants from another
life beyond, deposited upon a stage to facilitate an enactment before an
audience. In this way Friel elevates *Faith Healer* above conventional
naturalism. He also lifts it out of conventional time and lodges it in
artificial stage time where the improbable is possible and where

credibility can be created without corroboration. This accounts for one of the more poignant details of this play. Two of these voices are from beyond the grave. One conducts us with icy style towards his own horrible destruction. The other makes it perfectly clear why her suicide was inevitable. The MC who survives to preside over all this, the work's stage-manager, another of Friel's choric presences, is a tatty, vulgar man of quite extraordinary fidelity, in other words a fit-up Prospero, the spirit of Theatre itself.

Finally, to the nub of the play. This is a play about one of the most disturbing paradoxes in art, one which has bothered people through-out the history of civilization. It may be best stated interrogatively: how is it that persons of ugly, sordid even depraved character, persons with apparently no redeeming features in their personal lives are capable of creating great redeeming beauty in art, works of sustaining spiritual resource? Or, more temperately, why is it virtually impossible to connect the integrity of the work to the deviousness and pettiness of its creator? The whole style of *Faith Healer*, in particular its use of the ambiguities of story-telling, is based upon this crux. Art is, indeed, created out of concealment, illusion, fictiveness, a conscious reinven-tion of the self. If it is spun out of the common dross of the individual the web has such a finished, tensile and beautiful distancing from its source that its source is completely hidden. *Faith Healer*, in its bleak fashion, will not allow this forgetfulness. The bloodied, abandoned woman, the black foetus on the side of the road and the white healing hands are offered as part of the same ferment. From an entirely different angle the play is nevertheless a gloss on that great question in Herbert's poem 'Jordan I' on the mysterious deceit, the mysterious art, of false hair and painted chair.

BRIAN FRIEL: THE NAME OF THE GAME

SEAMUS DEANE

'. . . we can't say under what circumstances there would have been unicorns.'
(Saul Kripke)[1]

Naming is a kind of owning and a kind of knowing. Name a place and you have a reference; name a number of places and you have a system of relational references that can be organised into a map. The map itself can then be given a name – say, Ireland. We have a map of Ireland that contains within its boundaries a number of names of places. The triteness of this is deceptive. A map is a representation of a place and the representation itself needs a name so that we may know what it is that is represented. So we can take a map of Ireland and rechristen it 'Eire'; or name the two parts of it that are politically separate by any one or all of their soubriquets. A question arises here. If a place has two names, can't it be known by either or both? What then is the function of naming? Is it the description of a thing/place? Different names give different descriptions of the same place. Are these mutually compatible always or is it the case that one must disagree with the other? If so, a place, in being named, is described in such a way that its identifying features are represented to the namer in a specific manner. Is Burnfoot the same as Bun na h-Abhann? Each refers to the same place in different languages. No problem. But if we have two names in the same language for the same place – say the Six Counties or Ulster – is the problem not a little more twisted? Especially when some people would say that Ulster refers to nine counties, not six; and others that six counties, as a name, only has meaning if you are really thinking of 32. It is relational, in other words, to 26 and 32 (both places) and its significance as a piece of political numerology is political as well as geographic. But is there any naming of a place that would be wholly free of such considerations – these or others like them? If the answer is no, naming is an act of possession and of knowing but only in very specific circumstances. There is no rigid designator, as Kripke would call it, in a politically troubled country.

Could we rename what we call Ireland if we had a new language? Or would we always meet the same problem – that a name, to be acceptable as such, must identify certain inescapable or necessary

103

features of a place in such a manner that, no matter what the political or other views that may be held of it, it must be 'Ireland' that we refer to? Is a name a description of an essence that is unvarying? One can ask if the 'Ireland' that is referred to when people speak of a 'United Ireland' ever existed. Perhaps some names refer to non-existent places – not non-existent ideas because one can have an idea of a place, independent of others' versions of the place. And a place can be described in terms of a time – nineteenth-century Ireland is one example but so too is twenty-first century Ireland. Do either of these exist – or only one of them? Does a place exist only in time? Is naming only a rhetorical procedure that is part of a larger project; if so, can the project be described?

These questions and ruminations derive from a reading of Brian Friel as much as Saul Kripke. In Friel's work, naming is an important rhetorical strategy, but the status of the question it raises is difficult to determine. At one level, it is clear that the action of naming is historical. At another level, it is linguistic. What I propose to consider here is the extent to which these two levels fold into one another. Historical naming is a complex process but it is easier to deal with than the linguistic kind, because we can observe and analyse the forms it takes and the reasons for those particular formations. We can even see or ascribe a narrative to the history of naming. On the other, if naming is a linguistic operation, not bound by history, then the status of the issues raised is quite different. If a name necessarily belongs to a place – or a place to a name – that is, if the name in some sense embodies the essence of the place and therefore indicates, even ostensively, some radical aspect of that place's meaning, we are dealing with metaphysics not history. Or, more precisely, we are dealing with a metaphysics that is prior (logically) to history and in virtue of which historical narrative can be judged. In *Faith Healer* Friel is considering the question metaphysically; in *Translations* he is dealing with it historically; and in *Aristocrats* which precedes these two, he is moving from one level to the other. It may be that *Aristocrats* is the key to the later plays in that it combines in itself elements which each of the others treats separately. But this is no more than a speculation, a way of arranging or rearranging Friel's writings the better to see what they look like in this light.

Aristocrats is full of proper names of people but these people – all properly historical, like Daniel O'Connell, Cardinal Newman, Yeats, Sean O'Casey, G. K. Chesterton – are no more; their names have been given to things that they touched, sat on or fell off as the case may be. George Moore is a candlestick, Tom Moore is a book, Hilaire Belloc is the Bible or a Bible. Casimir, who is the chief nominator in the play, has his way with music too. The ten works by Chopin, all written for piano, can be identified by him after only a few bars have been played; some of them lose their own names and are Casimired or Ballybegged into, for instance, the McCormack Waltz (Waltz in G flat major, Op. 70, no. 1); and the posthumous Waltz in A flat major becomes the Bedtime Waltz. And when Eamon remembers the music he danced to in the Corinthian Ballroom in Derry he names the players too:

Tommy McGee on the sax; Bobby Kyle on piano; Jackie Fogarty on drums; young Turbet on clarinet. (*SP* 287)

As for Chopin's Sonata No. 2 in B flat minor, Op. 35, that is grand-father, no, great-grantfather O'Donnell's favourite because grandfather told Balzac to shut up when he (Balzac) tried to sing it in front of the glittering throng of musicians and literati at the famous 'party in Vienna'. These namings are all, of course, Irish or English or Euro-Catholic and their miscellaneous nature and chronological absurdities point up the spurious nature of a Catholic ascendancy tradition and the craving for authority and respectability involved. Besides, actual physical contact with the people here named is also a variation on the need to be assured that the tradition does exist for the O'Donnells of Ballybeg. The very items of furniture are contaminated by it although Casimir and his family are contaminated only by the need to believe in it. Cultural authority is as bogus in this play as political or parental authority. It is a neat irony that the father is a District Justice; this title minds us of his parochialism, his strictness and his injustice all at once. Just as the names are all askew, so too are the voices. The play is full of devices that separate the voice from the speaker – although it is precisely through a speaker that the father's voice is heard.

Names, voices, recorded music, recorded or reproduced voices all articulate a narrative about the ways in which different people learn to surrender grandiose notions of tradition for the more specific and actual experience of a context. According to Alice, 'love is possible only in certain contexts'. 'Have we a context?' asks Eamon. 'Let's wait and see' she replies. (*SP* 324) As usual, Friel doubles and triples his narrative, ironising it and yet permitting it to have its moment of final liberation from intricacy. Uncle George, whose mouth is always working as though he were eating, ratifies Alice and Eamon in their departure to London when he finally speaks in accepting their offer to come with them. This is an O'Donnell voice that is stimulated by an act of love. Eamon has been doubling as mock-historian of the O'Donnell family, mocking Tom Hoffnung's sober view of the family as a representative species. This is a family that has got a name for itself, but the name, in this instance, finally refers to an illusion. The confessions, the recognition that, as Eamon puts it, 'Something in us needs this . . . aspiration' (*SP* 319), that this slavishness to the idea represented by a Big House is what makes the Irish 'ideal for colonizing' (*SP* 318), immediately preface Casimir's first failure to identify a piece by Chopin as played by Claire. At last the naming can begin to stop. These are people on the verge of finding release from history and, free of the shadow of that patriarchal presence, beginning at last to live. *Aristocrats* is the proper name for common people; that begins as an irony and ends as a perception.

History, with all its inherited namings, is susceptible to reification when it is lived as aftermath, when the war is over, the crisis gone. It is less so when it is lived as origin, when the renaming is being done, when the war is beginning. *Translations* is, above all things, concerned with origins. It was itself originating for Field Day, the more appropriately so because it quite literally mapped a territory by writing about the remapping of a territory. As in *Aristocrats*, naming is dramatised as a crucial aspect of speaking; in the opening episode Sarah struggles to achieve her name. In this play, Ballybeg is not so much a hedge school as a language school. The first and the last lesson is the cost of learning what's in a name.

However, the issue is not quite the same as in *Aristocrats*. Not only is the play about a point of origin and, with that, implicit in it, a point of extinction; it is also concerned to explore the nature of naming in relation to place and to self as an act of possession and dispossession. Sarah loses her self-possession when she loses her name; she loses her name to herself when she loses her speech, even though she retains her name for others. Having one's name spoken is different from speaking one's own name, especially when one *cannot* speak that name. Although cast in the form of an historical parable, the play raises the issue of naming to a metaphysical level. The connection between a name and a person and between a name and a place is offered to us as something more than a historically derived relation. It is more intimate than that because it is prior to it. Is there, in truth, a connection between a name and the person or place indicated such that no other name, no substitute, transliteration or translation can operate satisfactorily in its stead? If so, does the area around Ballybeg disappear in the new Ordnance Survey map? Historically speaking, we can say yes, it does; this is one of the mutilating effects of colonialism. Mapping is an act of possession; techniques of mapping are not scientific in their aim, only in their methods. A Mercator projection of the world is a European act of possession; it is a political construct as much as a medieval map was a theological construct. So too, a British map of Ireland is a projection of a political situation. This is well-known. Less well-known is the ground of the opposition to such cartographical polemics. If a place is renamed and relocated, is it in some sense the same place as it had been or is it entirely, essentially, different? For a place is perhaps a site of interpretation and names are the commentaries by which it is revealed.

Friel's *Translations* broods on this appearance/disappearance motif. The quotations from George Steiner are sometimes used to startling effect. Hugh, for instance, announces that

... it can happen that a civilization can be imprisoned in a linguistic contour which no longer matches the landscape of ... fact. (*SP* 419)

This has usually been taken to mean that the language of Hugh's Ireland no longer corresponds to or can take account of the new Ireland that has emerged in the early nineteenth century. It is a perfectly respectable interpretation; but it surely cuts both ways. For it is also a description of English-speaking Ireland. Ballybeg seems to have the invidious choice of speaking an old language that cannot be mapped onto the new country or of speaking a new language that cannot be mapped onto the old country.

Hence the importance of translation. For the Ordnance Survey, and Owen's role in it, is specifically concerned with that aspect of the situation. The attempt is to find those names in English which would be the closest possible equivalent to the original (or earlier) Irish names. It is not the case that translation as such is impossible. Equivalence can be achieved; but it can never be identity. That is the problem of translation. It is, in effect, an interpretation. What haunts it is the belief that there is in the original name or text something which will not carry over, something that is untranslatable precisely because it is original. In being original, this untranslatable element is then understood to be essential. If there is a necessity in naming, if a place has an identity that is not only indicated but conferred by a name, then translation is an act of obliteration. Language speaks being; translated language speaks translated being. Linguistically speaking, you can't go home again. What has been renamed and mapped is a mutilated version of what was. Everything essential has been lost in the translation. Thereafter, the place is without the poetry of identity and is reduced to the prose of therapy.

The essentialist position is powerful in the fields of culture and politics. Origin is its fetish; priority is purity. It has a mystical view of culture, silently projected in the use of that very word as a single and singular ethos that is the product of many energies that somehow consolidate to form it. When threatened, the ethos becomes pathos. And it is always threatened because it relies so parasitically on the dream of origin. Of its nature, origin is always both first and past. The moment of authenticity is elusive because it has to be, like so many comparable moments – the moment when language emerged, the moment of the social contract – a heuristic fiction. Culture is both given by nature and developed in history, as silent in its formation as a coral reef. But it can be violated. For over two hundred years we have been told that the violation occurred when the 'modern' world, scientifically armed and bent on global uniformity, began to make war on the local, the regional, the traditional and the diverse. Nature was emptied and became an abstraction; history was flattened into the tarmacadam road of progress. Language, purged of its dissentient poetries and accents, became plain prose and received standard pronunciation. Culture withered into commerce; imperialism became the monoglot glutton that feasted on difference and regurgitated it as sameness. At the heart of this monstrous system, origin beat on, like a fading pulse.

Translations lives within that linguistic-historical frame but with ambivalence. The Latin and the Greek and the English of the play are spoken languages; the Irish is merely pronounced and always in relation to names. Even though Maire (and the others) are to be understood as speaking Irish, it is the English language that (for obvious reasons of dramatic necessity) represents their speech. Hugh tells Yolland that

We like to think we endure around truths immemorially posited. (*SP* 418)

Soon after Owen (or Roland as he is named by the English), rebukes this nonsense.

Is it astute not to be able to adjust for survival? Enduring around truths immemorially posited-hah! (*SP* 419)

In the interval between these remarks, Hugh, looking forward to his new post at the National School (the very school system that will play a vital role in destroying the Irish language), puts forward his theory that the Irish language is rich and ornate in inverse ratio to the poverty of the conditions of its speakers. Owen is simultaneously telling him that to get to the priest who will appoint him Hugh must go through a new landscape, not from Lis na Muc to Poll na gCaorach but from Swinefort to Sheepsrock. The Irish language is for Hugh a rich response to famished conditions; for Owen it involves a failure to adjust. Hugh sees language as a system in itself, not a mimesis but precisely a refusal of mimesis. It does not map an actual condition or territory; it creates an alternative. But his linguistic abilities manifest themselves merely as pedantry and pomposity. Hugh's English is bookish; the title of his proposed book, 'The Pentaglot Preceptor etc.', is an appropriate name for himself. The English he speaks is an anachronism. So too is his Irish, Latin and Greek. His territory is being renamed and he is displaced in time. So, having neither time nor place, he has no true existence. *Translations* explores the phenomenon of a society in which time and place do not intersect, by judging the power of language to name and thereby possess the world in which it is spoken. Irish nominates a world that is not there; English renames the world that has arrived.

This is the heart of the matter. The love between Maire and Yolland is spoken most eloquently as a litany of names and that moment is the most intense act of translation in the play. The Irish place names of Donegal, which Yolland and Owen have been translating into English equivalents, are now restored in all their potency as a love duet between the Irish and English lovers. Although it is a doomed love, spoken in the doomed names of the region, its language is as 'opulent with tomorrows' (*SP* 418), to use Hugh's Steineresque phrase, as Irish and yet free of the deceptions and delusions that Hugh also describes. Instead of the fake tomorrows of Hugh's Irish, it has Yolland's and Marie's 'always', a word that occurs ten times in brief space towards the end of their encounter. (See *SP* 429–30) The dominant idiom is once more that of place and time; the place is disappearing into its English names and the always is going to disappear brutally soon with Yolland's death at the hands of the Donnellys. Still, it is a true intersection, the only one in the play. The names of the lovers, the place names and the naming of the time they desire for each other is all the language they need. These are their co-ordinates and it is that attempt to define their own space which determines the fate of the village and all within it.

It is not, therefore, an ethos of 'culture' violated by brute force that governs the play's meanings. That dimension is there but its solidity is questionable. *Translations* seeks to establish the possibility of a time and a place for which there would be a correspondent language; the function of the language is to nominate, to specify the context in which human love is possible. It is at that level that 'culture' and 'politics', Irish and English, are reconciled. Everything else is 'after' – the world of division is, in a deep sense, always anachronistic. It is then, in that dislocated time, that Irish and English divide into languages of opulent tomorrows and of adjustings to the here and now. Only in the Yolland-Maire moment does language truly speak; it is only then that language is beyond translation.

Faith Healer concentrates on this moment. It forgoes the historical and political reverberations of *Aristocrats* and *Translations* and dwells exclusively on the strange phenomenon of a gift for healing that works with apparent randomness at a certain time in a certain place. The sojourns of Frank Hardy and his companions in Wales and Scotland unravel in litanies of names. Healing is not philanthropic:

... good God, no, nothing at all to do with that; but because the questions that undermined my life then became meaningless and because I knew that for those few hours I had become whole in myself, and perfect in myself, and in a manner of speaking, an aristocrat, if the term does not offend you. (*SP* 333)

This much is clear. Frank Hardy is not a do-gooder. Whatever he does is not directed towards the welfare of others but is instead the unpredictable expression of a gift that sometimes seems to be genuinely effective in its consequences and miraculous in its origin; more often, it seems like a con artist's routine, without miracle or effect and surrounded by the most squalid circumstances. It is inevitable that the faith-healing should be likened to the writer's gift and the audiences to his readership. Sometimes the relation is transforming; usually not. But the crux of the matter is not the gift itself; it has to do with the place of its exercise. Frank is so haunted by his odd capacity that everyone else is secondary – dead child, dead mother, Grace and Teddy. The place names of Wales and Scotland are his ritual prayer, his invocation of the muse. The ultimate test of his gift is home, Ballybeg. He straightens a man's finger and is destroyed because he cannot cure the twisted form of the once-savage McGarvey. It is a destiny that he sought:

... then for the first time I had a simple and genuine sense of home-coming. Then for the first time there was no atrophying terror; and the maddening questions were silent. At long last I was renouncing chance. (*SP* 376)

In this game of chance and choice, Hardy finally broods, before the dénouement, on Teddy's devotion, on Grace's, on a shaming memory of his father. These are receding emotions; he is facing into that bright knowledge of his doom. The question here concerns the gift and its ostensible analogy with writing.

If the analogy is pursued to Hardy's bitter end, it becomes opaque. Does Hardy, in choosing death, renounce the random and troubling gift? Or renounce the idea that this gift matters in any real sense – it might fix a finger but can do no more than that? Perhaps too we can hazard the guess that the emotional expense of the gift is so great for others and so inescapable for the faith-healer himself that it is a relief to be rid of it. These are possible implications, but they do not confront the fact that this is a homecoming, that it is this place, rather than those other places that have been chanted so ritually throughout, that ultimately matters. It is also possible to say that the gift of healing is complicit with violence; that the twisted bodies which are its subject-matter are also the consequences of violence. Violence, like Charity, begins at home.

Ballybeg is unavoidable. What makes it home, and therefore different, is that time and place converge there. Hardy heals himself in the end because he finally exists in that intersection. It is a moment of the sublime, when everything that had been random and accidental is finally configured as destiny. The name and the place, Ballybeg, matter; they are translated into choice. Healing is not displaced to someone else; it is an action performed by the healer on the healer; just before he dies he articulates himself. He authors himself in a final act of authority.

Reading the play in this way throws us back to the question of the subject, the protagonist. Hardy is indeed a subject to his sovereign gift; what he learns in Ballybeg is to become the subject of that gift. McGarvey and his friends are beyond curing, because they are people who want the gift to be validated in its effects. If the function of art is to cure, Hardy is only occasionally an artist. But Friel is preoccupied here with the nature, not the function, of the gift. The whole play is about a misreading, a mistranslation. Outside Ballybeg, in those desolate Celtic countries, the gift was only understood in terms of what it could or might do. It is in Ballybeg that Hardy realises that it is the relation between the gift and the world that is at the root of the whole problem. He was not born to put the maimed world right. His art is not a therapy. But because it is so understood, so tested, it is never known. The world that Hardy finally walks in on that morning of his death has at last been mapped, at last become known and possessed. It is the world before it had a name, Ballybeg before it was named, the country he belongs to before it was Ireland. It is in the very act of naming that the place, as it is in itself, is lost. As in *Aristocrats* and in *Translations* names and voices, languages and mappings, are all displacements of something that is prior to them. The problem is that the priority of what was before only becomes visible in the after-naming. The only true place is that which is coincident with time. Otherwise, people live in the permanent anachronism of history. It is only when here becomes a function of now that the gift truly exists; but when it truly exists is always just in that moment, dimension, before history and society come along to disfigure it, kill it, rename and remap it in the name of some violent longing for possession.

Friel's writing runs in parallel worlds. In one of them, it is profoundly historical, preoccupied with 'the matter of Ireland'. In the other, there is no historical dimension at all. It is a world in which the preoccupation is with writing and all the myths of origin, authenticity and strangeness that surround it. In one sense, we can say that the myths have no meaning unless he shows that they have reference to history and to Ireland. In another, we have to accept that the myths have no meaning because they have no satisfactory explanation or description of writing to recommend them. But writing is, above all, an act of naming, of saying what a thing or a place is; it is a subversive gift for in nominating everything that it comes to it reveals its own nature; but that nature can never itself be named. Writing is always about trouble because there is always trouble about what writing is. It is, historically speaking, as absurd as a fabulous creature like the unicorn. Could we imagine the conditions in which such a thing could exist? A philosopher like Kripke would have to say no, although it is a thorny, not a simple question. A writer like Friel would have to say yes – and then start naming the world in which it could exist. It is there, not in Ballybeg, but in the naming of a fictional place and coordinating that with an historical world and producing out of that a projection that includes both. Anything named does exist; not in itself but in virtue of the strange and fabulous act of naming. That is the name of the game. Time folds into place and place into time; in that postmodernist moment, we are in Ballybeg. After that comes Donegal, Ireland, history. These, politically speaking, can be as strange as unicorns in the view of those who read them on a different map, as belonging to another world where a Catholic Ascendancy, or a Greek-speaking hedge-school master or a wandering faith-healer exist and have meaning.

TRANSLATING THE PAST:
FRIEL, GREECE AND ROME

ALAN PEACOCK

As Brian Friel's career develops from play to play and from decade to decade, two things become apparent: a technical inventiveness, evident from *Philadelphia, Here I Come!* onwards, which is character-istically attuned to the dramatic needs of each successive project; and an accumulating breadth of outlook and frame of reference which universalizes his drama beyond the more localised themes and issues generated by its Irish setting. A graphic demonstration of these tendencies can be found in the utilization of the Greco-Roman Classics in his work where, in plays such as *Living Quarters* and *Translations*, dramatic invention and wide, trans-cultural allusiveness coalesce. The formulation of vital correspondences between nine-teenth and twentieth century Ireland and ancient Greece and Rome leads Friel to set himself technical challenges and, ultimately, to pro-duce plays of broad, resonating significance. What follows will be an attempt to suggest the nature and workings of this extra dimension.

In *Living Quarters* (1977) Friel explores a milieu which seems to have a special fascination for him – that of the Catholic, established middle-class in Ireland: those social strata which are sufficiently well-to-do to inhabit a large family house and to be within a palpable social pale vis-à-vis their humbler neighbours or (as in the more elevated milieu of *Aristocrats*, 1979), tenants and retainers. Because this is not the familiar, Ascendancy great-house society, the distinc-tions are social rather than religious or national; and even here, Friel is not centrally interested in socio-political discriminations. Rather, it is archetypal human questions of parent-offspring relationships, familial disaster and decay, thwarted ambitions and destinies, which preoccupy him. Because *Living Quarters* is worked out within a unitary Catholic culture and social milieu, the concentration on arche-typal issues is facilitated. Hence the possibility of parallelism with Greek Tragedy, for the play is 'after *Hippolytus*'. In making his starting-point a treatment of one part of a funded store of received cycles of ancient myth, sanctified in their essentials by tradition, Friel is, obviously, aggrandising the scope of his drama. He is also, particu-larly in his choice of Euripides' *Hippolytus*, inevitably broaching the endemic Greek tragic tension between determinism and individual

113

moral choice and action. (In the *Hippolytus*, the arbitrary, inevitable course of human destiny is set forth with notable clarity by Aphrodite at the beginning of the play and Artemis at the end.) There is of course no divine agency in *Living Quarters*, nor a conventional tragic chorus: indeed, many a spectator might well not tune in at all to the fact that the play is 'after' a Greek original. Moreover, it diverges, as will be seen, significantly from its model in the working out of the plot as well as in formal convention. It is not a translation, but an imaginative re-working in comprehensively modern terms of its ancient model. As such, it stands up well simply as a modern tragedy of provincial family life; but, like all such 'imitations', it accrues a special authority and irony in its full, dual impact – authority, because it draws on the prestige of its ancient exemplar; and irony, because it must also trade in the inevitable sense of disparity in such a project.

The pivot for much of Friel's manoeuvring in his technical and thematic revision of Euripides is the character Sir, who remains on stage throughout and is immediately introduced as a commentator on the action of the play. Dapper, efficient, impartial and, for the most part, impersonal, he is custodian of the 'ledger' which, as he informs us, the characters' collective 'deep psychic necessity' has conceived as a master-account of a particular day in their lives. Sir is in effect the voice of Fate, and the ledger codifies the unshakable destiny which the characters both assert and chafe against in their re-living of events in the course of the play. These events now lie in the past, and the participators in them are physically dispersed. The governing convention of the play is that they are re-united only at a psychic level.

Sir is obviously at one level, in his rapport and dialoguing with the protagonists, the chorus of Greek tragic convention; or perhaps more immediately a more informal, less ritualised modern derivative such as the chorus-figure in Anouilh's *Antigone*. Crucially however, and here is Friel's invention, he is the tutelary representative of a fate which the characters have worked out for themselves. The contents of the ledger were laid down by their own actions. Their fate is an historically defined necessity springing from their own moral and psychological make-up – not the abstract, impersonal Necessity of Greek tragic drama. Their fate is merely the actuality of the past as viewed from the vantage-point of the future.

Unlike the characters in conventional tragic drama, therefore, the characters are privy to their own destiny. Greek tragic irony, where the audience has pre-knowledge of the fate awaiting the unsuspecting protagonists, is reversed: they know, and indeed have rehearsed the events of the play 'a thousand times' over in their minds, whereas we do not. (Except, of course, to the extend that the developing parallelism with Euripides' *Hippolytus* may cue us; though here again, as will be seen, there are significant divergences.) This subtle re-tuning of the traditional tragic mechanism casts an influence over the whole tone of the play. The audience does not spectate on the inexorable sequence of the dramatic action as it impacts upon the protagonists and, though knowing the outcome, empathise with the characters through successive disclosures and recognitions. Rather, it spectates on the action in a psychodrama where, in Pirandello-like terms, characters in a dramatic text bring themselves, with varying degrees of willingness and difficulty, to enact an Ur-text which represents, in the conventions of the play, reality. In this sense, the treatment pivots into the realm of comedy: the tragic core is displaced into a secondary frame of reference by alienation techniques which lightly, and often comically, distance and to a degree defuse tragic intensity. This dimension is more than once asserted by Charlie's comically rendered attempts to infiltrate himself into scenes where he was not present (according to the ledger's unanswerable authority). From the first scene however, the tragi-comic formula is established as Father Tom quizzes Sir:

TOM: Sir

SIR: (*Busy*) What is it, Father?

TOM: I don't suppose it would be a breach of secrecy or etiquette if I – if you were to let me know how I'm described there, would it? You know – something to hang the cap on – 'good guy', 'funny guy', 'bit of a gossip'. Which of my many fascinating personas should I portray?

SIR: (*Still busy*) You'll be yourself, Father.

TOM: Of course. Naturally. But you've a description there, haven't you? And an objective view would be a help.

SIR: I don't think so.

TOM: As chaplain I've a right to – (*Pleasant again*) Please.

SIR: I think you shouldn't.

TOM: Please.
(SIR *regards him calmly.*)

SIR: Very well.

TOM: (*Breezily*) Soldier – man of God – friend of the boys – you name it.

SIR: 'Father Thomas Carty, sixty-four years of age, chaplain, Commandant, close friend of the Butler family.'

TOM: (*Saluting*) Yours truly. (*SP* 179)

The dialogue is comedic in form and tempo: but Sir's reluctant capitulation to the comic wheedling only discloses the full, unsparing summary of the ledger:

SIR: '– and that pathetic dependence on the Butler family, together with

his excessive drinking make him a cliché, a stereotype. He knows this himself –'
TOM: Cliché? For God's sake –!
SIR: '– but he is not a fool. He recognizes that this definition allows him to be witness to their pain but absolves him from experiencing it; appoints him confidant but acquits him of the responsibility of conscience –'
TOM: That's not how – ! O my God. . .

In assimilating Euripides into this tragi-comic mode Friel is of course making room for key aspects of his own dramatic outlook and manner; and by the same token he is meshing the Greek original with a dominant mode of twentieth century Irish drama. More generally, though, he is creatively facing up to the simultaneous sense of relevance and disparity which affects any attempt to recast an ancient drama in modern terms.

The middle-class, Chekhovian format, with its realistic character-motivation, naturalistic dialogue and socially specific setting is not so much an exercise in mock-heroic disparity, as an attempt to 'translate' an archetype into modern terms, preserving enough sense of correspondence or equivalence to draw on the power and authority of the original while at the same time effecting radical changes in idiom, theological and psychological premises, and plot. *Living Quarters*, like the best 'imitations' in all literary genres in the humanistic tradition, confidently recreates the original in contemporary terms. Euripides' tragedy of Phaedra's doomed passion for Hippolytus, her step-son and Theseus' royal scion, becomes a Donegal family's domestic tragedy, where a late-middle-aged Irish army commandant's son betrays him with his young second wife, partly it seems out of resentment for his father's sacrifice of his mother's health in pursuit of preferred career prospects. Just as the commandant, Frank, gains his career-crowning honours and posting after heroic action with the United Nations, his young wife Anna precipitates his suicide after candidly and rather matter-of-factly informing him of her infidelity. In the lead-up to this dénouement, the family's complex relationships and resentments are laid bare, with Friel's pet theme of non-communication between generations to the fore. The children enjoy a lively, bantering rapport, while the father remains cut off and ineffectual as a parent.

Ben's feelings towards his father are voiced only after his death:

And what I was going to say to him was that ever since I was a child I always loved him and always hated her – he was always my hero. And even though it wouldn't have been the truth, it wouldn't have been a lie either... (*SP* 245)

The non-communication is reminiscent of the situation between Gar O'Donnell and his father in *Philadelphia, Here I Come!*, just as the tenor of the dialogue between the sisters (with its moments of social communion, the shared anecdotes and conversational routines – and the more depressive moments when the routines break down, conversation falters and resentment or hopelessness registers within the claustrophobic family circle) looks forward to Friel's version of Chekhov's *Three Sisters*. The shot which kills the Commandant rings out, as in *Three Sisters*, in a world where:

Strange thing is that in the end it's never the great passions, the great ambitions that determine the course our lives take, but some trivial, piddling thing that we dismiss and refuse to take seriously; until it's too late. And then we recognise that the piddling little thing has manipulated us into a situation that is irrevocable and . . . final.[1]

A half-hearted love-affair symbolised in a pair of beach-shoes left in a caravan is the effective trigger of the Commandant's fate. The root causes however are the petty provincial aspirations, vanities and related emotional insensitivities which impair his human relationships. Friel has recognised implicitly that a genre may be 'translated' as well as a text, and that ancient convention may be mediated by modern cultural conditions and experience – as well as by intervening developments in theatre practice. Compare, for instance, Jules Dassin's cinematic translation of Euripides' *Hippolytus* in *Phaedra* and the chasm between Anna's casual request for the return of her beach-shoes (the only evocation of the love-affair in the play) and the stylised, emblematic love-making in front of the blazing hearth in the film. Dassin up-dates the action to modern Greece, but from the titles onwards, with their beautifully lit montage of details from the Parthenon sculptures, we are invited to seek high-style equivalence in his version. In Friel's more radical and ironic re-working, a sense of distance is generated: Euripides is mediated by a faithful sense of contemporary provincial Irish life, as well as by Chekhov's tragi-comic treatment of middle-class provincial life in nineteenth-century Russia.

At the same time, it remains important that the play is indeed 'after *Hippolytus*'. Friel is drawing on powerful and authoritative conventions, handed down over two thousand years; and the story-line broadly follows the Euripidean model. He makes use of modern alienation-techniques which emphasize the fact that the drama is at one level a contrivance – a matter of selecting, condensing and aesthetically ordering depicted human experience; at the same time, however, these effects are predicated on the conventions of a received dramatic ritual, sanctified by tradition and plumbing the paradigms of human experience enshrined in myth. The drama is aligning itself, as far as changed times, values and circumstances allow, with the Greek tragic tradition. For Friel, as for the Greek tragedians, drama is a religious event: powerful forces move through it.

Through the long scene in Act I, therefore, where Frank's daughters are gathered on the occasion of his public honouring, amidst the warm sisterly banter, the spring heat and the lazing on the lawn, we pick up threads of another story: the mother's death, Frank's re-marriage to a young wife, the son, Ben's estrangement, and Frank's vain intransigence in refusing postings considered below his dignity, but which might have helped his wife's health. The irony of the seductive garden scene, and the relaxed banter, is explicitly pointed out in Helen's protest:

HELEN: It's not right! It's not right!
SIR: Yes, it is.
HELEN: No, it's not. It's distorted – inaccurate.
SIR: I would tell you. Trust me.
HELEN: The whole atmosphere – three sisters, relaxed, happy, chatting in their father's garden on a sunny afternoon. There was unease – I *remember* – there were shadows – we've got to acknowledge them!
SIR: Why?
HELEN: Because they were part of it.
SIR: Don't you think they're aware of them? They're thinking the very same thing themselves.   (*SP* 188–9)

Something is wrong, something is impending; though of course in Friel's revision of Greek tragic irony only the characters re-enacting their fate are aware of the inevitable run of events. The audience (unlike the Greek audience) are not, as a basic premise of the event, aware of the tragic outcome. They may, as was said, progressively tune in to the parallelisms with Euripides' play, but the present-day realism of the re-working and the Chekhovian atmosphere will tend to render these equivocal.

Similarly, Sir's rôle as chorus is to a degree masked by its presentation in terms of a metaphor from the modern theatre as he progressively takes charge of the action like a theatrical producer, organising, commenting, outlining different possibilities of conduct; and the protagonists, like actors rehearsing a drama, share his rather dispassionate, thoughtful, practical approach to the task. He is a firm,

though humane taskmaster; and in Act II, where Ben's fateful relationship with Anna is briefly alluded to in their conversation at the beginning, he nevertheless allows the festive family surface to regenerate
itself in the re-enactment, even a little uncanonically (vis-à-vis the
'ledger's' authority), as he joins in the smiles at the shared set-piece
stories; and it is they, rather than he, who like a company of actors
collecting themselves to get on with the business in hand, initiate the
return to the canonical text: or, non-metaphorically, to enacting the
consequences of their own natures and actions.

Consistently through the play, the banter between the siblings as
they reproduce their practised intimacies preserves a light, and in
some ways seductive, domestic atmosphere which softens the disclosure of the tragic ingredients. We see Frank's doting conversation
with Anna after his return from the civic reception; Ben's dark
resentment against his father and the 'murder' of his mother is stated,
though not enacted; and Helen's grievance at the family's treatment of
her husband is similarly voiced. Always overlaying this however is
Friel's presentation of the insulated, articulate, seemingly carefree
social energy associated with this modestly well-to-do family and
their subtle, often unconscious exclusivity. Miriam, for instance, as her
husband observes, reverts instantly to type in their company. The
surface of their provincial middle-class lives which, even in their
psychic reincarnations, they still instinctively and pleasurably wallow
in is Chekhovian in inspiration: an affiliation which is also pervasively
felt in *Aristocrats* and definitively vented in the *hommage* of the version
of *Three Sisters*. The re-casting in Chekhovian terms is obviously
closely bound up with Friel's notable divergence from Euripides in
the final working out of the plot. Instead of the death of the Phaedra-
and Hippolytus-figures consequent on the momentous, divinely-
engineered infatuation of the former, we have the suicide of the
cuckolded Theseus-equivalent – a psychologically credible consequence (in modern terms) of the casual, banal liaison between Anna
and Ben.

In *Living Quarters*, Chekhov seems to have been a crucial mediating
influence in Friel's instinct as a 'translator' to interpret Euripides
boldly and decisively in terms of modern psychology and the social
and intellectual conditions of twentieth century provincial life (or
vice-versa). Ingeniously, while drawing on the archetypal authority of
the original, he has accommodated his own time and place and at the
same time his own dramatic talents and affiliations extrinsic to
Euripides. In particular he has introduced a comedic lightness of
treatment which avoids parody but allows the stark, arbitrariness of
myth to be tempered by a more socially and psychologically defined

view of human motivation and destiny. 'Well-well-well-well-well-well-well' says Sir, after the shot rings out which marks Frank's suicide: 'That wasn't too bad, was it?'

The Euripidean dimension of events in Ballybeg asserts much the same outlook as Patrick Kavanagh's famous insistence in the poem 'Epic' that:

> I have lived in important places, times
> When great events were decided, who owned
> That half a rood of rock, a no-man's land
> Surrounded by our pitchfork-armed claims.[2]

The imagined intervention of Homer –

> He said: I made the Iliad from such
> A local row. Gods make their own importance. –

memorably encapsulates Kavanagh's sense of the importance of the local which can stand, microcosmically, for the universal. In his introduction to an edition of the oral reminiscences of Charles McGlinchey, an octogenarian Inishowen weaver and tailor recorded in the late forties and early fifties by another Patrick Kavanagh, schoolteacher of Clonmany, Friel ends his appreciation by quoting the above first four lines from 'Epic'. He had previously noted how McGlinchey 'by his concentration on the everyday, the domestic, the familiar, the nuance of a phrase, the tiny adjustment to a local ritual, the momentous daily trivia of the world of his parish, . . . does give us an exact and lucid picture of profound transition: a rural community in the process of shedding the last vestiges of a Gaelic past and of an old Christianity that still cohabited with an older paganism, and of that community coming to uneasy accommodation with the world of today. . .'[3]

Inishowen is Friel's own adopted part of Donegal: he has lived there, in the village of Muff and in the town of Greencastle, during his years as a professional, full-time writer – close to his family roots in Omagh and Derry, and still within the natural hinterland of the latter. Somewhere near here, we should imagine the location of his composite Ballybeg, which draws on the whole of this background. It is the fictive vantage-point from which Friel chooses to view changes in Irish culture, history and social life with the local specificity of McGlinchey, but also with the generalising assertiveness of Kavanagh. Friel is 'parochial' in much the same complex way as Kavanagh in his defiant reversal of the normal pejorative connotations of the term. *Translations* is located in Donegal, was written in Inishowen – and premièred in Derry.

It is perhaps the high-point in Friel's career. It achieves precisely the objectives just intimated. It is parochial in a very literal sense – centring on a small parish in Donegal in the 1830s. It presents the village as a microcosm of the historical experience of the Irish people as their social and cultural world comes under stress through the impact of British colonial policy, and economic factors such as famine and emigration. In this sense, it reflects major national concerns and, by extension, the concerns of any community or nation suffering erosion of its cultural birthright. More than that, in its frame of reference, using Rome, Greece and Carthage as analogues for Irish historical experience, it transcends all local and national boundaries as a part of the tradition of Western culture. Though socially and historically specific to a given time and place in Ireland, it insists on larger perspectives.

It is not in fact so much a play of historical analysis and reconstruction as a play of ideas; and, laced as it is with echoes of modern literary theory, it is one way of coming to terms with the present predicament in Ireland – the questions of identity, allegiance and national and cultural birthright which have been revivified in the continuing crisis. Its frame of reference extends from Homer to George Steiner, and its linguistic repertoire ranges through Greek, Latin, Irish and English, tokening its breadth of intellectual purview; and yet, the parochial qualities, the focus on a single, small community and the attention paid to representing the life of that community in all its 'momentous daily trivia', keep the highly developed idea-content of the play firmly rooted in recognizable experience.

As with *Living Quarters*, the pursuit of this layering of historical, literary and cultural perspectives involves a notable technical and formal challenge; and *Translations* does some remarkable things by any standards. For one thing, it brings to the modern popular stage quotations from Homer delivered *in the Greek* (which is phonetically rendered in the published text); more than this, the characters from time to time communicate with each other in Latin. At the same time, though less surprisingly perhaps, the audience is also expected to digest snatches of Gaelic and take an interest in etymological speculation in all these languages – not to mention the fourth language, the language in which the play is largely delivered – English! Moreover, the play which demands this polyglot tolerance on the part of the audience also makes similarly complex demands in terms of theatrical convention in that it is established that Irish is the normal mode of communication between the characters, though the convention is that this is largely rendered in English. This in spite of the fact that a major thematic issue in the play is that they are actually speaking Irish rather than, specifically, English. To complicate matters further, English *qua* English is also used.

A recipe, it might be thought, for commercial disaster – particularly in a play aimed at a popular audience and premièred in 'provincial' Derry. For some kind of parallel we can perhaps look back to, say, Rattigan's *The Browning Version* where Greek (in Greek characters) is included in the text. But the meaning is heavily sign-posted, the quotations from Aeschylus are very limited, and there is nothing equivalent to the actual conversational exchanges in Latin which take place in *Translations*. In fact, the Greek in *The Browning Version* is a symbol of privileged public school accomplishments shared between master and pupils – something which the audience could recognize as a badge of an exclusive middle-class English cultural heritage.

Hence, in giving his characters their natural, unselfconscious, everyday familiarity with the ancient languages, while premièring the play in Derry, Friel has immediately made a telling point about the cultural potential of Irish life, as well as about metropolitan-based cultural élitism. Friel's long concern that stimulus should be given to activity in the arts, and particularly theatre, in the community of his own origin in the North West of Ireland is well enough known, and there is now the Field Day phenomenon to attest this (in which the original, creative, impetus of *Translations* was crucial); and to this extent the work is deliberately and explicitly given a local angling. It contains, for example, reference to a Burnfoot, and there is a hamlet of that name just across the border from Derry; and a similar reference to the 'cute' people of Buncrana (a little further down the same road) is obviously inserted for the sake of the local audience. All this however is 'parochialism', in the positive sense of the term espoused by Patrick Kavanagh, as opposed to 'provincialism': it is looking at the world through the known and assimilated prism of a given locale and community.

The 'parochial' focus, then, is concentrated rather than narrow, in a play which is about colonialism, vanishing cultures, vanishing languages and even the nature of civilisation and civilised values – important concerns within human culture. The general points are made microcosmically, by implication, and above all humorously. Central to everything, though, is the cultural phenomenon of language: in its various transformations more than anything else it impresses the play's issues upon us.

Translations makes words, language its central metaphor, and hence the generalising power of its implications: it is drawing upon a system of signs and symbols central to all human experience – normative in the structures of their usage and yet manifested everywhere with the same domestic, parochial focus as in the townland of Ballybeg.

Language exemplifies in its structures precisely the kind of 'parochial' potential defined by Kavanagh. Hence *Translations* avoids the difficulty in *The Freedom of the City*, where the Guildhall in Derry, focus of Unionist political ascendancy, is used as a central symbol. The symbol is perhaps too local in its associations: the invasion and occupation of town hall may not have the same political frisson in venues not tuned in to the particular local circumstances. Certainly when the present writer saw the play in its Royal Court run in London, this seemed an aspect of the play which did not travel well. The London production was, incidentally, interrupted by a (routine as I gathered) bomb-scare. I have not heard of such difficulties with *Translations*, even though this is a thorough-going indictment of its kind. *Translations* by its wit, brilliance and disarming good-humour tends to outflank such a response. It does not present itself as an overtly political play. It contains profound insights of course, but it is wrong to attempt to extract from the play any single, encoded *parti pris* message: Friel is following his own prescription of looking at what happens to people in particular historical or political circumstances. It is about culture before politics. It is elegiac rather than activist – humanistic rather than ideological.

The theme of the play is cultural dispossession, with linguistic dispossession as the symbolic focus. The Latin word *translatio*, apart from its familiar anglicised application for rendering speech or literature in one language into another, can also refer to other forms of transfer, transport or transformation out of one state or condition into another. The play harks back to a time when the Irish language was general in Ireland and when, even in the materially deprived and colonially depressed circumstances of the 1830s, there were still popular vestiges of the civilised qualities which made Ireland the 'land of saints and scholars'. There are no obvious saints in *Translations*, but plenty of scholars. Ballybeg is a community in which civilised values, typified in a disinterested zeal for the classical languages, have not yet been extinguished in favour of more utilitarian priorities such as learning English for personal advancement or in preparation for emigration to America. To this extent, there is an innocence about the characters – attending school at all ages like children with their slates and chalk, but notably conversant with points of grammar and philological tradition such as are nowadays limited to a few élite institutions. On the first page we are instructed that the waif-like Sarah could be anything from 17–35; and then immediately we are told that the 'infant prodigy' is sixty-five. It is a vision of an Arcadia of the intellect where humble peasants unassumingly perform the business of philological transmission (in which of course Ireland performed an historically important role in the Dark Ages). In their own way, the inhabitants of Ballybeg assimilate or 'translate' the legacy of Greece and Rome into the substance of their own lives in the kind of process of identification which was crucial for keeping the Classics alive in the cultural tradition of the Western world. In the same schoolroom, Sarah struggles with her five difficult words of Irish, while Jimmy Jack effortlessly carries on with his reading of Homer; and we the audience (presumably at most performances more or less 100% Greekless) hear Homer initially as a series of strange sounds, which have to be mediated by Jimmy Jack. *'Ton d'emeibet epeita thea glaukopis Athene. . .'* says Jimmy in the first Greek we hear; and then again: *'. . . alla hekelos estai en Atreidao domois. . .'* Eventually, his eagerness to communicate his enthusiasm spills over into translation:

JIMMY: *'Hos ara min phamene rabdo epemasset Athene –'* 'After Athene had said this, she touched Ulysses with her wand. She withered the fair skin of his supple limbs and destroyed the flaxen hair from off his head and about his limbs she put the skin of an old man . . .' The divil! The divil!   (*SP* 385)

Thus, in an idealised way it must be granted, the humble hedge school stands as a symbol of a remarkable Irish cultural tradition. The Classics are kept alive with a mixture of learning and innocence. This kind of effortless construing of Homeric Greek is beyond most of us now: the elderly, tramp-like 'Infant Prodigy' however reads his Homer with scholarly accuracy, but also with unaffected delight. Homer, the archetypal story-teller, is fully appreciated for his narrative drive: 'And wait till you hear! She's not finished with him yet!' Every reader, every writer, every culture in the Western tradition finds specific, live points of connection with the great literary exemplars of Greco-Roman culture (it is a truism that the Classics survive by translation), and it is clear enough why Jimmy is particularly keen on *Odyssey XIII*: 'The flashing-eyed Athene! By God, Manus, sir, if you had a woman like that about the house, it's not stripping a turf-bank you'd be thinking about – eh?' Jimmy, particularly when stimulated by some mildly lubricious interest, can react with immediacy to Greek or Irish goddesses; on the Judgement of Paris: 'No harm to Helen; and no harm to Artemis; and indeed no harm to our own Grania, Manus. But I think I've no choice but to go bull-straight for Athene. By God, sir, them flashing eyes would fair keep a man jigged up constant!' Jimmy's trans-cultural aplomb is founded on a sure sense of his own place in the world, which allows him to analogise unselfconsciously:

'Knuzozen de oi osse —' She dimmed his two eyes that were so beautiful and clothed him in a vile ragged cloak begrimed with filthy smoke. . .'! D'you see! Smoke! Smoke! D'you see! Sure look at what the same turf-smoke has done to myself! (*He rapidly removes his hat to display his bald head.*) Would you call that flaxen hair?

(*SP* 385)

Unencumbered by strict chronology, rapt by the marvels of the old tales, imaginatively anachronistic and yet philologically accomplished, Jimmy's mind is a throw-back to the world of the monkish scholars and copyists – innocently cloistered in the scriptorium and the limited social world of the monastery, and yet enjoying privileged access to the seductive world of pagan literature.

Even the less scholastic members of the Ballybeg community can put together the odd basic conversation in Latin. When Maire enters she can join in a brief Latin exchange with Jimmy: that is normal and routine enough – but then there is the practical necessity of coming to terms with English in all its baffling strangeness:

JIMMY: Esne fatigata?
MAIRE: Sum fatigatissima.
JIMMY: Bene! Optime!
MAIRE: That's the height of my Latin. Fit me better if I had even that much English.
JIMMY: English? I thought you had some English?
MAIRE: Three words. Wait – there was a spake I used to have off by heart. What's this it was? (*Her accent is strange because she is speaking in a foreign language and because she does not understand what she is saying*) 'In Norfolk we besport ourselves around the maypoll.' What about that! (*SP* 388)

There is of course a mischievous delight on Friel's part in relegating English to that strange other world where postillions may be struck by lightning or folk may besport themselves around the may-pole: it reverses common deferences. Even Jimmy has attained to only one word of English.

JIMMY: Sure you know I have only Irish like yourself.
MAIRE: And Latin. And Greek.
JIMMY: I'm telling you a lie. I know one English word.
MAIRE: What?
JIMMY: Bo-som.
MAIRE: What's bo-som?
JIMMY: You know – (*He illustrates with his hands*) – bo-som – bo-som –

you know – Diana the huntress, she has two powerful bosom.

(*SP* 388)

Jimmy's attitude to the classical languages is at a different level of seriousness altogether. He subscribes to the humanistic conviction that the Classics furnish a comprehensive guide to living ('Homer knows it all'). This is not just a literary conviction, but reaches into areas of practical initiative. When Doalty jokes that Nellie Ruadh is intending to call her illegitimate child Jimmy (after its putative father), Jimmy Jack is not let directly in on the joke, being treated as the stereotypical, unwordly scholar:

DOALTY: She told me last Sunday she was going to call it Jimmy.
BRIDGET: You're a liar, Doalty.
DOALTY: Would I tell you a lie? Hi, Jimmy, Nellie Ruadh's aul fella's looking for you.
JIMMY: For me?
MAIRE: Come on, Doalty.
DOALTY: Someone told him. . .
MAIRE: Doalty!
DOALTY: He heard you know the first book of the Satires of Horace off by heart. . .
JIMMY: That's true.

(*SP* 319–2)

The joke however is, in a sense, on Doalty, because the reference to the first book of Horace's *Satires*, intended as an instance of Jimmy's unwordly pedantry, is in fact to a volume which is racy in tone, full of worldly-wise observations – and which in particularly contains the second satire on adultery which is full of explicit sexual detail.

Jimmy knows too a more important matter: that Virgil's *Georgics* is a didactic poem containing practical agricultural lore:

JIMMY: Listen to this, Manus. 'Nigra fere et presso pinguis sub vomere terra. . .'
DOALTY: Steady on now – easy, boys, easy – don't rush me, boys – (*He mimes great concentration.*)
JIMMY: Manus?
MANUS: 'Land that is black and rich beneath the pressure of the plough. . .'
DOALTY: Give *me* a chance!
JIMMY: 'And with *cui putre* – with crumbly soil – is in the main best for corn.' There you are!
DOALTY: There you are.
JIMMY: 'From no other land will you see more wagons wending homeward behind slow bullocks.' Virgil! There!
DOALTY: 'Slow bullocks'!

JIMMY: Isn't that what I'm always telling you? Black for corn. *That's*
           what you should have in that upper field of yours – corn, not
           spuds.   (*SP* 392)

In spite of Doalty's fun at his expense, then, Jimmy knows things of a
practical nature about corn and potatoes. In this sense, he personifies
a key aspect of the survival of the Classics as, through the Middle
Ages and the Renaissance, a source of practical guidance in technical
as well as literary and philosophical matters.

In these implicit comments on the transmission of humanistic values
via the easy-going give-and-take of local Irish culture with its ragged
scholars, where the torch of classical civilisation is kept alive through
the Irish and ancient languages (and where English is wittily margin-
alised), Friel is of course reversing certain pre-suppositions about
Irish culture since Spenser and the Plantation: i.e. as barbarian, irre-
mediable, hardly Christian. It is achieved, however, with maximum
finesse and irony. Civilization is made the issue, and Ballybeg the
focus. Friel makes his points about cultural erosion not simply by
attacking the English colonizers, but by idealising the Irish achievement in terms of a humanism which is presented as an integrated part
of a way of life.

Of course, this may involve some weighting of the balance. The
hedge schools may not, generally, have been such model institutions
as that in Ballybeg; and English officers may not have been so
comprehensively ignorant of the Classics as Captain Lancey. There is
however an historical basis for the presentation of Hugh's hedge
school, and, as was said, we are dealing with an Arcadian vision
rather than a sociological or historical document. Arcadia is however
encroached upon in the play by violent historical reality – first hinted
at in the general, tense silence about the activities of the Donnelly
twins, the reported presence of the British troops and the damage to
their equipment, the ominous, sweet smell of the potatoes, and the
planned opening of the new National School which will operate
through the medium of English.

The latter event is directly relevant to Hugh, the head-master, who
arrives on stage conversing easily in Latin, inculcating etymologies
into his pupils, demanding on-the-spot parsing from them, and
speaking an educated Irish which is represented by a grandiloquent,
polysyllabically Latinate form of English. The Latin conversational
routines remain untranslated. The audience, though inevitably largely
uncomprehending of the meaning, is credited with an assumed understanding. Greek gets translated, Latin does not. It is an element of our
humanistic inheritance which is taken for granted in the play (just as

the audience must accept the convention that English may sound like incomprehensible gibberish). Hugh's polyglot banter with his students demonstrates, in its wit and good humour, the integration of learning and everyday life – Sophocles and sheep-dipping share the same cultural context: talk of the baptism of Nellie Ruadh's baby leads on to speculation on the derivation of the word 'baptise':

JIMMY: 'Baptizein' – to dip or immerse.
HUGH: Indeed – our friend Pliny Minor speaks of the 'baptisterium' – the cold bath.
DOALTY: Master.
HUGH: Doalty?
DOALTY: I suppose you could talk then about baptising a sheep at sheep-dipping, could you?   (*SP* 397)

When Doalty's arithmetic in the subsequent banter proves less sure than his philology, however, Hugh volunteers that 'Sophocles from Colonus would agree with Doalty Dan Doalty from Tulach Alainn: "To know nothing is the sweetest life." '

Close after this, we have Hugh's account of his encounter with the Captain Lancey who

explained that he does not speak Irish. Latin? I asked. None. Greek? Not a syllable. He speaks – on his own admission – only English; and to his credit he seemed suitably verecund. . .

More than this,

. . . he voiced some surprise that we did not speak his language. I explained that a few of us did, on occasion – outside the parish of course – and then usually for the purpose of commerce, a use to which his tongue seemed particularly suited . . . and I went on to propose that our own culture and the classical tongues made a happier conjunction – Doalty?
DOALTY: *Conjugo* – I join together.   (*SP* 398–9)

Doalty, though he has trouble with his nine-times table and is not one of the brighter members of the company, can construe well enough: he has the rudiments of culture in Hugh's view of the world. It is the same outlook as that of the returning Owen, delighted to be back among '*civilised* people'. However, the civilised irony of 'My job is to translate the quaint, archaic tongue you people persist in speaking into the King's good English' cannot mask the reality of his mission which is part of both a cultural and a military take-over. Nor is Hugh, for all his magisterial condescension towards English culture, insulated from the logic of events. Although he is capable of turning conversations which stray into topics such as the practical utility of English back into the more congenial vein of Latin parsing and construing, and is insistent on striking disdainful cultural postures –

Wordsworth? . . . no. I'm afraid we're not familiar with your literature, Lieutenant. We feel closer to the warm Mediterranean. We tend to over-look your island. –   (*SP* 417)

he is aware of what is happening, can lecture devastatingly *in English* on the complexity of linguistic and cultural identity; and, finally in the play, can use his classical learning not to switch off into dreams and assuaging preoccupations (Jimmy's route) but to analogise cogently and plangently between contemporary Irish experience and the ancient past.

With the collapse of their preferred world evident around them, Hugh and Jimmy, rather like Captain Boyle and Joxer in the last scene of *Juno and the Paycock*, are left to take stock of their situation. Jimmy in fact has already taken leave of reality. He is to marry Pallas Athene:

HUGH: The lady has assented?
JIMMY: She asked *me* – I assented.
HUGH: Ah. When was this?
JIMMY: Last night.
HUGH: What does her mother say?
JIMMY: Metis from Hellespont? Decent people – good stock.
HUGH: And her father?
JIMMY: I'm meeting Zeus tomorrow. Hugh, will you be my best man?
HUGH: Honoured, James; profoundly honoured.   (*SP* 443)

After his knowing sally to the departing Owen ('Take care, Owen. To remember everything is a form of madness') Hugh nevertheless reminisces:

HUGH . . . The road to Sligo. A spring morning. 1798. Going into battle. Do you remember, James? Two young gallants with pikes across their shoulders and the *Aeneid* in their pockets. Everything seemed to find definition that spring – a congruence, a miraculous matching of hope and past and present and possibility. Striding across the fresh, green land. The rhythms of perception height-ened. The whole enterprise of consciousness accelerated. We were gods that morning, James; and I had recently married *my* goddess, Caitlin Dubh Nic Reactainn, may she rest in peace. And to leave her and my infant son in his cradle – that was heroic, too. By God, sir, we were magnificent. We marched as far as – where was it? – Glenties! All of twenty-three miles in one day. And it was there, in Phelan's pub, that we got homesick for Athens, just like Ulysses.

The *desiderium nostrorum* – the need for our own. Our *pietas*, James, was for older, quieter things. And that was the longest twenty-three miles back I ever made. (*Toasts* JIMMY.) My friend, confusion is not an ignoble condition.   (*SP* 445–6)

Captain Boyle in the final moments of *Juno* . . . of course vaunted *his* supposed military exploits:

BOYLE: If th' worst comes . . . to th'worse . . . I can join a . . . flyin' . . . column . . . I done . . . me bit . . . in Eassther Week . . . had no business . . . to . . . be . . . there . . . But Captain Boyle's Captain Boyle![4]

Hugh's mock-heroics at the expense of himself and Jimmy are however in a different register: they are a device for honesty. Hugh is coming to terms with reality. He accepts their ineffectualness as soldiers, but nevertheless with controlled irony insists on a concept of dignified, if not heroic, failure: 'the need for our own' is both honourable in its way, and disabling. Nevertheless, in their own essentially quietistic terms, they did have their moment, and Hugh is conscious of both its glory and its comedy. The references to Virgil and Homer allow him to strike this wise balance with light, mock-heroic discrimination.

At the close of *Juno and the Paycock*, the famous malapropistic comic catch-phrase, repeated at various junctures in the play, in its final, drawn-out voicing by the Captain ('I'm telling you . . . Joxer . . . the'whole worl's . . . in a terr . . . ible state o' . . . chassis!') resonates beyond the limited moral purview of the Captain and Joxer, taking in the familial and general historical realities against which they still essentially insulate themselves, but which in their progressive disclosure have provided the tragic ingredients which inform the maudlin tragi-comic final scene. Hugh and Jimmy, in their final exchanges, are inevitably reminiscent of the Captain and Joxer in their tragi-comic presentation. Hugh however is quite distinct from the Captain in that he is the *conscious* vehicle for the deeper, tragic resonances. He has a capacity for growth and development denied Captain Boyle; and of course is quite differentiated in his intellect and academic attainments. Compare Hugh's moving reference to his wife as his 'goddess' in the passage quoted above, and Boyle's comically banal exegesis of his wife's name: 'You see, Juno was born an' christened in June; I met her in June; we were married in June, an' Johnny was born in June, so wan day I says to her, "You should ha' been called Juno," an' the name stuck to her ever since.'[5] We might compare also the comically rendered classical ignorance of another failed patriarch:

Tom Murphy's cowardly, hypocritical and mendacious Dada in *A Whistle in the Dark* in his drunken speech at the beginning of Act 3 caps a trivially opinionated disquisition on throat muscles and singing with the sole piece of Latin in the play – resoundingly mistranslated: 'Humanum est errare, there is truth in wine!'[6] The symbolism of this for Murphy's feuding, culturally lost, violent emigrés is the polar opposite of Friel's complex elegy for home, language and cultural birthright in *Translations*. Within his disintegrating world of Ballybeg, however, the economic and other forces behind the extreme dispossession of Murphy's twentieth century characters are already exerting their influence; and Hugh knows it.

Hugh's final words in the play translate a passage in Book I of Virgil's *Aeneid*:

HUGH: *Urbs antiqua fuit* – there was an ancient city which, 'tis said, Juno loved above all the lands. And it was the goddess's aim and cherished hope that here should be the capital of all nations – should the fates perchance allow that. Yet in truth she discovered that a race was springing from Trojan blood to overthrow some day these Tyrian towers – a people *late regem belloque superbum* – kings of broad realms and proud in war who would come forth for Lybia's downfall – such was – such was the course – such was the course ordained – ordained by fate. . .   (*SP* 447)

He falters, and repeats the same passage. He is of course indulging in the profoundest possible application of his discipline – to meditate on what can be learned from the literary and historical experience of a whole culture viewed in long, temporal perspective. The lines however resonate in complex terms, and their import is cryptic. Throughout the play, Hugh, with wit, learning and bravado, has likened Irish experience to that of Greece and Rome, 'overlooking' a thus diminished England, whose representatives have no competence in the ancient languages. If the identification is seen as continuing, then the lines quoted may, at least on first impression, read as a final act of intellectual wish-fulfilment and defiance – a prophecy of resurgence and renewal: just as Rome traced its ascendancy from the ashes of Troy, so will Ireland at some time renew herself. However, as the lines are repeated, another analogy asserts itself: that of Ireland with a tragically ruined Carthage, and England with an irresistible, imperial Rome.

We do not have to choose. Hugh is beyond political sloganising at this point. His is an inclusive vision. He is now in a completely unillusioned way tuned in to the historical and cultural reality of his own time and community: evasive irony, an insulated sense of cultural superiority wittily deployed against the English, the palliative of drink – none of these now cloud an acute assessment of the situation. He has assimilated his own lesson that 'it can happen that a civilisation can be imprisoned in a linguistic contour which no longer matches the landscape of . . . fact' and will now teach English to Maire. Owen, the agent of the re-naming of the territory by the English, reverts ultimately to atavistic assertion: 'I know where I live.' Hugh, however, will countenance change: 'We must learn where we live. We must learn to make them [the new names] our own. We must make them our new home.' This is no Ulysses (to pick up Hugh's own ironic comparison again) heroically setting his home and kingdom in order by violent action against importunate usurpers, but a responsible patriarch substituting wisdom and realism for cultural bravado. It is not a capitulation, but another kind of plan of action. The Classics, the constant symbol of cultural attainment throughout the play, are the indicator of Hugh's final insights. Crucially, now, they provide a projective as well as a retrospective vision, and it is informed by Virgilian pathos ('Sunt lacrimae rerum') and a tragic sense of the fate of nations. If the haunting cadences of Hugh's last, repeated quotation from Virgil portend equivocally both Irish and English fortunes, the ambiguity is richly suggestive beyond the pleading of a particular historical case. The Virgilian perspective allows Hugh a view of nation and empire in which, whatever identifications we make, *sub specie aeternitatis* the same fate awaits all.

Friel's achievement is to open up these perspectives suggestively and movingly, while simultaneously preserving a vital sense of the life of even the smallest community where these great movements are intimately worked out within a particular historical, social and cultural context. His concern for the larger processes of history and culture is indivisible from his interest in the specifically human, the specifically local or national experience within these processes. The play simultaneously embraces both perspectives, just as *Living Quarters* reconciled Greek myth and the world view implicit in Greek tragic convention with social realities in contemporary Ireland and a tragic formula tempered by intervening experience and theatrical practice. It is a humane drama in both the philological and ethical sense of the term. Whether Sarah, in *Translations*, will achieve the dignity of speech is an issue in the play alongside that of the threatened demise of a national language; and beyond this the Irish language question (and the culture which it represents in the play) becomes implicated in the fate of other languages and other cultures. In all these accumulating junctures between micro– and macro-cosmic viewpoints, between the individual case and the general law, the Classics provide a linkage, a frame of reference and the possibility of an encompassing vision. *Living Quarters* and *Translations* are complex and equivocal plays, capable of analysis at different levels and within different social, historical and cultural contexts; but Euripides, Homer and Virgil and the cultural perspectives which they entail are an integral element in the simultaneously intimate and detachedly analytical insights into Irish social and historical experience which Friel, here and elsewhere, is able to provide.

'ISN'T THIS YOUR JOB? – TO TRANSLATE?': BRIAN FRIEL'S LANGUAGES

ROBERT WELCH

At one point in *Volunteers* (1975), there is a particularly bravura piece of invention, during which a fantastic yarn is woven about the skeleton that dominates the archaeological site where the action is set. The volunteer who tells the story admits it is all pure improvisation and, as he breathlessly concludes, tells his audience (those on stage, those in the theatre) that he 'didn't know how that was going to end'. The tale he tells tempts us to allegorize: it is a tale of exile, hanging, sacrifice; a tale which is all too Irish. As Keeney interjects, during the unfolding of the story:

Ah, shure I can schmell dishaster comin'.

But when the tale concludes, Keeney, tired and worldly-wise, alive to the vices of allegory and the dreariness of the predictable message, says to Pyne, the narrator:

Not bad, Pyne. Fairly trite melody but an interesting sub-theme. Not bad at all.[2]

The core of a story takes good care to keep itself hidden; it does not yield its secrets to the facile probe of the allegorizing mind, that aspect of our uncertainty that reaches out for meaning and explanation, for the facts. If a story has a core it will have sub-themes or sub-texts relating it to other stories with their own undercurrents. It is those interrelations that are interesting, not the surface entertainment of the so-called 'story'. The sub-theme or sub-themes of a set of stories create reverberations that stir us, as possibilities interweave, meanings multiply, the thing that contains the stories, the form itself, acquires its fling, its ramification, its identity.

Friel is a dramatist with an impressive technique which he uses, expertly, to create that multiplying fling and ramification. If we go such to that scene in *Volunteers*, where Keeney questions Pyne's leaden predictability (who wants unthinking rhetoric about graves, exile, sacrifice?) we find Friel twisting the action around into another tale, immediately following this one, this time invented by Keeney, save that Keeney's narration is participatory, and funny. It is a tale, which is acted out, about two American matrons, who hugely enjoy their

134

holiday in an Ireland unsettled by civil commotion because it allows them to be frisked with tremendous zeal on all kinds of occasions by security men:

It was just frisk, frisk, frisk day and night for almost a week.[3]

Theatrically this is a superb turn, from the lugubrious to the carnivalesque; and Friel's theatre is asking you to test your reaction to these two narratives, not necessarily to spot the hidden connection, but primarily, simply to enjoy them; while at the same time delighting in the fluid variousness of which this art is capable. There is a connection, of course, but, for this writer at least, it cannot be sorted by means of a theoretical construct; the connection is rather that which obtains between quite different elements mutually coexistent in a unified field of cultural awareness.

Each of these two voices attempts to create a world. On this occasion the stories do not strive against each other for dominance, as they sometimes do in Friel; they are set side by side in the evolving physical relationship that only theatre can provide. And that relationship is often one of disjunction. The forces and tensions of those disjunctions, and the efforts language makes to express, repress, or heal them: these are the matters which concern us here.

Within a cultural system, the story itself, with its contents, themes, characters and so forth, while interesting enough in its own right, only serves as a vehicle for the conveyance of the complex of hidden contradictions, the tensions of which keep the system active. A story, therefore, if it is a significant one for a culture or an occasion, does not come cellophaned in transparent material, bearing a tag declaring its intent. It involves us and moves us precisely because it is resistant to easy formulation; we cannot readily translate its secrets. And we cannot do that because the story, if again, it is a powerful one, is various, manifold and in a crucial sense, uncertain. It can only carry its charge if the elements are active, which will mean they are mobile, shifting, impatient of the tired mind's desire to close down this uncertain activity. But although it may be a vehicle, a story can only be effective as such if it discovers a form which may hold these contradictions. A vehicle conveys nothing if it is crazy; a story needs must articulate, put together; it cannot be haphazard. Only then can it translate the contradictions and the disjunctive active elements, which is not to say that it explains them or sorts them out. A story translates the interior elements of culture most effectively when the form the translation discovers for the articulation encompasses the broadest possible scope. Time and again Friel's theatre holds in play the complexity of contemporary Irish culture: with its bleak parishes; its vociferous and timorous assertions; its hatred; its heartbreaking gentleness and affection; its obsession with the past; its ghoulish materialism and indifference; its fierce and casual passions.

An early short story of Friel's, 'Among the Ruins', gives us a clue to his understanding of the relationship between the form an artist creates, and the interior depths and labyrinths which it seeks to translate. A family, husband and wife, little boy and girl, travel back to the father's native place near Errigal in Co Donegal. The house is in ruins, the past a jumble of memories. The little boy, Peter, goes missing, and Joe, his father, eventually finds him in a small cluster of trees engrossed in play:

He was on his knees at the mouth of a rabbit hole, sticking small twigs into the soft earth.
'Peter! What the hell!'
'Look, Daddy. Look! I'm donging the tower!'[4]

The past is, to a large extent, unknowable; its conflicts and terrors, including those of childhood are often unresolved and hidden. There is a darkness. But the child's instinct, to create a frail interlocking structure over the dark hole, is that of the artist too. In the Elizabethan theatre the wooden structure of the stage itself had a door which opened into an area which, by convention, was recognised as hell. The little boy's grid of twigs is itself a tiny story with its own, semi-comic name; its image reverberates in the father's mind as he drives home. The child's structure over the unknown hole has entered into the network of human communication. The unknown is still not known, but the structure which would not be there without it, and which to some extent it articulates, translates, has entered the arena of human reasons and feeling.

He would ask him in the morning, but Peter would not know. Just out of curiosity, he would ask him, not that it mattered . . . And then a flutter of excitement stirred in him. Yes, yes, it did matter. Not the words, not the game, but the fact that he had seen his son, on the first good day of summer, busily, intently happy in solitude, donging the tower.[5]

A crucial (perhaps *the* crucial) preoccupation in Friel's work, which has both thematic and technical dimensions, is announced in these lines: something internal and hidden, which is related to the past, has been made manifest in the child's activity in the trees. It vibrates with meaning for the father: this construct signifies, it is a vehicle for connecting the past with the present, inner with outer, the inarticulate with form. But Friel's own writing, his own prose, is performing this function for that which the story is carrying for us: the writing is a translation for us, involving us.

Friel is an entirely social writer, in that his work remains always attentive to the minutiae of ordinary everyday life; but his calm and lucid realism is, in effect, born out of a responsibility to translate those interiors that are dark and hidden into a language that incorporates the world as we perceive it under normal conditions. The given world, the social contexts of family, politics, love affairs, administration, running a touring theatre company, are amongst the locations in which the private worlds of feeling are tested. So that Friel's art has a powerfully interior charge which is socialised by his classic realism. He was, inevitably, drawn to the theatre, because the theatre is the form which, above any other, tests the interior against the world of fact; and it does so in a way which holds up, for the audience's gaze and contemplation, the disjunctions between the stories people tell about themselves to themselves, and their actual conditions. We see people like ourselves inventing stories and so translating themselves; and we are asked to adjudicate on those narratives. The theatre is the most effective arena for contemplating the disjunctions narratives generate as they translate the varieties of individual and collective experience.

In *Philadelphia, Here I Come!* (1964) the disjunctions between inner and outer are effectively dramatized by splitting Gar O'Donnell into public and private versions of his personality. Private Gar continuously underlines the difficulty of adequately conveying, in the social context of life in a huxter's shop in Ballybeg, the complexity of a human narrative. People need to 'save the appearances', as when the 'lads' come round to visit Gar before he sets off to Philadelphia in the morning. No-one can face the reality of the departure, and the tension is resolved by bravado and heroic narratives of 'Greenock pieces' and two Dublin skivvies who, they say, chased one of the lads naked along the beach. Private's narrative clashes with this, now orthodox, fabrication:

We were all there that night, Ned. And the girls' names were Gladys and Susan. And they sat on the rocks dangling their feet in the water. And we sat in the cave, peeping out at them. And then Jimmy Crerand suggested that we go in for a swim; and we all ran to the end of the shore; and we splashed about like schoolboys. Then we came back to the cave, and wrestled with one another. And then out of sheer boredom, Tom, you suggested that we take the trousers off Crerand – just to prove how manly we all were. But when Ned started towards Jimmy – five foot nothing, remember? – wee Jimmy squared up and defied not only the brave Ned but the whole lot of us. So we struggled back home, one behind the other, and left the girls dangling their feet in the water. And that was that night. (*SP* 73)

None of the characters in the play can find a language capable of conveying their own view of how they are to any other character. They cannot 'translate all this loneliness, this groping, this dreadful bloody buffoonery.' (*SP* 88) But Friel's theatre *does* translate it, by making evident the gap between the realm of desire and that of necessity and by making that gap the object of our contemplation. We then see that the interaction and mutuality of social necessity is that by which the interior is constrained, and that it finds a voice in Friel's art.

We cannot but speak in our social context, but to speak is almost invariably to distort. It is extremely difficult, if not impossible, to find a just correspondence, a perfect 'congruence' between the words used and the material being expressed. (*Translations, SP* 445) Again, Friel's theatre is an arena for observing these lacks, so that it is, like Beckett's, a theatre obsessed with language; but unlike Beckett's this theatre conveys the difficulty of communication by underlining the normality of failure rather than the failure of normality.

Heidegger says that it is language, not man, which speaks,[6] and Friel's theatre shows us men and women tangled in the net of languages which speak to them rather than the other way around. The theatre is a space in which we observe men and women at a critical edge: they are creatures whose pasts are intersecting with the present during each moment of intensified time that is theatrical time. From these various pasts they bring the gear and baggage of languages, stories, narratives and in this critical present they are engaged in the testing of those languages as they seek to make them congruent with the facts as they evolve. They want to hold the line, they want to make or find 'a matching of hope and past and present and possibility', but invariably things will not cohere with the languages they bring with them. And those languages themselves are easily distorted or betrayed. Mistranslation is endemic.

In *Volunteers* Desmond, the young untenured academic who is supervising the prisoners engaged on the dig, finds out that the site is to be closed that evening because the developers want to get on with the building programme. The work isn't properly finished and the prisoners must return to gaol. Desmond is outraged, and in a speech from the verandah overlooking the hole where the prisoners are working (which is the stage floor itself) indulges himself in a bit of nationalist/Marxist rhetorical elevation:

I personally will write to every newspaper in the country and expose this act for what it is – a rape of irreplaceable materials, a destruction of knowledge that the Irish people have a right to inherit, and a capitulation to moneyed interests.

The self-aware Keeney's acid comment on this is:

That's good. That's impressive. God but I'm a sucker for that sort of stuff.

Stimulated now by the situation, by his own afflatus, by the intoxicating sense of being right and true and brave, Dessy the Red climbs to even greater heights; the language of politics takes over:

As for you men, no one knows better than myself how much toil and sweat you have put into this dig and I know that you are as angered by this news as I am. As to what form your anger will take, that is up to you . . .[7]

And so on. There is a perfect convergence here between Desmond's politics, the language, his view of himself; what is incongruous is the *fact* that he speaks to them of rights while they are prisoners without will. They are 'volunteers' only in the joke sense of that word; and their compliance with necessity will probably lead to their deaths (they will almost certainly be put to death when they return to prison as collaborators). Desmond's rhetoric, a language of power, translating his desire, promising to translate that into action, is out of touch with actuality. It isn't *real*. This disjunction is shown up later when Desmond returns. He went off intending to disrupt the Board at the University which was discussing the dig, but when he got there the meeting had concluded. He also has to admit he didn't know the full facts and that there is no alternative but to close. Now the men pretend to have taken him at his word, and there is much fun at his expense when they tell him they have written to the papers, so inspired were they by his speech, and his stand for them. The last thing he wants now is a convergence between word and deed. He is like them in that he is a victim; and like them that which victimises him is, at root, language. They are, in Keeney's words, casualties of language: 'which of us here isn't?'[8]

Desmond fails to stay in touch with his audience, the men, and vanishes into indignation's closed circle. Cass in *The Loves of Cass McGuire* (1966) is insistent that she will unfold her story in the way she wants to and tells the audience in the theatre that that is what she is going to do. She is emphatic that she lives in the present, the 'here and now'; 'Who the hell knows what happened in the past!' she exclaims to the audience later. But the past is all she can talk about; in a way what else can happen in a theatre except talk about various pasts?

Cass McGuire is in Eden House, a rest home for the elderly, or a workhouse, as she bluntly put it. Her narrative frames the action and when her memory flares the scenes from the past will not stay away: they are enacted on stage. This flashback technique adroitly indicates how her narrative control, her language, breaks down and shows that she is overwhelmed by that which she would command. Her return to Ireland and her family, both of which she has idealized for years in the

Bronx, is a terrible disappointment. Now, in Eden House, the scenes of her humiliation will not go away; they keep interrupting her attempt to hold the audience with her immediate vitality, her lavish, stage-Irish-Americanisms. Hers is a theatre for the voices she cannot keep under.

In the home there are two who have resolved the problem of accommodating the interior with the facts of actuality by creating an entire fantasy world of private invention. It is, needless to say, based on a story, the story of Tristan and Iseult. These two, named appropriately Trilbe and Ingram, are pathetic extensions of the storytelling 'lads' in *Philadelphia, Here I Come!*; or of Gar O'Donnell's hopeful citations from Edmund Burke in the same play. They are related to Fox in *Crystal and Fox* (1968), Casimir in *Aristocrats* (1979), everyone in *Faith Healer* (1979), Yolland and Hugh in *Translations* (1980), Senator Donovan in *The Communication Cord* (1982), Lombard in *Making History* (1988), and so on. Storytellers, narrators, talkers abound in Friel's theatre. But what marks Trilbe and Ingram is that their fiction is allowed, for once, to travel free and unchecked. And, in the end, they draw Cass into this mode of 'truth': 'our truth, our truth' they intone, which Cass, at last, picks up, giving up the struggle to keep in touch with reality, which, for her, is the audience in the theatre. As, in the third Act, she gravitates closer to the point where she will enter fiction, she loses contact with the auditorium. A stage direction reads: '*She takes a few steps towards the footlights, shades her eyes, searches the auditorium. She sees nobody*':

And I could ov swore there were folks out there. (*Shrugs*) What the hell.[9]

At last she joins the Trilbe and Ingram 'rhapsody' (Friel's word) to the strains of the 'Liebestod' from Wagner's *Tristan und Isolde*. She has sunk into the 'winged chair', reserved for these sterile flights, which is Friel's powerful critique on the danger of the autonomous imagination. It must be put to the test, otherwise the world of everyday experience, the actual, will cease to be real, to cite a distinction made by Seamus Deane in a discussion of the short stories which underlines Friel's moral intelligence.[10] Friel distrusts the storyteller, the maker of fictions, the word-spinner. In *The Loves of Cass McGuire* and to some extent in *Aristocrats* he is kinder to them in that he allows them dignity while at the same time making evident their pathos.

Cass McGuire, despite her desire for total presence, cannot stop the past from obtruding on to the space she wants to keep for herself, from which she projects to the audience, the playing area itself. Eden House is a place of voices, tales from the past or untrammelled dislocated fictions, which latter 'truth' she enters at last with relief, surrender and dignity.

In *Aristocrats* Friel takes one of the most haunting symbols in Irish writing, the Big House, and locates it in Ballybeg. The Hall is saturated with history, narratives; it is a 'bloody minefield' of stories: Yeats, Hopkins, Cardinal Newman, G. K. Chesterton – all have objects associated with them. The chaise-longue 'is Daniel O'Connell', the candlestick 'is George Moore' (*SP* 266–7). Casimir is the anecdotalist of these relics for the benefit of Tom Hoffnung, an American academic who is writing a history of the Catholic ascendancy families. He exhausts himself on his enthusiastic narration, and in making sure everything is in place. He desires there to be a complete 'congruence' between the past, his narration, and the present. He is fiercely active in the latter realm, which is of course that of the play, trying to keep everything under control, fully remembered, and explained. Claire, the youngest sister, is getting married, and he rushes about, trying to make sure that everyone is relaxed and happy. Historical forces, presences, and personalities have been reduced to objects: Yeats's cushion, Moore's candlestick. Curiously, his sick father's voice is also 'objectified' by the installation of an intercom, so that his needs can be attended to at once in the event of any emergency. That history may not be easily controlled is made powerfully evident at the end of the first Act when Casimir, as he brings a tray out into the garden for an *al fresco* lunch with the rest of the family, is struck rigid with terror as he hears his father's senile authoritarian blare from the ironically titled 'baby-alarm':

FATHER: Casimir!
          (*Casimir jumps to attention; rigid, terrified.*)
CASIMIR   Yes Sir!
FATHER: Come to the library at once. I wish to speak to you. (*Casimir now realizes that the voice has come from the speaker*)
CASIMIR: Christ. . . . Oh-oh-oh my God . . . Ha-ha . . .
          (*Judith, the eldest sister, comes in.*)
FATHER: At once, Sir! And bring your headmaster's report with you. I intend to get to the bottom of this.
CASIMIR   Judith?
JUDITH: What is it?
CASIMIR: Judith?
          (*She goes quickly outside, gets down beside him and takes him in her arms. He is crying now.*)
CASIMIR: I'm sorry – I'm sorry – I'm very sorry.
JUDITH: It's all right.
CASIMIR: I'm very sorry, very sorry.
JUDITH: Everything's all right – everything's fine.

Act Two opens with Casimir still gamely trying to create a convergence between the present and the past: he is crawling around on his
hands and knees trying to find the croquet holes in the lawn. The story
that Casimir wants to tell is that the past can be relived, just like that:
'hey presto' it's there again. The trouble is that the past contains within
it terror and uncertainty, whereas Casimir's language tries to be
cheerful and objective. He is enthusiastic and emphatic about each
identification he makes, whether he is naming the Chopin pieces
Claire plays, or finding the holes in the overgrown croquet lawn, or
naming the places where famous people damaged themselves in
Ballybeg Hall.

His narratives are challenged by Hoffnung in the last Act, when
the American points out that Casimir could not have ever seen Yeats,
whom he claims to remember so vividly, because Yeats in fact died
before Casimir was born. Tom walks off and Casimir, in nightmarish
uncertainty, starts to relate to Eamon, his brother-in-law, what they
both have just participated in, father's funeral. But even that now he
begins to doubt:

All that happened, didn't it, Eamon? All that happened?
Oh, yes, he would have been so gratified. (*SP* 309)

His uncertainty leads him to tell Eamon a story, yet another story,
about the past; this time of a childhood humiliation by his father when
Casimir began to realise, he tells Eamon, that he could live within
'smaller, perhaps very confined territories, without exposure to too
much hurt.' These are territories, however, that are maintained at great
cost, involving, as they do, incessant narratives which try to retain a
connection between past and present, inner and outer.

Ballybeg Hall itself is a fiction sustained by the various narratives of
the play: Casimir's, even Eamon's, the local man who has married
into the family. The latter's devotion to the Big House is, he acknowledges, grounded in 'all that is fawning and forelock-touching and
Paddy and shabby and greasy peasant in the Irish character'. That is
why, he concludes, 'we were ideal for colonizing'. Judith, who has
had the responsibility of looking after the house as well as taking care
of father, reveals, at the end, that the house is no longer an economic
proposition, nor has it been for a long time. All the complex historical
narratives, the ghosts of Newman and Hopkins, are contradicted; but,
strangely, at the play's end there is a curious air of jubilant relaxation.
The stories are all over; or at least the frantic need to sustain ones that
cost dear. The characters are all to move, but as the curtain falls they do
not stir. The people in the play have been brought into a secular, non-
fantastical world where what is actual is real; and it is no accident that

Uncle George has started to speak again after years of silence. They sing at the close:

They have fitted a slab of granite so grey
And sweet Alice lies under the stone . . . (*SP* 325)

As if to imply that death puts all narratives into perspective. Sombre, enigmatic, and curiously hopeful, *Aristocrats* brings a great deal of frenetic invention and interpretation to a strangely pacific conclusion on this minor chord.

In *Faith Healer* (1979) Friel completely aligns his technical concerns to his moral preoccupation with language. Starkly functional, the play consists of four monologues which recount, from their various per-spectives, the story of Frank Hardy, faith healer. They all differ; names change, crucial events are told in drastically different ways; the same person is said to be from different countries. Narration is unstable; language and memory distort. How can there be an accurate trans-lation of events, feeling, personality? But all are agreed on one thing: Hardy had a gift, a power to transform actuality, which functioned according to a law of its own. Hardy's art, though not linguistic, answers to a need, mute and unexpressed, in the people he ministers to, although it is as unpredictable and unstable as the narration through which it is conveyed. The audience never *see* Hardy performing; thereby avoiding scenes which would be unworkable theatrically, while at the same time reminding it how power is constructed in language.

Hardy's art of healing is put to the test of actuality in Donegal on the night he meets his death. Though it is not linguistic, this art is con-veyed to us through language; it is a story which people need. As ever with Friel's theatre the story is tested against other stories and against and in actuality. But this actuality, as conveyed in the words Friel gives Hardy in the last monologue, is both phenomenal and numin-ous; and entirely mysterious:

And although I knew that nothing was going to happen, nothing at all, I walked across the yard towards them. And as I walked I became possessed of a strange and trembling intimation: that the whole corporeal world – the cobbles, the trees, the sky, those four malign implements – somehow they had shed their physical reality and had become mere imaginings, and that in all existence there was only myself and the wedding guests. And that intimation in turn gave way to a stronger sense: that even we had ceased to be physical and existed only in spirit, only in the need we had for each other. (*SP* 375–6)

Hardy's act, which is going to fail, is tested against actuality. He is attempting, futilely, to translate that interior capacity he has for access to wholeness into the world of phenomena and he won't be able to do it. But that world is spoken of as mysterious in itself, one in which there is no difference between Hardy and his executioners. Friel, here, is creating a language for the ultimate translation of two terms into each other, a complete and secular sharing, a communion purged of liturgy.

Faith Healer, at the close, envisages a crossing of boundaries, of the limits between consciousness and other(s). In *Translations* (1980) the crossing of boundaries is explored in linguistic and cultural terms. Technique is most carefully attuned to function: a major source of pleasure in the play is the invigorating quasi-illusion Friel creates about the language the characters are supposed to be speaking. Apart from Latin and some Greek the only language the audience hears spoken is English, yet they accept a convention that for most of the play the language they are hearing is meant to represent Irish. So the audience are engaged in a translation game where they have all the pleasure and none of the effort.

The action revolves around the Ordnance Survey of the 1830's, during which Irish place names were translated into English and Ireland was mapped and surveyed. Lieutenant Yolland, the young English officer, and Maire, the local girl, cross boundaries in their affection for each other; but Yolland has identified completely with Ireland, the Irish language, and Irish tradition. One of the thematic cruxes of the play comes, appropriately enough, when Owen, the hedge schoolmaster's son, and Yolland, are working on the translation of the name of a crossroads, Tobair Vree. Old Hugh, Owen's father, has just left, on a wonderful exit line where he says that 'it can happen that a civilisation can be imprisoned in a linguistic contour which no longer matches the landscape of . . . fact.' (*SP* 419)

That statement is a very clear-sighted summary of what has happened. The landscape of fact is the one that is going to be created when Yolland and Owen have done their work. The language is changing, but Yolland is romantically attached to the old forms. Owen, just as realistic as his father, but no more so, points out that no-one, apart from him, knows how the crossroads Tobair Vree got its name: a man, called Brian, who had cancer fell into a holy well *near* the place where the crossroads is and drowned; but the well is now gone, and no-one remembers the man.

Translation, the carrying over of the depth of association, is a difficult business, because languages have quite different systems of awareness. People may not, but languages do. Maire and Yolland wave at each other across the fields, but the fields that lie between them are the fields of language, of discourse, and it takes a great deal of work to make the translation, before a field day is possible. They rush headlong, at each other and to disaster. Joyce gave it to the fatuous Englishman Haines to say in *Ulysses*: 'it seems history is to blame';[11] but Joyce knew, as does Friel, that the difficulty lies with language. Far from being a lament for the disappearance of the Irish language, *Translations* embodies an awareness of cultural differences, and the tragedies and violence they generate. It is an unsentimental analysis of the politics of language.

The Communication Cord (1982) is the farcical re-enactment of these concerns, as if Friel had felt the need to emphasise them by repetition, variation, and modulation into an outrageously comic mode.

The central image of the play is the set itself, an 'authentic' Irish country cottage, rebuilt to look exactly like the real thing. Like Ballybeg Hall this cottage is eloquent: it has a wealth of historical association, and rootedness; it is, in the words of Senator Doctor Donovan, 'the touchstone . . . the apotheosis'. It strikes a chord in every Irishman's breast; and it is the umbilical cord connecting us to the past. The trouble is everybody is using it for his (or her) own ends. The plot has the required complexity of farce, but to put it simply, everyone is confused and ends up, literally, in the dark when the light is blown out. The Senator, curious about the old-world implements attached to the wall, manages to lock a cow halter around his neck, thereby well and truly tying himself back into the umbilical cord. The confusion and mayhem arise because of the opportunity for exploitation the languages of tradition provide. The Senator is freed but at the end of the play as the young academic linguist, Tim, is making love to Claire ('Maybe silence is the perfect discourse'[12]) their friend Jack also gets the cow halter around his neck. At final black out the whole house, the prison-house of language, is falling down.

Language itself and the traditions, the 'images of the past,' (*Translations, SP* 445) it embodies may enslave us: the communication cord, the means of transmitting messages, the entire network of understanding, can become the halter of victimage. There is in Friel a profound distrust of language, because he understands its power.

In *Making History* (1988) O'Neill is someone who tries to resist this power. His situation is that of someone who is surrounded by people with very strong languages, who are trying to translate him into their terminology or into one they recognise. He doesn't have a stable language himself. He speaks with an English accent for most of the play, except in moments of anger, when he breaks into his native Tyrone. He is Irish but is also a product of the English and European High Renaissance, having been brought up in the Sidney House at

Penshurst, deliberately idealized in the play. He marries an English girl, Mabel, to the chagrin of Lombard and O'Donnell. Lombard, the Archbishop, has his version of O'Neill which is determined by the Roman Catholic politics of the Counter Reformation; as has O'Donnell, who is deliberately depicted as a patriotic enthusiast. O'Neill wants to stay out of these 'cords' although he does want to retain some inalienable right to be Irish in the country which is his. The trouble with that is that none of the available models will quite do. However, affectionate as he is in his memories of the pleasures and culture of Penshurst he cannot forget the racial slur delivered by Sir Henry Sidney, the evening of his departure, after all the years of generosity and kindness, when he was again, even if only for an instant, the 'Fox O'Neill', the traitorous unreliable Irishman.[13] But this does not mean that O'Neill is a victim of romantic or atavistic impulses. In a passage where, using a typical Renaissance trope, he translates various friends and allies into the language of flowers, he figures O'Donnell as borage and therefore as 'inclined to excessive courage, even recklessness.' This tropic set piece intervenes in another, larger discourse, which explores and attempts to translate the networks of opposition between Irish and English culture, 'two deeply opposed civilizations'. Maguire of Fermanagh is in rebellion and pressure is mounting on O'Neill to join him. Harry Hoveden, his secretary, asks:

. . . are you going to betray your old friend, Maguire?

O'NEILL: (*Roars*) 'Betray my old – !' For Christ's sake don't you start using language like that to me, Harry! (*Softly*) Maguire is a fool. He's determined to rise up and nobody can stop him and he'll be hacked to pieces and his people routed and his country planted with Upstarts and safe men. It happened to Fitzmaurice. And McDermott. And Nugent. And O'Reilly. And O'Connor. And O'Kelly. Their noble souls couldn't breathe another second under 'tyranny'. And where are they now? Wiped out. And what did they accomplish? Nothing.[14]

They are 'casualties of language', of words like 'tyranny', 'nobility', 'soul'. But the irony of all of this is that immediately after this outburst O'Donnell, the enthusiast, rushes in, afire with excitement, with the news that the Spanish have, at last, agreed to invade, with the consequence that O'Neill himself will indeed join Maguire.

The rebellion is crushed, and O'Neill and O'Donnell are, in the second act, isolated and on the run. Out in the Sperrins O'Neill writes his submission to the Queen and a most powerful and moving scene occurs when he recites the submission, to O'Donnell, a submission couched in the most elaborate and courtly English, a language of total abnegation, self-surrender and self-obliteration:

Most sorrowfully imploring her gracious commiseration and appealing only to her princely clemency, without presuming to justify my unloyal proceedings against her sacred majesty.[15]

O'Donnell, at first, enjoys this recitation and makes fun of the baroque extremism of the language of surrender but the mood darkens as it comes home to him how real, how *true* this language now is. There is now a perfect 'congruence' between word and situation. This language of victimage describes a situation which has come about because one culture, one language, has defeated another. So extreme is O'Neill's self-excoriation that one becomes aware that Friel is alive to the possibility that after defeat self-laceration may begin to have its own terrible attractions. The victim longs for the cord to tighten round his neck. Language may be not only a prison-house but a torture chamber where the complex transactions between victim and oppressor include masochism, self-disgust, self-contempt, acquiescence.

Lombard is a busy *naif*. He wants to write the history of O'Neill as a champion of the Counter Reformation, and as an Irish patriot. He is not interested in the 'truth', which O'Neill insists he must write. He wants to tell 'a story' which will make O'Neill a hero for 'a colonized people on the brink of extinction'.[16] O'Neill protests that he wants the truth, but when Lombard offers him the chance to make any changes in the outline he cannot or will not. He responds with silence.

The 'truth' the play has revealed is that there are different sets of cultural awareness which are conveyed in different languages: this truth relies upon the totality of those languages the play has set before us, its structure an arrangement of fragile interlinkings over the gulf between cultures and individuals. The end of the play is powerful in its unremitting focus on a man who is distrustful of all language, which means he is trustful of no-one, even Harry, who sells a pair of shoes to buy a cheap bottle of Chianti for his drunken master.

Friel's theatre is one in which language is held up for scrutiny. It reveals the power it has over people as individuals; and it shows that intensity and passion are, more often than not, created by language. He was drawn to the theatre because there the audience can see very clearly those disjunctions between the language someone displays and the contexts in which it is transacted. It is the place for realizing the *lack* of congruence between the word and the situation. The languages people use (or, more provocatively, by which they are used) embody sets of cultural awareness, which are translated or transacted as they speak. Friel's theatre is a laboratory of translations of different cultural and individual awarenesses interacting in a framework in which each strand is separate; but together, these strands are the interwoven form (the text or tissue) which stands before us in the theatre, just like the structure of twigs the little boy creates in 'Among the Ruins'. We are; and we are in the void, looking at that frail luminous structure which clings, with unremitting fidelity, to the formations of recognisable social life. But it is not social realism that Friel is interested in; he is obsessed by its making and unmaking in language.

Friel's theatre is concerned with many issues, such as, for instance, cultural identity or conflict. But these do not have a static presence in his work: they are taken up into the weave of the various languages that the plays hold in tension, and they become mobile, elusive, and all the more interesting for that. They are brought into the realisation of the intervoicings of the plays but they still retain complexity, a 'hiddenness' despite the fact that they are being explored. So that there is a sense in Friel's theatre of people or cultures *not* being reduced to formulae, an air, if one wishes, of spiritual generosity.

There is, as has been said, in Friel, a distrust of language, a preference for silence; yet he approaches language with a kind of reverence too. His dialogue is impacted with awareness; but he can also write an English cadenced like Burke's, and like his, one attentive to the need to control while at the same time retaining the potential for surprise. His English is spare too, and suspicious, written by someone intensely aware of the presence of a hidden language in modern Ireland: Irish.

TRANSLATING HISTORY: BRIAN FRIEL AND THE IRISH PAST*

SEAN CONNOLLY

Brian Friel has written two plays dealing directly with Ireland's past.[1] *Translations* (1980), set in a rural community in County Donegal in 1833, takes as its theme the decline of Irish language and culture. Friel himself has insisted that *Translations* is a play about language, utilising but not restricted by the 'necessary peculiarities' of its historical setting.[2] But the accuracy or otherwise of his presentation of cultural and linguistic change in early nineteenth-century Ireland has nevertheless been the subject of much debate. *Making History* (1988), set in the 1590s, deals with the last phase of the conquest of Gaelic Ireland by a newly centralised English state. Again Friel's reshaping of the historical record to suit his artistic purposes has given rise to some debate. Yet in this case what is involved is not just a play set in the past, but a play about history itself. Friel's theme of the inevitable distortion of the past as it is made to serve the needs of the present is an important issue in itself, and one that has an obvious relevance in contemporary Ireland. At the same time the play can also be read as Friel's response to the criticisms that have been directed against his own earlier practice in *Translations*.

I

Let us begin with Friel's presentation of cultural and linguistic change in the early nineteenth century. *Translations* depicts the arrival in a rural Irish-speaking community of two powerful new agencies. One, an off-stage but clearly delineated presence, is the new state-run national school, which will displace the 'hedge school' supported by the local community. The second is the officers and men of the Royal Engineers, who are engaged in mapping the area as part of the Ordnance Survey of Ireland. Between them these represent the forces that will destroy the Irish-speaking culture of the community to which they come. In the new national school instruction entirely through English will replace the teaching through Irish provided by the hedge schoolmaster Hugh O'Donnell. Part of the task of the Royal Engineers is to provide standardised and anglicised versions of local Irish place-

149

names: the 'translations' that supply the play's central metaphor. Both of these agencies, it is made clear, represent not just outside influences but the intervention of government. The national school will replace Hugh O'Donnell's establishment because it is backed by the power of legal compulsion – 'And every child from every house has to go all day, every day, summer or winter. That's the law' (p. 22) – and because the instruction it provides will be free. (In fact school attendance did not become compulsory in Ireland until 1892, and fees continued to be charged in the early national schools.) The Royal Engineers, equally, are cartographers but also soldiers. This point is hammered home at the play's climax, when they react to the disappearance of one of their number by initiating a policy of systematic reprisal against the local population as a whole. Whatever the broader ideas about language and mentality that Friel wants to put forward, his interpretation of linguistic change in early nineteenth-century Ireland is thus quite unambiguous: the Irish language declines because it is crushed by agencies of the British state, backed up where necessary by military force.

This picture of forcible suppression by an alien government has of course long been a part of Irish folk memory. Yet few historians working in the field would today explain the decline of the Irish language in such terms. From one point of view, it is true, Gaelic language and culture had been in decline ever since the native aristocracy and landed gentry, the losers in a series of military conflicts during the sixteenth and seventeenth centuries, had been dispossessed and broken as a social class. But the decisive period in the decline of Irish as the spoken language of ordinary people came much later, in the early and mid-nineteenth century. The proportion of persons recorded in later censuses as able to speak Irish falls from around 45 per cent of those born in the 1770s to 28 per cent of those born in the 1830s, and to only 13 per cent of those born in the 1860s.[3] The most straightforward explanation for this rapid fall may be found, not in official policies of cultural imperialism, but in processes of economic and social change. The first half of the nineteenth century saw, among other things, the development in Ireland of a more commercialised society, characterised by improved communications, greater mobility, and the penetration of new areas by the market economy. There was also a sharp rise both in permanent and in seasonal migration. In addition tens of thousands of Irishmen – perhaps 200,000 during 1793–1815 alone – served in the British army and navy, while many more were taken, through service in the militia, to parts of their own country they would otherwise never have seen. All this helped to disseminate both a knowledge of English, and a consciousness of its utility, among Irish-speaking populations. The appalling death toll of the Great Famine of 1845–51, concentrated as it was among the poorest regions and the lowest social groups, further reduced the proportion of Irish speakers. But it devastated a culture that was already in rapid decline.[4]

The irrelevance to the whole process of the sort of deliberate government intervention suggested in *Translations* may be illustrated by looking at an institution central to Friel's fiction: the school. The 1830s did indeed see the appearance in Ireland of a system of national schools. But the popular belief that these were wholly new institutions, designed by British government to reshape the character of Irish society, and representing a sharp break with the existing 'hedge' schools – an image faithfully reflected in *Translations* – is now known to be wholly misleading. The Commissioners of National Education appointed in 1831 did not create a purpose-built school system. Instead they offered financial support, on application, to schools, whether planned or already established, that could meet their minimum requirements. Of the 'national schools' that had been created by 1840, more than half had already existed before 1831; the majority of teachers in the early national schools, equally, had already begun teaching before the system was created.[5] This continuity in institutions and personnel was matched by continuity in curriculum. The national schools provided an elementary instruction, dominated by the basics of literacy and numeracy, entirely through English. But so had the 'hedge' schools they replaced. Some schoolmasters of the eighteenth and early nineteenth centuries were indeed students of Irish literature, preserving and transcribing manuscripts, and in some cases themselves composing poetry or other literary work. In the routine instruction of the sons and daughters of farmers and tradesmen that made up their staple employment, however, they taught through English. Nor is this surprising. By the early nineteenth century English was all too clearly the language of even modest success in life. It was the language of the law, of the employing and landowning classes, of the towns where goods were sold and bought, and where work might be had. It was also the language of the emerging Catholic establishment: of the increasingly influential bishops and clergy, as well as the new style of political agitation pioneered by Daniel O'Connell and his associates. It was thus what the great majority of parents, paying fees out of limited resources, wanted their children to be taught.[6]

A second feature of Friel's hedge school that few historians could now endorse is its status as an academy of classical erudition. The schoolmaster, Hugh O'Donnell, is an accomplished classical scholar, who composes verses in Latin. Jimmy Jack Cassidy, the elderly bachelor known as 'the infant prodigy', knows only one word of English, but is introduced 'contentedly reading Homer in Greek and smiling to himself' (p. 11). Other adult pupils are less accomplished, but are never-theless capable of supplying the Latin and Greek roots of the words that Hugh fires at them. None of this is Friel's own invention. Observers in the eighteenth and early nineteenth centuries commented regularly on the surprising existence in a mainly poor peasant society of schools providing instruction in Latin and Greek. Out of this grew the idea of a classically educated peasantry enshrined in pietistic works like Dowling's *The Hedge Schools of Ireland*, published in 1935 and ack-nowledged by Friel as a main source for his play. Yet the reality was rather different. The existence of schools where boys from relatively humble backgrounds could acquire the basics of Latin and Greek was quite clearly related to the need to train candidates for the Catholic priesthood: William Carleton, for example, whose account of his boyhood studies in Ovid and the Greek testament is quoted in Friel's programme notes to *Translations*, was originally intended for a clerical career. There was no question of a casual familiarity with the classics extending to the population as a whole. In the diocese of Raphoe, which takes in County Donegal, 9 schools out of the 262 operating in 1834 were reported to offer instruction in Latin and Greek. Between them they had a total of 241 pupils, not all of whom necessarily bene-fitted from the classical part of the curriculum. The remainder of the 14,500 children attending day schools in the diocese received an instruction confined to the basics of literacy and numeracy, with in some cases the addition of book-keeping for boys and needlework for girls. An even larger group received no formal instruction at all. In 1841 62 per cent of the adult population of County Donegal could neither read nor write.[7]

If Friel offers a distinctly elevated vision of the indigenous school system of his traditional Ireland, his account of the other major institution that plays a key role in his play, the Ordnance Survey, is a hostile caricature. The first comprehensive mapping of Ireland, and the standardisation of placenames that went with it, was indeed carried out, between 1824 and 1846, by army officers from the Royal Engineers and Royal Artillery, assisted by both soldiers and civilian employees. They approached their task, however, in a spirit wholly different to the crass colonial paternalism of Friel's Captain Lancey. The work of devising English equivalents for Irish placenames (most commonly by imposing an English orthography on the existing name, rather than by translating it into English) was done, not by a decultured utilitarian like Hugh O'Donnell's renegade son, Owen, but by John O'Donovan, widely regarded as the outstanding Irish scholar of his time. The survey's topographical department also employed another noted Irish scholar, Eugene O'Curry, as well as the archaeologist George Petrie and the poet James Clarence Mangan. At one point it was intended to accompany the maps with published 'memoirs' describing the physical features, economic life and social conditions in each parish. The scheme was eventually dropped, causing violent controversy, but the unpublished memoirs have since been recognised as a major source of information by historians seeking to reconstruct the lifestyles and mental worlds of the early nineteenth century. Even without the memoirs, moreover, the Survey's maps, with their wealth of antiquarian as well as cartographic detail, were praised by no less a person than Thomas Davis for the contribution they would make to raising the level of national consciousness in Ireland.[8]

These are some of the criticisms that an historian is likely to make of the presentation of the Irish past in *Translations*. To what extent do they matter? The answer depends in part on an assessment of Friel's intentions. One critic has argued that *Translations* and *A Paper Landscape*, the historical study of the Ordnance Survey by J.H. Andrews that served as one of Friel's main sources, should be seen as 'complementary texts'. *A Paper Landscape*, based on written documents, presents the history of the governing élite. *Translations* presents instead the history of the 'hidden Ireland', 'those who, defeated, are hidden from writing, hidden from written history'.[9] This is simplistic. History, like literature, has its subdivisions. *A Paper Landscape* is an administrative history, and works from sources appropriate to that enterprise. Other historians, using different sources, have made their own attempt to investigate the 'hidden Ireland' of the Catholic lower classes.[10] J. H. Andrews himself, passing lightly over the initial jolt he experienced on encountering the play's various departures from historical reality, suggests that *Translations* should be read, not as a recreation of a real moment in Irish history, but as a distillation of elements that have run through the experiences of several centuries. Captain Lancey, for example, is not intended to represent the true face of the army of the 1830s. Rather he stands for a particular tradition of British military administration, visible as far back as the wars of Elizabeth and Cromwell, and as recently as the current troubles in Northern Ireland.[11] All this, of course, fits neatly with Hugh O'Donnell's remark that 'it is not the literal past, the "facts" of history, that shape us, but images of the past embodied in language' (p. 66). Wolfgang Zach offers a somewhat different reading: that *Translations* deliberately reflects twentieth-century fantasy rather than nineteenth-century reality. It offers 'nostalgic and elegiac images from an imagined past', made into 'objective correlatives of present Irish issues'. The historical improbabilities of *Translations*, according to this view, foreshadow the coarser burlesque of the Irish obsession with an idealised past in Friel's next play, *The Communication Cord.*[12]

For Wolfgang Zach these points are enough to refute criticisms of
Friel's anachronisms and departures from the strict historical record.
Unfortunately other admirers of *Translations* have been unable to take
so sophisticated a view of the function of its historical dimension. To
see this one has only to turn to an earlier chapter of the book in which
Zach's own piece appears. Here Professor Brian John, without a hint of
caution or qualification, directs his readers to *Translations* for an
account of the way in which Ireland's rich mythology of famous places
'was finally lost before British colonial rule'.[13] A writer in the widely-
read *Eire-Ireland* goes further still in his tribute to the play's literal historical accuracy.

The Donegal peasant in Mr Friel's play is as familiar with the flashing-
eyed Athene of Greek mythology as with the Grainne of Irish legend. While
the master and his students cannot speak English [in fact the master can
and does], they can converse in the languages of Homer and Virgil. They
know nothing of Shakespeare, but they can quote Ovid. While this is an
authentic reflection of how things were, it may raise questions of dramatic
credibility.

The reviewer in the *Sunday Times* who objected (quite accurately) to
the suggestion that members of the British officer class in the early
nineteenth century would not have been ignorant, as Lancey and
Yolland are, of Latin and Greek, is accused of 'wounded ethnic pride',
and dismissed with massive sarcasm: 'Perhaps Mr Friel should have
taken some license in relation to historical accuracy as a sop to the
sensitivities of English critics'.[14] In the face of responses such as this, it
does after all seem necessary to set the record straight by indicating
just how little relation *Translations* bears to what is known of the reality
of linguistic and cultural change in nineteenth-century Ireland.

Brian Friel, of course, cannot be held responsible for the excesses of
his admirers. His own attitude to the historical reality of the Ireland he
presents in *Translations* remains unclear. At one point in the notes kept
while writing the play he comments: 'One aspect that keeps eluding
me: the wholeness, the integrity, of that Gaelic past. Maybe because I
don't believe in it.'[15] It is this which suggests to Zach that Friel's real
concern was to present a mythical rather than the actual Gaelic past.
But the passage could be read quite differently, as suggesting that
Friel wants to believe that this is what the Gaelic past was like, but is
having trouble doing so. (It must also be read in context: the preceding
sentences complain of the failure of the elements that make up the play
to fuse together and take on a life of their own.) There is also the
question of why, if Friel's aim was to recreate a purely mythical Irish

past, he should have decorated the programme notes to *Translations* with a series of quotations from both historians and contemporary writers, a gesture that has been taken at face value by at least one academic critic.[16]

Despite these uncertainties, Friel's declared aims in writing *Translations* are nevertheless clear enough. 'I don't want to write a play about Irish peasants being suppressed by English sappers. I don't want to write a threnody on the death of the Irish language. . . . the play has to do with language and only language. And if it becomes overwhelmed by that political element, it is lost.'[17] His theme is summed up in a sentence put into the mouth of Hugh O'Donnell but taken almost verbatim from another of Friel's source books, George Steiner's *After Babel*: '. . . it can happen that a civilisation can be imprisoned in a linguistic contour which no longer matches the landscape of . . . fact.'[18] For this purpose, Friel reminds himself in his diary, the 'cultural climate' of Ballybeg must be presented as 'a dying climate – no longer quickened by its past'.[19] And this sense of a dying culture is in fact conveyed in a number of ways. Hugh O' Donnell's hedge school, even before the opening of its state-funded rival, is an institution in decline. Pupils are drifting away. Hugh himself, with his Latin tags, his ponderous diction, his weakness for drink, is the object of some derision. Maire Chatach, the central female character, wants to learn English to prepare for her departure for America. The traditions behind the place names about to be obliterated by the Ordnance Survey are in any case fading from local memory (pp. 43-4). Most of all there is the character of Jimmy Jack Cassidy, 'the infant prodigy', whose obsession with his Greek texts provides a powerful symbol, not just of retreat from reality but also – in Jimmy Jack's use of these texts to feed the sexual fantasies of an aging bachelor – of impotence. But this takes us to the central problem. How is it that, despite such images, *Translations* has been widely read, by its critics and its admirers alike, as being precisely the play that Friel in his diary disclaims any desire to write: 'a play about Irish peasants being oppressed by English sappers', and a 'threnody on the death of the Irish language'?

The answer, it seems clear, lies in the conflicting messages that Friel builds into his text. The images of a dying culture are certainly there. But they are balanced at every stage by others of a very different kind. Jimmy Jack Cassidy may be both filthy and sexually frustrated: but there is nevertheless the careful note in the stage directions: 'He is fluent in Latin and Greek but is in no way pedantic – to him it is perfectly normal to speak these tongues' (p. 11). Maire Chatach and Owen O'Donnell may in their different ways articulate their sense of a cultural tradition in terminal decline. But their words are undercut by the mouths into which they are put. Maire's outburst about English is a pupil's rebellion, quickly crushed by Hugh's scorn and a diversionary sneer at the political and sexual opportunism of Daniel O'Connell, whom she had quoted in support of her claims. Owen O'Donnell is not quite an unsympathetic character, but he is a culturally maimed one, a symbol of the loss of values and cultural roots. His views are there to be rejected. By contrast Hugh O'Donnell, despite his moments of what we are carefully told should be seen as deliberate self-parody, is allowed a series of effortless verbal triumphs. A few of the local people, he reports himself as telling Captain Lancey, do speak English but 'outside the parish of course – and then usually for the purposes of commerce, a use to which his tongue seemed particularly suited' (p. 25). To Yolland, he cheerfully confesses an ignorance of Wordsworth: 'I'm afraid we're not familiar with your literature, Lieutenant. We feel closer to the warm Mediterranean. We tend to overlook your island' (p. 41).

Behind these encounters lies the in no way subtle contrast Friel draws between the cultural worlds represented by Hugh on the one hand and Lancey and Yolland on the other. The traditional culture of Ballybeg not only has its own language and mythology; it is also permeated by classical learning. The civilization that replaces it, by contrast, is crass, materialistic and uncultured. Of the two English speaking characters in the play, Lieutenant Yolland, the more sympathetic, is culturally as well as socially gauche, lost in simple-minded admiration for a culture so much richer than his own. His superior, Captain Lancey, is more self-confident, but if anything more culturally deprived. The main symbol of that deprivation is his total ignorance of the classical lore current among the peasants he seeks to patronise: addressed in Latin by Jimmy Jack Cassidy, he assumes the other is speaking Irish. Such ignorance, as already mentioned, is impossible to reconcile with the social and educational background from which British officers of the early nineteenth century would in reality have been drawn. Nor, in this case, is it easy to see how the departure from historical reality can be said to serve Friel's artistic purpose. On the contrary, it works against it. If the aim of the play is to present Hugh O'Donnell and the other inhabitants of Ballybeg as imprisoned in a dying culture, how is that purpose served by allowing him to score so many facile points? A culture dies because it ceases to make sense of the world in which its bearers live: or, as Friel (and Steiner) put it, because its linguistic contours cease to match the landscape of fact. But there is little real sense in *Translations* that this is what is happening. Instead the traditional culture of Ballybeg is presented as self-sufficient and organically complete: 'a consciousness', as Yolland puts it, 'that wasn't striving nor agitated, but at its ease and with its own conviction and assurance' (p. 40). Its downfall is a result of conquest, not of its loss of contact with reality.

All of these contradictions come together in the play's climax. Returning drunk from the funeral of the baby with whose birth the play began, Jimmy Jack Cassidy finally loses all hold on reality, announcing that he is to marry the goddess Athene. Hugh O'Donnell, on the other hand, agrees to start teaching Maire Chatach English, while he himself begins to study the new, anglicised place names in Owen's working papers: 'We must learn those new names. . . . We must learn where we live . . . . We must make them our new home' (p. 66). All this is consistent with Friel's declared theme, as is Hugh's warning to Maire that, although he can teach her the words and grammatical structures of English, he cannot guarantee that these will give her access to the cultural world that goes with them, that she will be able 'to interpret between privacies' (p. 67). Meanwhile, however, Lancey's soldiers have already begun their campaign of terror and destruction, trampling the corn and 'prodding every inch of the ground in front of them with their bayonets' (p. 57), as they search for the missing Yolland. And then comes Hugh's last speech: the tale of the ancient city of Carthage, loved above all others by the goddess Juno and intended by her to be the capital of all nations, but instead destroyed by a people 'kings of broad realms and proud in war' (p. 68). At a stroke – and these are the last words the audience hear, delivered twice as the curtain falls – we have moved once again from the obsolescence of a culture to its forcible destruction by superior military and political might.

How are these conflicting messages to be accounted for? One possible answer is suggested by the exchange, in 1983, between Friel and J. H. Andrews. Andrews, as a prologue to the subtle and sympathetic analysis of the play's historical dimension already summarised, identified as a feature that had given him particular initial difficulty the military reprisals that are in prospect when the action concludes. In reality, soldiers on survey duty would not have been armed with the bayonets referred to in the text, and Captain Lancey would never have contemplated launching, on his own authority, either house burnings, the slaughter of livestock or the eviction of another man's tenants. Friel, replying, took up the point:

I feel very lucky that I have been corrected only for using a few misplaced bayonets, and for suggesting that British soldiers might have been employed to evict peasants. I felt that I had merited more reprimands than that.[20]

This, of course, is a skilful distortion, behind a screen of disarming modesty, of Andrews's real point. But the tone is also suggestive. Friel may not have wished to write a play about 'Irish peasants being suppressed by English sappers'. But he clearly has little patience with the cavilling of historians who seem to imply that such oppression was not commonplace. Friel is of course right to insist that, for the creative writer, the imperatives of fiction must take precedence over those of historical accuracy. At the same time there are grounds for suggesting that he has not in fact freed himself from 'history' quite as fully as he would like to believe. 'Practical men', wrote John Maynard Keynes, 'who believe themselves to be quite exempt from any intellectual influence, are usually the slaves of some defunct economist.'[21] In this case, it might be argued, a practical playwright, consciously asserting the autonomy of his fiction, has nevertheless remained the prisoner of a particular image of the Irish past, an inherited folk history, in ways that actually work against his artistic purposes.

II

If a critique of the mythologising of the Irish past is – according to one interpretation at least – part of the purpose of *Translations,* it provides the central theme of *Making History.* Here Friel builds his story around two contrasting figures. Hugh O'Neill, an English-educated overlord in late Elizabethan Ulster, is a pragmatic survivor, acting out the traditional rôle of chief among his own people while at the same time avoiding an irrevocable breach with the English government and its local representatives. Eventually his stratagems fail; he is forced into a hopeless rebellion, defeated, and driven into exile. Peter Lombard, Catholic archbishop of Armagh, is Hugh O'Neill's biographer. His account, reflecting the spirit of the Counter Reformation and of an emergent Irish nationalism, recasts O'Neill's career as a heroic crusade for religion and fatherland. The play ends with O'Neill, now in Rome, confronting his biographer to protest at this glorification of a complex and in places unedifying reality. In reply Lombard argues that history can never be more than a version of the past, and that his version – an heroic legend – is what the Catholic people of Ireland need at this moment. In the end O'Neill, old, impoverished and drink-sodden, surrenders before his biographer's smooth self-assurance.

The programme notes to *Making History* include a short explanatory statement by Friel himself on the relationship between his fiction and the historical reality.

Making History is a dramatic fiction that uses some actual and some imagined events in the life of Hugh O'Neill to make a story. I have tried to be objective and faithful – after my artistic fashion – to the empirical method. But where there was tension between historical 'fact' and the imperative of the fiction, I'm glad to say I kept faith with the narrative. For example, even though Mabel, Hugh's wife, died in 1591, it suited my story to keep her alive for another ten years. Part of me regrets taking these occasional liberties. But then I remind myself that history and fiction are related and comparable forms of discourse and that an historical text is a kind of literary artifact. And then I am grateful that these regrets were never inhibiting.

Taken at face value, this may be read as an attempt to head off the sort of criticism directed at the handling of historical fact in *Translations*. Both tone and content are similar in many ways to those of Friel's earlier exchange with J. H. Andrews. We have the same mock contrition for the 'occasional liberties' taken with the facts, the same disingenuous attempt to reduce the issue to self-evidently trivial matters such as dating, and above all the same clear assertion that 'the imperatives of fiction' take precedence over considerations of historical accuracy. But the two cases are not in fact quite the same. In *Making History* the relationship between true and fictional versions of past events is no longer a side issue. It is now the central theme. For this reason it is worth looking a little more closely at what, on closer reading, emerge as some rather puzzling features of Friel's statement.

These concern what is in itself the relatively unimportant matter of chronology. The real Hugh O'Neill was born around 1550. During the 1570s and 80s he established himself, with the help of the Dublin government, as the most powerful figure in Ulster. He married his third wife, Mabel Bagenal, sister of the Queen's Marshall, in 1591. His aim throughout this period seems to have been to tap simultaneously into two sources of power: the English state, in which he was a peer and office holder, and the Gaelic tradition of Ulster, in which he was head of a powerful clan. In 1595, in response to the encroachments of central government on the one hand, and pressure from his fellow Gaelic lords on the other, he went into open rebellion, hoping for assistance from Spain and the papacy. When a Spanish invasion force eventually appeared in September 1601, O'Neill and his allies marched south to join it, but were decisively defeated at Kinsale on 24 December. O'Neill surrendered to government in 1603, left Ireland in 1607, and died in exile in 1616.

This outline may be set against the chronology offered in *Making History*. The play opens with O'Neill's marriage to Mabel Bagenal which is placed, correctly, in August 1591. In the next scene, 'almost a year' later, O'Neill, learning of a projected Spanish invasion, decides to risk all in open rebellion. Then, 'about eight months later', he is in hiding after the decisive defeat at Kinsale. So Friel has indeed taken 'liberties'. He has compressed the events of ten years, from 1591 to 1601, into somewhere under two. Nor could anyone other than the most blinkered pedant object to his doing this, in the interests of dramatic continuity. But there remain two problems. The first is Friel's programme note, with its apology for keeping Mabel Bagenal alive for ten years after her death in 1591. This would make sense if the battle of Kinsale had been presented as occurring, as in real life, in 1601. But in the play Kinsale has happened, and Mabel is dead, by Spring 1593. The second problem is that the real Mabel Bagenal died, not in 1591, or in 1601, but in 1595. Contradiction is piled on contradiction. One possibility is that there has been a mistake: a slip of the pen or a printer's error. But that, given the importance Friel evidently attaches to the whole matter, seems unlikely. The other possibility is that Friel has deliberately chosen to confuse the picture: partly, one assumes, to advertise even more clearly his liberation from the constraints of the historical record; partly, perhaps, to reinforce the play's satirical treatment of the pretensions of history, by means of a subtle practical joke at the expense of the hapless academic fact checker.

Chronology apart, how does Friel's Hugh O'Neill compare with what is known of the historical figure? Critical reaction to *Making History* has tended to start from the assumption that it offers a daring reassessment of patriotic legend. This is not in fact so. There is, in the first place, no radical new interpretation. Instead Friel follows very closely a book now almost half a century old: Sean O'Faolain's *The Great O'Neill*, first published in 1942. It was O'Faolain who first set out to demolish the myth of O'Neill as a dedicated patriot, returning from his education in England with no other thought but to prepare for the day when he could fling off the mask of loyalty and lead his people in a war of liberation. Instead he portrayed a supreme pragmatist, exploiting both English government and Gaelic tradition until events upset the equilibrium he had created. O'Faolain's book, in fact, provides not only the raw material for *Making History*, but also a clear outline of its theme, and even the suggestion that it should be written:

If anyone wished to make a study of the manner in which historical myths are created he might well take O'Neill as an example . . . a talented dramatist might write an informative, entertaining, ironical play on the theme of the living man helplessly watching his translation into a star in the face of all the facts that had reduced him to poverty, exile and defeat.

The play's final scene, in which a tipsy O'Neill rages helplessly against the falsification of his life enshrined in Lombard's history, is also based directly on an imagined episode sketched out in the last pages of O'Faolain's book.[22]

The critique of patriotic legend that some have detected in *Making History*, then, is not Friel's but O'Faolain's. In adapting the latter's material for the stage, moreover, Friel has to some extent softened its outlines. O'Faolain's Hugh O'Neill is presented as a man of wide vision, but also of primarily personal ambition. His aim was to establish himself as an 'Anglo-Gaelic earl', enjoying territorial ascendancy under the nominal authority of the crown. More recent historians have emphasised even more strongly the element of self-aggrandisement. They have also noted the extent to which O'Neill, far from being the last great champion of Gaelic Ireland, systematically promoted economic and cultural change within his territories in order to strengthen his own economic and military position.[23] Friel's O'Neill, by contrast, is a man with a largely selfless mission. He has tried, he explains to Mabel, to act as a buffer between the Gaelic population of Ulster and their English rulers, 'to hold together a harassed and a confused people by trying to keep them in touch with the life they knew before they were overrun', while at the same time trying 'to open these people to the strange new ways of Europe, to ease them into the new assessment of things' (p. 40). In other respects too Friel inches the picture of Elizabethan Ireland that he has derived from O'Faolain closer to, rather than further away from, the patriotic legend. O'Faolain presented the Gaelic civilization of the late sixteenth century as a 'decrepit and diseased antiquity'.[24] It was a fighting society but one without political vision. Wars were contests for territory and plunder. Chieftains were ready, for short term advantage, to aid the English state in destroying their fellow Gaels. More recent historians of Gaelic Ireland have similarly rejected the idea that even its intellectuals thought in terms of a national struggle between England and Ireland.[25] The Gaelic Ireland of *Making History*, as personified by Hugh O'Donnell, has its faults: rashness, indiscipline, and disunity. O'Neill complains of how, after his defeat at Kinsale, 'my brother Gaels . . . couldn't wait to strip me of every blade of grass I ever owned' (p. 66). Yet the underlying assumption is still that what was going on in the 1590s was understood by those involved as a national conflict between English and Irish.

None of this, of course, affects the validity of Friel's play. It is a work of fiction, and he has no need to be defensive about his departures from the historical record. The main weakness of *Translations*, it was suggested earlier, is its opposition between a wildly idealized Gaelic culture and an improbably debased and philistine English alternative. *Making History* is more restrained and even-handed. There are obvious links between the Gaelic culture portrayed in the two plays. O'Neill's

remark that 'it wasn't a life of material ease but it had its assurances
and it had its dignity' (p. 40) echoes, perhaps consciously, Yolland's
admiring comments in *Translations* (p. 40). Yet there is no attempt to
repeat the extravagant portrayal of a philhellenic Gaeldom. The new
English civilization, too, is this time given a fair hearing, as in the
scene where Mary Bagenal, Mabel's sister, contrasts the herb gardens,
orchards and reclaimed bog of her father's frontier estate in south
Ulster with the disorderly squalor beyond (pp. 20-23). If Friel's Hugh
O'Neill remains slightly green round the edges, his creator has
nevertheless moved far enough away from patriotic stereotype to give
credibility to his portrayal of a clash of cultures. (He has also, it seems
clear, done enough to alienate at least some sections of the audience
among whom *Translations* was most loudly acclaimed.[26]

What, finally, of the central theme of *Making History*: the critique of
the historian's function? The main thrust of Friel's argument is clear
enough. Confronted by O'Neill, Lombard admits that his biography
will be a 'narrative that has the elements of myth'. At the same time he
justifies the enterprise in terms of the needs of the audience for which
it is written:

Ireland is reduced as it has never been reduced before – we are talking
about a colonized people on the brink of extinction. This isn't the time for
a critical assessment of your 'ploys' and your 'disgraces' and your 'betrayal'
– that's the stuff of another history for another time. Now is the time for a
hero. Now is the time for a heroic literature (p. 67).

The historian, in other words, serves the cultural and political needs of
the society in which he lives. Here Friel is perhaps thinking less of the
seventeenth century than of his own day. The last twenty years or so
have seen a great deal of what has been termed 'revisionist' work in
Irish history. Economic historians have questioned both the uniformly
bleak picture painted of social conditions in earlier centuries, and the
extent to which poverty and underdevelopment were really the result
of oppression by landlord or state. Political historians have looked
more dispassionately both at the efforts of British government to cope
with the problems presented by Ireland, and at the real origins and
character of a range of movements, like Hugh O'Neill's revolt in the
1590s, that were formerly accepted simply as so many episodes in a
continuous struggle for national independence. To its supporters this
'revisionism' represents the belated professionalisation of the subject,
following decades in which enquiry was strangled by the combined
forces of intellectual isolation, an academic establishment starved of
funds, and a university appointments system dominated by political
and personal patronage.[27] To its opponents, on the other hand, it is a

political movement, by which establishment intellectuals have played their part in propping up a conservative status quo in Northern and southern Ireland alike. The debate has extended well beyond the ranks of professional historians. Even if it had not, the criticism directed at *Translations* – not all of it by any means as gently worded as the comments of J. H. Andrews – must have alerted Friel to the direction of much recent historical writing. Against this background it does not seem too far-fetched to suggest that Friel's attack on the pretensions of the historian has a contemporary relevance: that behind the ostensible satire on the patriotic myth-making of Lombard lies a comment on those modern historians who have in their turn rejected Lombard's myth, providing instead the 'other history for another time' to which the archbishop refers. Behind this again, of course, we may suspect a mild settling of scores with those who, in the name of the same revisionism, have criticised Friel's own earlier excursion into the Irish past.

If the basic theme of *Making History* is clear enough, its detailed working out is not entirely satisfactory. Archbishop Lombard, defending his handling of O'Neill's life, argues that all historical writing is 'a kind of story-telling . . . imposing a pattern on events that were mostly casual and haphazard and shaping them into a narrative that is logical and interesting' (p. 8). It follows that there is no one true history: only a range of possible interpretations that can be constructed from the available facts. For this theme to be followed through, however, it would be necessary to incorporate some sense of the 'casual and haphazard' into the reality against which Lombard's history is to be assessed. *Making History* does not really do this. Our image of Hugh O'Neill remains that which he himself outlines: a man caught between two opposing worlds, seeking to act as mediator between a defeated Gaelic culture and an advancing English civilization. O'Neill, in other words, does have a clearly defined history, and his complaint to Lombard, in the play's final scene, is that the archbishop has falsified this history, by omitting or glossing over certain portions of it. So we are back with the simpler proposition that historians commonly distort the past in order to serve the needs of the present. This is undeniable, but also rather obvious. Or at least it would need a more subtle illustration than the case of a Counter Reformation ecclesiastic engaged in the writing of an avowedly propagandist work. Friel's Lombard is allowed a degree of ironic self-knowledge, and through it a certain dignity. But in the end he is, like Captain Lancey in *Translations*, a purpose built target, permitting the scoring of numerous easy points, but less well suited to a proper development of the themes his creator has taken up.

FRIEL'S RUSSIA

RICHARD YORK

It is not surprising that Brian Friel's version of Chekhov's *Three Sisters* should have appeared soon after his *Aristocrats*. For the world of Friel's own imagination is very like that of the Russian writer, in many respects. His provincial Ireland resembles the provincial Russia of the nineteenth century, as it appears in Chekhov, with a disturbing closeness. There is the same emotional primacy of the family (a family dominated by a dead or dying father, and consisting of three sisters who long for significant life and of a brother who is reconciled to insignificance); there is the same sense of the apartness of the family, of its distinctiveness, its refinement and potential sensitivity, its capacity to profit from the missing fullness of life, and the same dissipation of its emotional energies in the activities of every day and in links with the simpler, more practical people of the surrounding community. There is the same sense of an 'elsewhere' which exercises pressure on the family's precarious seclusion and challenges its protectiveness. There is the alternation between the extrovert, active, hopeful characters who have knowledge of the world and confidence in its activities and those for whom indirectness and restraint are the normal modes of human contact. The personality structures of the characters within these worlds are akin: they have moments of half understood intensity, unformulated loves and hatreds that occasionally rise to consciousness and expression, often in a way disproportionate to the occasion; they have images of themselves, which involve fantasised images of their contact with others, and they are capable of a disturbing and often repressed recognition of their true isolation and frustration. The tension between image and truth makes for an ironic tenderness, half comic and half tragic, and for a sense that what makes the interest and drama of life is its inevitable limitations. The dramatic rhythms of the two playwrights are alike: they depict alike the desultoriness of conversation, the echoing recurrence of obsessive subjects, unpredictable moments of uninhibited expression, bleak anxious monologues. The whole tends towards a ceremonious self-display, in which private feeling and public sociability awkwardly mingle. There is, in both Chekhov and Friel, a dramaturgy of loss, of the wasted opportunity, of a confronting of inertia.

164

Friel, then, is a Chekhovian dramatist. The similarities are apparent not only in the works mentioned but also in, for instance, *Living Quarters*, with its three sisters and ineffective brother dominated by a military father eager to leave the provinces for the capital, or in *Translations*, where the gentle traditional world of Ballybeg is undermined by contact with the outer world, the more sophisticated and violent world of the military, of imposed political and cultural change, as well as by the real separateness and the various aspirations of its own members.

It is no surprise that Friel should have put his obvious sympathy for the Russian dramatist to the test by translating his work. Nor is it specially surprising that, after the clear theatrical success of *Three Sisters*, he should have gone on to adapt another nineteenth century Russian classic for the stage, namely Turgenev's *Fathers and Sons*. The challenge here is of course still greater: in addition to the translation from Russian to English, there is also the translation from novel to play, with the consequent need to communicate through purely dramatic means what is done in the novel by the narrator (and Friel has been meticulous in doing this: in other plays he actually approximates to narratorial comment, albeit sometimes ironically, with for instance the 'Sir' of *Living Quarters* or the academic commentators of *Aristocrats*, *The Freedom of the City* and *Making History*, but in *Fathers and Sons* there is no such quasi-authorial presence).

One should say here that Friel does not, apparently, produce his translations in the usual way by referring to the originals. His versions are in fact revisions or compilations of existing English translations. English here means, of course, almost entirely, British English. The implications of this process are very interesting and rather complicated. The spectator may come to the Friel works with no idea that there have been previous translations. In this (perhaps rare) case, he no doubt responds to them as new Irish plays about Russians; he will be struck by cultural similarity, by the sense that the two nations are alike sensitive to the hollowness and awkwardness of life, that, in short, there are general human experiences which are specially apparent in countries which have been marked by provinciality and by the exercise of remote power. Or he may come to them knowing that these versions are a riposte to the hegemony of British English, that when they lay claim to such depths of general humanity they do so in conflict with a previous approach; that they are a corrective to the assumption that truth speaks received standard English. And if he is aware of this polemic dimension, he will be aware of a curious paradox: these plays about inertia, about the acceptance of the status quo, are in fact acts, they do in fact attempt to change the cultural landscape; they can be seen as achieving a victory over cultural inertia.

How closely the audience is aware of the innovative force of the Friel translations will no doubt vary. One may guess that in *Three Sisters* there is for many spectators no more than an imprecise, generalised sense that this play is not quite what we're used to, that there is more animation and more specificness in it than we might expect from Chekhov. This sense should at least be sufficient to arouse in the audience an awareness that art is process and purpose in a context, that theatrical meaning comes into existence in the course of theatrical activity and is not flatly inherent in a text. In *Fathers and Sons* the changes are marked and immediately perceptible. Many of them were indeed commented on – often unfavourably – by the first reviewers, who for instance wanted Bazarov's death to be shown on the stage as it is directly narrated in the book, and objected to the suppression of this ready pathos. Here, then, the sense that the translator has actively intervened is inescapable. The first effect is a feeling that the actions depicted are oddly second-hand. Lively, even excessive as they may be, we are conscious that they are also an imitation of some remote, lost, nineteenth century Russian liveliness. The second effect is the feeling that the motivation of the translator's shaping of the text – since it produces stage actions which are intelligible, recognisable, normal – must lie in the world of translator and audience, rather than in that of author and characters; that the translator is saying to us, in essence, 'This is what Turgenev means – *for us, now*'.

And this can be seen in one of two ways. Friel's implicit claim may be seen as the establishment of a dialogue. Perhaps any good translation is – more or less openly – a dialogue between the translator, in his own moral, social, aesthetic world, and the author in his; perhaps any good theatrical performance or any good reading is a dialogue in some such way, and perhaps such dialogue is what gives life and relevance to the literature of the past. But Friel's claim can also be seen as a usurpation or exploitation, as an attempt to make use of Turgenev, to suppress those things in Turgenev that belong to the past and to another country, and to extract only those that talk to us of youthful radicalism and the continuity of the family, of the promise of renewal and the weight of tradition, of national hope and national hopelessness.

(A symptom of this ambiguity as between dialogue and exploitation lies in the fact that the plays have been performed in nineteenth century dress and décor, despite the frequent use of twentieth century terms in the characters' speech. This appears to lay claim to some loyalty to the period setting. But *could* the plays have been done in modern dress? Probably not, since the dialogue, the tension of past and present would have been lost, and this loss would have been regretted; but why exactly would it have been regrettable? what significance would have been lost?)

Undoubtedly, much of Friel's handling of the original texts does bear witness to a deep concern for fidelity to the originals, and to a close and productive familiarity with them. In *Three Sisters* this may appear unproblematic; it simply means that, to a very large extent (though not entirely), the speeches in the Friel version correspond one by one to the speeches of the Chekhov play. At most one might say that the temptation to expand or modify has been checked. But this is obviously not the case with *Fathers and Sons*, where the change in genre has necessitated quite major modifications. And yet one may be struck, beyond all the modifications, by the persistence of motifs and details, and in general by the extraordinarily adroit processes of condensation and reordering by which a novel of moderate length is reduced to a much shorter dramatic scope with minimal loss of texture.

Examples are easy to find. There is the green tea which Pavel Petrovich Kirsanov asks his brother Nikolay's mistress and housekeeper Fenichka to order for him from the city in chapter VIII of the novel. The detail neatly symbolises Pavel's fastidious tastes and his reliance on the practicality of the peasant woman Fenichka; the conversation gives him the chance to make some conversation about the son she has just borne to his brother, and this conversation very delicately hints at his own attraction towards her, masked as it is by the proprieties of family relationship. The tea is there in Friel: it appears in the very first scene (and may be more prominent than it is in the novel). It again reveals Pavel's aristocratic consumerism (now complicated by the foreignness of green tea) and the restrained master-servant relationship. But the conversation, as theatrical exposition requires, is much more open: the initial contact is more obviously embarrassed and hesitant, the baby is already on stage and therefore an inevitable subject of conversation, and Pavel actually tells Fenichka of her beauty, though phrasing his remarks in French so as to inform the audience of his feelings without informing their object. Friel's dramaturgy is an efficient, direct one; meaning is crowded into the scene, whereas it emerged gently and uncertainly from the Turgenev chapter.

This economy of communication is apparent throughout. In Turgenev, to take a second example, Nikolay recalls tenderly his dead wife's piano-playing, and also admires the musical skills of Katya, who is eventually to marry his son Arkady. In Friel we see Nikolay (there spelt Nikolai) and Katya playing a piano duet. The sympathy of the two characters, separated by age and background, but united in their concern for family affection rather than political passion, is dramatically shown, not left for the spectator to intuit; it is further contrasted with the unsteady relationships of the more intense characters, whose conversation occupies the foreground of the scene as Nikolay and Katya play. All in all, the music has become a focus of dramatic life. In Turgenev it is, largely, incidental: music is simply a normal accomplishment; in Friel it is the bearer of constant significance.

In places this dramatically effective condensation can prove thematically awkward. The clearest example lies in the turning point of the relationship between the central character, the radical Bazarov, and the woman he reluctantly falls in love with, Anna Sergeevna Odintsova. In chapter XVIII of the novel Bazarov declares his love for her and attempts to kiss her; she rejects his embraces, with signs of fear and agitation. Deeply disappointed, he leaves her house and goes to stay with his parents. He then leaves them and in chapter XXIII meets again Fenichka; he has a friendly, relaxed conversation with her, in the course of which he kisses her. She does not resist (she corresponds more nearly to one side of his character, she is more natural and direct than the self-conscious aristocrat Anna Sergeevna) – but they are observed by the jealous Pavel Petrovich, and this leads to the duel between him and Bazarov which dissolves the moderately agreeable society of the Kirsanov group. This has taken some forty pages of reading (say one fifth of the whole length of the novel) and some days of narrated time. In Friel all this happens in one scene (Act II, sc. i): rejected by Anna Sergeevna, Bazarov overhears a brief conversation between the young lovers Arkady and Katya (perhaps two minutes on stage) and then meets and kisses Fenichka; Pavel, on his incursion, immediately proposes the duel, which takes place offstage before the next scene. Turgenev's Bazarov is certainly brusque and business-like; he acts impulsively and efficaciously with little regard for formalities and little tolerance of delay; but his disappointment in Anna Sergeevna is nevertheless much less promptly put behind him than it is in Friel. Friel's characters rush on towards conclusions; in Turgenev – as in Chekhov – people avoid conclusions, events occur unpredictably, through chance and weariness, and not through the inexorable pressure of the rhythm of the stage.

Moreover, Friel's fidelity to his texts may at times seem strange in itself, since it often goes side by side with an incongruous modernisation or transplantation of them; it may seem to verge on parody, whether of the oddity of these old foreigners, or of the oddness of a modern dramatist reproducing those old characters. Some suspicion of parody may appear, for instance, with the retention of Russian cultural references in *Three Sisters* (to which many non-Russian cultural references have been disruptively added). Thus, in the first scene of

Chekhov's play, Chebutykhin complains of his own ignorance of the work of Dobrolyubov. Dobrolyubov being one of the best known literary critics and polemicists of nineteenth century Russia, the original audience – even if some members happened to share Chebutykhin's ignorance – could be expected to know what is deplorable about it. But it is not especially deplorable for a modern Irish audience to know nothing about Dobrolyubov (some people might even think that it shows a healthy freedom from pedantry). And Friel demonstrates the fact:

For example I see here that there is a critic called – (*Reads*) – Nickolai Dobrolyubov. Now there's an important-sounding name for you! But what Nickolai Dobrolyubov 'criticises' I'm afraid I don't know and I'm afraid I don't care.[1]

This dimension of strangeness grows more playful in *Fathers and Sons*. Thus the retention of the servant with his earring and his parti-coloured hair will inevitably suggest to a modern audience a quite incongruous punk; the addressing of a character by the absurd combination of 'Fenichka Fedosya' suggests mockery of foreign nomenclature as such; and – most insidiously of all – the 'black sherry', which in Turgenev is served to the young men by Bazarov's impecunious father and tastes like a mixture of copper and turpentine, is in the Friel version promised to them by the more sophisticated and properous Nikolay Petrovich as a means of 'dissipating'.

There is much fidelity to the originals, then, but perhaps it is, at least sometimes, an ironic fidelity. Because Friel does not just accept the vision of Chekhov or Turgenev; he rewrites, and the rewriting implies a coherent strategy. It reflects a number of persistent elements in Friel's own dramatic conceptions; from the emphasis of the Russians on the sheer separateness of people and on the ineluctability of change, we move in Friel to a sense of continuity, of community and of a lasting core of social identity, and thereby to a greater sense of assertive individualism, of open self-expression and interaction, or even of shared lamentation.

It is not only with *Fathers and Sons* that we move into a theatrical world, one in which social contact is made conspicuous; even in *Three Sisters*, we move to a world which, in a sense, is more fully and wholly theatrical than the world of Chekhov's play – and perhaps more Irish for that reason. The distinction is naturally more obvious with Turgenev. In his novel, much of the interest is in something that could hardly be shown concretely, theatrically, since it is negative in quality and so has to be left for the reader to recognise in the process of his reading: the gradual lapsing of contact, shown in the barely perceptible growing apart of Arkady and Bazarov, in the misunderstandings of Katya and Arkady, or of Bazarov and Anna Sergeevna – so that, for instance, Anna Sergeevna's visit to the dying Bazarov is not just moving but surprising, as a stoical reassertion of concern against the essential strangeness of the two characters. But in Friel the quarrels and disagreements do not come very close to apathy; connectedness may take the form of conflict, but it never lapses.

Friel's society is, accordingly, one marked by continuity, by redundancy and repetitions. There is constant communication, between the characters and between the stage and the audience, and the significance of this communication is readily recognisable because it involves so much recurrence of words, phrases, attitudes. The literature of Chekhov and Turgenev is, to a considerable extent, a literature of gaps; but it is in the persistence of sounds and words that much of Friel's dramatic effect lies.

His interest in music, very apparent in both these plays, as in many of his own creations, and most especially perhaps in the cello music of *Fathers and Sons*, makes for a continuity of tone. Whatever the vagaries of language, however unpredictable the things people may say, they are homogenised, to an extent, by the melancholy lyricism of the cello. But in any case, what they say is not always unpredictable; in Friel characters are constituted to quite a large degree by habit, and especially by habits of language. In *Three Sisters* a number of repeated phrases have been built in that have no antecedent in the work of Chekhov, as with Tusenbach's 'to coin a phrase' or his 'if I understand you correctly', or Irina's addressing Chebutykhin as 'dopey doctor' (in Russian, 'Ivan Romanich'), or Natasha's repetition, in her final triumph, of the ironic reproach of wearing 'distinctive' dress – a reproach addressed to her in the first act by Olga. In *Fathers and Sons* this goes even farther: there is Nikolay Petrovich's encouragement to 'dissipate', his reiterated wish to 'organise our lives', Vassily Ivanovich's heavy use of Latin phrases; there is the repeated joke of Nikolay's calling for the servant Piotr, who never answers in time – until the last act when he answers before he is called. As so often in Friel, this is a matter, in part at least, of dramatic craftsmanship; the audience can admire and appreciate the skill with which the sameness of the character is made perceptible.

Similarly repeated elements of dramatic interest may symbolise or encapsulate the relationships of characters, as with the litter of pups which forms a common interest for Katya and Arkady, and shows their likeness to each other in their innocent appreciation of the animal world, and whose growth does something to trace the passing of time in the play. These pups are Friel's invention; in Turgenev, Katya has a

Borzoi which is already fully grown and is alluded to only occasionally. The point that needs to be stressed here is not just that a substitution has been made; it is that the substitution is one that favours a
sense of permanence. It is the sameness of the characters that is made
manifest in such ways, or the continuous development of their relationship. Turgenev is much less confident that people and their
relationships can be unchanging or continuous; life and individuality
are, in his work, much more uncertain.

As is society. People in Friel live in a world of constant bustle;
people are always arriving and talking. And people include, very
prominently, servants. The change is somewhat apparent in *Three
Sisters*, where Anfisa and Ferapont get a little more prominence than
they do in Chekhov. So a speech of Anfisa's in Act I of Chekhov might
be literally translated like this:

Dear people, there's a colonel I don't know! He's already taken off his coat,
children, and is coming in here. Arinushka, you be polite and friendly. . .

Friel gives us this:

Colonel Somebody-or-Other has arrived. Never clapped eyes on him
before. He's taken off his coat if you don't mind and he's on his way
upstairs. Irina, you just behave yourself now, madam.[2]

Anfisa is certainly never discreet; but she seems rather more confident
in Friel that she is the star of the occasion. In this play, however, the
shift of emphasis is marginal. The rise in prominence of servants is
very much more marked in *Fathers and Sons*. The jokes there about
Piotr's idleness and vanity do arise from Turgenev, but are much
expanded in Friel; the expansion is still more marked with the surli-
ness of Prokofyich; and Dunyasha becomes quite a major character in
Friel, where her fascination with Bazarov and her acceptance of
marriage to the land-manager Adam contrast significantly with
Natasha's love for and marriage to Nikolay, whereas she appears only
occasionally in the novel: her attraction to Bazarov is sketched by
Turgenev but undeveloped, and her romance with Adam (himself
unnamed) has no foundation in the original. Two things can be said
here: Friel's picture of the relationship of masters and servants may be
accurate – for nineteenth century Ireland; certainly Somerville and
Ross, say, would largely support it. But in nineteenth century Russia,
even if these relationships were less formal than they might have been
in England at the time, the sense of hierarchy was obviously much
more strongly maintained. Secondly, what this implies is that Friel's
vision is of a total society; Turgenev's is of an aristocratic society –
which is framed by a peasant society. So it is that our vision of Friel's

Pavel is influenced by the frequent references to him, originating with Dunyasha, as a 'Tailor's Dummy'. We find out that this label is a simplification, that there is much more to him than his dandyism; but it is significant that our initial view is through the unsophisticated characters, whereas, in the novel, our first substantial impression of him comes from the detached – if modestly ironic – view of the narrator.

It is this concern for social unity that leads also to one of the major modifications in the play: Nikolay's ailing farm is restored by the energetic intervention of Anna Sergeevna. Her contact with Nikolay's family is in the novel extremely tangential, and hardly extends beyond the marriage of her sister to his son (after which she immediately departs for Moscow); in Friel marriage involves whole families, and leads to economic well-being as well as to social harmony. It also accounts for the grave and pathetic dignity of the final scenes of the play. Whereas the novel dies away with a summarising chapter recounting the later life of the surviving characters – and making it clear that they are really just surviving beyond their time of real excitement, the time of decision and conflict presented in the plot – the play ends with a celebratory farewell, in which speeches are made, truth is told, a new moral order declared and the family union finally celebrated as Nikolay and Katya join in song. In Friel people live together, consciously and proudly; in Turgenev, they live apart. Again, the effect is a deeply theatrical one; the society of Friel's Russia is a spectacle, one in which social communion is displayed and celebrated.

As people are more social, so they express themselves more openly. They are more explicit, more articulate about their motives. Feeling is closer to the surface; it does not have to penetrate hesitantly through a veil of restraint, but is there for immediate sharing. This extrovert disposition is very frequently apparent in the two works. It goes with a tendency to general lengthening of dialogue, as each interchange becomes, in Friel, more a matter of repeated demonstrations of continued contact. An instance is the account of the quarrel between Solyony and Tusenbach in Act IV of *Three Sisters*. A literal translation might be this:

IRINA: Ivan Romanich, darling, my dear, I am terribly disturbed. You were on the boulevard yesterday, tell me what happend there?
CHEBUTYKIN: What happened? nothing. Trifles. (*Reads newspaper*) It's all the same.

This is the Friel version:

IRINA: Dear, darling, dopey doctor –
CHEBUTYKIN: You haven't called me that in ages.

IRINA: I'm worried sick.
CHEBUTYKIN: My own little sweetheart, what is it?
IRINA: You were in town last night, weren't you?
CHEBUTYKIN: I was.
IRINA: What happened?
CHEBUTYKIN: What do you mean?
IRINA: Outside the theatre – there was a row of some sort.
CHEBUTYKIN: Was there?
IRINA: You know there was. Between the baron and Solyony.
CHEBUTYKIN: Oh, that.
IRINA: What happened?
CHEBUTYKIN: That was nothing. (*Opens his paper.*) Nothing. Hot air. Big
                words. Nothing. Nothing.[3]

There is increased dramatic tension, no doubt, as the audience is kept waiting to find out (from Kulygin's next speech) that a duel is planned. But there is also a conspicuous expression of a leisurely concern for making relationships manifest: they are manifest in expressions of anxiety, of affection, of insistence, delaying manoeuvres, indirect elicitations. Being together matters, not just sharing information.

The general terseness and practicality of Turgenev's Bazarov is very radically modified as a result of this shift towards a constant self-dramatising on the part of Friel's characters. One sign of this is the treatment of sexuality. Bazarov, in the novel, is no believer in romantic love – until he actually falls in love with Anna Sergeevna – and summarises his views succinctly in chapter VII:

And what about the mysterious relationships between man and woman? We physiologists know what these relationships are. You study the anatomy of the eye: why should you be captured, as you say, by an enigmatic gaze? All that's romanticism, nonsense, rubbish, art.

and he returns, fairly brutally, to the question in chapter XVII:

'If a woman pleases you,' he said, 'try and get some results. If you can't, well, don't worry, go somewhere else. The world's not that small.'

In Friel, this cynicism is open and hedonistic; and Bazarov energetic-ally seeks to enlist Arkady in enjoyment of it: there is the running joke about the list of women they would like to seduce, and there are 'Dr Bazarov's Principles Concerning the Proper Ordering of Relationships between Men and Women'. These are the principles just quoted from Turgenev, but announced in a very different spirit:

One. Romantic love is a fiction.
Two. There is nothing at all mysterious between the sexes. The relationship is quite simply physical.
Three. To believe that the relationship should be dressed up in the

trappings of chivalry is crazy. The troubadours were all lunatics.
Four. If you fancy a woman, any woman, always, always, try to make love
to her. If you want to dissipate, dissipate[4] (I,i).

This is showmanship; Friel's Bazarov is proud of his scepticism and
sees it as an entertainment, and as a weapon against the half-hearted
'dissipation' of the essentially respectable Nikolay Petrovich. He is
interesting – and he thinks himself interesting – because he has the
irresponsibility to treat sexuality as a subject of clowning (the view is
of course one very offensive to feminist spectators, since it treats
women as an object of clowning, too, and is excusable only in the light
of its later collapse); he has the self-possession of the person who needs
– so far – to take nothing seriously.

Characters in Friel, then, tend to assume simple and conspicuous
forms, readily grasped by the other characters and by the theatrical
audience: the camp Roddey, the brash Natasha, the naively admiring
Arkady. Each is more readily recognised and categorised than his or
her equivalent in the Russian, because each lives through a relatively
fixed projection of a self-image upon the surrounding circle.

And this leads, even in the more subtle and searching passages, to a
readiness to externalise what is alien to the original. This externalising
may amount to what appears to be a declaration of the themes of the
play, as in the comments of Pavel to Anna Sergeevna in *Fathers and
Sons*:

We all want to believe at least in the possibility of one great love. And
when we cannot achieve it – because it isn't achievable – we waste our lives
pursuing surrogates; at least those of us who are very foolish do[5] (II, iv).

This corresponds to no single speech in the novel, and it may be a little
surprising in view of the gentlemanliness and reticence of Turgenev's
Pavel; but it does summarise a crucial element of the whole work. The
effect is important. On one hand it is part of the density of the play;
things that emerge slowly and almost accidentally from the novel are
foregrounded in the play, which makes open the things that in the
novel are covert. The relation of the play to the audience is an
authoritative one: the audience's task is now to interpret the events it
has seen in the preceding scenes – and notably the death of Bazarov –
in the light of this general hypothesis. And on the other hand, this
explicitness is part of the closeness of the characters: two people who,
in the novel, never meet, here share their deepest thoughts.
Theatricality is intimacy – intimacy of characters, intimacy of play and
audience; it is an openness of experience.

The point is apparent in a different way in the farewells of Bazarov and Arkady. In Turgenev these are firm, and precise, if not without a certain rhetorical ostentation:

And now I'll repeat my farewell . . . because there's no point in deceiving ourselves: – we are saying goodbye for ever, and you yourself feel it. . . . You have behaved sensibly; you aren't made for our bitter, harsh, solitary existence. In you there is no toughness or wickedness. There is youthful boldness and youthful ardour; that's not enough for our work. Your type, the gentry, can't attain beyond noble humility or noble agitation, and that's a trifle. . .

The speech continues. But the corresponding section of the Friel version will suffice to illustrate a change of key:

BAZAROV: We won't be getting together again, Arkady. We both know that. We are saying goodbye now. From your point of view you're making all the sensible choices because instinctively you know you're not equipped for our harsh and bitter and lonely life.

ARKADY: Who the hell do you mean by 'our', Bazarov? I'm a Nihilist, too, remember?

BAZAROV: When you were a student. But your heart never really forsook the gentry and the public decencies and the acceptable decorum. Of course you have courage and of course you have your honest passion. But it's a gentleman's courage and a gentleman's passion. You are concerned about 'difficult issues' but you believe they are settled by rational, gentlemanly debate and if that doesn't work, by gentlemanly duels. But that's not how real change, radical change, is brought about, Arkady.[6]

There are two things to say about this. Firstly, the rhetoric of the original is appreciably strengthened and extended. The listing 'bitter, harsh, solitary' becomes, more emphatically, 'harsh and bitter and lonely' (the last term producing the alliteration 'lonely life'); the patterned phrase 'youthful boldness and youthful ardour' is itself abandoned but gives rise to the more conspicuous repetitions of *gentleman* and *gentlemanly*, *courage* and *passion*. Secondly, this is a rhetoric of provocation. It manifests the self-image of the speaker, his view of his own capacity as a judge, and his image of his hearer, his sense of his hearer's need to be instructed, and it challenges Arkady to admit Bazarov's rightness and authority. So it is full of marks of certainty: the hyperbole 'all the sensible choices'; the acutely chosen adjectives, which are partly derived from the original, but which become in the Friel version so frequent and insistent as to suggest a speaker who has, before speaking, categorised and defined his subject and the person he is addressing: 'harsh', 'bitter', 'lonely', 'public', 'acceptable', 'honest'; the self-confident antithetical form 'Of course . . . but . . .'; the masterly shifting of rhythm between concise statements of determination and more expansive expressions of complaint; the subdued metaphorical system of the verbs, 'equipped', 'forsaken'; the direct address by name; the reminder of the actual duel that has been fought in the play. Arkady is being shown what he is, in relationship to his class and in relationship to the uncompromising outsider Bazarov. Turgenev's Bazarov is, of course, doing essentially the same thing; but he is doing it without such a display of profound and decisive moral categorisation, and so without any implicit claim to be an interesting character meriting attention and respect because of his clarity of moral-political vision. His manner is precise, informative, conclusive, perhaps regretful: he is repressing, as he admits, his 'romanticism'. Friel's Bazarov has his own sort of romanticism, which expresses itself precisely in this ostentatious challenge. And the challenge is addressed to the audience as well: the spectator has to decide how he feels about the outsider, how far he himself belongs to the restrained, intellectual, sensitive, passive sort of people who sometimes form the audience of plays, and how far to the brash, decisive kind – the Bazarov kind – who sometimes appear on the stage.

In *Bazarov* challenge is made spectacle. And this is nothing new in Friel. In his original plays there are a whole series of characters who challenge the decencies, the inhibitions and masks of Irish society: the wits, the jokers, the rebels, the voices of an uncomfortable, sometimes vulnerable, very self-conscious truthfulness that is in search of acceptance by an uncomprehending traditionalist society: Keeney in *Volunteers*, Skinner in *The Freedom of the City*, Eamon in *Aristocrats*. Ireland, it seems, for Friel, is a strange compound of uneasy refinement and anxious aggressiveness. Friel's Irish people live close to each other, and are forced into self-knowledge by the theatrical quality of their intimacy. And this, one may well feel, is a genuine part of Friel's fidelity to his own society, of his love for the Irish nation, which he perceives as a nation in which personal contact is strong, vital, intense, demanding, and above all as a nation where speech matters. Ireland, it seems fair to say, is a verbal country: it is one where speech is esteemed for its ingenuity, self-confidence, originality, for the physical presence it manifests, and for the direct, dynamic human contact it ensures; and this Irish love of speech has been imported into Brian Friel's translations.

But there is a certain strain involved in this importation. The Irish ease and enjoyment of speech does not quite fit into the character of Russia as we see it in Turgenev and Chekhov (it is much more nearly part of the character of Dostoevskii's Russia); for them, truth comes from a recognition of the limits of human contact, from disappointment and arrests of action. Perhaps Friel's Russia, in essence, is Friel's Ireland. But for the spectator there remains an awareness of the difference of the two countries, as well as of their similarities, a recognition of the gap between Turgenev's melancholy and Friel's melancholy; and with that recognition goes a sense of the boldness, even the desperation of Friel's attempt to make a Russia of his own.

STAGING FRIEL

JOE DOWLING

'Words are signals, counters . . .' Hugh Mor O'Donnell reminds us in one of Friel's most accomplished plays, *Translations*. This is a useful starting point in looking at the staging of any writer, particularly a playwright for whom language has always been used to convey the emotional landscape of the play. For the actor working in Friel, language is a vital consideration and the most important way for signals to be conveyed to the audience. In discussing any dramatist, it is important to remember how incomplete the work is until it is performed on stage by actors. The value of any piece for the theatre cannot be assessed fully until the skill of the actor is used to explore the sub-text and reveal the emotional truth behind the surface dialogue.

Themes and ideas may be analysed and dissected by an academic study of the text, but the essence of all drama lies in whatever emotional response can be created by the interaction between actor and audience in the theatre. Some texts, which on the page can seem trite and superficial, in the hands of skilled actors have a depth and meaning which even the writer only hints at. For the actor to realize the full value of a character, it is essential to go beyond the language of the text and delve into the sub-text. Guided by the director's overall vision of the production, the actor must explore aspects of the characters' life which do not appear as part of the text. Together, the actor and director can uncover the unspoken thoughts which help to identify the imaginative life of the rôle. Exploration of this kind can take the actor into difficult areas of his own personality and psyche. Through the work of rehearsal, the actor must find parallels with his own experience which provide a common thread of understanding with the character he is playing.

The work of rehearsal is devoted to the careful piecing together of the text and the world behind the play. Essentially, whatever the complexities of form and theatrical style, the function of the writer in the theatre is to tell a story, to weave the imaginative narrative fabric which actors can then stitch together into a multi-coloured quilt. A writer without interpreters can only tell half the story. Great theatre is created from a lively combination of the author's imaginative world and the actor's emotional discovery. Very often, plays which on first reading seem uninspiring can, in the hands of good actors and a sensitive director, turn into vibrant and exciting theatrical events. Similarly, a fine play can be destroyed by the failure to convey its real quality in performance. The history of the theatre is littered with plays which needed to be rescued from their first disastrous productions.

Brian Friel is a writer whose work always demands a particular quality of acting and direction. With each new Friel play, the director and actor are presented with major challenges of staging, of characterisation and often of language and its theatrical possibilities. The staging difficulties usually relate to a correct balance between realism and an instinctive theatricality which is part of each play, no matter how naturalistic the basic story. The characterisation must always be based on a sense of reality and truth. The language is often heightened to a point where the actor must find a way of making the poetic vocabulary seem real without losing the rhythm.

A typical example of this stylistic and linguistic balancing act occurs in *Translations*, perhaps Friel's most complex play. There is a real challenge of interpretation for the actor playing the character of Yolland, the young British soldier whose enchantment with Ireland and with the local girl Maire leads to such tragic results. He speaks of his first impression of Ballybeg and the society which the Hedge School represents:

It wasn't an awareness of *direction* being changed but of experience being of a totally different order. I had moved into a consciousness that wasn't striving nor agitated, but at its ease and with its own conviction and assurance. (*SP* 416)

The language used here is more literary than conversational and the actor must find the correct way to present it so that the enthusiasm of the young man and his fascination with the place and the people is palpable and at the same time not lose the structures of the sentences and the stylistic integrity of the language.

The great value of Friel's language is that it is always possible for the actor to find the correct imagery behind the line. In this case, there is a sharp contrast with the world which Yolland's father expected for him. A world of exciting possibilities, a new world. His father was born on the day the Bastille fell:

I've often thought maybe that gave his whole life its character. Do you think it could? He inherited a new world the day he was born – The Year One. Ancient time was at an end. The world had cast off its old skin. There were no longer any frontiers to man's potential. Possibilities were endless and exciting. . . . I'm afraid I'm a great disappointment to him.

Taking this expectation of dynamic achievement with Yolland's own desire for a quieter energy, one can immediately see how the archaic world of Ballybeg would appeal to him and make him feel at ease with himself and with his surroundings. The clear contrast between the forceful language of this speech and the fluidity and poetic flow of the description of Ballybeg gives the actor the clue to the delivery. There is always a sub-text to be found and a context for the attitudes in each scene. No matter how formal the language, there will always be a psychological root to the character and the situation which allows the actor a clear direction as to its meaning.

Friel is an exceptionally fine storyteller who uses the characters and their place in his carefully structured image of society to advance his narrative. The world of his plays unfolds gradually and without obvious force. Where violent actions occur, as they do often in his work, they are used as an indication of the brutality of the world surrounding the play. The savagery and almost inevitable violence of *The Gentle Island* comes as a shock and is used in ironic counterpoint to the physical beauty of the island. The same effect is used in *Translations*, where a stranger becomes enchanted with the atmosphere of the Donegal countryside without ever realizing the depth and the intensity of his isolation from the community. The death of Frank Hardy in *Faith Healer* is a similar shock and happens at the hands of people who are strangers to him and who seem at first glance to be unlikely murderers. Frank describes their first appearance:

When we came downstairs to the lounge in the pub we got caught up in the remnants of a wedding party – four young men, locals, small farmers, whose friend had just gone off on his honeymoon a few hours earlier. Good suits. White carnations. Dark, angular faces. Thick fingers and black nails. (*SP* 339)

Within a few lines, Friel creates a whole picture of the men who later demand Frank's life in return for the inevitable failure of his healing gift. This counterpoint between the simplicity of the situation, the ordinary nature of the people and the effects of extreme violence, gives *Faith Healer* a heightened theatricality which makes it attractive to audiences and triumphs over the unconventional nature of the monologue structure. In the majority of the plays, however, it is the unspoken things, the silences, the misunderstandings, the deliberate confusions and the tricks of memory which tell us the stories and maintain the narrative drive.

For the actor and the director, it is the minutiae of the work which provide its most important exploration. The actor must always delve behind the line, examine the sub-text and then accurately reproduce the sound of the character as Friel has written it. His ear for dialogue is uncannily accurate and the actor will find that the speech of the character will always feel right on the tongue. Witness the girlish chatter of Mags in *Lovers*, with her references to nuns ('screams if you don't take them seriously') and the other details of her crowded young life such as the concern for the baby she is carrying:

I think now, Joe, it's going to be nineteen days overdue. And in desperation they'll bring me into the hospital and put me on the treadmill – that's a new yoke they have to bring on labour; Joan told me about it. An aunt of a second cousin of hers was on it non stop for thirteen hours. They keep you climbing up this big wheel that keeps giving away under you. Just like the slaves in olden times. And after the baby's born they'll keep it in an oxygen tent for a fortnight. And when we get it home it'll have to be fed with an eye dropper every forty-nine minutes and we'll get no sleep at all and –[1]

This breathless and fervent imagination contrasts with the formality of language and the bleakness of imagery in the final monologue of *Faith Healer* where Frank Hardy goes out to a willing death

And although I knew that nothing was going to happen, nothing at all, I walked across the yard towards them. And as I walked I became possessed of a strange and trembling intimation: that the whole corporeal world – the cobbles, the trees, the sky, those four malign implements – somehow they had shed their physical reality and had become mere imaginings, and that in all existence there was only myself and the wedding guests. And that intimation in turn gave way to a stronger sense: that even we had ceased to be physical and existed only in spirit, only in the need we had for each other.(*SP* 375–6)

Friel has a remarkable capacity to convey dialogue which actors can speak with ease and which yet provides a sense of beauty and round-ness. The rhythms of speech are not only created to carefully indicate the meaning of the speech but also to convey the essence of the charac-ter. Each character is given the right level of articulateness and just the right vocabulary to illustrate social and educational background.

Lily in *The Freedom of the City* speaks with a different flow and a different vocabulary to Hugh O'Neill in *Making History*. Lily's world is described with a colloquial ease which immediately sets her social status for both actor and audience:

D'you see our place? At this minute Mickey Teague, the milkman, is shouting up from the road, 'I know you're there, Lily Doherty. Come down and pay me for the six weeks you owe me.' And the chairman's sitting at the fire like a wee thin saint with his finger in his mouth and the comics up to his nose and hoping to God I'll remember to bring him home five fags. And below us Celia Cunningham's about half-full now and crying about the sweepstake ticket she bought and lost when she was fifteen. And above us Dickie Devine's groping under the bed for his trombone and he doesn't know yet that Annie pawned it on Wednesday for the wanes' bus fares and he's going to beat the tar out of her when she tells him. (*SP* 141)

The world of the Earl of Tyrone is somewhat different and is expressed in a language so far removed from Lily's patois:

O'NEILL: Do I grasp the Queen's Marshal's hand? – using Our Henry as a symbol of the new order which every aristocratic instinct in my body disdains but which my intelligence comprehends and indeed grudgingly respects – because as a boy I spent nine years in England where I was nursed at the very wellspring of that new order – think of all those formative years in the splendid homes of Leicester and Sidney and indeed at the Court itself – hence the grand accent, Mary –
MABEL: Hugh, I think –
O'NEILL: No – allow me – or – or do I grip the hand of the Fermanagh rebel and thereby bear public and imprudent witness to a way of life that my blood comprehends and indeed loves and that is as old as the Book of Ruth. My dilemma. Help me, Mary. Which hand do I grasp? Because either way I make an enemy. . . .[2]

Yet both characters speak with conversational ease and in a way which at once provides the exact context for the character. By following both the intelligence of the speech and the traits of language, of phraseology, and even the punctuation, the actor and director can easily find the character. The next step is to reproduce it with the same accuracy as it appears on the page. In Friel's work, there is never a word astray and if the actor finds the line hard to say, it is usually because he has not analyzed the sub-text of the speech. Such examination must be conducted with a fine-tooth comb as clues to the character can be found throughout the text.

There is no consistency of theatrical style or a defined approach to language and characterization which a director and actors can fall back on. From the device of the two Gars in *Philadelphia, Here I Come!*, where both actors must be aware of the thinking of the other if the performances are to have a necessary unity of character, through to the equally innovative monologues in *Faith Healer*, where the actors must believe diametrically opposed accounts of the same events, Friel always makes enormous demands of the actor. The stylistic devices force him to find new ways of expressing the character and frequently demand a detailed offstage life which must be understood and imaginatively explored. Essentially, Friel is a master story teller and the rôle of the director and actors is to convey that narrative in as direct a way as possible for the audience. Any deviations from what is implicit in the text can do great harm to the intentions of the author.

Directors who see Friel's work as a way of making their own theatrical statements without taking very careful note of the nuances of the text will inevitably do considerable damage to the concise and accurate theatrical imagination which is always evident. It is vital for the director to approach the text of any Friel play with scrupulous attention to detail. The way of producing the play is always to be found within the work itself. It rarely requires extraneous production ideas. The director has to listen to the music of the text. The actor can often find the clues to the characterisation in the dialogue, not only of his own character but that of others. Friel's characters are always rooted in a detailed psychological reality, and however heightened the language may be, it is ultimately in that area of emotional truth that the impact will be made on an audience.

Actors can sometimes find this textual orthodoxy constricting as they must restrain their own creativity and become interpreters of the music of the text rather than the inventor of fresh new ideas. The rôle of an actor in a Friel play is analogous to the members of an orchestra who respond to the music of a symphony. The director is the conductor and is responsible for the accuracy of the sound on the stage. In Friel's work, there is no room for sloppy intentions on the director's part. If the whole piece is to have an accurate resonance, the value of each line must be understood and realised as the author intended. The main thing the actor can rely on is that Friel will have a particular sound in his head in writing the line and if that is found, the line will be correct.

In *Philadelphia, Here I Come!*, we find out the details of Gar O'Donnell's life largely from the information given by his private self. On the surface, he seems a quiet, almost reticent man of 'average' intelligence, as his old schoolmaster reminds him. However, if we listen to the cynical, sensitive and at times bitter commentary of the private persona, we can appreciate a depth of feeling which the public man cannot express. This must affect the way the actor approaches the character of the Public Gar. While we focus particularly on the evidence of the private self, another witness who can indicate his personality is Madge the faithful housekeeper who has been a mother substitute for the young Gar in that house of silence, of things unspoken. If the actor playing Public only listens to the evidence of his more extroverted Private self, he will miss out on a whole aspect of the character which Madge reveals.

When the boss was his age, he was the very same as him: leppin, and eejitin' about and actin' the clown; as like as two peas. And when he's the age the boss is now, he'll turn out just the same. (*SP* 98)

With this information, the actor now knows that the silent and unloving father, whom Gar thinks of as 'Screwballs' once had the same energy and vitality which his character displays. He must now seek points of similarity with the character of the father and areas of the text where the truth of Madge's words can be conveyed. Similarly, the actor playing S. B. O'Donnell also has a sub-text which informs his actions. While the body may be old and the memories different, there still exists somewhere inside him, the young man so lovingly described by Madge. All the way through the play, there are similar hints for the actor and it is only by listening carefully to the text that they can be found and applied.

In *Aristocrats*, the character of Casimir is revealed to us slowly and carefully and his real eccentricities are not obvious from the start. Friel is quite emphatic about this in the stage directions when he first appears:

One immediately gets a sense that there is something different about him – as he says himself, 'peculiar'. But what it is, is elusive: partly his shyness, partly his physical movements, particularly the way he walks – rapid, jerky, without ease or grace – partly his erratic enthusiasm, partly his habit of suddenly grinning and giving a mirthless 'ha-ha' at unlikely times, usually when he is distressed. But he is not a buffoon, nor is he 'disturbed'. He is a perfectly normal man with distinctive and perhaps slightly exaggerated mannerisms. (*SP* 255)

Casimir is not an idiot and the temptation for the actor to play the obvious comedy in the opening scene must be very carefully avoided. The director must maintain a discipline in that first scene and allow the details to emerge slowly and effortlessly. Often, an inexperienced director will want to rush the pace and get to the heart of the action quickly. That is a terrible mistake and completely unbalances the play. For the first twenty minutes he is on stage, we know that something is astray but we are not sure what it is. Casimir talks of the delights of Ballybeg Hall where, for him, the sun always shines, the doors and windows are always open and music is a constant companion. It is essential that the actor does not play the complete character in the opening scene. He must persuade us that his memories are accurate and that his recollection of the many distinguished visitors to the Hall is also true. Friel destroys our first impressions of the character when he introduces the father's voice on the baby alarm. This gives us a more telling image of the damage caused to Casimir's confidence and personality than all the enthusiastic protestations of an idyllic childhood.

Finally, it is Alice who reveals the truth behind Casimir's present bleak situation:

Began law in the family tradition but always hated books. So he left home – went to England – worked at various 'genteel' jobs. Then he met Helga and she took him off to Germany. I think he works part-time in a food-processing factory – I don't want to ask him; Helga's the real bread-winner: she's a cashier in a bowling alley. (*SP* 271–2)

Eamon casts further doubt on Casimir's veracity when he questions even the existence of Helga and the children '– all a fiction, all a game'. Suddenly the audience's perception of Casimir changes significantly and gradually the actor can present the whole figure. The actor knows all the strands of the character in advance but can only allow them to emerge piecemeal so that the author's intention in the stage direction is realised. The first real indication of the depth of the childhood trauma is given at the end of Act One when he reacts so desperately to the voice of the father on the baby alarm. The dramatic effect of that moment will be destroyed if the character seems eccentric or perse-cuted. The skill of the actor and the responsibility of the director is to allow that frightened, damaged personality to slowly emerge so that the impact of his 'great discovery' in Act Three can be as significant for the audience as for Eamon.

In Friel's work, for an actor, there must be more than what Stanis-lavski describes as 'the shallow physical life of the role'. An inner life which takes us behind the language and into the soul of the character must be created and sustained throughout the performance. The actor and director must find that life within the text and then work out-wards. Friel's work, which has so often been compared with Chekhov, demands an application of the artistic principles of the great Russian teacher and director, Constantin Stanislavski whose collaborations with Chekhov created a new awareness of the strengh of emotional naturalism in the theatre. It was he who first identified the need for an actor to work from the inside of a character out to the external details. He demanded that actors should find an inner life for the characters, a sense of a life separate from the immediate world of the play. Perfor-mances should not start simply at the moment the actor walks on the stage. The actor must be familiar with the daily routine of the character's life as much as with his deeper psychological realities.

With a new approach to the reality behind the character's life, Stanislavski swept away the whole artificiality of 19th century acting where gesture and attitude were used as a substitute for truth and emotional directness in the actor's repertoire. He laid the foundation for the theatrical realism which we have come to take for granted in modern theatre and which also influenced the development of the cinema. This search for honesty demanded a sense of the spiritual meaning which motivated the characters as well as the more obvious material functions which affected the surface of the text. For Stanislavski, the aim of acting was the creation of the human spirit in artistic terms. This the actor could do only if he fully absorbed the inner life of the character and, in imaginative terms, understood the internal drives and motivations which dictate the action of the play. To this end he created a series of exercises and games which allow the actor to explore his own attitudes and reactions and to apply them to the character he is playing. This use of an emotional memory allows the actor to find parallel feelings and emotional responses in his own personal experience which can then be made to apply to the work of the writer.

As Stanislavski outlines in his seminal work, *An Actor Prepares*:

Our whole creative experiences are vivid and full in direct proportion to the power, keenness and exactness of our memory. . . Sometimes impressions once received continue to live in us, grow and become deeper. They even stimulate new processes and either fill out unfinished details or else suggest altogether new ones.[3]

Memory is often a theme in Friel's work, whether the false memories which trick the mind and shape present bitterness, or the shared memories which bind families in an endless repetition of the past. Gar O'Donnell remembers the blue boat with its paint peeling and the simple gesture of fatherly concern in placing a coat around his shoulders as protection against the rain. S.B. has no such recollection and can only piece together the bare facts of the boat colour and the pleasure of the fishing. Similarly, he can remember the sailor suit worn by a chatty child on his way to school, hand in hand with an adoring father. Madge, the centre of their lives and their emotional go-between, knows that no such suit existed.

Memory is used here to serve the particular emotional recall. If the actor wishes to fully realise the character of Gar or the father, he must decide on a particular memory from his own experience, a parallel situation which may not link directly with the play but will be sufficiently strong to allow a similar emotional response. By such a juxtaposition of emotional memory, the actor can convey the depth of feeling implicit in the scene. So often the memories of the characters in the plays are presented in graphic detail or have an ambiguity which leaves the audience unsure of the exact truth behind them. To play that ambiguity, the actor needs to believe the text fully and allow it to speak directly to the audience without frills and intrusions. The plays demand a discipline and a honing of the emotional truth to fully engage an audience's attention.

Technical problems rarely occur in Friel's work. With the exception of *The Freedom of the City*, his plays usually demand only one setting or a composite set which allows for few scene changes. In *Translations*, where the famous 'love scene' takes place in a field near the school, he suggests in the stage directions that it 'may be played in the schoolroom, but it would be preferable to lose – by lighting – as much of the schoolroom as possible, and to play the scene down front in a vaguely "outside" area.' (*SP* 426) This lack of concern for the visual environment is typical of a writer who creates mainly through the language and the characterisation rather than through extraneous theatrical effects.

In spite of his early apprenticeship with Tyrone Guthrie, one of the most innovative and visually exciting directors of this century, Friel never really developed a sense of the possibilities of stage design as a way of expressing the imagery of his plays. He is usually very literal in his demands for the physical environment, describing in detail exactly the type of setting he requires. This rarely allows for an imaginative approach from the designer and demands a clear naturalism – even in plays which have a more expressionistic possibility. His most recent play, *Dancing at Lughnasa*, is an example of the potential of modern stage design to illuminate a script and to provide an audience with a range of signals which can add to the pleasure of the evening in the theatre. The play contains some of the most exciting visual and theatrical possibilities in the frenzied dancing of the sisters and the continual hints of pagan ritual and African customs. However, the stage directions demand a detailed realism against which the domestic ordinariness of the sisters' lives and the exotic activity described by Fr Jack's memories are seen in contrast.

Essentially, the plays demand productions which concentrate on the performances without much emphasis on the externals. Directors who ignore this reality about Friel can do untold damage to the integrity of the work without adding anything substantial in its place. On the other hand, modern theatre demands a visual awareness and a sense of the set as more than a mere backdrop to the actors. Striking the balance between Friel's demands and the expectations of the audience in contemporary theatre creates the biggest challenge to the director and the designer. Without making statements, they must reflect the essence of the piece and widen the possibilities for the audience.

Friel is not only one of the most significant voices in contemporary Irish theatre, he is also one of the most important writers on the world's stage. With his constant exploration of both form and theme, he is one of the most innovative theatrical writers in the English speaking theatre without ever falling into the murky territory of the 'experimental'. While many contemporary writers eschew the use of narrative and find contact with their audience by use of disconnected images and intense physical activity, Friel has never abandoned the central rôle as storyteller. His methods of telling the story may change with each new work, but the starting point is always rooted in a naturalistic reality.

While many lesser writers make obfuscation a virtue and confuse their audiences with contradictory signals, Friel is always clear in both meaning and form. He writes to communicate with the audience rather than alienating them and holding them at bay. Few playwrights working in the contemporary theatre can match the elegance of his language, the breadth of his vision and the remarkable understanding of the emotional power of the theatre which he brings to each character he creates. It is this capacity to create such wonderful, rounded and complete characters which makes his work so popular with actors. In theatrical terms, he is an 'actor's writer' rather than one who can be manipulated by a director's vision. This means that his writing does not fit into a modern concept of Director's Theatre where the director sees himself as co-creator of the dramatic piece. With so much of the modern theatre, critics place as much emphasis on the 'concept' behind the production as on the value of the text. With the majority of Friel's work, such a conceptual approach in the production would seriously affect the integrity of the author's intentions.

This is not to suggest that a director is not an essential ingredient in every production. Rather it affirms the crucial and delicate nature of the relationship between writer and director. Without a strong director shaping each scene, finding the correct pace and rhythm for each character, dictating a sense of momentum which the play requires, the plays may not realise their potential. Actors cannot find that objective realisation of a scene without the careful and intelligent reading of the text by a director who respects the text. It is not always essential to see the hand of the director in an obvious way in a production, but it must always be there and it must have a strong influence on each element of the performance. The directorial function is to draw the best from all the elements – actors, designers, technical crew, in order to fully realise the intentions of the text. To play the music of the text as clearly as the writer has composed it must always be the overriding objective of any production of a Friel play. Extraneous production ideas, novel and unnecessary bits of theatrical 'business', bizarre settings and costumes have no place in the performance. Just as the writing is always disciplined and controlled, so the production must be solidly based on the evidence of the text and the imaginative power of the actors.

As Friel's work develops, the demands on the directors and actors will change. The evidence of his most recent play, *Dancing at Lughnasa*, suggests a more theatrically expansive framework which must be filled with a non-naturalistic detail. However, the essence of the work remains emotional and human and these features will continue to be the strengths of this unique Irish writer.

'HAVE WE A CONTEXT?': TRANSITION, SELF AND SOCIETY IN THE THEATRE OF BRIAN FRIEL

TERENCE BROWN

Brian Friel's drama has always attended to precise social moments in the history of the Irish people. And his imagination has repeatedly been drawn to those phases in Irish social experience that can be reckoned as transitional. His earliest success achieved in *Philadelphia, Here I Come!* (first performed at the Gaiety Theatre, Dublin in 1964) accordingly took as its ostensible subject Irish emigration as social fate, at the very moment when altering economic conditions and communications were to make the act of departure from the native place altogether less absolute and definitive than they had traditionally been. Ten years later Gar O'Donnell would have had the chance of university in Galway, Dublin or Coleraine (to which many Donegal students flocked in the 1970s) and twenty years later he would have lobbied for a Green Card and spent his summers in Ireland reckoning Boston to Shannon a comparatively inexpensive, short flight. *The Loves of Cass McGuire* (first performed in New York at Helen Hayes Theatre in 1966) also caught a poignant moment of transition in Irish/Irish American relations focussing at just that point in social history when an economically resurgent country, with its eyes on membership of the European Community, was beginning to recover from its infatuation with all things American (that infatuation reaching hysterical proportions during John Kennedy's all too brief Presidency and a kind of orgasmic intensity during his visit to the land of his forbears in 1963). Poor Cass McGuire, vulgar, ebullient, every bit the returned Yank in 1966, finds her family well able to do without the money she has faithfully despatched to them during her impoverished years in New York. 'We never really needed it' her brother informs her in a cruel kindness which lets her (and a whole generation of Irish American exiles) know, that they don't really need *her* either.

It was in 1970 however that Friel himself made clear that he thought of himself as a socially conscious artist in a transitional society, drawing explicit attention to what had only been implicit in his earlier work, even if the dramatic power of his early successes came rather more from their ability to explore emotional ramifications of social fact than from their analytic presentation of a social dimension. In that year Friel expressed the ambition 'to write a play that would capture the peculiar spiritual, and indeed material, flux that this country is in at the moment. This has got to be done, for me anyway, and I think it has got to be done at a local, parochial level, and hopefully this will have meaning for other people in other countries'.[1]

Within two years grim events across the Donegal border with County Derry and Northern Ireland gave him ample opportunity to dramatise a society in flux by focussing on the inhabitants of a particular district, the Bogside in Derry, as its inhabitants were caught up in the waves of a violent political crisis. *The Freedom of the City* (first produced in the Abbey Theatre in 1973) represents Friel's most explicitly social drama of that troubled decade, as it addresses the dilemma of the citizen when he or she is confronted by the manipulative power of the state to mould a disintegrating reality to its own purposes. That play, in which we see the actual lives of three victims of violent political repression denied any social significance by a state which must define them as legitimate targets of its claim to exercise control in a society undergoing revolutionary transition, is Friel's most damning indictment of contemporary society. But its stark theme does in fact alert us to a dominant feature of his work as a whole – that is the inability of his characters to express themselves as social beings in any context other than the family or the local community. In *The Freedom of the City* we see indeed the local, distinctive identities of three Derry citizens, who as such might be expected to enjoy the rights of civic space, denied any mode of self expression in a political system which finally takes their lives, reputation and very individuality. 'I must', the judge at the play's end announces as he gives the State's judgement on its own actions, 'accept the evidence of eye-witnesses and various technical witnesses that the three deceased were armed when they emerged from the Guildhall, and that two of them at least – Hegarty and the woman Docherty – used their arms. Consequently it was impossible to effect an arrest operation'. But *The Freedom of the City* is only the most graphic statement of a problem with which Friel has grappled throughout his career. For a sense of the dislocation between public definitions of the self, of personhood, of citizenship, and the actual life of the affections is something which is present in almost all his work, at its most explicit in Friel's dramatic stratagem of Private Gar and Public Gar in *Philadelphia*. It is very much a concern, for example, of *Living Quarters* (first produced in the Abbey theatre in 1977).

In *Living Quarters* a career soldier in the Irish army who has won distinction serving with a United Nations' peace keeping force cannot resolve the ambiguities involved in his rôle as public hero and private participant in familial discomforture. He has just been presented with

a celebratory parchment by the people of Ballybeg, the Donegal village
near which he has been stationed for many years; this public moment
draws from him the pained cry 'Yes, I suppose the intention was good.
But being addressed by the people of Ballybeg – "You are our most
illustrious citizen" sort of stuff – my God they don't know me and we
don't know them'. There is a sad irony in his sufferings as the middle-
aged man whose young wife has had an affair with his son while he
was away on the one piece of active service his career has demanded.
And for the Irish public, which in the 1960s had gained in confidence
as economic growth replaced the stagnation of the past four decades,
which took especial pride in the 1970s in the dutiful exercise of its
peace keeping responsibilities in the Middle East, the sufferings of
Commandant Frank Butler were a troubling reminder of the defeated
quality of so much Irish life even in a decade which seemed to see
Ireland escaping from the impotent isolation of its recent past. That the
hero of such a mission as that undertaken by the Commandant is seen
in this play to be deeply flawed as a man and, incapable of resolving
his emotional and familial crises, chooses suicide, is peculiarly
shocking. For it highlights (suicide being rarely admitted as a cause of
death in Ireland) the disjunction between the public and the private in
contemporary Irish experience in an immediate way. There is even the
suggestion in the play that the quality of Irish civic life, the role it
offers its army officers for example, simply awaiting promotion from
one year to the next in some provincial town or village, works its
poison on the private and familial worlds:

Walking over here from the camp, d'you know what I was thinking: what
has a lifetime in the army done to me? Wondering have I carried over into
this life the too rigid military discipline that – that the domestic life must
have been bruised, damaged, by the stern attitudes that are necessary. . . .
                                                                        (*SP* 194)

So Friel's theatre in its social dimension is a theatre of societal transformations, of transitions. But it is also a theatre in which the individual
characters are beset by manifold difficulties when they seek to define
themselves as anything other than members of a family or of a markedly local community. The society in which they live, move and have
their being affords little or no civic space for such self-expression and
at moments of transition this becomes strikingly evident. For transition
itself confronts the familial and local worlds of Friel's characters (in
which they seek such meaning as seems available to them) with
fundamental challanges. George O'Brien has written of Friel's theatre,
'It speaks on behalf of its characters' inner lives rather than for their
social existence'[2], accurately highlighting the essentially subjective

concerns of Friel's dramaturgy. But the fact that almost all his characters must perforce ground their sense of personal meaning in the emotional life in its familial and local contexts is an aspect of their social existence to which Friel's writings consistently bear a pained and poignant witness. They can do no other, Friel's work implies, since the public life of a transitional Ireland, its institutions, professions, self-definitions, social modes, offer them nothing commensurate with their capacity to demand fulfilment and a sense of personal and collective significance.

A number of Friel's most remarkable plays of the last two decades exhibit how perennially Friel has been concerned as a dramatist with the problematic I have outlined in these terms. *Aristocrats* (first performed in the Abbey Theatre in 1979) and *Translations* (first performed in Derry by the Field Day Theatre Company in 1980) both in their different ways addressed the crisis of transition and suggested how profoundly that involved, for the individual, problems of public, societal definition.

Aristocrats was a Chekhovian elegy, lyrical and redolent of pathos, for the life of a Catholic family which has long inhabited a Big House near Friel's quintessential Donegal village, Ballybeg. A dynasty that has served both the British and Irish state in meeting and doling 'unequal laws unto a savage race' in a spirit of Victorian duty, the O'Donnells are reaching a point of terminal decline. The old judge is senile following a stroke and the house and all that it stands for can no longer exist in the new Ireland of slot machine empires, entrepreneurial greengrocers who supply the tourist hotels and political violence across the border. The family has returned for the marriage of one of the daughters of the house to the widowed greengrocer many years her senior who is scarcely a suitable match for the depressive, sensitive, musically gifted young woman who can see no other future for herself in the diminished, unfulfilled world she has inherited. Through the action of the play, which sees the death and burial of the old judge (a funeral is the focus of the family reunion rather than the anticipated wedding, in a nice dramatic irony), we slowly learn of the family's history and of the lives of the dispersed children of a marriage which imprisoned a vibrant young woman of the theatre in the living death of respectability until she took her own life. None of the children has been able to make any sort of life in Ireland. Casimir, the son of the house, is the repository of family traditions and mythology. It is he who remembers, misremembers, invents its significant social past as a centre of aristocratic Catholic influence in the district and an island of literary and intellectual cultivation in a sea of rude peasant life. His imagination is drawn to a fiction in which his family represented the epitome of Catholic Victorian and Edwardian civilisation (Hopkins rested on one of their armchairs and read from *The Wreck of the Deutschland*, Chesterton and Belloc were family friends, the O'Donnells arranged John McCormack's papal knighthood). But Casimir, the nostalgic celebrant of all this imaginary tradition (his evocations of past familial occasions are an anachronistic mélange which he scarcely troubles to authenticate in his instinctively mythological animadversions on the past), is a failed lawyer who has married a German woman and he now works in a food-processing factory in his wife's country where she works as a cashier in a bowling alley. The O'Donnells have become a little German family and Casimir cannot even converse with his own German-speaking children. He is adrift between the fictional social existence of the family's past and its actual life in a new European consumer and leisure society, without satisfactory public meaning. He has, in a bemused transition, forsaken a dying dynasty for the nuclear family and consequently spends much of the play on the long distance telephone trying to communicate across unbridgeable cultural and social gulfs.

The women of the house in their various ways embody the dynastic crisis and the improbability of a social rôle for themselves in the Ireland of the later twentieth century. Judith is a martyr to her father's illness and her illegitimate child (the fruit of an affair with a Dutch reporter who had no doubt covered the seige of the Bogside in which she had participated) is in an institution, unacceptable to the one man, an owner of mobile homes for tourists, who might wish to marry her. Claire has had her belief in herself as a musician crushed by her overweening father in just the way he crushed the life of her mother and Alice who married a village boy is an alcoholic who keeps her probation officer husband on permanent duty. Her husband Eamon is perhaps the most interesting character in the play and he asks the most pertinent question in this drama of the transitional crisis and failed social possibility. One of the new Irish, a young man of humble birth who has married into a good family and embarked on a promising career as a diplomat, he has thrown it all away because of an injudicious involvement with the republican cause in Northern Ireland (which would scarcely have pleased his superiors in the Department of Foreign Affairs in the 1970s during the Coalition Government led by Liam Cosgrove, when Northern Policy was being articulated by Conor Cruise O'Brien). He now works in London at a job he does not really enjoy. It is he who, as the play ends and we know the house will have to be sold, expresses the hope that it may in some way be saved. His wife Alice by contrast feels a sense of release. She acknowledges that the death of the house is harder for Eamon than for herself because she recognises that he has always been regretfully in love with her sister Judith (to whom he first unsuccessfully proposed):

ALICE: You and Judith always fight.
EAMON: No we don't. When did you discover that?
ALICE: I've always known it. And I think it's because you love her; and that's the same thing. No, it's even more disturbing for you. And that's why I'm not unhappy that this is all over – because love is possible only in certain contexts. And now this is finished, you may become less unhappy in time.   (*SP* 324)

'Have we 'asks Eamon in reply 'a context?' in a question which goes to the heart of the play. Do any of the O'Donnells and those associated with them have a context where they can experience the meaningful social existence without which love cannot blossom in innovative and creative life. Love in the oppressive atmosphere of Ballybeg House, cut off from the life which surrounds it, has bred suicide, madness, neurosis, alcoholism, confusion and loneliness. As the world changes the audience wonders can anything really change for these hurt human beings who desperately need 'a context'.

   Translations is a play of contexts too and dramatises a moment when social transition presses acutely on the individual who seeks a mode of social existence that has substance in public and private reality. Friel himself has supplied a succinct summary of the play's contents:

Translations is set in a hedge-school in Ballybeg, County Donegal. The year is 1833. The British army is engaged in mapping the whole of Ireland, a process which involves the renaming of every place name in the country. It is a time of great upheaval for the people of Ballybeg: their hedge-school is to be replaced by one of the new national schools; there is a recurring potato blight; they have to acquire a new language (English); and because their townland is being renamed, everything that was familiar is becoming strange.[3]

And in this journal which he kept while he was working on the play Friel identified the social and cultural significance of the historical matter which preoccupied him in his work:

In Ballybeg, at the point when the play begins, the cultural climate is a dying climate – no longer quickened by its past, about to be plunged almost overnight into an alien future. The victims in this situation are the transitional generation. The old can retreat into and find immunity in the past. The young acquire some facility with the new cultural implements. The in-between ages become lost, wandering around in a strange land. Strays.[4]

Owen, the play's principal character, is most fully the victim of this transitional state of affairs. It is he who has left Ballybeg and its tribal, communal satisfactions for Dublin and a life of commerce which has made him a man of some substance. Just the sort of person, with the local knowledge to boot, that the imperial power would happily recruit to aid it in its progressive and yet colonially inspired mission, the mapping of the country and the changing of place-names from Irish to English. But it is Owen's mistake, as he comes to recognise, to believe that he can negotiate with impunity between the two contexts which constitute his social experience, Ballybeg and the new order which is asserting its authority in cartography, a system of national schooling and in taxation. By the end of the play he knows he cannot. He is left without any context in which he could live with integrity other than that offered by the armed rebellion of the Donnelly twins, whose menacing shadow hangs over the entire play. So the play's primary concern is alienation from the modes of social existence which are possible in a society enduring transition under the impetus of colonial government. The theme of language explored here with its disjunctions, in a period of fundamental change, between a linguistic contour and social fact, is, I would argue, subsidiary to the dominant theme which preoccupies Friel in this as in so much of his work. Disjunction between an Irish language consciousness and a social reality being recreated from English language moulds is just another reason proffered by Friel why it is impossible in Ireland to achieve a creative and fulfilling relationship between public and private experience. So emigration (represented here in the person of Maire, who wants to learn English so that she can seek work in America), cultural nostalgia of a frozen and self-delusive kind (represented here by Jimmy Jack the polymathic classicist), complacent accommodation (represented by Hugh who would take a job at the national school if he could get it) and internal exile (the innocent Manus, suspected of complicity in the murder of the English soldier Yolland, flees to an Irish outback) are all hopelessly inadequate social and imaginative contexts within which to confront the realitites of an Ireland shaped and controlled by the experience of colonialism. Such an Ireland leaves no room, allows no real civic space for its Owens, its Manuses, its Maires. At the end only three alternatives remain apparent: the acquiescence of Hugh ('Take care, Owen. To remember everything is a form of madness'); emigration; or making contact with the mountainy men.

Such a reading of course does some damage to the play as a theatrical experience. For it is the peculiar power of the best moments in the play (the dual language love scene between Maire and Yolland, as touching as anything in Irish drama since Christy Mahon met Pegeen Mike, Maire reciting in wonderment the magical names of an England she knows only in the person of the murdered Yolland, Hugh remembering his unheroic role in '98) to suggest the privacies of the human heart even as it dramatises a complex socio/cultural situation. Friel himself when writing the play advised himself to avoid the too obviously political and public issues which the situation in Ballybeg in 1833 inevitably raises. 'The play' he reflected 'must concern itself only with the exploration of the dark and private places of individual souls'.[5] But the play as written and performed shows those private places as determined by the prevailing conditions of public life and consequently as places where pain, loss, a sense of betrayal prevail, and where the right to privacy itself, most immediately expressed in the right to one's own name and mother tongue, is publicly denied. In focussing most obviously on the language question in *Translations* Friel wrote a play for contemporary Ireland which would inevitably touch on a pressure point in a society that still reckons itself in transition between a Gaelic order in which the Irish language determined reality and an English language context which, although it affords economic opportunity, is somehow out of step with the needs of the Irish spirit. That fact together with the dramatic power of some of its most affecting scenes in which individual, private feeling is tenderly revealed on stage, I believe distracted audiences from the more searching critique Friel was offering of late twentieth century Ireland. The work was neither a lament for a vanished civilisation (a kind of *aisling* as Edna Longley has posited), nor an historical investigation of the roots of our distress (the anachronisms which critics have noted and the self-conscious modernity of the dialogue, all semiotics and ethnography, signal that) but a fiction in which is inscribed the social and cultural dilemma of living in a society which offers no ready means for the individual to negotiate between the private life of feeling and the public life of action, in which even language which might supply a negotiatory instrument, is implicated in the social problematic. The Ireland of *Translations* was therefore an Ireland in which it was impossible to imagine any satisfactory social reality emerging from the processes of change which the play dramatised. It was at its most reflective moments marked by a bleak pessimism that the Irish context could be anything other than disabling and destructive to its confused inhabitants. All it could offer by way of hope was Hugh's resigned commitment to continue his wrestling with words and meanings as an alternative to his son's determination ('I know where I live') to cast in his lot with the forces of rebellion which must resist the coloniser's theodolytes as well as his bayonets:

But don't expect too much. I will provide you with the available words and

the available grammar. But will that help you to interpret between privacies? I have no idea. But it's all we have. I have no idea at all.   (*SP* 446)

Friel's most recent play *Dancing at Lughnasa* (first performed in the
Abbey Theatre in 1990) is once more a play of social transition. But this
time the sense of contextual inadequacy, which so dominated his work
in the seventies and eighties, is replaced, in a striking shift in Friel's
career, by a vision of Irish life that suggests there are residual energies
in its culture which can enhance individual and collective experience.
It is perhaps the most warmly celebratory of any of this dramatist's
works and represents a moment in his imaginative development when
he reckons the Irish context not wholly without spiritual resources in
which the individual can discover personal and collective meaning.

The time is August 1936 in the home of the Mundy family, two
miles outside the village of Ballybeg. Five sisters (the youngest twenty-
six, the oldest forty) live together in the family home, along with the
seven year old child of Chris the youngest sister and their brother Jack
who has recently returned from a missionary parish in Uganda, his
health apparently broken and his mind in disarray. There is only one
wage-earner in the household, the pious, strait-laced oldest sister Kate.
Maggie at thirty-eight is the housekeeper, Agnes, thirty-five, and the
simple-minded Rose, all naivety and sexual innocence at thirty-two,
supplement the family income by knitting gloves at home. Chris,
mother to the illegitimate Michael (who as a young man narrates the
action of the play as a personal memory) has given birth to the son of
a devil-may-care Welsh travelling salesman (one possessed of an
English accent) and adventurer who visits Ballybeg very occasionally.
Change is in the air. The family has fun with the new wireless on
which the dance music of the thirties (subject in the Ireland of that time
to much ecclesiastical censure) supplies a steady diet of syncopated
frivolity (interrupted only when the valves overheat or the batteries
give out). But, more threateningly, old ways of life seem at risk. A new
Arcade is opening in the town, no doubt disturbing local shopkeepers,
and a new factory has started up making machine gloves, thus under-
cutting the cottage industry in which our two sisters are engaged. A
war in Spain will also take Chris' n'er-do-well lover off in quest of
excitement. There is almost a hint indeed in the precision of the
historical detail in *Dancing at Lughnasa* that Friel is humorously
poking a little sly fun at those who noted the anachronisms of
Translations. This most definitely is thirties rural Ireland. But it is also
of course Ireland in 1990, since the country still reckons itself essentially rural and judges traditional modes of life to be at risk from the
forces of economic growth and rapid social change. Much of contem-

porary Ireland is Ballybeg writ large.

At the end of the play we learn of the many disasters which overtake the Mundy family and we realize that the vibrant, colourful, exuberant, comic two days we have, imaginatively, spent in their company are only the nostalgic memories of the narrator who has composed the past into a personal myth of individual fulfilment and content. It is the constituents of this myth which are the most challenging aspects of the play for they amount to a way of thinking about modern Ireland as a context, which excitingly augments Friel's analysis of Ireland as a colonised society in his earlier play *Translations*.

The play is set at harvest time during the feast of Lugh, the pagan god of the sun worshipped by the ancient Celts. There are rumours of strange rites, involving fire and dance in the hills, at which a local boy has been terribly burnt. As we get to know the brave-spirited bunch of women who confront a life of hardship and economic insecurity with wit and dignity in their simple home we realize that there stirs within them a love of life and an unexpressed sexual energy which makes them unconscious pagans even as they accede to the pieties of conventional religion and the rule of the parish priest. Father Jack, the repatriated missionary, is the character whom Friel employs to articulate the vision of Ireland's pagan vitality in this work. He has it transpires gone native in Africa. He found there the ceremonial of native religion, its efficient polygamy and communal ritual all too easy of synthesis with his own life-enhancing version of Catholicism and has accordingly been forceably retired by his Church. The suspicion that attends his return inevitably falls on the family as a whole and Kate will, as summer ends, lose her job as a teacher in the parochially controlled local school because of her brother's heterodoxy. But for a moment Jack's vision of African life and the exuberant, vitality of the five women of the house seem to provide a way of thinking about Ireland which sets it apart from the developed world and hints at a shared experience with the colonised socieites of the third world where indigenous religion has not been completely overlaid by alien concepts. In a poignant fancy the women ask Jack if he could find them husbands in Africa. He replies that they would have to live polygamously there, sharing the same man. They are less than appalled by such a prospect, frustrated as they are by the manless parish of Ballybeg. And Chris, who in the course of the play, 'marries' her son's father in a dance of perfect communion (which 'marriage' saves her from depressive illness when he leaves for Spain) is in fact sharing Gerry with a wife and child in Wales. Or so Michael the narrator discovers after the death of his father. A bigamous relationship in Ireland seems as oddly workable as the polygamy of

Africa. Sexual and familial needs in traditional societies, it is implied,
are not to be contained within the conventional bounds of orthodox
monogamy, whatever the clergy and an anti-divorce vote in a referendum may say (*Dancing At Lughnasa* is among other things a powerful
post-referenda statement).

It is in the extraordinary dance scene in Act One of *Dancing At Lughnasa* that the pagan energies of Ballybeg are allowed their freest
expression. Marconi's magical invention, which brings the strains of an
Irish dance tune over the ether to a cottage kitchen, presides like some
lord of misrule over an increasingly uncontrolled outbreak of unihibited celebration and carnivalesque exuberance. In the Abbey performance this was a moment of unambiguous joy for actors and audience
alike, the communal female world of the Mundy family raised to
ecstatic self-forgetfulness. The text in fact suggests a more complex
occasion and indicates that Friel's aligning of Irish life with third world
experience in this work is not merely sentimental evasion of the crisis
of Ireland's transitional condition for some pastoralism of the primitive. The pagan notes, to which the Mundy family are made individually and collectively subject, beat out, Friel indicates in his stage
directions, a tune with dark as well as liberating implications. Maggie
is first to fall under their hypnotic power: 'her head is cocked to the
beat, to the music. She is breathing deeply, rapidly. Now her features
become animated by a look of defiance, of aggression; a crude mask of
happiness'. For ten seconds she dances alone 'a white-faced, frantic
dervish'. All the sisters but Kate, horrified that Chris tosses Jack's
surplice over her head, then join her in a wheeling dance that Friel
indicates should be 'almost unrecognisable' and 'grotesque'. Suddenly
Kate is overwhelmed, the tart piety of her persona abandoned for
some more authentic expression of her essential nature:

Kate dances alone, totally concentrated, totally private; a movement that is
simultaneously controlled and frantic; a weave of complex steps that takes
her quickly round the kitchen, past her sisters, out to the garden, round the
summer seat, back to the kitchen; a pattern of action that is out of character
and at the same time ominous of some deep and true emotion.

And Friel advises of the dance as it reaches a crescendo of noise and
violence:

With this too loud music, this pounding beat, this shouting – calling –
singing, this parodic reel, there is a sense of order being consciously subverted, of the women consciously and crudely caricaturing themselves,
indeed of near-hysteria being induced.[7]

Their dance is the dance of the misplaced, of proud, gifted, bravely energetic women whose lives are misshapen by an Irish society that will, as it changes, destroy the life they have struggled to achieve. A key word in the play is ceremony. It is the word Father Jack struggles to remember (his mind failing) as he recalls the efficacy of an African sacrificial ritual. Michael invokes the 'marriage' of Chris and Gerry as a 'ceremony' and in Act Two Father Jack offers a vision of the cere-monial richness of tribal life and the 'magnificent ceremonies' of the Ryangans in Uganda: 'And the interesting thing is that it grows naturally into a secular celebration; so that almost imperceptibly the religious ceremony ends and the community celebration takes over'. But the dance in the first act, so like and yet unlike the tribal dancing Father Jack recalls from his Ugandan days, indicates that Friel does not believe Irish life can readily be transposed to the ceremonial innocence of some third world context. Nevertheless the play with its highlight-ing of the pagan aspects of the Irish tradition suggests a context within which it may be possible to read the colonial experience of the country in a more benign light than Friel's work has hitherto deemed possible. Ballybeg – with its feasts of Lughnasa, the mask-like designs a child paints on a toy kite, the vibrant and yet dangerous call of its music, the instinctive animism of its feeling for the material world which makes of a wireless a whimsical presiding deity and a gramophone (Gerry thinks he'll make a killing selling them in Ireland) appropriately named a Minerva (Minerva was an Italian goddess of handicrafts) – functions here as a vision of some alternative to the world of appar-ently inevitable dislocation and familial disruption represented by the economic and social changes that destroy the Mundy household as summer ends. It hints at residual springs of Irish energy and per-sonality which, if tapped, might allow self and society to flow more readily together, carried along as they must be in the changeful waters of our post-colonial history.

MARKING TIME: FROM *MAKING HISTORY* to *DANCING AT LUGHNASA*

FINTAN O'TOOLE

When someone asks me where I live, I remember where I used to live.
Someone asks me for directions, and I think again. I turn into
A side-street to try to throw off my shadow, and history is changed.
 Turn Again, Ciaran Carson

1.

At the start of both plays it is already August, summer in full bloom but about to become overblown, the year just about on the turn, time ripening into decay. The heads of the households are in the August of their lives, too: O'Neill is 41, Kate Mundy is 40. And these points in time – a year on the turn, a life on the turn – are more important than turning-points in history. If Brian Friel were Shakespeare, these plays would be sonnets, full of time and decay and the delaying tactics on the march to death rather than history plays full of alarums and kings, battles and stratagems. The tone is 'When to the sessions of sweet silent thought, I summon up remembrance of things past', not 'Now is the winter of our discontent. . .' And to read them as history plays rather than sonnets is to misread them. Brian Friel does not write history plays, but plays that mock history. He looks for a time that is outside history, a personal time, the time of our lives.

To take Friel's work as a whole is to deny the operation of history. At first glance, his work has the sweep of centuries, from the sixth century of Saint Columba (*The Enemy Within*) to the 1980s of *The Communication Cord*. Not only is there this seeming sweep through history, but the work also seems to brush up against historical highlights from the formation of Irish Christianity as a supra-tribal force to the end of Gaelic civilisation in *Making History*, the 1798 rebellion and the death of the Irish language in *Translations*, the emergence of a newly Americanised Ireland in *Philadelphia, Here I Come!* and *The Loves of Cass McGuire*, the Bloody Sunday massacre in *The Freedom of the City*, and the corruption of southern Irish politics in *The Mundy Scheme* and *The Communication Cord*. To look at the plays like this is to see Friel's work as a composite history of Ireland, or to go further and say, as many have done, that plays like *Making History* and *Translations* are not merely history plays but plays 'about history'.[1]

Yet such a view denies the extent to which Friel's plays are less about historical sweep than they are about the excavation of unchanging places, people and dilemmas. It is always Ballybeg. It is, in *Translations*, *Making History*, and *Dancing At Lughnasa*, the August of the year, the point at which the cycle of the seasons is beginning to turn. From the beginning of Friel's work to *Dancing At Lughnasa*, taking in *Translations* along the way, there are schools closing down or teachers finding the schools closed to them. This may be happening because of economic change in the 1950s, because of the introduction of the National Schools in the 1830s, because of the scandal of Father Jack in the 1930s – the times and reasons, the historical context, matter hardly at all. What matters is the image. And basic situations recur, regardless of the time in history. Gar O'Donnell, Manus in *Translations*, Agnes and Rose in *Dancing At Lughnasa* are all trapped into the same escape from Ballybeg. The christening of Nellie Ruadh's baby at the start of *Translations* in 1833 is repeated in the comic christening of the radio at the start of *Lughnasa* in 1936, and in the eternal, placeless present of *Faith Healer* which begins with Frank Hardy's act of naming. And in each case, even this act of naming, of christening, does not really set time in order by marking a proper commencement. What is christened or inaugurated is what is already dying: Nellie Ruadh's baby will soon be waked; the baptised radio will hover between life and death throughout the play; the places named by Frank Hardy are 'all those dying Welsh villages'. History changes nothing. Sarah's struggle to speak in 1833 is Father Jack's struggle a hundred years later. The golden late afternoon in the mid-1970s with which *Aristocrats* ends but which itself 'may go on indefinitely' is the same golden, indefinite, unending late afternoon with which *Dancing At Lughnasa* ends in the mid-1930s. The drive is not towards history, but towards a collapse of past and present into the eternal suspension of memory.

Hugh's contention in *Translations* that 'it is not the literal past, the "facts" of history that shape us, but images of the past embodied in language' is supported by Friel's work. The great events of history collapse into each other in comic or ironic conflation. The French Revolution is a snatch of prose about Marie Antoinette that runs around in Gar O'Donnell's head like an advertising jingle or, in *Translations*, a distant event that helps to explain someone who is doubly distant, Yolland's father. Homer's heroics are set against the fall of Hugh's hedge school. Hugh O'Donnell in *Making History* is more concerned with 'the shit O'Doherty' than with the politics of the counter reformation, and the timbers of the Armada, the stuff of history itself, merely provide new floors for his house in Donegal. Even the nature of historical events does not change through history. The trek south into battle undertaken by two Hughs – in *Translations* and in *Making History* – ends in the same way, with the same disgrace, sitting in Phelan's pub in Glenties or running away like rats. 1798 seen from 1833 looks the same as 1591 seen from the 1610s. The facts of history seem to shape nothing and to change nothing.

In these plays, history has neither unbroken continuity nor the power to effect a genuine breach with itself. Lombard's memorialisation of the crowning of The O'Neill – 'six hundred and thirty continuous years of O'Neill hegemony' – is dismissed by O'Neill himself as nothing more than 'a political ploy'. The opposite of that continuity, an apocalyptic or teleological view of history, seems to be present at times in Friel's work, but it, too, is powerfully contradicted. The world in Friel's plays is always about to end and never does. The conflict between English and Gaelic civilisations in *Making History* is 'life-and-death', the Gaelic people 'on the brink of extinction'. The loss at Kinsale should therefore be a final one. Yet, two and a half centuries later, in *Translations* we still have a civilisation and a people on the brink of extinction, still barely alive. Its clash with English civilisation also seems irrevocable and ultimate, as all-or-nothing as the Trojan wars which peep through its screen. The Homeric ending of the play talks in absolutes: there is no future for this ancient city. And yet, a hundred years later in *Dancing At Lughnasa*, the old civilisation is not dead, the 'rituals and ceremonies and beliefs these people have practised since before history' of *Making History* are still pulsing through the lives of the Mundy sisters in 1936. If nothing can really change, then nothing can really die. The workings of the inner logic of history are always subverted in Friel by the workings of the force that torments Frank Hardy and all of his characters – the force of chance. It is the random, the inexplicable, the accidental with its tantalising illusions of freedom, and not the iron laws of history that are most at stake. The new is a version of the old: Gar O'Donnell, as Madge tells us at the end of *Philadelphia* is as his father was and will be as his father is, 'as like as two peas'. The future is already contained in the past. And there is therefore no trajectory of time towards death: Frank Hardy, alive and dead simultaneously, present before us after he has embraced his own death, is the ultimate anti-historical character, existing in a ghostly but continual present tense.

2

To misread Friel's plays as history plays, or even as plays about history, is to see Friel as a writer of commitment, an *écrivain engagé*, as some of those who praise his work have done.[2] Because his work deals in the stuff of history, and sometimes in that of politics, it is tempting to understand him as a fundamentally political writer. In his introduction to Friel's *Selected Plays*, his friend and Field Day collaborator Seamus Deane feels it necessary to point out that Friel's work is not 'wholly political in its motivations and obsessions'[3] (which implies, of course, that it is largely so). He goes on to regard *Faith Healer* as 'one of his most important if also one of his most unexpected plays'. He avoids the question of whether, if a play that is arguably a writer's most important and essential is so unexpected, there might not be something wrong with the expectations. The point is an entirely central one, because if it is not possible to understand Friel as an anti-historical and anti-political writer, it is very difficult to understand what happens in the move between *Making History* and *Dancing At Lughnasa*, or, indeed, to understand those plays themselves. The committed writer is a writer who has faith in politics, in history, and above all in the power of language, not merely to communicate things but also to change them. Friel is a writer in despair at, or in flight from, all of these things. *Making History* and *Dancing At Lughnasa*, far from being plays which set out to analyse society or history, are plays which deny the power of rational analysis at all. Mary Bagenal's belief in *Making History* that 'superstition must yield before reason' is not merely challenged by O'Neill's calculated defiance of reasonable action as both insufficient and impossible, it is answered directly in *Dancing At Lughnasa* in which superstition has its reasons and they are given their due.

History and politics, like O'Donnell's Armada timbers, may well floor Friel's house, but they do not contain the drama that happens in that house. Consistently throughout Friel's plays the writers, the chroniclers, the analysts, and the historians are insufficient, and more or less incapable figures. Far from being an engaged writer, Friel is a writer who doubts even the possibility of writing. Dr Dodds the sociologist in *The Freedom of the City*, Sir in *Living Quarters*, Hoffnung in *Aristocrats*, the mutually contradictory narrators of *Faith Healer* and Peter Lombard in *Making History* lose much more than they capture in their spinning of one or other of the available narratives. O'Neill in *Making History* could speak for all of them: 'The overall thing – we don't even begin to know what it means.' The act of writing itself in many of the plays has about it a ridiculous or comically inept air: Owen and Yolland writing in their Name-Book as they get more and more hysterically drunk; O'Neill writing out his lavish and crawling apology for his rebellion; Michael in *Dancing At Lughnasa* writing at the wrong time of year to a Santa Claus who doesn't exist, asking for a bell for the bike he doesn't have; Peter Lombard writing his pompous and lying history of O'Neill and O'Donnell. The writers are doomed to fail, to be ridiculous, to tell lies without necessarily meaning to. What is left is the figure, not of the writer, but of the priest, the one who can curse or bless, cure and heal, rather than the one who can analyse. This, too, is an ambiguous enterprise, but it is the power which represents the only possible way out of failure in Friel's hall of mirrors in which fictions reflect on each other. Frank Hardy, the secular priest, has that power in his healing hands. Father Jack, the unorthodox priest, has it in his simple sense of blessing. And to the extent that Peter Lombard has any power on his side it is because he is, as he says of himself, 'half priest, half schemer'. In the schemer part, he is a writer-historian and a dramatist, making a play of heroes and villains out of the confusions of events. And in that part he is a more or less contemptible failure. But in the priest part, he is acting out of a desire to bless, to heal the wounds of subjugation, to make of O'Neill a latter-day Jesus who did great works, was crucified and rose again. To the degree that he, too, is an unorthodox and secular priest, Lombard is absolved from the bitter judgement on the previous historians and analysts of Friel's plays. To the degree that he is a writer, a maker of narratives, he is not. Writing and failure go hand in hand.

What happens when Friel writes a play which makes use of certain historical events, therefore, is that he denies the possibility of writing truthfully about those events. *The Freedom of the City* is not a play about Bloody Sunday. It is a play about the impossibility of writing a play about Bloody Sunday. And *Making History* is not a play about O'Neill. It is a play about the impossibility of writing a play about O'Neill. Not only does the play literally tell lies about the historical events of O'Neill's rebellion (conflating the events of 1591–1602 into two years), it also implies that even a straight, historically accurate narrative of these events would still be a lie, a narrative which leaves out and distorts as much as any other. In Friel, even one's own history, the things that have happened in one's own life, is untrustworthy – think of Gar O'Donnell's most important 'memory' of the day in the boat with his father, or of the conflicting accounts of events by those involved directly in them in *Faith Healer* – and it follows that anyone else's account of what happens must be all the more so. As Friel's work progresses, the basic tools of that work – language, narrative, the shaping force of imaginative fiction – all become more and more suspect to the man who wields them. *Making History* is a culmination of this process of self-doubt, this imprisonment in untrustworthy fictions. A writer who cannot trust his own fictions will find it more and more difficult to make compelling drama from those fictions. This is what happens in *Making History* and what *Dancing At Lughnasa* leaps away from.

3

This turning away from history and politics is not unparalleled in the modern theatre, and the parallels are important to the way we approach *Dancing At Lughnasa*. One obvious parallel is with Beckett's self-conscious pursuit of 'an art . . . weary of its puny exploits, weary of pretending to be able, of being able, of doing a little better the same old thing, of going a little further along a dreary road . . . and preferring the expression that there is nothing to express, no power to express, no desire to express, together with the obligation to express'.[4] But more fruitful and much more pertinent to *Dancing At Lughnasa* are the parallels with the American dramatists who emerged out of the collapse of the hopeful left-liberalism of the 1930s: Arthur Miller and in particular Tennessee Williams. In America the leftism in which both Miller and Williams shared in the 1930s gave way to the collapse of such hopes in the post-war mixture of frantic materialism and anti-communist witch-hunting. The playwrights found themselves unable either to disavow the public world or to claim it as their own. Their strategies were ones which turned on the transformation of public categories into personal ones. Denied the vision of a better future, they turned instead to the continuous present of both *Death of A Salesman* and *The Glass Menagerie*, a conflation of past, present and future tenses in which time is effectively frozen. Denied the consolations of a belief in history, they replaced history with memory. Denied the external turning-points of political change, they created personal turning-points, the moments at which it becomes the August of life and the year shifts into decline. Denied the possibility of the liberating breakdown of order which revolution brings, they turned instead to things falling apart, the ineluctable disintegration of personality and community and family. And their work became reflexive: the political imagination became the imagination pure and simple, language, not the world, needed to be saved, history and society became fictions, the real and the imagined collapsed into each other, and lyrical evocation took the place of analytic description.

All of these things are true of Brian Friel, too, and for analogous reasons. For Friel, not only is there no functioning politics, there is no polity. He refuses to posit fealty in either the Republic of Ireland or Northern Ireland, to see either as the context for his work. His best work swims in the backwash of nationalism, in the aftermath of the straightforward aspirations which ceased to be straightforward and became nightmarishly circular after 1968 and the first phase of the present Troubles. Neither the politics of the Republic, which are seen in a series of plays from *Philadelphia* to *The Mundy Scheme* and *The Gentle Island* to *The Communication Cord* as at best ridiculous and at worst viciously corrupt, nor the tribal warfare of the North offer a ground on which history can operate, on which a future can be posited. Like Yeats and the Irish Revivalists after the fall of Parnell, Friel has seen art, and in particular theatre, as filling a political vacuum. Filling a vacuum, though, also means operating in one. In the same sense, and with the same consequences, that Miller and Williams are post-socialist playwrights, Friel is a post-nationalist one.

This connection becomes important only when you see how strongly connected *Dancing At Lughnasa* is to Williams' *The Glass Menagerie*. It is significant that the influences on *Lughnasa* are not primarily Irish ones at all. Whereas in *Translations* or *Making History*, the influences of, say, Sean O'Casey (the last scene of *Translations* in which Jimmy Jack and Hugh play the roles of Captain Boyle and Joxer from *Juno and the Paycock*) or Thomas Kilroy (the device whereby O'Neill's accent switches from upper-class English to bog Irish is strongly reminiscent of the figure of Brendan Bracken in *Double Cross*) are strong, *Lughnasa*, even at the reflexive level of theatrical style, tends to move out of an identifiable Irish idiom just as it moves out of a specific historical Irish context. As a disavowal of history, the play is also a disavowal of a specifically Irish cultural context. Just as it hangs suspended in time, between past and future, so it hangs suspended in contradictory influences, those of First World modernity (through the borrowings from Williams and Miller) and those of Third World magic realism and atavism. One set of images in the play – the work-ings of narration and memory – are strongly connected to American drama, particularly to *The Glass Menagerie*. But another – the centrality of ritual and magic – is obviously African and tribal. In a play which dramatises a relationship between memory and forgetfulness, the images of memory are First World, the images of forgetfulness are Third World: Father Jack's inability to remember the words for things and specifically Maggie's suggestion that Agnes should put roses on his windowsill 'with a wee card – "ROSES" – so that the poor man's head won't be demented looking for the word,' comes directly from the imagery of cultural amnesia in Gabriel Garcia Marquez's *One Hundred Years of Solitude*. This suspension between two worlds – the world of Tennessee Williams and the world of Gabriel Garcia Marquez – helps to give the play its sense of a suspended, placeless time.

The connections between *Lughnasa* and *The Glass Menagerie* are reasonably obvious ones. The use of the narrator as a device for the suspension and conflation of time, the elegiac tone of the narration, the use of a mentally disturbed young woman (Laura, Rose) whose sexuality takes on a critical edge, the guilty departure of the narrator, the sense of a family trapped as an anachronism in an increasingly hostile world, the persistence of old ceremonies, and, above all, perhaps, the use of music, all link the plays together. The use of lyricism as antithetical to history and society is the same in both Friel and Williams. The suspension of time as a way of rescuing historically marginal people is shared by both writers, and Williams' expression of its purpose is close to what is happening in *Lughnasa*: 'it is the continual rush of time, so violent that it appears to be screaming, that deprives our actual lives of so much dignity and meaning, and it is, perhaps, more than anything else, the *arrest of time* which has taken place in a completed work of art that gives to certain plays their feeling of depth and significance'.[5] In *Lughnasa*, time is corroding the Mundy sisters in the simplest sense that as spinster women they are getting past their sell-by date for marriage and children. Their romance is all in the past and the arrival of figures from that past – Maggie's friend Bernie O'Donnell, Gerry Evans, Father Jack – serves not to re-unite them with the past but to mark their distance from it. The absence of marriages – Gerry Evans will not marry Chris; Kate will not get Austin Morgan; Maggie will pine on; Danny Bradley and Rose can never be a respectable couple – is a failure to arrest time in the way that marriages do, making a bond now, which, theoretically at least, will last forever. So much is this the case that marriage itself fractures in the play, presenting us with alternative forms of marriage: the eventual unorthodox wedding of Chris and Gerry, the African marriage customs described by Father Jack, the separated marriage of Danny Bradley, the other, metaphorically adulterous marriage of Gerry Evans in South Wales which we learn of towards the end of the play.

There are sociological, even historical, aspects to this corrosive action of time on the Mundys. Kate's sense that 'hair cracks are appearing everywhere; that control is slipping away; that the whole thing is so fragile it can't be held together much longer' is linked to the onset of social change. The arrival of the Industrial Revolution in Donegal in the form of the factory that will replace the hand-knitting cottage industry from which Rose and Aggie earn their keep is clearly one of the cracks. The radio which is such an important character in the play, reminiscent of the Hi-Fi, TV and drinks cabinet which is such an important prop and metaphor in Williams' *Cat on a Hot Tin Roof*, is used in the same way that Williams uses his prop: as an image of a rural society giving way to the stirrings of an urban one. What Christopher Bigsby has written of Miller and Williams is, in this respect, largely true of Friel's work as a whole and partly true of *Lughnasa*: 'The individual who cannot adjust to the new materialism is celebrated and deplored simultaneously. He or she is associated with a simpler, and, indeed, as both writers admit, even a simplistic model of society. Theirs is thus a tainted lyricism. Indeed such characters are often seen as verging on the psychotic. The fault lies not only with the system which destroys them, but also with the individual who clings to myths and dreams discarded by history'.[6] This ambiguity is at work in Friel's plays (most notably in *Translations*) and the loyalty to older ways, to the paganism of Lughnasa, is located in those who are, if not psychotic, then certainly disturbed: Rose and the youths of the back hills. Yet 'fault' is not the right word to describe Friel's attitude to those who cling on to something beyond history. *Lughnasa* treats them with more gentleness, with a more gentle sense of elegy than Williams treats, say, Laura in *The Glass Menagerie* or Blanche in *A Streetcar Named Desire*.

Yet this nexus of sociological and historical forces is not the central one in *Lughnasa*. The sense of the play is that the Industrial Revolution is merely an aspect of the breakdown that is under way, not a cause of it. If anything, the play is even more a disavowal of history than *Making History* is. The play does not happen on the margins of history, history happens on the margins of the play. World history and Irish history are introduced as if they are about to become important, but only in order that we may see that they are not. The First World War is a battered and absurd hat that Father Jack, once a chaplain in the British Army, swaps for Gerry Evans' straw one. The Italian invasion of Ethiopia is a decidedly unheroic and unhistoric jingle sung by Rose:

> Will you come to Abyssinia, will you come?
> Bring your own cup and saucer and a bun.

And even this in turn is further undercut by being repeated as a jingle about De Valera and Baltinglass, which makes it both ridiculous and anachronistic. Similarly Kate's involvement with the Irish War of Independence is mentioned as an aside and, instead of being a central fact of her life, is utterly irrelevant to it. Gerry Evans' decision to join up in the Republican forces for the Spanish Civil War is personally, rather than politically motivated, and again the historic force of that conflict is reduced and undercut by his description of his recruitment. Great historical forces are conjured up only to be dismissed. It is the things that are set against them, the things out of which the play works, which are infinitely more important to the world of *Dancing At*

Lughnasa: memory and ritual.

The tension which provides the drama of *Dancing At Lughnasa* (the play is almost entirely without direct conflict) is the tension between the onrush of time, on the one hand, and the frame within which time is frozen and contained on the other. Its brilliance lies in its ability to structure the falling apart of things, the terrible widening of the hair cracks, within a form which is the opposite of these things: full of ease and gentleness and apparent stasis, a form in which time seems suspended. This tension is also the tension of Friel's own playwrighting, and in this sense the play is as reflexive, as much about the dilemma of playwrighting, as *Faith Healer* is. It is the tension between the desire to lift certain lives out of time, to memorialise them in the theatre, on the one hand, and the fact that time itself is the medium of theatre on the other. Only by being placed in a time-filled form can the lives in question be brought out of time. This contradiction is the motor of the play, the engine of conflict which drives it. And since the play is at this level 'about' the dilemma of its author, it makes sense that the play should also work within the form of autobiography. The autobiographical dimensions of the play are acknowledged by its dedication to the memory of 'those five brave Glenties women' and by Friel's making Michael, the boy, the same age (seven) as he himself would have been in 1936. The play is, for Friel, the same act of memory and tribute as the narrator's calling of that time to mind is to the narrator. This form of autobiographical memory play, this device of a continual present in which history is replaced by memory is what Friel takes from *The Glass Menagerie*. What he does with that form, the brilliance and subtlety and daring with which he uses its freedom to collapse the distance between past, present and future, is entirely his own.

4

Dancing At Lughnasa could, had Friel not used the title already, have been called *Translations*. In moving to *Lughnasa* from *Making History* he performs the acts of translation which are necessary for him to work his way out of the hall of mirrors that *Making History* has become. *Making History* is so reflexive that it ceases to have any dramatic tension or much theatrical force. If nothing can be said, nothing can be enacted, and if nothing can be enacted, then the main condition of the play is stasis. That stasis affects *Making History* deeply: a play which is, at its centre, about the impossibility of writing, it is also a play which doesn't get written, which argues itself into submission. In order to write, Friel had to translate many of its categories into another dimension: history into memory, language into movement and sound, reality into appearance. It is through these translations that *Dancing At Lughnasa* works.

By moving out of history and into the personal time of autobiography *Lughnasa* gains the essential freedom with time which Friel is seeking. Almost from the beginning of the play, past and future are conflated in a sentence like 'He had come home to Ballybeg – as it turned out – to die.' What will happen to Father Jack after the action of the play is uttered in the past tense. The opening monologue prefigures in words, again in the past tense, much of what is for us as audience the future, the things we are about to see happen. Lughnasa itself is an image of ahistorical time. Not only is it pre-historic, immemorial, but it also operates on two different time scales. It is at once both a specific day, a specific time of *this* year now, and a part of a vast sweep of time from unrecorded eras to the present. The terrible ending of Rose and Agnes is prefigured in apparently harmless ways by the early presence of London as a place in the play and by Gerry's seemingly casual remark about women making better drifters. And this freedom with time culminates in the stunning switch forward to the future that lies ahead for these characters and then back to their present frozen moments of golden calm with which the play culminates. Here Friel captures precisely the tension which is at the heart of theatre itself, its ability to keep alive its characters only so long as they are on the stage, its pervading irony that to freeze people in time is to mimic the action of death, that even the most pleasurable conjuring up of memories on the stage is evanescent and must lead on to death.

What *Dancing At Lughnasa* does is to embrace the failures of theatre. Instead of agonising over the innate inadequacies of language, the uncertainty of all fictions, the untrustworthiness of narrative, as a line of plays from *Faith Healer* to *Making History* does, *Lughnasa* takes these failures for granted and looks instead towards ways of making them enjoyable at least for the duration of the play. This is what gives the play its peculiar bittersweet taste, its sense of a gentle, and in some respects pleasurable, slide into tragedy. This is done in two ways. In the first place the lack of congruence between how things are and how they are shown, the inability of the theatre to reflect anything truly and with accuracy which haunts so much of Friel's work, is embraced and enjoyed. In *Dancing At Lughnasa*, the play itself ceases to be an attempt to reflect the world and becomes instead an attempt to ritualise it, to give the shape and significance of a ceremony while accepting the lack of power of the theatre to affect it. Where a play like *Making History* attempts to affect the world by understanding it, and recoils in static despair at its own failure to do so, *Lughnasa* attempts to affect the world as a ceremony does – magically, by the power of analogy and metaphor. 'Attempts' is the right word, for the rituals of the play are not, in fact, effective. The ceremonies of Lughnasa don't stand up to the Industrial Revolution or the power of the parish priest, the new religion, to sack Kate. The ceremony between Jack and Gerry is, after all, only an exchange of hats, a swapping of outward appearances. And the marriage ceremony of Chris and Gerry may make her feel temporarily like his wife, but doesn't in the end hide the fact that he has another wife and another son. Yet ceremonies are entered into not just for their effectiveness but for their own sake, the shape and beauty of their form, just as plays are entered into. In *Dancing At Lughnasa* Friel is avowing the importance of theatre outside of its responsibilities, saying that it can have its place even when it is incapable of changing the world.

Where previous Friel plays, most notably *Making History,* have concerned themselves with the failure of theatrical or fictional appearance to do justice to reality, *Dancing At Lughnasa* makes reality evaporate into appearance. The play does not present itself as reality but as appearance, as a series of figments of memory and imagination. The broken looking glass at the beginning of the play is a disavowal of the power of the play to reflect things as they really are or were, an embracing of the fractured constructs of the imagination. And the play goes on to enact this by making imagined absence as powerful in the action as real presence. The young Michael, who is not there, is as much a character as any of those who are present on the stage. The play often seems to operate on Berkeley's *Esse est percipi* principle: to be is to be perceived. The young Michael exists because he is perceived by the others, and in a daring extension of the theme, the perceived Michael himself becomes the eye which perceives Chris and Gerry from behind the bushes and gives their love existence. And this imagery is extended in the play's action. The non-existent Michael fools Maggie with a non-existent rat. She fools him with a non-existent bird. Curly McDaid is called Curly not because of his hair, but because he is 'bald as an egg'. Things can be defined as much by what they are not as by what they are. Absence is as potent as presence. The lack of congruity between how things are and how they seem – what the narrator announces at the start of the play as 'a widening breach between what seemed to be and what was, . . . things changing too quickly before my eyes' – can be a source of fun as much as it is the play's source of tragedy.

And as with reality, so with time. Time cannot be stopped, history cannot be escaped. But it can be shaped, given the pleasurable if irrational form of music and dance. What music and dance do is to take time and mark it, make it aesthetic, give it significance and shape. In dancing we cease to resist the passage of time, but choose instead to fall into step with it, to shape our movements to it, in an act of active surrender rather than of resistance. The play's most vibrant moments – the wild dance in the first act – are moments of surrender by the sisters to the force of the music, the urge of the dance, a force at once joyous and tyrannical, a dance of grief and liberation. We remember that this is a memory play and that in memory it is images and movements and colours, not words, which come to mind. 'In memory' as Tennessee Williams says in the preface to *The Glass Menagerie*, 'everything happens to music'. The surrender of language to movement which the close of the play celebrates, the swaying to the music of memory which holds at bay the fate that is to come, is also the surrender of history to marked time. Time, once marked, can be replayed and re-enacted, always passing but always re-constituting itself, like the flow of our memories, like the act of theatre itself.

'A KIND OF *COMHAR*': CHARLES
MACKLIN AND BRIAN FRIEL

JOHN McVEAGH

Brian Friel's *The London Vertigo* is a 'vigorously' shortened version –
the description is his own[1] – and also an updating of Charles Macklin's
comedy *The True Born Irishman*, first produced in Dublin in 1761.
Macklin's play succeeded in Dublin, but failed six years later when the
author re-named it *The Irish Fine Lady* and tried staging it in London.
English audiences in the 1760s were not interested in Dublin satire.

Macklin accepted this verdict. He commented that there was a
'geography' in humour as in other things,[2] and did not repeat the
experiment. Instead he adapted his comic writing more closely to the
daily experience of London people. The plays still came with an Irish
theme, but theatre audiences themselves figure as characters on stage
(as in some of Fielding's plays), and so do English aristocrats, Scots-
men and naturalized British Jews. Thus Macklin shifts the centre of
gravity from Dublin to London. As a result, his later plays like *The Man
of the World* and *Love-à-la-Mode* achieved greater success, and kept the
stage for a lengthy period.

Yet the differences between *The True Born Irishman* and Macklin's
other plays do not obscure a fundamental similarity. His remark about
a geography in humour hints at this. What obsessed Macklin, both as
an actor and a writer, was the issue of nationality. Cultural difference,
race, the politics of class, creed and sex in eighteenth-century Britain
were his field of interest. These topics re-emerge, of course, with special
force in Brian Friel's own dramatic writing, and his affectionate tribute
to Macklin as a kindred spirit in the Introduction to *The London Vertigo*
comes as no surprise. Without seeking to reiterate Brian Friel's own
points on Macklin's personality and career, the present essay offers
further details on Charles Macklin which, it is hoped, readers of *The
London Vertigo* may find of interest. What kind of person was this
actor-playwright of two centuries ago, whom Brian Friel salutes as a
neighbour and a comrade? What characterises his plays?

2

Brian Friel explains that, for him, Macklin's interest lies in his system-

215

atic re-making of his own personality. He sees Macklin's life as an exercise in metamorphosis, in which process the man, the actor and the writer were all bound up together. Macklin did in fact change himself from an Irish speaking, poor Catholic peasant boy born in the late seventeenth century in the Inishowen peninsula on Donegal's north coast into a famous and highly paid London actor, teacher and playwright. He ran an actors' school, taught stage elocution and acting to members of the aristocracy and was on friendly terms with many influential people in the capital, not all of them limited to the theatrical and literary coterie. The street named after him near Covent Garden (like those named after Betterton, Garrick, Kemble, Kean and others) was a sure sign of success; it still exists. Despite all this, Brian Friel perceives in Macklin an ingrained timidity; and here I am not so sure I agree. Thus he imagines we can detect in Macklin's apology to the irritated London audience in 1767 his 'terrified voice' and 'clipped Donegal vowels'.[3] Certainly if a modern author were driven on stage to placate an irate pit he would be seen as grovelling, but things did not work quite like that in the eighteenth century. Macklin was only doing what was expected of him, and what others frequently did. Friel implies that fear and ambition drove Macklin to re-invent his personality, and that his fear of England never left the Irish boy. If this is true – if Macklin was constitutionally or culturally timid – then he made an extraordinarily good job of covering it up. But was he, really? Might we not interpret him differently? Noting the stream of quarrels which characterised Macklin's life and the aggressive satire of his writing, we might call him an angry more than a fearful man – the anger, perhaps, fuelled by resentment, if indeed he had to suppress or deflect his natural instincts.

There is uncertainty about Macklin's precise origins. His earliest biographer J. T. Kirkman, writing immediately after Macklin's death, tells us that he was born in 1690, two months before the battle of the Boyne, into an aristocratic Catholic Irish family which had lost property in the seventeenth century confiscations, and that his father had fought for King James.[4] Kirkman also says that Macklin's mother then married a Williamite soldier called Luke O'Meally, who bought a Dublin tavern and carried his wife and family to live in the capital city. Macklin was placed in a boarding school by his stepfather, where, Kirkman goes on, he developed a powerful dislike of his Scottish schoolmaster and extended this in later years into a hatred of the whole Scottish nation. (Anti-Scottish feeling is certainly a feature of Macklin's later plays.) In the early 1700s Macklin ran away to London for a brief acting spell, then a little later took up with strollers in the west country before gradually making his way into the London theatre (including Goodman's Fields when Fielding wrote for it) towards the end of the 1720s and in the early 1730s.

Kirkman's biography of Macklin has been challenged, no doubt correctly, as myth-making. He makes Macklin 107 years old at his death in 1797 – not impossible but unlikely; and suspiciously convenient is the identification of his birth year with that of the battle of the Boyne. Although Kirkman knew Macklin well and claimed to be using his own material, collected, it was said, for an autobiography, modern biographers are sceptical of him. There is no other evidence that Macklin came from the dispossessed aristocracy of Ireland, nor that he was born in 1690, and indeed his latest biographer, W. W. Appleton, states flatly that 'almost nothing' can be established of Macklin's early working life. According to him the first unambiguous evidence is that Macklin was engaged in the 1720s as a Drury Lane actor. Appleton suggests he came from the middling classes in County Donegal.[5] *A Biographical Dictionary* accepts this account.[6]

Thus the romantic legend finds little modern favour. Nevertheless, if Kirkman's version, semi-fictitious though it may be, represents what Macklin claimed about himself, we may note that he would not be the first to invent a grand ancestry in order to cover up an obscure origin. More serious are the politics of the claim. The Macklin of the early stories, though a committed Protestant and Hanoverian in his middle and later life, identified himself throughout with the defeated culture of Catholic Ireland. He preserved an Irish sense of loss, an awareness of national difference. These themes do indeed run through his work like threads in the fabric. In a review of Appleton's pragmatic biography, the Irish scholar J. O. Bartley comments as follows:

I am not sure that Mr Appleton fully appreciates Macklin's personality. We know the inaccuracies and legend-building of the early biographies, but for antecedents there is nowhere else to go, and they contain elements of psychological probability. Macklin, being an Irishman and a Gael, would never have regarded himself as of 'low origin'. If in fact his family had been crushed by the Williamite wars, and he had been brought up in a household religiously divided, disappointed of higher education, and forced to make his way by his talents and toughness, much of his behaviour would be explained. His unwillingness to compromise, his pride and arrogance, his insistence on his rights, and his magnanimity in victory are qualities which, if not necessarily aristocratic, he may have felt to be so, and therefore to belong to his *persona*.[7]

'Elements of psychological probability': it is a good phrase. Macklin, we shall see, both as actor and dramatist, does indeed explore the sense of dispossession, social rejection, political subjection and cultural loss – and, occasionally, imagines their magical reversal. His greatest coup as an actor came in his re-interpretation of Shylock in *The Merchant of Venice* in 1741.[8] This performance catapulted him into fame, and soon afterwards, when he turned dramatic writer on his own account, he continued to explore the same theme of the politics of the outcast. But what brought him to Shylock? What do we know of his acting life before that moment?

By the 1720s, Appleton writes, he was acting at Drury Lane. Soon he became an established secondary comic actor, playing Teague in *The Committee*, Lord Foppington in *The Relapse*, the Prince in *1 Henry IV* (and also Francis in the same play), Jerry Blackacre in *The Plain Dealer*, Ben in *Love for Love* and Marplot in *The Busy Body*. Most of these are anything but star roles, but neither are they merely walk-on parts. Teague may be an undemanding stereotype, but Lord Foppington, Jerry Blackacre and Marplot are individualised characters needing to be intelligently interpreted and performed if the plays in which they figure are to succeed. Interesting are the Prince in *1 Henry IV* and Ben in Congreve's *Love for Love*; both are witty but serious roles in which, one might say, Macklin looks to the future. They show him as an actor interested in the individual who is pulled two ways – interested in serious drama.

This seems to lead directly on to Shylock. But let us first recapitulate. Macklin by the time of his fortieth birthday – by the late 1730s – had come a long way. He had undergone, in Brian Friel's word, a 'metamorphosis'.[9] He had changed his name from MacLochlainn (or in English, McLaughlin) to Macklin. He had changed from being a Catholic to being a Protestant. He had changed his country from Ireland to England. He had changed his language from Gaelic Irish to English. None of these has been a unique experience then or since but taken together they must constitute an unusually deep self-examination, involving the repression of a good deal of early experience. If the thoroughgoing self-reconstruction called for by this process testifies to Macklin's extraordinary mental strength, as it surely does, it may also explain his quarrelsome personality as a professional actor and writer, as well as the residue of anger evident in all he wrote.[10] Macklin's prickly nature shows in his difficulty in getting on with colleagues, his litigious habit of mind, his vengeful attacks on those who challenged his copyright. He was unable to stay out of trouble. He accidentally killed the actor Thomas Hallam in 1735 by driving a stick into his eye after a row in the green room; Hallam had presumed to take Macklin's wig. Eight years later in 1743 he fell out with Garrick and other colleagues over the defeat of the actors' rebellion against the manager Fleetwood. When the conflict was patched up Garrick and the other actors were taken back into employment but the manager refused to re-employ Macklin; since the actors had agreed to stand by one another, he felt let down by his colleagues. It may be hard to take a different view on that incident, but Macklin remained peculiarly accident-prone. For example, five years after the Garrick row, in March 1750, his simmering pay disputes with Thomas Sheridan, the manager of Smock Alley Theatre in Dublin, erupted when the latter sacked him from the company. In 1763–4 Macklin quarrelled with Henry Mossop, again over salary arrears, again at Smock Alley Theatre. He did so yet again in 1770–71 on the same subject, but this time at the Capel Street Theatre in Dublin, which was then being managed by William Dawson and Robert Mahon.[11] This aspect of Macklin, in my view, Brian Friel underrates. He refers to the marvellous 'ease and assurance'[12] of Macklin's new identity as an English actor, an ease, however, which collapsed in panic when *The Irish Fine Lady* failed at Covent Garden. Considered as a description of Macklin's literary activity, the summary may appear no less odd. None of Macklin's plays strike me as easy and assured; they are knottily intelligent, and somewhat stiff. And as I suggested above one can overstress his self-abasement before the audience. Eighteenth-century managers and actors were in the hands of the audience, and would sack a performer, cancel a show or apologise unjustifiably, sometimes on their knees, if they wished to save their theatre from being torn apart.[13] By the standard of the times, Macklin was a tough, even defiant character. In 1775 he took some of the audience to court for conspiring to barrack him in *The Merchant of Venice*, and argued that they were trying to deprive him of his livelihood. He conducted his own case, and won it, then waived his damages with a theatrical or even corny generosity which remains oddly endearing and impressive even after two hundred years.[14] This was the act of a proud but not a timid man.

There is a hint of what all this cost Macklin, of his repressed side, in a story told by Kirkman on the subject of speech. Macklin's first language was Irish and when he first became an actor in the English west country his extremely marked accent – what Kirkman calls 'strong vernacular' traces of Irish in his speech[15] – proved an obstacle to his advancement. Macklin therefore took elocution lessons. After six months of these he re-applied for work but was told by the manager of the Bristol theatre that he would still need to 'cut three or four inches more of the brogue from his tongue' if he was going to make a success of his profession. To this Macklin made the laconic reply: 'Cutting off tongues was a dangerous experiment'. Kirkman adds that Macklin felt 'a lingering pain in his mind' because of 'his accent and provincial expressions'. It is an ambiguous statement. A lingering pain: was this because the Irish speech had been removed, or because its removal had been so hard?

Macklin's rather plodding acting career suddenly took off in 1741 when he was given Shylock to play at Drury Lane. He transformed the part and made of the performance the sensation of the theatrical year – if not of the century. He turned Shylock into the tragic figure we know today by rejecting out of hand the conventional eighteenth century interpretation of the Jew – usually played in Granville's 1701 adaptation of *The Merchant of Venice* – as a farcical buffoon. Instead Macklin went back to Shakespeare's text, drew from his own expatriate experience and studied Jewish literature and history so as to gain a personal insight into the psychology of the outcast race. The resulting realism of Macklin's performance deepened the impact of the play and swept aside the conventional interpretation for good.

The realism of Macklin's Shylock took everyone by surprise, but there had been hints of it before. In the 1730s, we read, friction grew between Macklin and some of his colleagues (such as Quin) because he refused to bow down to the older, sing-song acting style. 'He was guilty of inventing bits of naturalistic business which upset traditionalists and distracted attention from their stately movement and pompous declamation'.[16] Macklin's emphasis on realism (followed by Garrick, who built upon his work) sounded the death knell of this fashion. But for us the important thing is what drew Macklin to Shylock in the first place: his perception of the tragic potential of the Jew. Shylock had always been laughed at. Macklin did not laugh. He took seriously the foreigner in Venice, the Jew among Christians, the businessman among lounging aristocrats. His emphasis on the outsider turning on his persecutors coupled with the internalised and deeply studied rendering which he gave of the Jewishness of Shylock's mind, deepened the superficial Shylock of farce into a tragically impressive figure. Perhaps a truer staging of Shakespeare was going to happen anyway, but few actors at the time can have been so well qualified as Macklin to revitalise that particular text. It was no accident that he chose *The Merchant of Venice* to experiment with, rather than *Richard III* or Falstaff in *1* and *2 Henry IV* (both similarly undervalued plays at the time). Shylock suited Macklin because his story dramatized the theme of national and racial antagonism. This subject, both as actor and writer, he would continue to explore.

3

Macklin wrote eight plays, and they had mixed fortunes. His first was *The Alternative, tyranny or liberty* (1745), an anti-Jacobite propaganda piece which failed on its first performance and failed again after being revised. Macklin then laid the work aside, but in fact it gives us a good idea of some of the mixed feelings and preoccupations which underlay Macklin's Hanoverian loyalties. For this piece designed to damn the Jacobites Macklin chooses a plot drawn from sixteenth-century Scottish history in which, on the one hand, the Catholic forces of Continental Europe – the Pope and the King of France – seduce the Scottish court into an alliance, while, on the other, a band of 'rebels' rejects this Catholic conspiracy, pushes for an alliance with England which will preserve Scotland's national integrity, and brands the court leaders as the real traitors to their country. Macklin wrote the piece to uphold the established power of England against the Scottish Jacobites and their English sympathisers, and with this end in view champions in the play an English-Scottish alliance. However, his historical metaphor also pulls the other way. He casts the rebels against kingly power as the true patriots; by contrast, king and court are revealed as the corrupt half in the political struggle taking place. This is capable of ambiguous interpretation in Hanoverian Britain in the 1740s. Macklin does not contradict himself as such, but allows the story, as it unfolds, to draw him into unexpected utterance. The rebel leader Huntley illustrates what is happening when he speaks out against the sale of Scotland to France and Rome and invokes the neglected traditions of his race, now extinguished by cynical politicians drawing support from a foreign source. Within the historical metaphor of the play, this is the patriot speaking. But an extinguished culture was to be the Jacobites' experience, not the fate of the English; Macklin writes as if seeing the forthcoming Highland clearances, and as if penning their elegy. More likely, a pressure of feeling drawn from seventeenth-century Ireland informs Huntley's words. He mourns a land in which freedom and ownership, once secure, have been undermined, and in their place 'Arrests, Imprisonments, / And Confiscations compose your Subjects Dreams, / And break their restless Sleep'.[17] Huntley then goes on to summarise 'Scotland's' condition; lost leaders have been replaced by sycophantic administrators no longer ruled by a deluded government:

I see my Country bleeding in her vital Vein;
I see her Nobles banish'd, imprison'd, and assassin'd;
I see Scotland's Dregs compose her Councils;
All Concerns, sacred, civil, and military,
Sold and huckster'd as in a public Mart.
I see Majesty – deluded Majesty,
Hem'd in by a Band of crawling Parasites,
Who taint his royal Mind with a King's bluest Plague,

Seditious Jealousie of his best Subjects.

When Huntley is condemned to death as a rebel – that is, re-reading the metaphor, signalised as a patriot – the old blood of Scotland under Sir David Bruce rallies to his support, gathers the clans, and damns the court's foreign alliance as an injustice 'entailed upon Posterity' (iv). Speculation it remains, but some pressure of feeling from Irish history seems to enter the writing process here.

Perhaps Macklin was aware of this undercurrent himself. Again and again in his subsequent plays he returns to the theme of weak-minded Irish men and women allowing themselves to be seduced by English fashion into betraying their country. He contrasts with them one or two representatives of genuine Irish patriotism like Sir Murrough O'Dogherty in *The True Born Irishman*, the original of Friel's *The London Vertigo*. Patriotism here always seems to mean old Irish patriotism, never Anglo-Irishism. Although all Macklin's plays after *King Henry the VII* (which is the revised version of *The Alternative, tyranny or liberty*) are comedies, they are aggressive and darkly satirical affairs in which a political anger is discernible. Thus in *The New Play Criticiz'd* (1746; later retitled as *The Suspicious Husband Criticiz'd*) Macklin holds up for savage ridicule in Sir Patrick Bashfull a new kind of stage Irishman who is actually a stage Anglo-Irishman. Bashfull is an insecure, blustering expatriate seeking acceptance in London fashionable circles but disabled by a feeling of incapacity in the strange milieu. In order to impress his acquaintances he denies his nationality and gives out that he was born in France; but his blunders only make things worse, as when he sings an Irish song to attract attention. Fashionable English society is also a target in this play, but Macklin treats Bashfull – a traitor to his nation as well as a fool – with particular savagery.

Macklin was by no means an Irish-obsessed writer. He was very observant of English life in its own right. He was also naturally interested in the politics of the green room, and in the relations between audience and performers in London theatres. Both subjects are covered in the play just discussed, *The New Play Criticiz'd*, which in spite of its superadded Irish theme was conceived in the first place as a reflection upon audience reactions to another dramatist's work. Theatrical and dramatic satire also figures in Macklin's play *A Will and No Will* (1746), a translation from Regnard's *Le Légataire Universel*, which satirises scandal-mongering among theatre audiences (Macklin here, perhaps, taking a hint from Fielding, and passing it on to Sheridan). And the theme is repeated in his next play, *The Covent-Garden Theatre* (1752) – if it is a play at all. Macklin calls the piece, which is largely plotless, a

'Dramatic Satyr'. Pasquin mounts a rostrum in the theatre and satiric-
ally catalogues public nuisances too subtle for the law: obstructive
patrons, pretenders to taste, damners of new plays, self-professed
critics, shameless ladies – all the members of the audience itself. The
piece has spirit, but reveals Macklin's chief problem as a dramatist:
construction. Macklin found it difficult to invent a convincing story. So
far, as a dramatist, he had got round this problem by lifting his plots
from history, or from the French drama, or by dispensing with plot
altogether (as in *Covent-Garden Theatre*). When he produced *The School
for Husbands* nine years later he tied sentimental drama with satirical
comedy and produced a work which enabled him to get in some blows
against political careerism in England (as represented by the ministerial ambitions of Lord Belville) while keeping the satire embedded in
a story of personal relationships (the Belvilles' uncertain marriage).
Although the play deals with English politics, Ireland still seems to
enter when the aristocratic Belville, caught in disguise, is forcibly
recruited into the army by an Irish corporal and an Irish private. The
scene is unexpectedly drawn-out. Is Macklin making a symbolic point?

Macklin's plays, it will be plain, may be farcical and under-
organised but they are never innocuous. Instead they are highly politically charged. They show Macklin to be a writer obsessed with the
vexed issue of national confrontation, especially with the historically
troubled political and cultural rivalries between England, Ireland and
Scotland. Macklin directs his scorn at two prime targets: the mental
slavery (Swift's term)[18] of those Irish men and women who have
willed away their national pride for a spurious Englishness, and,
secondly, the Scottish adventurers elbowing their way under the
influence of Lord Bute into prominent positions in British politics, thus
disadvantaging still further the 'injured lady' of Ireland.[19] This political
aggression could land Macklin in trouble. We may see this by the
reception given to his next play *The True Born Scotsman* (later called *The
Man of the World*). Macklin staged it in 1764 at the Crow Street Theatre
in Dublin but then failed to get it past the English censor for seventeen
consecutive years; *The Man of the World* only appeared in London in
1781, when its anti-Scottish satire had been watered down and its title
made less pointed.[20] This play can still impress by its narrow, furious
attack on Scottish adventurism, personified in the new man of the
world in the third quarter of the eighteenth century: not Lien Chi
Altangi, Goldsmith's urbane philosopher, but the gross careerist Sir
Pertinax MacSycophant, all elbows, greed and bluster.

The Man of the World includes no Irish character and lacks a specific
Irish dimension. Perhaps Macklin thought British political corruption
a sufficient handful on its own. But he returns to the subject of national

difference in his last complete play *Love-à-la-Mode* (1784). Four lovers pursue Charlotte Goodchild in marriage – an English sporting gentleman, a genteel Jew, an insolent Scotsman and an Irish rover. In the Irishman (who predictably wins the contest) Macklin counterbalances the pathetic Anglo-Irishman of his first play, Sir Patrick Bashfull, with an old Irish aristocrat who represents in an idealised form the historic culture of his race. Sir Callaghan O'Brallaghan is 'one of the true old Milesians',[21] with a lineage as honourable as any in the three kingdoms. Here Macklin risks dullness, for a paragon may be just as uninteresting on the stage as a satirical stereotype, but what he is seeking to do is depict an Irish character which bears some relation to the historical reality, and this is a rather new enterprise. Where Irish men and women were concerned, eighteenth-century English drama before Macklin had seen little but variations on the Teague caricature. Macklin seeks to move beyond this, just as, forty years earlier, he had rejected the Jewish stereotype in Shylock and replaced it with a historically and culturally convincing representation of the Jewish character.

Let us return to *The True Born Irishman* of 1761 – produced in Dublin three years before *Love-à-la-Mode*. It is obvious from Brian Friel's adaptation of this play, from his comments upon it, and from what has been said above, that in *The True Born Irishman* Macklin re-examines what was, for him, familiar ground. He ranges against the authentic Irish figure Sir Murrough O'Dogherty a number of Englishmen in Ireland or spurious Irish types (including O'Dogherty's Anglophile wife), and satirises the latter as seduced by English fashion and English power away from their true Irish responsibilities. There is Lord Oldcastle, the absentee landowner. There is Count Mushroom, his English agent. There is Oldcastle's brother, Counsellor Hamilton. To these, and to Mrs O'Dogherty, the hero's wife, add the lesser figures Lady Kinnegad, Lady Bab Frightful, Mrs Gazette, Mrs Jolly, and Major Gamble. As the range of these characters indicates, Macklin launches in *The True Born Irishman* not just an entertaining social satire, but an attack on the political mismanagement and careerist intrigue mixed inextricably, as it seems, with a moral laxity which he sees as characteristic of the entire cultural-political establishment of Anglo-Ireland. In O'Dogherty he combines, on the one hand, the personality of Gaelic Ireland in its historical reality (fast disappearing as he wrote),[22] while adding to him, on the other, an awareness of the immediate priorities needed in any political programme intended to deal effectively with Ireland's mid-century problems. As elsewhere in Macklin's plays, where economic, social and moral discussion comes to the fore, his language recalls Swift. Here, for instance, O'Dogherty's speech recalls the King of Brobdingnag's definition of truly useful public work. The allusion suggests a source for some of Macklin's political ideas:

Take this judgement from me, and remember that an honest quiet country gentleman who out of policy and humanity establishes manufactories, or that contrives employment for the idle and the industrious, or that makes but a blade of corn grow where there was none before, is of more use to this poor country than all the courtiers, and patriots, and politicians, and prodigals that are unhanged – so there let us leave them, and return to my wife's business.[23]

This speech illustrates another feature of Macklin's play, and plays – a key feature, which, as it happens, returns us to Brian Friel. The lines quoted are moralistic rather than dramatic, and in fact they hold up the drama by looking beyond the stage and addressing themselves not to Counsellor Hamilton, O'Dogherty's interlocutor within the play proper, but to the politicians outside and inside the theatre: the critics, the essayists, the intellectuals, the reading and writing public, the members of Parliament in Dublin and in London. They are, in short, rant. That Macklin himself is half aware of this we can see from the wrenches with which he brings his audience back to the drama by giving O'Dogherty the line: 'so there let us leave them, and return to my wife's business'. But meanwhile Mrs O'Dogherty's business has gone dreadfully cold. Why does Macklin not delete the speechifying? Because his wish to hit the Irish 'patriots' has prevailed over his dramatic instinct. He could not bring himself to dispense with a piece of political propaganda. Macklin lacked Pope's 'art to blot'. It may be a reason why he remains a minor dramatist.

Here, compare Brian Friel. The basic difference between *The True Born Irishman* and *The London Vertigo* is that Friel has produced out of Macklin's lively but cumbersome text a leaner, funnier script. As Friel remarks in his preface, one of his changes is technical: the reduction of fourteen characters to five to fit in with the economic stringencies of a modern theatre. But of course this trimming of the cast makes for an important dramatic difference too. When Friel cuts out the walk-on characters who satirise fashionable types in eighteenth-century Dublin (such as Mrs Jolly, Lady Kinnegad, Fitzmungrel and others) he sharpens the focus on the essential subject of Irish nationality. When he abolishes the supernumerary men servants James, John and William and collapses their roles into the single servant figure Katty Farrell, she, of course, grows enormously in significance. No less interesting is Friel's excision of those political and moral speeches in Macklin's version in which, as we have seen, drama yields to rhetoric. By laying down the mallet and taking up the rapier, he achieves a deeper penetration. Take the following exchange, in which Macklin's woodenly nationalistic writing is deleted or trimmed back into subtle suggestion, with a noticeable sharpening up of the drama. Here, first, is Friel:

O'DOGHERTY: Then let us be rid of your London English with your neems and your teestys and your veestlys and your imminselys.

MRS DIGGERTY: They're dispinsed with – dispensed with now.

O'DOGHERTY: And above all things, pray never again call me Diggerty. My name is Murrough O'Doherty and I am not ashamed of it. But that damned name Diggerty, my dear it – it – it dements me.

MRS DIGGERTY: Then upon my honour, Murrough O'Doherty, you'll never be demented again. (Friel, p. 36)

And here is Macklin:

O'DOGHERTY: And as to yourself, my dear Nancy, I hope I shall never have any more of your London English; none of your this here's, your that there's, your winegars, your weals, your vindors, your toastesses, and your stone postesses; but let me have our own good, plain, old Irish English, which I insist is better than all the English English that ever coquets and coxcombs brought into the land.

MRS DIGGERTY: I will get rid of these as fast as possible.

O'DOGHERTY: And pray, above all things, never call me Mr Diggerty – my name is Murrough O'Dogherty, and I am not ashamed of it; but that damned name Diggerty always vexes me whenever I hear it.

MRS DIGGERTY: Then, upon my honour, Mr O'Dogherty, it shall never vix you again.

O'DOGHERTY: Ogh, that's right, Nancy – O'Dogherty for ever – O'Dogherty! – there's a sound for you – why they have not such a name in all England as O'Dogherty – nor as any of our fine sounding Milesian names – what are your Jones and your Stones, your Rice and your Price, your Heads and your Foots, and Hands, and your Wills, and Hills and Mills, and Sands, and a parcel of little pimping names that a man would not pick out of the street, compared to the O'Donovans, O'Callaghans, O'Sullivans, O'Brallaghans, O'Shaghnesses, O'Flahertys, O'Gallaghers, and O'Dogherty's – Ogh, they have courage in the very sound of them, for they come out of the mouth like a storm; and are as old and as stout as the oak at the bottom of the bog of Allen, which was there before the flood – and though they have been dispossessed by upstarts and foreigners, buddoughs and sassanoughs, yet I hope they will flourish in the

Island of Saints, while grass grows or water runs.
(Bartley, pp. 111–12)

Notice that although Friel cuts out this undramatic last speech he does not lose the national point Macklin is at such pains to make. He places it less in view, but like the oak under the bog in O'Dogherty's simile the Irish dislike of English linguistic and cultural imperialism remains present in the text. In fact it could be said to be strengthened. On one level Friel's 'let us be rid of your London English' may appear just the slightest re-working of Macklin's 'I hope I shall never have any more of your London English'. But a second glance shows it to be suddenly ambiguous. Is the English language still being talked about, as before, or is the author now writing about the English people? If we are still discussing language, it is still true that Friel's revised line transforms a mere individual feeling into something more general. 'Let us be rid of' is not quite the same as 'I hope I shall never have any more of'. It has a more general application. It turns O'Dogherty's private dislike into a general, and perhaps a national, rejection. I don't know whether this is the case of a meaning being imposed on *The London Vertigo* by an individual reader, or whether it is an explosive implication ticking away in the text like a time bomb, having been placed there deliberately by the author. Either way it shows how advantageous it can be for a playwright to understate rather than overstate a dramatic idea.

In 1780, when a ship went down in the Irish Sea, Macklin lost a mass of unfinished writings, including draft plays. What would these have been like? They *could* have contained surprising developments, it is true, but Macklin's existing work does not suggest that his themes – social satire, political indignation, Irish pride – were going to change very much. He certainly had not become less political as the years went by; nor would he have written with less edge, to judge by the tendency of some of his commonplace jottings, published after his death. These rather suggest a continuing, dominant interest in the subject of national culture, and racial antagonism.[24] For example, take the following sketch for a new play from his commonplace book, possibly one of those plays which drowned:

THE ENGLISH MISANTHROPE. Of the noblest nature – angry with vice – in love with virtue – sees the vice of his country – knows what it must come to – loves it – would die for it – he has a great fortune. The materials of the TRUE BORN ENGLISHMAN would do for him and the fable. THE MISANTHROPE is a better character than the TRUE-BORN ENGLISH-MAN. – Query, but misanthropy is a fine active character for satire, and for myself.[25]

Macklin's allusion here to *The True Born Englishman* is puzzling

(Defoe's poem? Not easy to see how.) Possibly he refers to a planned work of his own. But what is clear is that he intended to give the proposed work a very sharp political slant.

Right to the end therefore Macklin was planning to explore and express the same basic feelings he had been concerned with all his acting and writing life: political authority, the Scots, Ireland, national culture and English fashion. All that Macklin wrote was a response to the colliding national sensibilities of mid-eighteenth century Britain. He explores the life of an alien in a foreign land. In particular, he illustrates some of the pressures which Irish artists lay under, living and working in England after the cessation of the Williamite wars, with their awareness of displacement and dispossession. The aggressive nature of his writing reflects this, and perhaps even his plays' jerky structure may be traced to a satiric overplus in the writer's mind, militating against urbane statement. Certainly the plays' sense of the unfairness of history and of the uncharming nature of English power politics, their sympathy with the culturally deprived and also – perhaps the other side of this sympathy – their scornful obsession with high fashion, London-based and emotionally arid, could well be seen as coming out of an Irish awareness.

Macklin made a great success of his career in England but never lost his central concern with the psychology of the rejected. Was he, in the end, as a writer, too political for his own good? His restless mind seems very close indeed to the stuff of his drama, and he was perhaps, it might be judged, too obsessed with historical and political argument, too locked into fact, to achieve a really lucid expression. Compare Goldsmith. In spite of its generic difference *The Deserted Village*, written on precisely the same topics as those of Macklin's plays, achieves a generality Macklin lacks because the writer severs his poem from too actual a connection with a real place and a real time.

Or, to end where we began, compare Macklin with Friel, all of whose plays show how much stronger it can be, artistically speaking, to leave things implied rather than explicitly and laboriously hammered out. Beside such a dramatist, Macklin can seem like a crude pioneer, chopping down a whole tree when he wants to make a single shelf. Pioneers, however, as Pound acknowledged in relation to Whitman, do clear the ground; without Macklin, later Irish dramatists might have found their subject matter harder to put into words. But if the finished work is what counts, we may concede finally that in rewriting *The True Born Irishman* as *The London Vertigo* Brian Friel has taken over from Charles Macklin a powerful, lumbering juggernaut, stripped it down to its essentials, and turned it into a racer.

FOR LIBERATION: BRIAN FRIEL AND THE USE OF MEMORY

SEAMUS HEANEY

> This is the use of memory:
> For liberation – not less of love but expanding
> Of love beyond desire, and so liberation
> From the future as well as the past. Thus, love of a country
> Begins as attachment to our own field of action
> And comes to find that action of little importance
> Though never indifferent. History may be servitude,
> History may be freedom. See, now they vanish,
> The faces and places, with the self which, as it could, loved them,
> To become renewed, transfigured, in another pattern.[1]

When T. S. Eliot says in *Little Gidding* that the use of memory is 'for liberation', he is not thinking of memory as an escape mechanism. What he has in mind is something more akin to that readjustment and repossession of the ability to understand experience which Aristotle called *catharsis*, that momentary release from confusion which comes from seeing a drama complete itself in accordance with its own inner necessities rather than in accordance with the spectator's wishes. The satisfaction which art gives resides in this sense of rightness which is wholly independent of the happiness of the characters, and separate from what the audience would wish for itself. What an audience experiences at the final curtain of Brian Friel's *Faith Healer* or *Translations* is just such a sensation of rightness; even though things have manifestly gone wrong for the people on the stage, the people in the stalls go away happy because of something completely rendered, a single meaning precipitated from a whole swirl of different elements. Their elation comes from the perception of an order beyond themselves which nevertheless seems foreknown, as if something forgotten surfaced for a clear moment. Whatever they knew before that moment then becomes 'renewed, transfigured, in another pattern.'

The other terms which Eliot employs in his celebrated meditation are equally suggestive in relation to the plays of Brian Friel. Servitude to history or freedom from it, lives subsiding, lives reviving, faces vanishing, patterns renewing – all these ways of seeing apply to Friel's presentation of Colmcille, Cass McGuire, the O'Donnell family who are the aristocrats of Ballybeg and those other far from aristocratic

229

O'Donnells, Gar and Screwballs, also of Ballybeg; and they equally apply to Hugh O'Donnell, the hedgeschoolmaster, of *Translations*, and Hugh O'Neill, the Earl of Tyrone, in *Making History*. All of these characters, and their fates as they are resolved by the dramatist, constitute aspects of a single vision; and that vision opens a path within us, individually and as a society, towards what Eliot called, in another memorable phrase, 'an overwhelming question.'

The question might be formulated like this: how does the fully conscious human life find its bearings in order to navigate between what Hugh O'Donnell calls 'privacies' and what Mabel Bagenal calls 'the overall thing'?[2] Between the allure of inherited affections and inexplicably meaningful memory, on the one hand, and on the other, the command to participate intelligently in the public world of historical process. How are the contours of a validating personal language to be moulded to the landscape of fact? One half of the consciousness, after all, is inclined to relapse, to repose on the cushion of the sixth sense, in the illogic of old attachments and defensively extravagant gesture, even as the other half is busily at work in the mammon of emotional iniquity, networking, politicking in relationships, abiding in compromise, vigilantly observing the decorum of the tribe.

Nobody is more exact in the presentation of this common predicament than Brian Friel. He gives a perfectly recognizable anatomy of the social life, the domestic life and the emotional life – tender, bewildered and punitive – of the semi-country people who inhabit his small towns and the city people who end up unexpectedly in the Guildhall or the archaeological site or 'the gentle island'. Friel knows these people and their inner demons completely. But he also knows, in the illuminating words of Seamus Deane, that what they live by is not what they live for.[3] The constrictions of the moral code and social manners of Irish life are experienced by them as a set of reflexes and caveats, but their sense of their ultimate meaning arrives as a tantalizing intimation of a freedom beyond the pale of the usual, beyond the routines of the day-to-day. We may therefore employ another distinction formulated by Seamus Deane and say that Brian Friel's work is always alert to the gap between the actuality of event and the reality of imagination,[4] and that as a consequence of this, his writings are intent upon showing forth the different tensions, transgressions and transfigurations that occur once the line between the realm of actuality and imagination is crossed.

Some of the most affecting and reticent expressions of the tension between the way his characters habitually conduct themselves and the need they intuitively feel for an ampler understanding and a more liberated experience occur in Friel's short stories. These stories constitute a beautifully fashioned pivot upon which the great intricate structure of the plays turns, and much of the complexity and tragedy of the mature work is implicit in their quieter atmospheres and incidents. Yet the subtlety of the stories is not bought at any expense of seriousness. What they do is to trace what William Wordsworth called, in a memorable phrase, the primary laws of our nature, and they do it by the methods which Wordsworth said he employed in composing the *Lyrical Ballads*. Like the poet, Friel also chooses incidents from common life, incidents which allow him to focus upon their psychological import for the characters; and then, by throwing over them a certain colouring of imagination, he proceeds to trace, truly though not ostentatiously, those primary laws – in particular, the laws of love and all their complicated relations to the operations of memory.

The consolations and distortions which memory provides, and the consequences, destructive and creative, which flow from those processes, are obviously a central concern of Friel's plays also. A great deal of his dramatic writing demonstrates the way his characters either retrieve or reconstruct a past, sometimes in order to indulge and absolve the characters, sometimes to expose and judge them, but mostly in order to exercise judgement and absolution at the same time. Friel is intent upon showing how easy it is for them to evade reality by taking the wrong memory-turn; and he is also intent upon confronting audiences and readers with the possibility that they too have been prone to the same evasions and false trails. But his effort is by no means all negative, since he also wishes to show that there are vitally necessary resources to which memory alone, in its true operations, will give access; so the problem which Friel, his characters and his audience face constantly is this: how to decide between a tender-minded allowance of memory's authentic reinforcements and a tough-minded disallowance of its self-serving deceptions.

From the beginning, Brian Friel's work obviously abounds in instances of the latter kind of memory-work, where a flattering distortion of the facts is laid like an unction to the soul – as, for example, in the story 'The Illusionists,' in which the schoolteacher father and the itinerant magician rehearse drunkenly and antiphonally their ideal fictions of themselves. Likewise, in *Aristocrats*, the O'Donnells of Ballybeg conspire half-consciously in the creation of a past which is partly a social benefit conferred harmlessly by themselves upon themselves, and partly a dangerous flight from reality which they reflexively and obstinately maintain. And then there is Cass McGuire, with all her protective fictions and resultant excoriations. These kinds of diagnoses occur everywhere in his work, but my main concern here is with the other, value-creating function of memory, memory as a mythological resource rather than a deceptive compensation. This is a function which Brian Friel can explore and affirm with enviable credibility since he is elsewhere so scrupulous about rejecting all that is spurious in appeals to the past. And when it is being explored, the writing tends to gain in concentration and lucidity, as in the following passage from *The Enemy Within*. Here Colmcille, self-exiled on Iona, is accusing himself of breaking the monastic rule that he lives by, but in doing so he also reveals very poignantly what it is he lives *for*:

Out at the corn there, Cormac was cutting, and I was behind him tying, and the sun was warm on my back, and I was stooped over, so that this bare, black exile was shrunk to a circle around my feet. And I was back in Tirconaill; and Cormac was Eoghan, my brother, humming to himself; and the dog that was barking was Ailbe, our sheepdog; and there were trees at the bottom of the field as long as I did not look; and the blue sky was quick with larks as long as I did not lift my head; and the white point of Errigal mountain was behind my shoulder as long as I kept my eyes on the ground. And when we got to the bottom of the field, Cormac called to me, 'Look what I found! A horse shoe! That's for luck!' But I did not look up because he was still Eoghan, my brother, and the earth was still Gartan earth; and the sound of the sea was the water of Gartan Lough; and any minute mother would come to the head of the hill and strike the iron triangle to summon us in for food. And when Cormac spoke I did not answer him because I could not leave them, Caornan. As God is above, I could not leave them![5]

This passage, perhaps, could be read as evidence of a lapse into disabling nostalgia on Colmcille's part rather than an enabling pilgrimage to the sources of his emotional stamina. I believe, however, that it does represent this latter positive phenomenon, because the Donegal memory is something that the character re-enters not in order to avoid the present but because he wishes to fortify himself so as to deal with the present in a more competent and empowered way. In such a case, memory is recognized as an element where consciousness refreshes and verifies itself, an element where energy and vision are given new sharpness and confirmation, and for such salubrious purposes it is even occasionally allowable that memory should play tricks.

There are moments in *Philadelphia, Here I Come!* where the dramatist and the audience must abide by their tender-minded impulses. When, for example, Gar Private remembers fishing with his father in a blue boat, and his father all the time singing 'All Round My Hat I'll Wear a Green-coloured Ribbono', the integrity of that memory is not diminished by Councillor O'Donnell's staid enumeration of the facts – first in relation to the song:' "All Round my Hat"? No, I don't think I ever knew that one. It wasn't "The Flower of Sweet Strabane," was it? That was my song.' And then, in relation to the boat: 'And you say the boat was blue. . . there was a brown one belonging to the doctor and before that there was a wee flat-bottom – but it was green – or was it white?' (*SP* 95) As I say, the Councillor's humdrum grip upon the facts does not and is not meant to deny the creative truth of Gar's memory of a blue boat. Instead, the dramatist is implicitly insisting upon the authenticity of that visionary, transformative faculty which reinforces and gives energy to a life in touch with its impulses towards individuation. In other words, Gar O'Donnell – Gar Public and Gar Private united by action and in total self-consciousness – this whole Gar derives a confidence of identity from his image of the past, an image whose contents may be questionable but whose truth has been proved acceptable. And it is acceptable because the intelligence has been at work upon the psychic matter, a process which Brian Friel shows happening in slow motion by presenting us with the constant, vigilant negotiations between Gar Public and Gar Private.

Elsewhere, he also shows this process happening within the consciousness of Joe, the unpretentious hero of that low-key but subtle story, 'Among the Ruins'. When Joe returns with his wife and children to his childhood home, he has some kind of experience from which he can wrest no satisfactory meaning until he is driving back home in the car. His wife is irritated by his inarticulateness about why he cherishes memories of the little bower where he played as a boy; he himself is let down by the gap between the aura of the place in his recollections and the plain, small factuality of its topographical existence; and during the course of the visit, his disappointment at all this was only banished by a panic that his son Peter had been lost in the fields. That panic ended, however, when he came upon the child playing a strange private game called 'donging the tower', and the story ends like this:

What did Peter mean, he wondered dreamily; what game was he playing, donging the tower? . . . not that it mattered. . . . And then a flutter of excitement stirred in him. Yes, yes, it did matter. Not the words, not the game, but the fact that he had seen his son, on the first good day of summer, busily, intently happy in solitude, donging the tower. The fact that Peter would never remember it was of no importance; it was his own possession now, his own happiness, this knowledge of a child's private joy. Then, as he turned the car into the road that led to their house, a strange, extravagant thought struck him. He must have had moments of his own like Peter's, alone, back in Corradinna, donging his own towers. And, just as surely, his own father must have stumbled on him, and must have recognized himself in his son. And his father before that, and his father before that. Generations of fathers stretching back and back, all finding magic and sustenance in the brief, quickly destroyed happiness of their children. The past did have meaning. It was neither reality nor dreams, neither today's patchy oaks nor the great woods of his boyhood. It was simply continuance, life repeating itself and surviving.[6]

This conclusion enacts that process of rumination and internalisation of knowledge which I had in mind when I spoke of intelligence being at work upon psychic matter, and it is a process, of course, which is repeated every time a writer carries through successfully a work of imaginative composition. In fact, some things which Carl Gustav Jung writes in the 'Prologue' to his autobiographical *Memories, Dreams, Reflections* are particularly apposite to this discussion of Friel as an explorer and illuminator of the human psyche. Obviously Friel's writings are also critically and profitably alive to the social and historical dimensions which his characters inhabit, and his oeuvre has been both illuminating and steadying for those of us who have lived with it as it appeared over the past three decades. The deformations and needs brought on by narrowness in social and religious affairs in Ireland, the motives and consequences of political violence, emigration, the Irish language, the attitudes to be taken towards Irish history – all of these topics have been addressed by him and been revivified for his audience. Here, however, I want to supplement the view of Friel as an interpreter of Irish society with a glance at Friel the myth-maker, the mental fortune-seeker who has fared forth in imagination and come back with a story to tell, which is the story of the effort and price of becoming whole. And this is why Jung seems apposite: his 'Prologue' begins as follows:

My life is a story of the self-realisation of the unconscious. Everything in the unconscious seeks outward manifestation and the personality too desires to evolve out of its unconscious conditions and experience itself as a whole.[7]

This could be the voice of Frank Hardy in *Faith Healer* or Grace Hardy or Gar O'Donnell or the dumb-struck Sarah of *Translations*. But what Jung says a couple of paragraphs later could surely be the voice of Brian Friel himself.

Thus it is that I have now undertaken . . . to tell my personal myth. I can only make direct statements, only 'tell stories'. Whether or not the stories are 'true' is not the problem. The only question is whether what I tell is *my* fable, *my* truth.

Obviously, neither Jung nor Friel mean to abscond from the evidence when they insist on the right to tell a personal truth. The evidence is what we are all up against, and when Jung writes of telling 'a personal myth' which will be 'my fable, my truth', he is not proposing to enter the realm of fantasy or to shirk his responsibility to face facts. He is insisting rather that the evidence and the facts be confronted afresh, that the individual consciousness take the measure of reality in a first-hand, unmediated encounter, that the panaceas and alibis and stereotypes offered by convention be avoided and the impact of the real be received directly and registered in an authentic voice. For example, it is because Hugh O'Neill connives in what he knows to be an inauthentic story of his life being propounded by Peter Lombard that he weeps and asks forgiveness of the dead Mabel Bagenal at the end of *Making History*; conversely, it is because of the authenticity of the transition from narrative presentation to reverie and narcotic dream-life at the end of *Dancing at Lughnasa* that we can respect Michael's entrancement as an adequate response to 'the evidence'. At the end of *Making History*, Peter Lombard's 'story' is unacceptable because it is rigged for political purposes and told as a cover-up, whereas at the end of *Lughnasa* the fiction of transition into the eternal world of dance, the tír-na-nóg of memory itself, is acceptable precisely because it has been demonstrated to be a personal truth. It is Michael's own fable, constructed in face of but not in avoidance of the evidence:

And so, when I cast my mind back to that summer of 1936, different kinds of memories offer themselves to me.

But there is one memory of that Lughnasa time that visits me most often; and what fascinates me about that memory is that it owes nothing to fact. In that memory atmosphere is more real than incident and everything is simultaneously actual and illusory. In that memory, too, the air is nostalgic with the music of the thirties. It drifts in from somewhere far away – a mirage of sound – a dream music that is both heard and imagined; that seems to be both itself and its own echo; a sound so alluring and so mesmeric that the afternoon is bewitched, maybe haunted, by it. And what is so strange about that memory is that everybody seems to be floating on those sweet sounds, moving rhythmically, languorously, in complete isolation; responding more to the mood of the music than to its beat. When I remember it, I think of it as dancing. Dancing with eyes half closed because to open them would break the spell. Dancing as if language had surrendered to movement – as if this ritual, this wordless ceremony, was now the way to speak, to whisper private and sacred things, to be in touch with some otherness.[8]

Those lines from the conclusion of *Dancing at Lughnasa* mesh perfectly with other lines from Jung's 'Prologue', and taken together with them, they can lead us towards a deeper understanding of the homeopathic function of Brian Friel's drama within our lives and our historical moment. Jung writes:

When we think of the unending growth and decay of life and civilisations, we cannot escape the impression of absolute nullity. Yet I have never lost a sense of something that lives and endures underneath the eternal flux. . . . In the end the only events in my life worth telling are those when the imperishable world irrupted into this transitory one. . . . Similarly, other people are established inalienably in my memories only if their names were entered in the scrolls of my destiny from the beginning, so that encountering them was at the same time a kind of recollection.[9]

These sentences seem applicable to the way in which many of Friel's most significant characters are impelled within themselves and understand the import of what happens to them. At the end of *Volunteers*, for example, as Keeney goes out, intelligent and hopeless, to meet the death which he knows his prison comrades have arranged for him, what he walks towards is indeed 'a kind of recollection'. At that point, we are witnessing the 'self-realization of his unconscious'; the laws of his nature and the inexorable laws of the drama are in accord. All the recklessness and nihilism which his vivid, cynical behaviour has manifested grow pointed, definite and purposeful as he heads offstage for the last time, having dismissed the audience's culpable security and their avoidance of the violent underlife of their society in one final, maimed, ironical limerick:

> Five diggers examined their plight
> But a kangaroo court
> Gave a final report. . .
> They were only a parcel of. . .[10]

And if Keeney goes to encounter a fate which seems like a recollection, how much more inescapably is this the case at the end of *Faith Healer*. All through that play's rememberings and misrememberings, the contradictory inventions and fictionalizing of Frank Hardy and Grace and Teddy are symptoms of a destiny – or, in Jung's terms, an unconscious – trying to realize itself; and the play's function is to reveal both the achievement of this realization and the awful price it entails.

Frank Hardy is a Colmcille without a monastic rule, a martyr without a metaphysic, a man tossed about in a world of relative values and uncertain motives until he returns to Ireland and meets the absolute McGarvey, his unrealized, dumb other. What he experiences in that meeting corresponds to those events where, in Jung's words, 'the imperishable world irrupted into this transitory one.' In *The Enemy Within*, Colmcille may cry out with a certain self-knowledge and a certain theatricality, 'What more do you demand of me, damned Ireland? My soul? My immortal soul? Damned, damned, damned Ireland! (*His voice breaks*) Soft, green Ireland – beautiful green Ireland.. . .'[11] but in spite of that emotional rhetoric, there is still a certain illustrative element in the saint's outcry. In the early play, Friel is intent on showing that the inherited circumstances of family and memory and love – the 'privacies' – have become the enemy within and create the pain of Colmcille's adjustment to 'the overall thing.' Thus, the whole action of the play has the force of a parable, and the conclusion offers the satisfaction of expectations fulfilled – the saint has mastered his daimon and is ready to begin again within the discipline of his monastic vows. But the conclusion of *Faith Healer* has the radiance of myth, it carries its protagonist and its audience into a realm *beyond* expectation, and it carries the drama back to that original point where it once participated in the sacred, where sacrifice was witnessed and the world renewed by that sacrifice.

What Frank Hardy does is to sacrifice a future of uncertainty and tawdriness as a travelling faith-healer to the idea of himself as a redemptive figure. Yet the sacrifice is utterly un-transcendent; Frank expects no flow of grace or benefit for himself or the survivors; all he expects is all that he achieves, a failure which constitutes a fidelity. He accepts, indeed he embraces the failure of his gift to transform reality, yet he also reveals an exemplary fidelity in himself to the *idea* of transformation. The conclusion of *Faith Healer*, in other words, is the ultimate manifestation of the convergence of opposites, the point of intersection between imperative vision and incontrovertible evidence, in that Hardy lives out to the death his own personal myth, fully conscious of the evidence that is there all the time, evidence which says that he will fail to cure McGarvey and the consequences will be fatal.

All of the characters in *Faith Healer* speak out of a kind of afterlife, a kind of post-fatal depression, as it were. All of them exhibit the workings of memory, its capacity to re-arrange the facts in a self-serving or self-protective or compensatory way. The loss of Grace's child and her solitary suicide are the cruel ground note of the action, and they impugn the character of Frank Hardy: he is a self-absorbed and destructive protagonist as well as a self-destructive one. But it is only Frank who is capable of turning the workings of memory into 'the use of memory', and revealing how the world can be 'renewed, transfigured, in another pattern,' which is the ancient pattern of tragic art itself.

The tragic emotion subsumes all kinds of loss and disappointment into itself, and there is a sense in which *Faith Healer* is a play of triumph and affirmation. The performer in Frank Hardy comes to his rescue at the very end so that he takes his destiny into his own hands even as he hands himself over to the deadly custody of the dangermen at first light. There is a shine off the writing in this finale, a cathartic brilliance.

But at the end of *Translations*, the disappointment is unmitigated and it is amplified very resourcefully and deliberately by the dramatist's play upon the audience's own literary and historical memory. Obviously, the end of *Translations* coincides with the end of its central character's world. Hugh O'Donnell is drunk and affected by the pathos of his own decline so that, dramatically speaking, his recitation of the passage from Virgil's *Aeneid* is an apt and characteristic response to his situation. Virgil's anticipation of the fall of Carthage and the rise of Rome at its expense comes naturally into the mind of an old classics teacher as an analogy for the fall of Irish-speaking culture before the economic and military power of England and English-speakers. But there is another way in which Friel has amplified the theme of defeat, one which reinforces Hugh O'Donnell's literary allusion to Virgil and which constitutes a further instance of the use of memory by the playwright.

Surely the end of *Translations* is meant to echo the end of another play where a Juno wreaks her vengeance, one which also ends with two drunk men philosophizing on the floor. Neither Hugh nor Jimmy Jack actually does say that the world is in 'an awful state of chassis', but their situation inevitably recalls that of Captain Boyle and Joxer Daly at the end of *Juno and the Paycock*. Once again, in the aftermath of a death and a domestic collapse inside the larger context of a violent political crisis, two marginalized boozers are left to represent the human condition, two contenders who should be ridiculous but who actually manage to be heartbreaking. There is, however, a greater intellectual valency about the conclusion of the Friel play, not least because of its self-conscious translation of the famous O'Casey scene into an historical context almost a century before the moment in which O'Casey set it. Suffice it to say that Friel is here obeying the great reminder which Hugh gives to Owen earlier in the scene when he tells him that we are shaped by images of the past and that we must therefore never cease renewing those images. What the end of *Translations* does is to disallow too much sentimental indulgence for those two old tragi-comic codgers in the earlier play: their beloved theatrical images are being ironized, and certain stereotypes from the historical memory are also being revised – stereotypes of the learned hedge-schoolmaster and the prodigiously educated country scholar, the wild earth of whose speech is richly stored with the fragmented ware of classical literature. Moreover, Friel here reveals himself as the more purposefully inventive dramatist because he is not simply designing an anti-heroic curtain. He is attempting instead the theatrical equivalent of Jung's intuition that 'something lives and endures under the eternal flux.'

Jung's words, in isolation, may sound like a shaky proposition, but we are bound to take them more seriously when we have heard Hugh O'Donnell not only recite his Virgil but also recollect the mythic inevitability of his faring forth in the spring of 1798, a recollection which operates to provide character and audience alike with what Wordsworth called 'intimations of immortality'.

Everything seemed to find definition that spring – a congruence, a miraculous matching of hope and past and present and possibility. Striding across the fresh, green land. The rhythms of perception heightened. The whole enterprise of consciousness accelerated. We were gods that morning, James; and I had recently married my goddess, Caitlin Dubh Nic Reactainn, may she rest in peace. And to leave her and my infant son in his cradle – that was heroic, too. By God sir, we were magnificent. We marched as far as – where was it? – Glenties! All of twenty-three miles in one day. And it was there, in Phelan's pub, that we got homesick for Athens, just like Ulysses. The *desiderium nostrorum* – the need for our own. Our *pietas*, James, was for older, quieter things. And that was the longest twenty-three miles back I ever made. (*Toasts* JIMMY.) My friend, confusion is not an ignoble condition. (*SP* 445-6)

Of course, that wonderfully absolving line about confusion is directed to Jimmy Jack, and is not meant to let the audience off the hook. The characters in the play may be indulged in their nostalgia, but the play itself is intent upon liberating both the audience and the playwright himself from any consolation in the backward look. Nevertheless, to anatomize the problem as a condition of confusion rather than a 'state of chassis' is to direct attention to one central reason for Friel's major importance as a dramatist, for Ireland and for the world, in the late twentieth century.

At this stage, we no longer think of human beings as a conjunction of the animal and the angel, or as the convergence of supernatural essences and sublunar substance. Even in Ireland, that older religious understanding of human nature has been replaced by a post-Christian understanding of ourselves as creatures who include inside our minds all that was once imagined beyond ourselves, outside time and space, in the hell and heaven of eternity. Yet it is true to say that we and our language still possess a religious unconscious, whether we are striving consciously to secularize ourselves or are being secularized, willynilly. What were once confidently referred to as 'the values of Western civilization' may have been deconstructed and unmasked as mere contrivances by which élites have heretofore mystified the basis of their power. A newer economic and political understanding may have replaced the theological and moral emphases of an older world. But even so, the necessity to be a single person is still felt as an imperative, a necessity to get some self-integrating hold upon our 'confusion', upon the randomness and contradictoriness of what we experience. We refuse to abandon ourselves totally to a relativistic flux even as we concede the inadequacy of older systems of order and authority, whether they were invested in a faith or a family or a motherland. Friel's plays ultimately recognise this modern solitude of the person within the universe, and they search for minimally trustworthy bases upon which to situate a spiritually purposeful and value-engendering existence. In this search, memory and its transformations are sometimes the guide, sometimes the misguider; memory remains, at any rate, one of the thresholds where the quester for truth undergoes a test. False memory sends the quester into the land of self-deception, into the limbo of meaningless invention; but true memory gives access to the dancing place, the point of eternal renewal and confident departure.

Brian Friel's plays are poetic and mighty because they make these generalities palpable and affective. They reflect their region, and make images which are as elaborate as our intuitions, images which are moreover true to their maker and to his wise, lucid, uncompromised understanding. For finally, in the words of a Wallace Stevens poem which I have already echoed, 'the image must be of the nature of its creator'; so I shall conclude by quoting further from 'A Mythology Reflects its Region.' These lines are meant to reaffirm, in an idiom different from the idiom of Carl Jung, that by telling stories Brian Friel has made a triumph out of the telling of his personal myth. By telling *his* fable and *his* truth, he has given his audience access to their own possibilities and reminded them also of their limitations:

> The image must be of the nature of its creator.
> It is the nature of its creator increased,
> Heightened. It is he, anew, in freshened youth
> And it is he in the substance of his region,
> Wood of his forests and stone out of his fields
> Or from under his mountains.[12]

NOTES

INTRODUCTION

Alan Peacock

1   D. E. S. Maxwell, *A Critical History of Modern Irish Drama* (Cambridge, Cambridge University Press, 1984), p. 201.
2   D. E. S. Maxwell, *Brian Friel* (Lewisburg, Bucknell University Press, 1973), p. 109.
3   Des Hickey and Gus Smith, *A Paler Shade of Green* (London, Leslie Frewin, 1972), p. 223.
4   *Ibid.*, p. 224.
5   Brian Friel, 'The Theatre of Hope and Despair', *Everyman*, 1 (1968), pp. 19–20.
6   Friel, *A Paler Shade* . . . , p. 222; George O'Brien, *Brian Friel* (Dublin, Gill and MacMillan, 1989), p. 53.

' "DONGING THE TOWER" — THE PAST DID HAVE MEANING': THE SHORT STORIES OF BRIAN FRIEL

John Cronin

1   *TLS*, 28 April 1966, p. 361.
2   D. E. S. Maxwell, *Brian Friel* (Lewisburg, Bucknell University Press, 1973), p. 50.
3   Brian Friel, 'The Theatre of Hope and Despair', *Everyman*, 1 (1968), p. 19.
4   Seamus Deane, *Brian Friel: Selected Stories* (Dublin, The Gallery Press, 1979), Introduction, p. 9.
5   *TLS*, 19 April 1963, p. 261.
6   Brian Friel, *The Saucer of Larks* (London, Victor Gollancz, 1962), p. 20.
7   *Ibid.*, pp. 27–28.
8   *Ibid.*, pp. 24–25.
9   *Ibid.*, p. 26.
10 *Ibid.*, p. 29.
11 *Ibid.*, p. 30.
12 Brian Friel, *The Loves of Cass McGuire* (Dublin, The Gallery Press, 1984), p. 49.
13 *The Saucer of Larks, op. cit.*, pp. 21–22.

14 Maxwell, *op. cit.*, p. 31.
15 *The Saucer of Larks*, op. cit., p. 57.
16 *Ibid.*, p. 63.
17 *Ibid.*, p. 65.
18 Brian Friel, 'Self-Portrait', *Aquarius*, 5 (1972), p. 18.
19 *Ibid.*, p. 17.

THE PENALTIES OF RETROSPECT: CONTINUITIES IN BRIAN FRIEL

Neil Corcoran

1 Seamus Deane (ed.), *Selected Plays of Brian Friel* (London, Faber and Faber, 1984), p. 15.
2 Edward Said, *Beginnings: Intention and Method* (New York, Columbia University Press, 1985), p. 40.
3 Seamus Heaney, *Death of a Naturalist* (London, Faber and Faber, 1966), p. 43.
4 Brian Friel, *The Enemy Within* (Dublin, Gallery Books, 1979), p. 70.
5 Brian Friel, *The Loves of Cass McGuire* (London, Faber and Faber, 1967), p. 14.
6 Brian Friel, *The Gentle Island* (London, Davis-Poynter, 1973), p. 37.
7 Seamus Deane, *op. cit.*, pp. 21–2.
8 *See* Edna Longley, *Poetry in the Wars* (Newcastle upon Tyne, Bloodaxe Books, 1986), pp. 190–1.
9 Declan Kiberd, 'Irish Literature and Irish History' in R. F. Foster (ed.), *The Oxford Illustrated History of Ireland* (Oxford, Oxford University Press, 1989), p. 331.

THE FIFTH PROVINCE

Elmer Andrews

1 Blurb on dustjacket of *Ireland's Field Day* (London, Hutchinson, 1985).
2 Friel quoted in John Gray, 'Field Day Five Years On', in *The Linen Hall Review*, vol. 2, no. 2 (Summer 1985), p. 7. The 'Fifth Province' was a concept originally explored by Richard Kearney (one of the Field Day pamphleteers represented in *Ireland's Field Day*) and Mark Hederman in the first issue of *Crane Bag* (1977). They noted that the Irish word for province — 'coiced' — meant, literally, a fifth, and that 'although Tara was always the political centre of Ireland, this middle or fifth province acted as a second centre which though non-political, was just as important, acting as a necessary balance'. It was 'the secret centre . . . where all oppositions were resolved. . . The constitution

of such a place would require that each person discover it for himself within himself'. Friel, in an interview in the *Irish Times* (18 September 1984), confirms that Field Day appropriated the phrase, suggesting that the ' "Fifth Province" may well be a province of mind through which we hope to devise another way of looking at Ireland, or another possible Ireland' — one that first must be 'articulated, spoken, written, painted, sung', but then may be legislated for.

3 This, and subsequent citations, are from *The Gentle Island* (London, Davis-Poynter, 1973).

4 Seamus Heaney, 'Viking Dublin: Trial Pieces', *North* (London, Faber and Faber, 1975), p. 23.

5 Derek Mahon, 'The Last of the Fire Kings', *Poems 1962–1978* (Oxford, Oxford University Press, 1979), p. 65.

6 This, and subsequent citations, are from *Volunteers* (London, Faber and Faber, 1979).

7 Heaney, 'Punishment', *North*, p. 38.

8 Heaney, 'Viking Dublin: Trial Pieces', *North*, p. 23.

'FIGURES IN A PEEPSHOW': FRIEL AND THE IRISH DRAMATIC TRADITION

Desmond Maxwell

1 From *On the Boiler*, *Explorations* (London, MacMillan, 1962), p. 446.

2 *Autobiographies* (London, MacMillan, 1955), p. 524.

3 *Essays and Introductions* (London, MacMillan, 1961), p. 170.

4 *Ibid.*, p. 224.

5 *Explorations*, p. 250.

6 *Ibid.*, pp. 74 and 247.

7 *Ibid.*, p. 254.

8 Its Board of Directors has since added Seamus Deane, David Hammond, Seamus Heaney, Tom Kilroy and Tom Paulin.

9 Field Day productions: Brian Friel, *Translations* (1980), *Three Sisters* (1981, adapted from Chekhov), *The Communication Cord* (1982), *Making History* (1988); Athol Fugard, *Boesman and Lena* (1983); Tom Paulin, *The Riot Act* (from *Antigone*) and Derek Mahon, *High Time* (Translation of *L'École des Maris* (1984); Tom Kilroy *Double Cross* (1986); Stewart Parker, *Pentecost* (1987).

10 Seamus Deane, 'Field Day', *Ireland Today*, June 1985.

11 Seamus Deane, programme note to *Translations*.

12 *The Dramatic Works of Denis Johnston*, Vol. I (Gerrards Cross, Colin Smythe, 1977), p. 80.

13 The other plays are *The Communication Cord* — described by Seamus Deane as 'a farce which undermines the pieties sponsored by' *Translations*; the stage adaptation of Turgenev's *Fathers and Sons*; and *Dancing at Lughnasa*, produced by the Abbey in 1990.

14 Brian Friel, *Making History* (London, Faber and Faber, 1989), p. 70.
15 *Explorations*, p. 167.
16 *On Poetry and Poets* (London, Faber and Faber, 1957), p. 77.
17 'All Change: Contemporary Fashions in the Irish Theatre' in M. Sekine, *Irish Writers and the Theatre* (Gerrards Cross, Colin Smythe, 1986), p. 36.
18 'The Essential and the Incidental', *The Bookman*, LXXXCI (1934), repr. *Disjecta*, pp. 82–3.

FRIEL'S 'EMBLEMS OF ADVERSITY' AND THE YEATSIAN EXAMPLE

Christopher Murray

1 Conor Cruise O'Brien, 'An Unhealthy Intersection', *The New Review*, 2, No. 16 (July 1975), 3–8. Also *The Irish Times*, 21 August 1975, p. 10.
2 W. B. Yeats, 'The Man and the Echo', *Collected Poems* (London: Macmillan, 1950), p. 393.
3 Fintan O'Toole, 'The Man from God Knows Where: An Interview with Brian Friel', *In Dublin*, 28 October 1982, p. 22.
4 Eavan Boland, 'Brian Friel: Derry's Playwright', *Hibernia*, 16 February 1973, p. 18.
5 *See* Seamus Kelly, 'New Friel Play at the Abbey', *Irish Times*, 21 February 1973; Desmond Rushe, 'Friel's "Freedom" Ironic Commentary', *Irish Independent*, 21 February 1973; Gus Smith, 'For Whom the Bells Tolled', *Sunday Independent*, 25 February 1973; Mary Manning, 'Freedom of the City', *Hibernia*, 2 March 1973, p. 28.
6 *See* Sean Cronin, 'Letter from New York: Storm over Friel Play on Broadway', *Irish Times*, 4 March 1974, p. 13. See also Elizabeth Hale Winkler, 'Reflections of Derry's Bloody Sunday in Literature', in *Studies in Anglo-Irish Literature*, ed. Heinz Kosok (Bonn: Herbert Grundmann, 1982), pp. 411–21. The play 'Constitutes a bitter accusation of the injustice of the Widgery Report' (p. 415).
7 Seamus Kelly, drama critic for *The Irish Times*, concluded his review of *Volunteers* on 6 March 1975 (p. 11) with the querulous query, 'Your point, Mr. Friel — your point?'
8 Seamus Heaney, 'Digging Deeper', *Times Literary Supplement*, 21 March 1975, p. 306. The reference was to Gus Smith, 'Friel Must Dig Deeper', *Sunday Independent*, 9 March 1975, p. 11.
9 Lynda Henderson, 'A Dangerous Translation', *Fortnight*, 235 (10–23 March 1986), p. 24.
10 Edna Longley, 'Poetry and Politics in Northern Ireland', *The Crane Bag*, 9.1 (1985), p. 29. The subsequent quotation is from the same page.
11 Brian Friel, John Andrews and Kevin Barry, '*Translations* and *A Paper Landscape*: Between Fiction and History', *The Crane Bag*, 7.2 (1983), p. 123. Subsequent references to Andrews's comments refer to this source, for which page numbers are given parenthetically.

12 Sean Connolly, 'Dreaming History: Brian Friel's *Translations'*, *Theatre Ireland*, 13 (1987), p. 43.
13 Brian McAvera, 'Profile of Brian Friel', *Fortnight*, 215 (4–15 March 1985), p. 20.
14 Quoted by James W. Flannery, *W. B. Yeats and the Idea of a Theatre: The Early Abbey Theatre in Theory and Practice* (New Haven and London: Yale University Press, 1976), pp. 332–3.
15 *Uncollected Prose by W. B. Yeats*, ed. John P. Frayne and Colton Johnson (London and Basingstoke: Macmillan, 1975), II, p. 308.
16 W. B. Yeats, *Explorations* (London: Macmillan, 1962), p. 241.
17 Lady Gregory, *Our Irish Theatre: A Chapter of Autobiography* (Gerrards Cross: Colin Smythe, 1972), p. 91.
18 *Ibid.*, pp. 94–5.
19 Fintan O'Toole, 'The Man from God Knows Where', p. 23.
20 James Fenton, 'Ireland: Destruction of an Idyll', *The Sunday Times*, 28 September 1980, p. 40.
21 Ernest Blythe, *The Abbey Theatre* (Dublin: National Theatre Society Ltd., n.d.), no pagination, section headed 'Influence in Public Affairs'. The subsequent quotations are also from this section.
22 Philip Edwards, *Threshold of a Nation: A Study in English and Irish Drama* (Cambridge: Cambridge University Press, 1979), p. 211. Space does not here permit the exploration in Friel's plays of this repudiation of the future, but it is a significant emphasis.
23 'Voice from Ireland: Victoria Radin talks to Brian Friel', *The Observer*, 1 March 1981, p. 34.
24 Brian Friel, 'Plays Peasant and Unpeasant', *Times Literary Supplement*, 17 March 1972, p. 306.
25 W. B. Yeats, *Explorations*, p. 108.
26 *Ibid.*, p. 210.
27 Ulf Dantanus, *Brian Friel: The Growth of an Irish Dramatist* (Göteborg: Acta Universitatis Gothoburgensis, 1985), p. 34. *See also* pp. 37–8.
28 W. B. Yeats, *Explorations*, p. 2·2.
29 J. M. Synge to Frank Fay, April 1904, quoted by Ann Saddlemyer, ed., *J. M. Synge Collected Works*, III (London: Oxford University Press, 1968), p. xxvii.
30 W. B. Yeats, *Explorations*, p. 164.
31 'Finding Voice in a Language Not our Own: Brian Friel in interview with Ciaran Carty', *Sunday Independent*, 5 October 1980, p. 16.
32 ' "Talking to Ourselves": Brial Friel Talks to Paddy Agnew', *Magill*, 4.3 (December 1980), p. 60.
33 W. B. Yeats, *Essays and Introductions* (London: Macmillan, 1961), pp. 519–20.
34 Brian Friel, 'Extracts from a Sporadic Diary' [on *Translations*], in *Ireland and the Arts*, ed. Tim Pat Coogan (London: Namara Press, n.d.), p. 58.
35 'The Saturday Interview: Elgy Gillespie talked to Brian Friel', *Irish Times*, 5 September 1981, Weekend, p. 6.

36   Brian Friel, *Anton Chekhov's Three Sisters: A Translation* (Dublin: Gallery Books, 1981), p. 81.
37   Brian Friel, 'Extracts from a Sporadic Diary' [on *Aristocrats*], in *The Writers: A Sense of Ireland*, ed.. Andrew Carpenter and Peter Fallon (Dublin: O'Brien Press, 1980), p. 40.
38   Brian Friel, 'The Theatre of Hope and Despair', in *Everyman*, 1.1 (1968), p. 21.
39   W. B. Yeats, *Essays and Introductions*, p. 224.
40   Seamus Deane, *Celtic Revivals: Essays in Modern Irish Literature 1880–1980* (London: Faber and Faber, 1985), p. 168.
41   W. B. Yeats, *Essays and Introductions*, p. 224.
42   *Ibid.*, p. 245.
43   W. B. Yeats, *Collected Plays* (London: Macmillan, 1952), p. 289.
44   *Ibid.*, p. 593.
45   Robert Cushman, 'Taking a Look at Tribal Customs', *The Observer*, 8 March 1981.
46   It may not be immediately apparent that *Calvary* is a dream play, but this is suggested by the First Musician's lines: 'Good Friday's come, / The day whereon Christ dreams His Passion through. / He climbs up hither but as a dreamer climbs.' See *Collected Plays*, p. 450.
47   Robert Hewison, 'Forces of Persuasion', *Times Literary Supplement*, 20 March 1981, p. 310.
48   W. B. Yeats, *Purgatory*, in *Collected Plays*, p. 689.
49   W. B. Yeats, *Essays and Introductions*, p. 221.
50   Brian Friel, *Dancing at Lughnasa* (London and Boston: Faber and Faber, 1990), p. 71.

BRIAN FRIEL: THE NAME OF THE GAME

Seamus Deane

1   Saul Kripke, *Naming and Necessity* (Cambridge, Mass., Harvard University Press, 1980), p. 24.

TRANSLATING THE PAST: FRIEL, GREECE AND ROME

Alan Peacock

1   Brian Friel, *Three Sisters* by Anton Chekhov (Dublin, The Gallery Press, 1981), p. 101.
2   Patrick Kavanagh, *The Complete Poems*, ed. Peter Kavanagh (Newbridge, The Goldsmith Press, 1984), p. 238.
3   Brian Friel (ed.), *The Last of the Name: Charles McGlinchey* (Belfast, The Blackstaff Press, 1986), pp. 1–2.

4 Sean O'Casey, *Three Plays* (London, Pan Books, 1980), p. 72.
5 *Ibid.*, p. 27.
6 Thomas Murphy, *A Whistle in the Dark* (Dublin, The Gallery Press, 1984), p. 53.

'ISN'T THIS YOUR JOB? – TO TRANSLATE?':
BRIAN FRIEL'S LANGUAGES

Robert Welch

1 Brian Friel, *Philadelphia, Here I Come!* in *Selected Plays* (London, Faber and Faber, 1984), ed. Seamus Deane, p. 88.
2 Brian Friel, *Volunteers* (Dublin, Gallery Books, 1989), p. 63.
3 *Ibid.*, p. 64.
4 Brian Friel, *Selected Stories* (Dublin, Gallery Books, 1979), p. 103.
5 *Ibid.*, p. 106.
6 Martin Heidegger, *Poetry, Language Thought* (New York, Harper & Row, 1975), p. 198.
7 *Volunteers*, pp. 45–6.
8 *Ibid.*, p. 28.
9 Brian Friel, *The Loves of Cass McGuire* (Dublin, Gallery Books, 1984), p. 58.
10 *Selected Stories*, 'Introduction', p. 15.
11 James Joyce, *Ulysses* (London, The Bodley Head, 1954), p. 18.
12 Brian Friel, *The Communication Cord* (London, Faber and Faber, 1982), p. 86.
13 Brian Friel, *Making History* (London, Faber and Faber, 1989), p. 35.
14 *Ibid.*, p. 30.
15 *Ibid.*, p. 49.
16 *Ibid.*, p. 67.

TRANSLATING HISTORY: BRIAN FRIEL AND THE IRISH PAST

Sean Connolly

* Some of the material in this essay first appeared in S. J. Connolly, 'Dreaming History', *Theatre Ireland*, 13 (1987). I am grateful for permission to reproduce it here.
1 *Translations* (London, Faber, 1981); *Making History* (London, Faber, 1989). All page references in the text are to these two editions.
2 Brian Friel, 'Extract from a Sporadic Diary', in T. P. Coogan (ed), *Ireland and the Arts* (London, Namara Press, 1983), p. 58.
3 Garret Fitzgerald, 'Estimates for Baronies of Minimum Levels of Irish-Speaking amongst Successive Decennial Cohorts: 1771–81 to 1861–71'; *Proceedings of the Royal Irish Academy*, sect. C, 84 (1984), p. 127.

4 This broad interpretation goes back to Maureen Wall's 'The Decline of the Irish Language', in Brian O Cuiv (ed.), *A View of the Irish Language* (Dublin, Stationery Office, 1969), pp. 81–90. For a more recent account see V. E. Durkacz, *The Decline of the Celtic Languages* (Edinburgh, John Donald, 1983).

5 M. E. Daly, 'The Development of the National School System 1831–40', in Art Cosgrove and Donal Macartney (eds.), *Studies in Irish History* (Dublin, University College, Dublin, 1979).

6 L. M. Cullen, *The Emergence of Modern Ireland 1600–1900* (London, Batsford, 1981), pp. 131–2.

7 *Second Report of the Commissioners of Public Instruction, Ireland* (British Parliamentary Papers, 1835, vol. XXXIV), pp. 4–5, 384–400.

8 J. H. Andrews, *A Paper Landscape: The Ordnance Survey in Nineteenth-Century Ireland* (Oxford, Oxford University Press, 1975), p. 142.

9 Kevin Barry, in Brian Friel, John Andrews and Kevin Barry, 'Translations and *A Paper Landscape*: Between Fiction and History', *Crane Bag*, VII, 2 (1983), p. 119.

10 The literature in this area is now very large. For one sample see the essays in Samuel Clark and J. S. Donnelly (eds.), *Irish Peasants: Violence and Political Unrest 1780–1914* (Madison, University of Wisconsin Press, 1983).

11 Friel, Andrews and Barry, '*Translations* and *A Paper Landscape*' pp. 120–2.

12 Wolfgang Zach, 'Brian Friel's *Translations*: National and Universal Dimensions', in Richard Wall (ed.), *Medieval and Modern Ireland* (Gerrards Cross, Colin Smythe, 1988), pp. 77–8. A similar argument is developed in David Cairns and Shaun Richards, *Writing Ireland: Colonialism, Nationalism and Culture* (Manchester, Manchester University Press, 1988), pp. 147–9.

13 Brian John, 'Contemporary Irish Poetry and the Matter of Ireland', in Wall (ed.), *Medieval and Modern Ireland*, p. 45.

14 Desmond Rushe, 'Derry Translations', *Eire-Ireland*, XV, 4 (1980), p. 128.

15 Friel, 'Extracts from a Sporadic Diary', p. 58.

16 Christopher Murray, review of *Translations* in *Irish University Review*, XI, 2 (1981), pp. 238–9.

17 Friel, 'Extracts from a Sporadic Diary', 58–9.

18 *Translations*, p. 43. The use of Steiner is noted by Murray (above n. 16) and Zach, 'Brian Friel's *Translations*', p. 77.

19 Friel, 'Extracts from a Sporadic Diary', p. 59.

20 Friel, Andrews and Barry, '*Translations* and *A Paper Landscape*', p. 122.

21 Quoted in Michael Stewart, *Keynes and After* (2nd ed. Harmondsworth, Penguin, 1972), p. 25.

22 Sean O'Faolain, *The Great O'Neill* (London, Longmans, Green & Co. 1942), pp. vi, 280–81. In reality Peter Lombard published his *De Regno Hiberniae Commentarius* in 1600, when O'Neill's rebellion was still in progress. He did not become archbishop of Armagh until the

following year. O'Faolain's portrayal of O'Neill as spending his last years in drunken, demoralised exile has also been undermined by subsequent research. Micheline Kerney Walsh draws on official Spanish records to portray 'a man of unbroken spirit, politically-minded, active and astute, with a clear grasp of contemporary international affairs' ['*Destruction by Peace': Hugh O'Neill after Kinsale* (Armagh, Cumann Seanchais Ard Mhacha, 1986), p. 5].

23 Nicholas Canny, 'Hugh O'Neill, Earl of Tyrone, and the Changing Face of Gaelic Ulster', *Studia Hibernica*, X (1970).

24 O'Faolain, *The Great O'Neill*, p. 230.

25 Bernadette Cunningham, 'Native Culture and Political Change in Ireland 1580–1640', in Ciaran Brady and Raymond Gillespie (eds.), *Natives and Newcomers: The Making of Irish Colonial Society 1534–1641* (Dublin, Irish Academic Press, 1986).

26 See for example the very hostile review in one of the most prestigious of the Ulster local history journals, *Seanchas Ardmhacha*, XII, 2 (1989), 291–3.

27 This is the case argued in S. J. Connolly, 'Revision and its Reasons: Changing Views of Irish Economic and Social History', in *Irish History in the Classroom: Research, Resources and Realisation* (Belfast, Dept. of Education, Northern Ireland, 1987), pp. 33–49.

FRIEL'S RUSSIA

Richard York

1 Brian Friel, *Three Sisters* by Anton Chekhov (Dublin, Gallery Books, 1981), p. 15.

2 *Ibid.*, p. 18.

3 *Ibid.*, p. 91.

4 Brian Friel, *Fathers and Sons* (London, Faber and Faber, 1987), p. 19.

5 *Ibid.*, p. 87.

6 *Ibid.*, p. 67.

STAGING FRIEL

Joe Dowling

1 Brian Friel, *Lovers* (London, Faber and Faber, 1969), p. 43.

2 Brian Friel, *Making History* (London, Faber and Faber, 1989), p. 28.

3 Constantin Stanislavsky, *An Actor Prepares*, trans. E. R. Hapgood (London, Geoffrey Bles, 1937), pp. 186 and 188.

'HAVE WE A CONTEXT?': TRANSITION, SELF AND SOCIETY
IN THE THEATRE OF BRIAN FRIEL

Terence Brown

1 Quoted in George O'Brien, *Brian Friel* (Dublin, Gill and MacMillan, 1989), p. 126.
2 O'Brien, *op. cit.*, p. 126.
3 Brian Friel, 'Extracts from a Sporadic Diary', in *Ireland and the Arts*: a special issue of *Literary Review*, ed. Tim Pat Coogan (London, Namara Press, n.d.), pp. 56–7.
4 *Ibid.*, p. 596.
5 *Ibid.*, p. 60.
6 *See* Edna Longley, *Poetry in the Wars* (Newcastle upon Tyne, Bloodaxe Books, 1986), pp. 190–91.
7 Brian Friel, *Dancing at Lughnasa* (London, Faber and Faber, 1990), p. 22.

MARKING TIME: FROM *MAKING HISTORY* TO
DANCING AT LUGHNASA

Fintan O'Toole

1 *See* for instance the back-cover blurb on the published edition of *Making History* (London, Faber and Faber, 1989).
2 *See* in particular Ulick O'Connor, Brian Friel: the Writer and Commitment (Dublin, Elo Press, 1990).
3 *Selected Plays of Brian Friel*, Introduction (London, Faber and Faber, 1984), p. 12.
4 Quoted in Martin Esslin, *Mediations: Essays on Brecht, Beckett and the Media* (London, Abacus, 1983), p. 76.
5 Tennessee Williams, *Five Plays* (London, Secker and Warburg, 1962), p. 127.
6 C. W. E. Bigsby, *A Critical Introduction to American Drana*, Vol. 2 (Cambridge, Cambridge University Press, 1984), p. 11.

'A KIND OF *COMHAR*': CHARLES MACKLIN AND BRIAN FRIEL

John McVeagh

1 Brian Friel, *The London Vertigo* (Oldcastle, Co. Meath, Gallery Books, 1990), p. 11. For title quotation, see p. 12.
2 *Ibid.*, p. 11.
3 *Ibid.*, p. 11.
4 J. T. Kirkman, *Memoirs of the life of Charles Macklin*, 2 vols, (London, 1799), I, pp. 12, 9..
5 W. W. Appleton, *Charles Macklin. An Actor's Life* (Cambridge Mass., Harvard University Press, 1960), pp. 2–6. For further details of Macklin's life see William Cooke, *Memoirs of Charles Macklin*,

Comedian (London, 1804) and F. A. Congreve, *Authentic Memoirs of the late Mr Charles Macklin, Comedian* (London, 1798). Neither of these is completely reliable. A brief, sensible and acute biography is E. A. Parry, *Charles Macklin* (London, K. Paul, Trench, Trübner & Co., 1891). See also Denis Donoghue, 'Charles Macklin: Actor, Dramatist, Producer' (unpublished master's thesis, University College Dublin, 1952).

6 *A Biographical Dictionary of Actors, Actresses, Musicians, Dancers, Managers and Other Stage Personnel in London, 1660–1800. Volume 10: M'Intosh to Nash*, by Philip H. Highfill, Jr., Kalman A. Burnim and Edward A. Langhans (Carbondale and Edwardsville, Southern Illinois University Press, 1984), p. 2.

7 J. O. Bartley, *Theatre Notebook*, 16 (1961), pp. 23–4.

8 For details of Macklin's first Shylock performances in *The Merchant of Venice* see *The London Stage 1660–1800. Part 3: 1729–1747*, ed. by Arthur H. Scouten (Carbondale, Illinois, Southern Illinois University Press, 1961), II, p. 889.

9 Friel, pp. 9–10.

10 *See* Robert R. Findlay, 'The Comic Plays of Charles Macklin: Dark Satire at Mid-Eighteenth Century', *Educational Theatre Journal*, 20 (1968), pp. 398–407.

11 For further details on these and similar squabbles throughout Macklin's unquiet life, *see* the Macklin entry in *A Biographical Dictionary*, X, pp. 2–37.

12 Friel, p. 10.

13 For further discussion of the relationship between theatre managers and audiences in the eighteenth century see Leo Hughes, *The Drama's Patrons. A Study of the Eighteenth-Century London Audience* (Austin and London, University of Texas Press, 1971), pp. 4, 17–20, 26–30, 41, 51 and elsewhere; Cecil Price, *Theatre in the Age of Garrick* (Oxford, Basil Blackwell, 1973), pp. 84–101; Allardyce Nicoll, *The Garrick Stage. Theatres and Audience in the Eighteenth Century* (Manchester, Manchester University Press, 1980), pp. 87–91.

14 On 24 February 1775 the five Covent Garden theatre rioters Clarke, Aldus, Leigh, James, and Miles tried before Justice Aston were found guilty of having entered into a conspiracy to endanger Macklin's livelihood. It was revealed that they had primed certain individuals with drink on 18 November 1774 and paid for them into Covent Garden Theatre to halt the performance of *The Merchant of Venice*. Macklin, who was playing Shylock in this performance, was required to come on stage and kneel in submission. He refused to do so. A riot ensued which damaged the playhouse. George Colman then dismissed Macklin from the company so as to save his theatre from further damage. It was in answer to this stroke that Macklin took the ringleaders to law. *See A Biographical Dictionary*, X, pp. 18–20.

15 *See* Kirkman, *Memoirs*, I, pp. 58–9.

16 *See A Bibliographical Dictionary*, X, p. 6.

17 *King Henry the VII*, I, 3. The quotation in the text is taken from the microcard version of the Larpent Manuscript copy of Macklin's play, reproduced in *Three Centuries of drama (microform)*, *American and English, 1500–1800*, ed. by Henry W. Wells (New York, Readex Microprint Corp., 1956). This microcard text archive accompanies G. Williams Bergquist, *Three Centuries of English Drama* (New York, Hafner, 1963).

18 *See* the third of Swift's *Drapier's Letters*, 'Some Observations Upon a Paper, called, the Report', etc. in *The Drapier's Letters and other works 1724–1725*, ed. by Herbert Davis (Oxford, Basil Blackwell, 1966), p. 31 and passim.

19 *See* 'The Story of the Injured Lady', in *The Prose Works of Jonathan Swift*, ed. by Herbert Davis (Oxford, Basil Blackwell, 1968), IX, pp. 1–12.

20 On Macklin's struggles with the censor over this play see 'The Censorship in the Case of Macklin's *Man of the World*', *Huntington Library Quarterly*, 10 (1936), pp. 79–101.

21 J. O. Bartley, *Four Comedies by Charles Macklin* (London and Hamden, Connecticut, Archon Books, 1968), p. 59.

22 As J. O. Bartley points out, O'Dogherty's catalogue of Irish names recalls important personages from Ireland's past and asserts the under-valued historical tradition. *See* Bartley, *Four Comedies*, p. 112 (footnote).

23 Bartley, *Four Comedies*, p. 87. *See also* Jonathan Swift, *Gulliver's Travels*, Book II chapter 7.

24 *See The Monthly Mirror*, 4 (1797), pp. 339–340; 6 (1798), pp. 71, 220; 7 (1799), p. 276; 8 (1799), p. 15. Of interest too is Macklin's remark that Shakespeare was a bad actor but a good writer. He goes on: 'His acting, indeed, was bad. Why? Because he was a writer. The qualities and habits of each are opposite, and in contest for superiority. This I have experienced:— Colley Cibber experienced it' [*The Monthly Mirror*, 9 (1800), p. 167].

25 *The Monthly Mirror*, 4 (1797), p. 337.

FOR LIBERATION: BRIAN FRIEL AND THE USE OF MEMORY

Seamus Heaney

1 T. S. Eliot, *Four Quartets* (London, Faber and Faber, 1944), p. 55.

2 Brian Friel, *Translations* (London, Faber and Faber, 1981), p. 67; *Making History* (London, Faber and Faber, 1989), p. 39.

3 *The Diviner: The Best Stories of Brian Friel*, ed. Seamus Deane (Dublin, The O'Brien Press, 1983), Introduction, p. 9.

4 *Ibid.*, pp. 9–10.

5 Brian Friel, *The Enemy Within* (Dublin, The Gallery Press, 1979), p. 21.

6 Brian Friel, *The Saucer of Larks* (London, Victor Gollancz, 1962), pp. 29–30.
7 C. J. Jung, *Memories, Dreams, Reflections*, trans. R. and C. Winston (London, Fontana, 1967), p. 17.
8 Brian Friel, *Dancing at Lughnasa* (London, Faber and Faber, 1990), p. 71.
9 Jung, *op. cit.*, pp. 18–19.
10 Brian Friel, *Volunteers* (Dublin, The Gallery Press, 1989), p. 88.
11 *The Enemy Within*, p. 70.
12 Wallace Stevens, *Opus Posthumous* (London, Faber and Faber, 1959), p. 118.

SELECT BIBLIOGRAPHY

PUBLISHED PLAYS

The Enemy Within (Newark, Delaware, Proscenium Press, 1975).
Philadelphia, Here I Come! (London, Faber and Faber, 1965).
The Loves of Cass McGuire (London, Faber and Faber, 1967).
Lovers (London, Faber and Faber, 1969).
Crystal and Fox (London, Faber and Faber, 1970).
Crystal and Fox and The Mundy Scheme (New York, Farrar, Straus and Giroux, 1970).
The Gentle Island (London, Davis-Poynter, 1973).
The Freedom of the City (London, Faber and Faber, 1974).
Living Quarters (London, Faber and Faber, 1978).
Volunteers (London, Faber and Faber, 1979).
Aristocrats (Dublin, The Gallery Press, 1980).
Faith Healer (London, Faber and Faber, 1980).
Translations (London, Faber and Faber, 1981).
Three Sisters by Anton Chekhov: A Translation (Dublin, The Gallery Press, 1981).
The Communication Cord (London, Faber and Faber, 1983).
Selected Plays, ed. Seamus Deane (London, Faber and Faber, 1984).
Fathers and Sons: After Turgenev (London, Faber and Faber, 1987).
Making History (London, Faber and Faber, 1989).
Dancing at Lughnasa (London, Faber and Faber, 1990).
The London Vertigo (Dublin, The Gallery Press, 1990).

FICTION

The Saucer of Larks (London, Victor Gollancz, 1962).
The Gold in the Sea (London, Victor Gollancz, 1966).
Selected Stories, with an Introduction by Seamus Deane (Dublin, The Gallery Press, 1979).
The Diviner: The Best Stories of Brian Friel, with an Introduction by Seamus Deane (Dublin, The O'Brien Press; London, Allison and Busby, 1983).

EDITIONS

Charles McGlinchey, *The Last of the Name*, with an Introduction (Belfast, The Blackstaff Press, 1986).

GENERAL

Andrews, J. H., *A Paper Landscape: The Ordnance Survey in Nineteenth-Century Ireland* (Oxford, The Clarendon Press, 1975).

Bell, Sam Hanna, *The Theatre in Ulster* (Dublin, Gill and MacMillan, 1972).

Bertha, Csilla, 'Tragedies of National Fate: A Comparison between Brian Friel's *Translations* and its Hungarian Counterpart, András Sütö's *A szusai menyegzö*', *Irish University Review*, Vol. 17, No. 2, Autumn 1987, pp. 207–22.

Bigsby, C. W. E., *Contemporary Dramatists* (London, St. James Press, 1977).

Birker, Klaus, 'The Relationship between the Stage and the Audience in Brian Friel's *The Freedom of the City*', in *Harmon*, pp. 153–58.

Boland, Eavan, 'Brian Friel: Derry's Playwright', *Hibernia*, 16 February 1973, p. 18.

Brown, Terence, *Ireland: A Social and Cultural History 1922–1985* (Glasgow, Fontana Press, 1985).

Browne, Joseph 'Violent Prophecies: The Writer and Northern Ireland', *Eire-Ireland*, Vol. 10. No. 2, Summer 1975, pp. 109–19.

Cairns, David and Richards, Shaun, *Writing Ireland: Colonialism, Nationalism and Culture* (Manchester, Manchester University Press, 1988).

Carpenter, Andrew (ed.), *Place, Personality and the Irish Writer*, Irish Literary Studies 1 (Gerrards Cross, Colin Smythe, 1977).

Connolly, Peter (ed.), *Literature and the Changing Ireland*, Irish Literary Studies 9 (Gerrards Cross, Colin Smythe, 1982).

Connolly, Sean, 'Dreaming History: Brian Friel's *Translations*', *Theatre Ireland* 13, Autumn 1987, pp. 42–4.

Dantanus, Ulf, *Brian Friel: The Growth of an Irish Dramatist*, Gothenburg Studies in English 59 (Gothenburg, Acta Universitatis Gothoburgensis, 1985; Atlantic Heights, New Jersey, Humanities Press, 1986).

— *Brian Friel: A Study* (London, Faber and Faber, 1988).

Deane, Seamus, 'The Writer and the Troubles', *Threshold*, No. 25, Summer 1974, pp. 13–17.

— 'Brian Friel', *Ireland Today* (1981), pp. 7–10.

— 'Brian Friel: The Double Stage', in *Celtic Revivals: Essays in Modern Irish Literature, 1880–1980* (London, Faber and Faber, 1985), pp. 166–73.

Dowling, P. J., *The Hedge Schools of Ireland* (Cork, The Mercier Press, 1968).

Etherton, Michael, *Contemporary Irish Dramatists*, Macmillan Modern Dramatists (London, MacMillan, 1989).

Field Day Theatre Company, *Ireland's Field Day* (London, Hutchinson, 1985).

FitzGibbon, Emelie, 'All Change: Contemporary Fashions in the Irish Theatre', in *Sekine*, pp. 33–46.

Fitz-Simon, Christopher, *The Irish Theatre* (London, Thames and Hudson, 1983).

Foster, John Wilson, *Forces and Themes in Ulster Fiction* (Dublin, Gill and MacMillan, 1974).

Friel, Brian, John Andrews and Kevin Barry, '*Translations* and *A Paper Landscape*: Between Fiction and History', *The Crane Bag*, Vol. 7, No. 2, 1983, pp. 118–24.

Grene, Nicholas, 'Distancing Drama: Sean O'Casey to Brian Friel', in *Sekine*, pp. 47–70.

Harmon, Maurice (ed.), *The Irish Writer and the City*, Irish Literary Studies 18 (Gerrards Cross, Colin Smythe, 1984).

Heaney, Seamus, 'Digging Deeper', Revies of *Volunteers*, *TLS*, 21 March 1975, p. 306.

Henderson, Lynda, ' "The Green Shoot": Transcendence and the Imagination in Contemporary Ulster Drama', in *Across a Roaring Hill: the Protestant Imagination in Modern Ireland*, ed. Gerald Dawe and Edna Longley (Belfast, The Blackstaff Press, 1985), pp. 196–217.

Hickey, Des and Smith, Gus, *A Paler Shade of Green* (London, Leslie Frewin, 1972).

Hogan, Robert, *After the Irish Renaissance* (London, MacMillan, 1968).

— 'The Year in Review: 1967 — Theatre', *University Review*, Vol. 5, No. 1, Spring 1968, pp. 103–12.

— '*Since O'Casey*' and Other Essays on Irish Drama, Irish Literary Studies 15 (Gerrards Cross, Colin Smythe, 1983).

Hunt, Hugh, *The Abbey: Ireland's National Theatre 1904–1979* (Dublin, Gill and MacMillan, 1979).

Kearney, Richard, 'Language Play: Brian Friel and Ireland's Verbal Theatre', *Studies* 72, Spring 1983, pp. 20–56.

Kelly, Colm, 'Homecomings and Diversions: Cultural Nationalism and the Recent Drama of Brian Friel', *Studies*, 76, Winter 1987, pp. 452–62.

Kenneally, Michael (ed.), *Cultural Contexts and Literary Idioms in Contemporary Irish Literature*: Studies in Contemporary Irish Literature 1, Irish Literary Studies 31 (Gerrards Cross, Colin Smythe, 1988).

Kiberd, Declan, 'Brian Friel's *Faith Healer*', in Masaru Sekine, *Irish Writers and Society at Large*, Irish Literary Studies 22 (Gerrards Cross, Colin Smythe, 1985), pp. 106–21.

King, Kimball, *Ten Modern Irish Playwrights: A Comprehensive Annotated Bibliography* (New York and London, Garland Publishing, 1979).

Kosok, Heinz (ed.), *Studies in Anglo-Irish Literature* (Bonn, Bouvier Verlag Herbert Grundmann, 1982).

Lehmann, Elmar, 'England's Ireland: An Analysis of Some Contemporary Plays', in *Kosok*, pp. 431–38.

Levin, Milton, 'Brian Friel: An Introduction', *Eire-Ireland*, Vol. 7, No. 2, 1972, pp. 132–36.

Longley, Edna, 'Poetry and Politics in Northern Ireland', in *Poetry in the Wars* (Newcastle upon Tyne, Bloodaxe Books, 1986), pp. 185–210.

McGowan, Moray, 'Truth, Politics and the Individual: Brian Friel's *The Freedom of the City* and the Northern Ireland Conflict', *Literature in Wissenschaft und Unterricht*, Vol. 12, No. 4, 1979, pp. 287–303.

McMahon, Sean 'The Black North: The Prose Writers of the North of Ireland', *Threshold*, No. 21, Summer 1967, pp. 158–74.

Maxwell, D. E. S., *Brian Friel* (Lewisburg, Bucknell University Press, 1973).

— 'Imagining the North: Violence and the Writers', *Eire-Ireland*, Vol. 8, No. 2, Summer 1973, pp. 91–107.

— Introduction to *The Enemy Within, The Journal of Irish Literature*, Vol. 4, No. 2, May 1975, pp. 4–6.

— *A Critical History of Modern Irish Drama, 1891–1980* (Cambridge, Cambridge University Press, 1984).

Murray, Christopher, 'Irish Drama in Transition 1966–1978', *Études Irlandaises*, Nouvelle Série No. 4, December 1979, pp. 287–308.

— 'Recent Irish Drama', in *Kosok*, pp. 439–46.

— 'The History Play Today', in *Kenneally*, pp. 269–89.

Niel, Ruth, 'Digging into History: A Reading of Brian Friel's *Volunteers* and Seamus Heaney's "Viking Dublin: Trial Pieces" ', *Irish University Review*, Vol. 16, No. 1, Spring 1986, pp. 35–47.

— 'Non-Realistic Techniques in the Plays of Brian Friel: the Debt to International Drama', in Zach, Wolfgang and Kosok, Heinz (eds.), *Literary Interrelations: Ireland, England and the World* II (Tübingen, Gunter Narr Verlag, 1987), pp. 349–59.

O'Brien, George, *Brial Friel* (Dublin, Gill and Macmillan, 1989).

O'Connor, Ulick, *Brian Friel: Crisis and Commitment — The Writer and Northern Ireland* (Dublin, Elo Publications, 1989).

ÓhAodha, Michael, *Theatre in Ireland* (Oxford, Basil Blackwell, 1974).

O'Malley, Conor, *A Poet's Theatre* (Dublin, Elo Press, 1988).

Ormsby, Frank, 'The Plays of Brian Friel', *The Honest Ulsterman*, No. 23, 1970, pp. 27–31.

O'Toole, Fintan, 'Island of Saints and Silicon: Literature and Social Change in Contemporary Ireland', in *Kenneally*, pp. 11–35.

Pine, Richard, *Brian Friel and Ireland's Drama* (London, Routledge, 1990).

Rafroidi, Patrick; Popot, Raymond; Parker, William, *Aspects of the Irish Theatre* (Lille, Publications de l'Université de Lille III, 1972).

Richards, Shaun, 'The Changing Landscape of Fact: English as "Necessary Sin" in Contemporary Irish Literature', *New Comparison*, No. 7, Summer 1989, pp. 88–98.

Robbins, Ronald, 'Friel's Modern "Fox and the Grapes" Fable', *Eire-Ireland*, Vol. 21, No. 4, Winter 1986, pp. 66–76.

Robinson, P. N., 'Brian Friel's *Faith Healer*: An Irishman Comes Back Home', in Zach, Wolfgang and Kosok, Heinz (eds.), *Literary Interrelations: Ireland, England and the World* III (Tübingen, Gunter Narr Verlag, 1987), pp. 223–27.

Roche, Anthony, 'Ireland's *Antigones*: Tragedy North and South', in *Kenneally*, pp. 221–50.

Rollins, Ronald, 'Friel's *Translations*: The Ritual of Naming', *The Canadian Journal of Irish Studies*, Vol. 11, No. 1, June 1985, pp. 35–43.

Sekine, Masaru (ed.), *Irish Writers and the Theatre*, Irish Literary Studies 23 (Gerrards Cross, Colin Smythe, 1986).

Throne, Marilyn, 'Brian Friel's *Faith Healer*: Portrait of a Shaman', *The Journal of Irish Literature*, Vol. 16, No. 3, September 1987, pp. 18–24.

Timm, E. F., 'Modern Mind, Myth, and History: Brian Friel's *Translations*', in *Kosok*, pp. 447–54.

Todd, Loreto, *The Language of Irish Literature* (London, MacMillan, 1989).

Toolan, Michael, 'Language and Affective Communication in Some Contemporary Irish Writers', in *Kenneally*, pp. 138–53.

Warner, Alan, 'Introducing Brian Friel', *Acorn*, No. 14, Autumn 1970, pp. 25–8.

Winkler, E. H., 'Brian Friel's *The Freedom of the City*: Historical Actuality and Dramatic Imagination', *The Canadian Journal of Irish Studies*, Vol. 7, No. 1, June 1981, pp. 12–31.

— ' "Eejitin" About: Adolescence in Friel and Keane', *Eire-Ireland*, Vol. 16, No. 3, Fall 1981, pp. 138–44.

— 'Reflections of Derry's Bloody Sunday in Literature', in *Kosok*, pp. 411–21.

Zach, Wolfgang, 'Brian Friel's *Translations*: National and Universal Dimensions', in Richard Wall (ed.), *Medieval and Modern Ireland* (Gerrards Cross, Colin Smythe, 1988), pp. 74–90.

NOTES ON CONTRIBUTORS

ELMER ANDREWS, Lecturer in English at the University of Ulster at Coleraine, gained his M.A. and Ph.D. degrees from Queen's University, Belfast. He has taught in Greece and at Mohammed V University in Rabat, Morocco. He is the author of *The Poetry of Seamus Heaney: All the Realms of Whisper* and editor of *Seamus Heaney: A Collection of Critical Essays* and *Contemporary Irish Poetry: A Collection of Critical Essays*. He is currently working on a full-length study of Brian Friel.

TERENCE BROWN, Associate Professor of English in Trinity College, Dublin and Fellow of the College, has published widely on Anglo-Irish Literature. His most recent book is *Ireland's Literature: Selected Essays*. He is currently at work on a critical biography of W. B. Yeats.

SEAN CONNOLLY, Reader in History at the University of Ulster, has written *Priests and People in Pre-Famine Ireland 1780–1845* (Dublin, Gill and MacMillan, 1982), *Religion and Society in Nineteenth-Century Ireland* (Dundalk, Economic and Social History Society of Ireland, 1985), and *Religion, Law and Power: The Making of Protestant Ireland 1660–1750*, forthcoming from Oxford University Press.

NEIL CORCORAN is Senior Lecturer in English Literature at the University of Sheffield. His publications include *The Song of Deeds: A Study of 'The Anathemata' of David Jones* (1982), *Seamus Heaney* (1986) and *The Chosen Ground: Essays on the Contemporary Poetry of Northern Ireland* (1991).

JOHN CRONIN, Professor of English at the Queen's University of Belfast, has taught previously at the University of Witwatersrand, Johannesburg. He is author of *Somerville and Ross* (Lewisburg, 1972), *Gerald Griffin (1803–1840): A Critical Biography* (Cambridge University Press, 1978), *The Anglo-Irish Novel, Vol. 1, The Nineteenth-Century* (Appletree Press, 1980) and *The Anglo-Irish Novel, Vol. 2, 1900–1940* (Appletree Press, 1990).

SEAMUS DEANE is Professor of Modern English and American Literature at University College, Dublin. His books include *Selected Poems, Celtic Revivals, A Short History of Irish Literature, The French Enlightenment and Revolution in England 1789–1832*. He is General Editor of *The Field Day Anthology of Irish Writing*.

JOE DOWLING joined the Abbey Theatre while still a student at University College, Dublin. He founded Ireland's first theatre-in-education group, The Young Abbey which later became TEAM Theatre Company. He was

Director of the Peacock Theatre from 1973–1976, Artistic Director of the Irish Theatre Company from 1976–1978 and Artistic Director of the Abbey (National) Theatre from 1978–1985. In 1985, he joined the Board of Gaiety Stage Productions, founded The Gaiety School of Acting in 1986 and became Managing Director of The Gaiety in 1987. As well as working in Ireland, he has directed in New York, London, Montreal and Washington.

SEAMUS HEANEY has taught at Queen's University, Belfast; Carysfort College, Blackrock; and since 1981 has spent one term a year at Harvard University, where he was subsequently appointed Boylston Professor of Rhetoric and Oratory. His book of poems include *New Selected Poems* and *Seeing Things* (1991) and his recent critical prose was collected in *The Government of the Tongue* (1988). In 1989, he was elected as Professor of Poetry at Oxford University.

THOMAS KILROY is a playwright and novelist. His most recent play is *The Madame Macadam Travelling Theatre* (Methuen), first produced (1991) by the Field Day Theatre Company, of which he is also one of the directors.

DESMOND MAXWELL was born in Derry and graduated from Trinity College, Dublin in 1947. He has taught in Ghana, Nigeria, Dublin, Belfast and Canada. Among his books are *Brian Friel* (1973) and *A Critical History of Modern Irish Drama 1891–1980* (1984).

JOHN McVEAGH was born in Pontefract, Yorkshire and educated at Birmingham University. He has taught in Ibadan University, Nigeria and is currently Senior Lecturer in English in the University of Ulster. His publications include *Tradefull Merchants* (1981), *All Before Them* (1990) and (with Andrew Hadfield) *Strangers to that Land* (forthcoming).

CHRISTOPHER MURRAY is Lecturer in English and Director of the Drama Centre at University College, Dublin. Editor of *Irish University Review*, he has published widely on Irish theatre and drama. With Masaru Sekine, his *Yeats and the Noh* was published in 1990 (Colin Smythe) and with the late Barbara Hayley he edited *Ireland and France, A Bountiful Friendship: Literature, History and Ideas: Essays in Honour of Patrick Rafroidi* (Colin Smythe, 1991).

FINTAN O'TOOLE has been theatre critic for *In Dublin* magazine, *The Sunday Tribune* and *The Irish Times*, for whom he is also a columnist on social and political affairs. His books include *The Politics of Magic: The Work and Times of Tom Murphy, No More Heroes: A Radical Guide to Shakespeare* and *A Mass for Jesse James*, a selection of his journalism. In 1991 he was Literary Adviser to the Abbey Theatre.

ALAN PEACOCK is a graduate of Birmingham University and is a Lecturer in English at The University of Ulster at Coleraine, having spent time at Manchester University and Magee University College, Derry. He has written a range of articles on English poetry from the seventeenth to the twentieth century and has published on modern Irish writers such as Kavanagh, MacNeice, Longley and Heaney.

ROBERT WELCH was born in Cork and is Professor of English in the University of Ulster. He has taught in Leeds, Ife and Cork. He has published *Irish Poetry from Moore to Yeats, A History of Verse Translation from the Irish* and other works, including *Muskerry* (poems). He is editor of *The Oxford Companion to Irish Literature*.

RICHARD YORK is Reader in Modern Languages in the University of Ulster. He has published *The Poem as Utterance* (Methuen, 1986) and articles on language and form in modern literature.

INDEX